Neither Sharks Nor Wolves

Neither Sharks Nor Wolves

The Men of Nazi Germany's U-boat Arm, 1939–1945

TIMOTHY P. MULLIGAN

Naval Institute Press   *Annapolis, Maryland*

Library of Congress Cataloging-in-Publication Data

Mulligan, Timothy.
    Neither sharks nor wolves : the men of Nazi Germany's
U-boat arm, 1939–1945 / Timothy P. Mulligan.
        p. cm.
    Includes bibliographical references (p. 311) and index.
    ISBN 1-55750-594-2 (alk. paper)
    1. World War, 1939–1945—Naval operations—Submarine.
    2. World War, 1939–1945—Naval operations, German.
    I. Title.
    D781.M85 1999
    940.54'51—dc21   98-53659

Printed in the United States of America on acid-free paper ∞
06 05 04 03 02 01 00 99   9 8 7 6 5 4 3 2
First printing

To my teachers and mentors, past and present

Contents

Tables

Preface

More than fifty years after the last German submarine slipped silently into Allied custody at the end of World War II, the U-boat retains its grip on the popular imagination. New books on U-boat aces and battles continue to appear; cable television regularly offers new film documentaries; the making of a domestic feature film on the subject commands a cover story in Germany's leading news magazine; and the internet features a growing number of U-boat websites. On display at Chicago's Museum of Science and Industry, the *U-505* draws hundreds of thousands of visitors each year, most of them born long after the submarine's capture at sea by U.S. naval forces in June 1944. In Halifax, Nova Scotia, older residents still relate stories of captured U-boat crewmen with tickets to local dances in their pockets. And New Zealand newspapers investigate allegations that the crew of *U-862* came ashore to milk cows in sight of the port of Napier.

The last examples illustrate how fact and fiction have blended into legend, the apocrypha and exaggerations of which do not obscure the truth that German submariners carried the war to the shores of every Allied power. Alone among the branches of the Wehrmacht, U-boat crews fought their battles without respite from the first day of the war to the last, a period of five years and eight months that spanned the Second World War's longest campaign. Yet their ability to project an image of omnipresent menace contrasts sharply with the reality of the tremendous odds against them, a disparity that led the navy's commander-in-chief, Grand Adm. Erich Raeder, to observe on the third day of the war that his forces were "so inferior in number and strength to the British fleet . . . they can do no more than show that they know how to die gallantly."[1] Die they did, whether gallantly or not, and at a horrific rate. During World War II U-boat crews endured losses unequaled in modern military history, yet continued to put out to sea in search of targets through the last hours of the conflict.

Ironically those who manned the U-boats remain almost invisible, with little more substance than the ghostly images of bearded young men glimpsed briefly in stock newsreel footage. "No roses bloom on a sailor's grave," laments an old German seafaring song, an appropriate description as well for the state of research into their collective identity. Biographical studies and memoirs focus on the "aces," the submarine commanders skillful or fortunate enough to have experienced success in sinking Allied ships and who have dominated U-boat historiography since the First World War. In these accounts, and in narratives of convoy battles and technical treatments of U-boat types, the crewmen who made possible those successes and operated the complex equipment rarely emerge from the background except as the source of colorful anecdotes or sweeping generalizations.[2] New reference works appear at an ever-increasing rate, detailing the histories, operations, and fates of individual U-boats, but in them the crews furnish only a precise casualty statistic for every boat destroyed.[3] Only in the exceptional novel may a general reader glimpse the reality of routine, grime, and terror for the average U-boat crewman of World War II.[4]

Even in the best examples of these categories, the portrayals of U-boat officers and men are limited in time or space, crews manning individual submarines or fighting specific battles. Incidents are generalized and crew characteristics are assumed as representative of the German submarine service throughout the war, rather than as unique to a particular period. When treated collectively, U-boat crews have been alternately hailed as heroes, branded as criminals, and mourned as victims; though their ranks included some of each of these, such simplifications reveal much more about the commentators than of the submariners allegedly described. Consistently U-boat sailors have been treated as a single entity rather than as a succession of cohorts that evolved over time, whose character changed as their numbers grew and contracted. Their war is here perceived as one campaign with several phases, in which each unique successive force fought its own war distinct from the others.

This book is an attempt to tell their story.

More specifically, it is an effort to understand the character of the U-boat service. This encompasses the leadership and command of the force, the process by which men were selected and transformed into submariners, and the manner and means by which the U-boat arm fought the war. Above all it is a study of those who manned the U-boats—where they came from, what occupations they held, which characteristics they shared. For both officers and enlisted men, we shall review their specialized career-tracks in naval service and the associated functions they performed on board a submarine. This study moreover finds new answers to questions that have never been systematically treated, including: How many men served on U-boats? Were they all volunteers? Did morale truly remain high throughout the conflict? And did the U-boat force gradually deteriorate into a "children's crusade"?

Our study also addresses the broader context of U-boat warfare and those who waged it. The book's twelve chapters are loosely grouped into three parts, the first of which establishes the foundations: the organization and routine of a U-boat crew, the mixed legacies of World War I, and the framework and chronological patterns of the World War II campaign. Chapters 5 through 8 concern the men themselves, their backgrounds and career specialization, selection and training as submariners, and variations in their ages and combat experience. The final chapters examine specific aspects of the war and their service, including the general conditions of morale, the conduct of submariners toward Allied survivors, and the relationship of the navy to National Socialism, with a concluding summary of their experiences at war's end, in captivity, and during the postwar period. Separate appendices describe the questionnaire survey of U-boat veterans used in this book and the question of numbers and losses in the U-boat service during the war. Scattered throughout are discussions of such familiar issues as Grand Adm. Karl Dönitz's leadership, operations of individual U-boat captains, and characteristics of specific U-boat types, but always linked to our central theme.

This work began as a consequence of the author's earlier research into the story of U-boat ace Werner Henke and his command of *U-515*. Henke's veteran crew played a crucial role in their mutual success and survival, as reflected in the commander's attempt to maintain his crew intact for as long as possible. A later study indicated that many distinctive characteristics of *U-515*'s crewmen were shared by U-boat sailors in general, leading to the decision to undertake the present effort.[5]

The initial ambitious goals of this study had to adjust to the problematic state of primary source documentation on individuals. Except for fragments, the records of neither the U-boat Personnel Department nor the U-boat flotillas survived the war, and those of the *Marinepersonalamt* are also incomplete.[6] Kriegsmarine central personnel files are not held by the Bundesarchiv at Kornelimünster with those of the other armed forces, but by the Deutsche Dienststelle (WASt) in Berlin, where U-boat crewmen's' service records are mixed with those of all other naval personnel and, as of 1993, were not accessible for the research planned.

Yet at a deeper level, it is still too early for the most significant personal papers to emerge. The letters, diaries, photographs, and retained official materials of U-boat crewmen remain locked away in attics and closets as they pass through the transition from treasured memories of loved ones to disposable curiosities of distant relatives. With time, too, will come perspective and the interest of future generations to study these men further. Only then will such personal records gain the status of valued historical sources; only then will their authors' voices speak again to reveal their experiences, values, beliefs, fears, and hopes at the moments they lived them.[7]

Lacking access to these sources, this study created one of its own, a collection of survey questionnaires distributed to U-boat veterans with the assistance of the privately run U-Boot-Archiv in Cuxhaven, Germany. Each questionnaire asked no more than basic biographical and service data to establish personal backgrounds, ages, ranks, dates of entry into the navy and into submarine duty, and length of service aboard specific U-boats. Over a period of three and one-half years, more than 1,100 veterans responded—167 former officers and 937 former noncommissioned officers and enlisted men. The questionnaires were accordingly divided between those categories and thereunder arranged by career-track (e.g., line or engineering officer, torpedo mechanic, seaman, or radioman) and then by rank. Much of our analysis and a majority of the tables used in this work derive from these data.

Other primary sources that complemented the survey include German Navy organizational records maintained at the Bundesarchiv-Abt. Militärarchiv (Freiburg i.Br.) or available on microfilm at the National Archives (College Park, Maryland); interrogation reports of captured survivors of sunken U-boats (including copies of British interrogations) among the records of the U.S. Navy's Office of Naval Intelligence, also at the National Archives; and interviews and correspondence with U-boat veterans in Germany, Canada, and the United States. For specific operational aspects, this study relies on the war diaries of Dönitz's command, of the Naval Staff's Operations Department (*1/Seekriegsleitung*), and of the U-boats themselves. All are supplemented by information furnished in memoirs and research presented in many secondary works.

Throughout the text an effort has been made to allow the voice of the U-boat crewman to be heard directly. The survey data offer an indirect means to the same end by presenting collective evidence on shared or distinctive traits and characteristics, usually to test the accuracy of observations and commentaries made by historians.

Some apologies are in order. Readers will, I hope, forgive the absence of technical discussions of U-boats and their weaponry, the lack of detailed narratives on U-boat operations or the contributions of signals intelligence, and the relative paucity of data on Allied forces. Excellent accounts are already available on all of these subjects, and I have attempted to identify the standard works for further reference. The thematic approach in the chapters inevitably involves some overlap, and consequently some significant items are repeated. Finally I have retained the use of German terms and ranks as much as possible, first as this represents their language and military culture, and second because many of these words have no precise English equivalent. It is the coin for admission into the vanished world of the *U-Boot-Fahrer* (a figurative but not literal term for U-boat sailors).

And if the children of their former enemies decide to make the visit, the story of these submariners might find a meaning they could never imagine.

AN UNDERTAKING of this type necessarily incurs many debts. As with many other historians of the German U-boat service, mine begins with Horst Bredow, director of the U-Boot-Archiv (*Stiftung Traditionsarchiv Unterseeboote*) in Cuxhaven-Altenbruch. Not only did he and his wife Annemarie extend their extraordinary hospitality to me during several visits to his unique archives, but his cooperation in circulating my questionnaire survey of U-boat veterans was indispensable to this work.

I am also deeply indebted to the more than 1,100 U-boat veterans who took the time to complete questionnaires disseminated through the U-Boot-Archiv. Many added details or specific experiences on their own initiative. The willingness to share personal information with a foreigner—a national of a country against whom these individuals fought—testifies to an inner peace and understanding that is humbling.

A number of veterans and their families graciously accommodated an inquisitive historian over prolonged periods. These especially include Werner Hirschmann and his wife Diana, the late Carl Möller and his wife Irmgard, Hans and Hannelore Schultz, and Hermann and Inge Molzahn. Mrs. Molzahn in particular granted the use of personal photographs taken by her father, *Kaptlt.* Hans Karpf. Mr. Hirschmann and Pete Petersen not only shared memories and insights, but read and critiqued specific chapters. The surviving crew members of *U-515* and their wives always extended an enthusiastic welcome and invaluable assistance at their annual reunions. Wilhelm Müller-Arnecke, Reinhard Hardegen, and Eduard Vogt all took time from their schedules for lengthy interviews. Veterans Rolf Güth and Heinz Trompelt generously contributed copies of materials they had written or collected.

Prof. Eric Rust, whose pioneering work with Crew 34 provided one of the inspirations for this project, also assisted with some key information and insights from his research. Mr. Eberhard Schmidt kindly provided access to materials at the *Wehrgeschichtliches Ausbildungszentrum* of the German naval academy, *Marineschule Mürwik*. At the Bundesarchiv-Abt. Militärarchiv in Freiburg i.Br., Dr. Maierhöfer and his colleague Herr Döringhoff put forth a much-appreciated extra effort to identify some crucial records. The staffs of the National Archives' Central Reference and Still Pictures Branches (particularly Ms. Dale Connelly and Mr. Fred Pernell at the latter) and the reference staff at the Library of Congress's Manuscript Reading Room unfailingly furnished efficient and courteous assistance regarding their holdings.

At different times Dr. Charles Burdick, Jak Mallmann Showell, Philip Lundeburg, Keith Gill, Mary Kay Schmidt, Eva Krusten, Maarja Krusten, Fynette Eaton, Robin Cookson, and Sam Lewis all offered ideas, commentaries, and support for this project at moments when they were most needed. Renie Wallace and Blaine Madison assisted with the formatting and typing of the glossary and table of comparative ranks. Mr. Lawrence Humphries and the staff at Computer Support Systems electronically "packaged" the final product at short notice.

Finally my deepest thanks to Bonnie, whose active daily support alone makes everything possible.

Glossary

Because the U-boat service represents a part of German military culture, the text relies on an extensive use of the original German military terminology to identify ranks, organizations, and concepts. A translation is provided the first time a term is used, but the glossary below provides a ready reference to most of the terms used. Intermixed are standard abbreviations in English for military terms (e.g., CO, NCO). Most German terms are italicized, but the names of services (Wehrmacht, Luftwaffe, Waffen-SS, Kriegsmarine, Bundesmarine) have either become familiar vocabulary in English or are used so frequently in the text that a special font would be inappropriate.

Whenever a U-boat is identified, the name and rank of her commanding officer for the period or incident described (rather than the officer's final rank or the name of a later commander) is also given. In later references where no change of commander has occurred, the U-boat is identified only by number. A table of comparative ranks immediately follows the glossary.

All distances are given in nautical miles (approximately 6,080 ft.) and speeds in knots (nautical miles per hour). Figures for tonnage of merchant ships reflect gross registered tons, without regard for weight of cargo.

Endnote citations to secondary sources are reduced to short titles, with complete citations given in the bibliography. Exceptions are citations to works used only once and not reproduced in the bibliography, in which case the full publication data are provided.

Provided below are terms, abbreviations, and acronyms used in the text and endnotes, as well as some terms not found in the text but useful for general reference in regard to U-boats.

Aal Eel, slang for a torpedo

Agru-Front Abbreviation for *Technische Ausbildungsgruppe für Front-U-Boote,* the Technical Training Group for Combat U-boats, responsible for training U-boat crews under simulated emergency conditions

Alberich Code name for an experimental rubber coating used on a U-boat conning tower to neutralize Allied radar (not generally used)

Aphrodite A radar decoy used by German U-boats

Asdic British term for sonar, after the Allied Submarine Detection Investigation Committee that invented the device in 1917

BA-MA *Bundesarchiv-Abt. Militärarchiv,* located in Freiburg i.Br., Germany

B-Dienst Beobachtungsdienst, the German Navy Signal Intelligence Service

BdU *Befehlshaber der Unterseeboote,* Commander in Chief of Submarines

BdU/Op Operations Staff under BdU, directed by *Konteradmiral* Eberhard Godt for most of the war

Bold A device released by a submerged U-boat to decoy Allied sonar

Bugraum Forward torpedo room

CO Commanding officer (or *Kommandant*)

Crew German naval designation for a class of naval officer cadets by year of entry (e.g., Crew 36 = officers who entered the navy in 1936)

Dräger A combination breathing apparatus and life vest used to escape from a sunken U-boat

E.K. (I, II) *Eisernes Kreuz,* Iron Cross (First, Second Class)

Enigma Designation for the cipher machine used by the German armed forces to encode security-classified messages

FAT *Federapparat Torpedo,* spring-operated torpedo

FdU *Führer der Unterseeboote,* Commander of Submarines; Dönitz's original title until the redesignation BdU on 19 September 1939, thereafter used for a regional U-boat command, e.g., *FdU Italien* (Commander of Submarines, Italy)

Frontboot Combat or front-line U-boat

FuMB *Funkmess-Beobachtungsgerät,* radar-detection equipment

Funker Radioman

GHG *Gruppen-Horch-Gerät,* "group listening apparatus," an array of hydrophones installed on a U-boat's bow

Hecktorpedoraum Aft torpedo room

HF/DF High-frequency/direction-finding ("Huff-Duff"), an electronic apparatus for locating a U-boat by its radio transmissions

Hohentwiel The manufacturer and common name for a type of primitive radar carried aboard U-boats

HSO *Handelsschiffsoffizier,* a merchant marine officer who entered the German navy after 1933

I.W.O. *Erster Wach-Offizier* (colloquially *Eins* W.O.), First Watch Officer (equivalent to a U.S. Navy Executive Officer)

II.W.O. *Zweiter Wach-Offizier,* Second Watch Officer

Konfirmand Slang for a "commander-in-training" aboard a U-boat commanded by another

Kriegsmarine Official designation after May 1935 of the German navy, which was known as the *Reichsmarine* during the interwar period and the *Kaiserliche Marine* from its foundation through the end of World War I

KTB *Kriegstagebuch,* war diary

Laufbahn Career-track, indicating specialty branch within the navy

L.I. *Leitender Ingenieur,* Chief Engineer

Lords Collective nickname for naval enlisted men

LUT *Lageunabhängiger Torpedo,* "bearing-independent torpedo," developed to run a straight course into a convoy and then begin a back-and-forth course until striking a ship

Marine-Hitler-Jugend "Naval Hitler Youth," a branch of the Hitler Youth for those interested in nautical activities, membership in which eventually became a basis for conscription into the navy

Metox The manufacturer and common name for a primitive type of radar detection gear (FuMB) mounted on U-boats

Mittelstand Literally "middle class," but in the German context of the interwar period defined here as the lower-to-middle middle class, excluding artisans and skilled laborers

Mixer Slang for a torpedo mechanic

NA National Archives, College Park, Md.

Naxos Code name for a type of radar-detection gear (FuMB)

NCA *Nazi Conspiracy and Aggression,* a published series of translated captured German documents from the Nuremberg Trial

NCO Noncommissioned officer

NID Naval Intelligence Division (British)

NS National Socialism

NSDAP *Nationalsozialistische Deutsche Arbeiterpartei,* the "National Socialist German Workers' Party" or Nazi Party

Oberbootsmann/Nummer Eins Boatswain (Bosun)/Number One, a senior

NCO generally responsible for the conduct of the seaman division aboard a U-boat

Oberfeldwebel Senior NCOs in the German military and navy

Obersteuermann Chief navigator or helmsman, a senior NCO aboard a U-boat; also the designation for a specific naval career-track

OKM *Oberkommando der Kriegsmarine,* Naval High Command

ONI Office of Naval Intelligence, U.S. Navy

Op-16-Z Office designation for the Special Activities Branch within ONI, responsible for the interrogation of prisoners of war and the evaluation of captured equipment

Pi-2 German term for a type of magnetic detonator used with torpedo warheads

PK-Mann *Propaganda-Kompanie Mann,* term for a war correspondent

POW Prisoner of war

RAF Royal Air Force (British)

RG Record Group, used by the National Archives to indicate the records originated by a specific agency or department

Ritterkreuz Knight's Cross of the Iron Cross

Rudeltaktik "Group (or pack) tactics," attacks on convoys by concentrations of U-boats after contact had been made and the necessary strength massed via radio control at BdU headquarters

Rudergänger Crewmen who operated the hydroplane controls on a submerged U-boat; the *Gefechtsrudergänger* were the most experienced operators who manned the controls during battle stations

SA *Sturmabteilung,* Nazi party storm troopers

Schlosser Usually translated as "locksmith," but also the common term for nonspecialized (and often apprentice) metalworkers, so frequently recruited by the German navy

Schnorchel Snorkel, a tube that could be extended above the water's surface from a submerged U-boat, taking in oxygen and releasing exhaust fumes, thereby allowing U-boats to recharge their batteries and use their diesel engines underwater

Schulboot U-boat used only for training purposes

Skl *Seekriegsleitung,* Naval Staff, the executive department of the Naval High Command; references in the text are to 1/Skl, the Operations Section, responsible for coordinating naval operations

Smut or Smutje Cook on a German vessel

SS *Schutzstaffel,* "Guard Echelon," Nazi party security organization

T-5 German acoustic torpedo, also known as the *Zaunkönig* ("wren") to the Kriegsmarine and the "Gnat" to Allied intelligence

Techniker Collective term for those serving in technical career-tracks within the navy, including engineering personnel, torpedo mechanics, and radiomen aboard U-boats

TMWC *Trial of the Major War Criminals before the International Military Tribunal Nuremberg, 14 November 1945–1 October 1946,* a forty-two-volume transcript of the Nuremberg Trial that includes copies of many documents introduced in evidence

Torpedovorhaltrechner Torpedo attack calculator, a primitive computer mounted on the wall within the conning tower into which data were fed to calculate the proper torpedo release time

U-Boot-Waffe Submarine Service, U-boat Arm

ULTRA Code name for the Allied interception and decryption of secret German radio communications

Unteroffiziere Noncommissioned officers, which in the German navy includes both chief petty officers and petty officers

UZO *Überwasserzieloptik,* a device used on the U-boat bridge for surface torpedo firings

Volksoffizier An officer risen from the ranks

Wabos Contraction of *Wasserbomben,* German for "depth charges"

Wanz or Wanze Contraction of *Wellenanzeiger* ("wave detector"), the common name for a type of radar search receiver that replaced the Metox FuMB

"Warschau!" Expression used to alert others of one's imminent descent down a ladder or passage through a hatch, similar to "Coming through!"

Wintergarten The aft section of a U-boat's bridge on which the antiaircraft guns were mounted

Zentrale Central control room in a U-boat

Comparative Ranks of World War II Navies

German Navy	Royal Navy	U.S. Navy
Matrose (II)	Ordinary Seaman	Apprentice Seaman
Matrosen- or Mechanikersgefreiter	Able Seaman	Seaman 3d Class
Maschinengefreiter	Stoker	Fireman 3d Class
Matrosen- or Mechanikersobergefreiter	Able Seaman	Seaman 1st Class
Maschinenobergefreiter	Stoker 1st Class	Fireman 2d Class
Funkobergefreiter	Telegraphist	Radioman 3d Class
Bootsmannsmaat	Leading Petty Officer (Seaman's Branch)	Petty Officer 3d Class, Coxswain
Mechanikersmaat	Leading Petty Officer (Gunnery/Torpedoman's Branch)	Torpedoman's Mate, 3d Class
Maschinenmaat	Leading Stoker	Fireman, 1st class
Funkmaat/Oberfunkmaat	Leading Telegraphist	Radioman, 2d Class
Oberbootsmannsmaat	Acting Petty Officer (Seaman's Branch)	Petty Officer, 2d Class Boatswain's Mate, 2d Class

German Navy (cont.)	Royal Navy (cont.)	U.S. Navy (cont.)
Obermechanikersmaat	Acting Petty Officer (Torpedoman's Branch)	Torpedoman's Mate, 2d Class
Obermaschinenmaat	Acting Stoker	Machinist's Mate, 2d Class
Bootsmann	Petty Officer (Seamen's Branch)	Petty Officer, 1st Class / Boatswain's Mate, 1st Class
Obermechaniker/Mechaniker	Petty Officer (Torpedoman's Branch)	Torpedoman's Mate, 1st Class
Maschinist	Acting Stoker	Machinist's Mate, 1st Class
Oberbootsmann	Warrant Officer (Seaman's Branch)	Chief Petty Officer / Chief Boatswain's Mate
Obersteuermann	Chief Petty Officer (Navigation)	Warrant Quartermaster
Obermaschinist	Chief Stoker	Machinist (Warrant Officer)
Fähnrich zur See	Midshipman	Midshipman
Oberfähnrich zur See	(Senior Midshipman)	(Senior Midshipman)
Leutnant zur See	Junior Sublieutenant	Ensign
Leutnant (Ing.)	Junior Sublieutenant (Eng.)	Ensign–Eng.
Oberleutnant zur See	Sublieutenant	Lieutenant (j.g.)
Oberleutnant (Ing.)	Sublieutenant (Eng.)	Lieutenant (j.g.)–Eng.
Kapitänleutnant	Lieutenant	Lieutenant
Korvettenkapitän	Lt. Commander	Lt. Commander
Fregattenkapitän	Commander	Commander
Kapitän zur See	Captain	Captain
Kommodore*	Commodore*	Commodore*

*Courtesy title for captains holding flag rank

German Navy (cont.)	Royal Navy (cont.)	U.S. Navy (cont.)
Konteradmiral	Rear Admiral	Rear Admiral
Vizeadmiral	Vice Admiral	Vice Admiral
Admiral	Admiral	Admiral
Generaladmiral	—	—
Grossadmiral	Admiral of the Fleet	Fleet Admiral

Neither Sharks Nor Wolves

A Community Bound by Fate

When writer Nicholas Monsarrat saw his first U-boat prisoners of war as a World War II sailor with the Royal Navy, his feelings reflected both surprise and contempt:

> They seemed an insignificant and unexciting lot: Water dripped from their hands and feet onto the deck, and above their nondescript and sodden clothes their faces were at once woebegone and relieved. . . . No heroes, these: Deprived of their ship, they were indeed hardly men at all. . . . Was this really all that was meant by a U-boat's crew?[1]

But appearances, as so often in war, can be deceiving.

The Crew

A World War II U-boat crew in fact represented a complex and interdependent team of seamen, technicians, and weapons specialists whose combined efforts converted the world's most unorthodox warship into one of history's deadliest weapons. Their supreme commander, Grand Adm. Karl Dönitz, once characterized a submarine crew as a *Schicksalsgemeinschaft*, a "community bound by fate," for each man—regardless of rank—held in his hands the key to life or death for all. "If one crewman errs," wrote Dönitz, "if he fails as a lookout, improperly closes a valve, or forgets a seal, he jeopardizes his boat's success, his life, and the lives of his crewmates. Thus is each dependent on the other, and is thereby sworn to one another."[2] In these pages we shall examine who these men were and what kind of war they fought.

First it is necessary to understand the organization and functions of a typical U-boat crew. The men who manned a U-boat could be divided by rank into three groups—officers, noncommissioned officers, and enlisted men—and by function into two divisions, seamen (*Seemänner*) and technical personnel (*Techniker*). The standard German navy organizational chart in table 1 reflects this dual arrangement for the forty-eight to fifty men crammed into the 220-foot-long tube that was a Type VIIC U-boat, including four officers, three or four senior noncommissioned officers (*Oberfeld-webel* or *Unteroffiziere mit Portepee*), fourteen petty officers (*Unteroffiziere*), and twenty-six to twenty-eight enlisted men (*Mannschaften*). The exact number of officers and men could be as high as sixty, especially for the Type IX and larger U-boats. The basic tasks performed by designated personnel, however, remained essentially unchanged among the submarine models most commonly used in the war.

The variation in crewmen's ranks served as an informal index of their experience level: A preponderance of enlisted men who held the rank of *Maschinen-* or *Matrosenobergefreiter*, for example, usually indicated a veteran crew.[3] And it was the need for specific numbers of specialized personnel— seamen, radiomen, diesel and electrical engineering personnel, torpedomen—at varying ranks for every fifty-man crew that would eventually compel the navy to abandon the notion of a purely volunteer submarine force.[4]

The most important individual—the boat's "soul," as expressed by Dönitz —was of course the *Kommandant* (commanding officer), who usually held the rank of *Kapitänleutnant* (lieutenant) or *Oberleutnant* (lieutenant [j.g.]), the latter with the suffix *zur See* to indicate an executive or line officer. To him fell the ultimate responsibility for the submarine's success or failure. A U-boat captain drew upon his individual character, skills, training, and experience to master the challenges of seamanship, battle tactics, and above all leadership of his men. Every combat patrol tested a commander's abilities daily, whether in the intricacies of maneuvering to obtain the best firing position, the split-second decisions in eluding a depth-charge attack, or the constant effort to maintain his crew's morale and efficiency. His severest test required him to set the proper example while under attack, cracking a joke or ostentatiously reading a novel as depth charges detonated around them. As one commander recalled, "If you had the confidence of your crew, you were almost a god."[5]

If so, circumstances often required a captain to act like one. Whatever his skills as seaman and hunter, a U-boat commander and his officers had

TABLE 1 **PROFILE OF A TYPICAL U-BOAT CREW**

Officers

Commander *(Kapitänleutnant or Oberleutnant z.S.)*
Chief Engineer *(Oberleutnant [Ing.])*
First Watch Officer *(Oberleutnant/Leutnant z.S.)*
Second Watch Officer *(Leutnant z.S.)*
(On occasions: Commander-in-training; Doctor)

Seaman's Division *(Seemänner)*

Senior NCOs *(Oberfeldwebel or Unteroffiziere mit Portepee)*
- Chief Helmsman/Navigator *(Obersteuermann)*
- Bosun *(Oberbootsmann or Oberbootsmannsmaat)*
- One or two midshipmen *(Fähnrich z.S.)*

Chief and other petty officers *(Unteroffiziere)*
- Chief Bosun's Mate *(Oberbootsmannsmaat/Bootsmaat)*
- Bosun's Mate *(Bootsmaat)*
- Torpedoman's Mate *(Obermechanikersmaat/Mechanikersmaat)*

Enlisted Men (Seamen)
- Two to ten Seamen 1st Class *(Matrosenobergefreiter)*
- Two or three *Mechanikersgefreiter* (no exact USN equivalent)
- Two to twelve Seamen 2d Class *(Matrosengefreiter)*
- One or two Apprentice Seamen *(Matrose)*

Technical Division *(Techniker)*

Senior NCOs
- Chief Diesel Machinist *(Diesel Obermaschinist)*
- Chief Electrical Machinist *(Elektro Obermaschinist)*
- Chief and other petty officers
- Two to six Machinist's/Electrician's Mates *(Maschinenmaat,* including one Central Control Room Mate or *Zentralemaat)*
- Two Radiomen *(Oberfunkmaat/Funkmaat)*

Enlisted men
- Two to eight Firemen 2d Class *(Maschinenobergefreiter)*
- Two or three Radiomen 2d/3d Class *(Funkobergefreiter/Funkgefreiter)*
- Three to eight Firemen 3d Class *(Maschinengefreiter)*

to exude confidence and control at all times and under any conditions, setting constant examples while never letting down their guard. Always visible, he had to demonstrate his mastery of every situation that arose. In times of crisis he had to calm his men's fears and never take counsel of his own. As we shall see, the strain sometimes proved too much.

The commander inhabited his submarine's central sections: the *Zentrale* or central control room, which was the U-boat's command and nerve center; the cramped conning tower, where he sat at the attack periscope to conduct submerged torpedo firings; the bridge, where he usually joined the watch every dawn and dusk, the periods of limited visibility that rendered a U-boat most vulnerable to attacking aircraft; and his own quarters located just forward of the control room, where a cloth curtain afforded him his only privacy. During torpedo runs on the surface, he supervised his first officer in conducting the attack. Although the *Befehlshaber der Unterseeboote* (BdU, commander of U-boats) nominally directed his movements, a U-boat captain ultimately exercised his own judgment. In his cabin he recorded the daily entries for the boat's war journal, took advantage of a small washstand to clean and shave (if he wished), and grabbed what sleep he could.

Whatever his general abilities, the captain's marksmanship skills and luck often determined the submarine's ultimate success and the crew's morale. Although U-boats achieved most of their sinkings on the surface through 1942, submerged attacks sometimes provided the only opportunity for success or survival and from 1943 increasingly became the only possible means of attack. Peering through the lens of the attack periscope, the commander above all required a keen eye for estimating his target's size, course, and speed during a few seconds' observation—a talent that might be enhanced but rarely acquired through training and experience. "If a commander is successful, his crew will love him more, even if he is an idiot, than one who isn't," observed U-boat ace Wolfgang Lüth, but he added: "In the final analysis, if anything goes wrong it is always the captain's and the officers' fault."[6]

Second in importance stood the chief engineer (*Leitender Ingenieur*), universally known as "L.I." by his initials (pronounced "ell-ee") or "Chief" (*Chef*) by his function, usually with the rank of *Oberleutnant (Ingenieur)*. In contrast to his counterpart aboard an American submarine, the L.I. stood almost equal to the captain as the officer responsible for the submarine's operation as a vessel. "The L.I. carried the commander on his shoulders," remarked a senior engineering officer, adding: "The cooperation between the two must be that of a good marriage."[7] Accountable for all aspects of the boat's propulsion systems, diving capabilities, and underwater control, the L.I. also closely advised the commander on all technical matters. He kept the submarine trimmed and maneuverable while submerged, a task often rendered difficult by descending depth charges and bombs. This also required him to educate the entire crew on appropriate conduct while submerged, especially in maintaining sound discipline and strict control of weight shifts that might affect the boat's trim. Like the captain, he had no specific watch but was on constant call, and he maintained both the diving data log and his own war diary for the operation of the vessel's engines.

A German war correspondent who served aboard U-boats observed that, more than mere technical ability, the L.I. required "a special sense which will enable him to anticipate the boat's every tendency to sink or rise, because by the time these show up on instruments it is usually too late."[8] In short, a good chief engineer developed a "feel" for the unique characteristics that slightly but definitely distinguished every submarine's handling. "Without a competent L.I.," wrote one veteran captain, "a U-boat is a lame duck."[9] Entrusting the routine operation of the engine spaces to his subordinates, the L.I. spent most of his time in and around the control room. On longer patrols he was often assisted by an apprentice (or "second") engineer, usually a *Leutnant (Ingenieur),* who thereby gained experience for eventual promotion to L.I. on his own boat.

Two watch officers assisted the *Kommandant* in command functions and relieved him of many administrative duties. The first watch officer *(Erster Wach-Offizier,* usually abbreviated to I.W.O. or *Eins WO),* equivalent to a U.S. Navy executive officer, held responsibility for (1) organizing the bridge watches and directly supervising the first watch for eight out of every twenty-four hours, and (2) maintaining the readiness of the submarine's torpedoes and associated fire-control systems. Under the commander's general supervision he conducted surfaced torpedo attacks—and because this was the most effective means of attack, more Allied merchant ships could thus be claimed by I.W.O.s than by captains.[10] First officers also assumed direct command in the event of the captain's death or incapacity. According to Lüth, the I.W.O. also acted as the confidant of both the captain and the crew, to keep all on the same wavelength and identify potential morale problems before they could develop.[11] Performing these duties usually served as the final rung on the ladder to submarine command.

The second watch officer *(Zweiter Wach-Offizier,* or II.W.O.), usually an ensign *(Leutnant zur See),* exercised primary responsibility for the readiness of the U-boat's deck guns (important early in the war) and flak armament (vital after 1942), as well as for the boat's provisions and administrative matters. Responsible for communications, he kept in close touch with the radiomen and when necessary encrypted and decrypted classified radio messages. His daily duties centered on supervising the second bridge watch for two four-hour periods every day. Both watch officers and the L.I. shared a forward compartment, which doubled as the officers' mess, when mealtimes offered the opportunity to discuss aspects of command with the captain—or from which the commander absented himself to allow his officers freedom to grouse.

Sometimes a *Kommandantenschüler* ("commander-in-training"), also known as a *Konfirmand* (the designation of an adolescent receiving his religious confirmation), joined an outbound U-boat for a combat patrol. As a rule, these officers had showed great promise in training but had not previously served as watch officers; the "confirmation cruise" acquainted them with the everyday realities of submarine life and the opportunity to observe a veteran skipper in action. They stood watches on the bridge, observed the loading and cleaning of torpedoes, read all the radio messages, and above all stayed out of the way of the crew when necessary. After one or more such cruises, these officers usually qualified for their own commands.[12]

Specialist officers sometimes accompanied U-boats into combat to perform specific tasks. For a particular period of the war, naval surgeons were assigned to many U-boats, in part to attend to medical problems that arose on extended voyages and in part to treat the growing number of casualties suffered from Allied air attacks. Often they stood a watch in the radio room or took over one of the lesser duties of one of the watch officers.[13] Another common class of passengers consisted of war correspondents, combat artists, and photographers who belonged to the *Marine-Propaganda Abteilungen* (Naval Propaganda Sections), known collectively—and somewhat derisively—to submariners as "PK-Männer" (*Propaganda-Kompanie* men). These individuals maintained the image of the indomitable U-boat before the German public, in newspapers, magazines, radio broadcasts, and the weekly newsreels of *Die Deutsche Wochenschau*. Long after the war, these writers continued to mold the perception of the U-boat war, most through popular histories that mirrored their earlier narratives, one in a brutally realistic and controversial novel that became the international best-seller *Das Boot*.[14] At the height of the campaign, however, these passengers brought no joy to U-boat crewmen: "Whenever a surgeon or *Wochenschau*-reporter came on board, we knew we were in for some heavy action," recalled one veteran.[15]

Passengers on board submarines also included meteorologists; teams of signals intelligence experts from the German navy's intercept and crypt-analysis service, the *B-Dienst;* liaison officers for Japanese forces; and even political figures (for example, Indian nationalist leader Subhas Chandra Bose, borne by *U-180* (*Kapt.z.S.* Werner Musenberg) to a rendezvous with a Japanese submarine in the Indian Ocean). On some occasions U-boats carried agents, saboteurs, and commando teams, but these occurred far less frequently than imagined by British and American journalists of the time or novelists today. A survey of war diaries indicates a total of only twenty-five such missions among approximately 2,700 completed patrols con-ducted by U-boats in the Atlantic theater. More common were rescues of survivors, whether of destroyed Allied merchant ships (recorded in war di-aries of sixty submarines), sunk or damaged Axis vessels (thirty-two boats), downed Axis aircraft (fourteen boats), and eventually German refugees from Danzig Bay (at least twelve boats). Most unusual was *U-380's* (*Kaptlt.* Josef Röther) improvised rescue of four German infantrymen from the Tunisian coast on 10 May 1943 as Allied forces cleared North Africa of the last Axis forces. In all of these instances, accommodations for unplanned passengers were found in the already cramped quarters by officers and men voluntarily yielding their bunks.[16]

By 1941, U-boat crews often included a midshipman (*Fähnrich zur See*) or two to understudy the watch officers or the L.I. They might work on charts, stand watch as lookouts, and temporarily relieve watch officers and petty officers during quiet periods. If a senior midshipman (*Oberfähnrich*), he might supervise the third bridge watch and assume an officer's duties. Regular midshipmen, however, did not enjoy officer status on board, rank-ing instead as the highest-paid noncommissioned officers (NCOs). One veteran captain quartered them among the crew and gave them extra du-ties, to maximize their learning experience and demonstrate to the crew how much was required of these future officers.[17] The inevitable and often basic mistakes they made, however, drove exasperated veterans to ponder the "sheer stupidity [of] having these green kids on board."[18] Wise midship-men kept out of the way and learned anything they could from everyone.

In this their chief tutors consisted of the senior NCOs or *Oberfeldwebel,* officially designated (but rarely called) *Unteroffiziere mit Portepee* (literally "noncommissioned officers with sword-knot"), who performed the func-tions equivalent to those of warrant officers, a category gradually dropped by the German navy by 1936. Often older and more experienced than the officers who commanded them, the senior NCOs carried nearly the same re-sponsibility as regular officers in the daily routine of submarine operations. At the beginning of the war, a U-boat typically carried four senior NCOs; the expansion of the submarine fleet after 1940 reduced the average to three. Together they shared a small compartment aft of the bow torpedo room for meals and sleep, but on duty they operated in different areas of the boat.[19]

Most senior was the *Obersteuermann* (chief helmsman or navigator), re-sponsible for navigational matters and the boat's provisions. Usually an ex-perienced sailor in his late twenties to mid-thirties (and thus often the old-est man on board), he generally supervised the third bridge watch and spent most of his time in the control room, charting the vessel's course and position. Daily he recorded the boat's position by sun or starlight with a sextant on the bridge or using the sky periscope; in overcast or stormy weather, he had to use dead reckoning on the basis of the vessel's presumed course and speed. He also assumed responsibility for the storage plan of provisions throughout the submarine and worked out with the cook a schedule for their consumption. In the pursuit of a convoy and in attacks he played a major role, determining the appropriate intercept course and assisting the captain to establish the most advantageous attack position as quickly as possible. In working with his maps, charts, and sextants, he might be assisted by a petty officer from the seamen's division.[20]

Another senior NCO, the *Oberbootsmann* (coxswain, or more popularly "bosun"), generally referred to as *Nummer Eins* (Number One), exercised a wealth of onboard duties that kept him the busiest of the crew. He had responsibility for the crew's clothing and equipment and the daily cleaning of the vessel. During attacks, his station was the conning tower, where he entered relevant data into the torpedo attack calculator (*Torpedovorhaltrechner*). Above all, however, his duties concerned the conduct of the seamen's division of the crew. In keeping with German navy tradition, the bosun served as a scowling but protective "mother hen" to the sailors, with authority to handle disciplinary problems before they reached the level of the commander. The great expansion of the U-boat fleet, however, diluted the supply of available *Oberbootsmänner* and gradually resulted in the bosun's replacement (in function) by a chief petty officer (*Oberbootsmannmaat*).

Assisting the bosun were one or two mates (*Bootsmannsmaat* or *Bootsmaat*), sometimes but not usually referred to as *Nummer Zwo* (Number Two, pronounced in this way rather than "zwei" to avoid confusion with "drei") and *Nummer Drei* (Number Three). The former had to account for all ammunition stored aboard the submarine, whether for deck or flak guns, machine pistols, or officers' pistols; any ammo use required his countersignature. Number Three attended to administrative and personnel issues of the seamen's division, and the final cleanup and removal of property after the boat returned to port. The bosun and his two mates each served on one of the bridge watches.[21]

The two remaining senior NCOs, a *Diesel Obermaschinist* (chief diesel mechanic) and an *Elektro Obermaschinist* (chief electrical mechanic), respectively, ran the diesel engine and electrical motor compartments located aft of the control room. Reporting directly to the L.I., each was assisted by one or more petty officers (typically a *Maschinenmaat*, machinist's mate) and two or three men (usually at the rank of *Maschinenobergefreiter* or

Maschinengefreiter, equivalent at the time to the U.S. Navy's fireman 1st and 2d class, respectively). Swathed in heat and noise, these men devoted all their energies to engine maintenance and smooth operation. Standard procedure called for them to work watches of six hours on and six hours off, although this could be mixed with four-hour shifts at the L.I.'s discretion, particularly for U-boats operating in the tropics. During an *Alarm* (crash dive), their ability to switch propulsion from the two diesel engines to the electrical motors in a few seconds' time could mean life or death for everyone aboard. Except for an occasional smoke or the rare opportunity for a saltwater shower in southern waters, they rarely came up on deck.

Most taxing for engineering personnel were repairs of damaged engines, essential to the boat's survival. Often performed while under attack, this always demanded exhausting physical labor and frequently required imaginative improvisation of otherwise-unavailable replacement parts. Aboard *U-124 (Kaptlt.* Wilhelm Schulz), for example, ingenious engineers fashioned replacement ball bearings for the diesel engines from the tin foil wrappings of cigarette packages. Machinists on one of *U-515's (Kaptlt.* Werner Henke) patrols welded together sections of a badly damaged exterior hull despite constant vomiting caused by the acetylene torches' fumes. Sometimes duty exacted the extraordinary, as when two mechanics on *U-178 (Kaptlt.* Wilhelm Spahr) exposed themselves to injury by interposing their bodies to prevent a free-swinging piston from puncturing the fuel-oil tank.[22]

Long-term physical effects of engine-room duty only became apparent to U-boat doctors relatively late in the war. Temperature records maintained in these compartments consistently remained the highest on board a submarine. For example, on an October day with an external water temperature of 64° F., readings aboard a U-boat submerged at forty meters would stand at 74° in the control room and 73° in forward torpedo room, but 82°–85° in the engine room spaces. In the tropics at summer, temperatures often exceeded 100° with a relative humidity of over 90 percent. The decreased efficiency of those working six-hour shifts in these conditions could be measured in direct proportion to the heat and humidity index; in tropical waters, a number of men collapsed from the heat.

Other tests demonstrated damage to eardrums caused by the noise of the diesel engines, with measurable hearing loss that usually proved temporary but sometimes was permanent. Still more tests revealed that exposure to high levels of carbon dioxide intake and the physiological effects of diesel engine vibrations led to decreased mental alertness and efficiency. How these factors might have contributed to U-boat losses will never be known.[23]

In addition to the engine-room personnel, several other crewmen qualified as technical staff. The *Funker* (radio operators) originally comprised two petty officers (*Oberfunkmaat* and *Funkmaat*), each paired with an enlisted man on four-hour watches in transmitting and receiving radio communications. The radio had to be manned around the clock; messages could still be received while at periscope depth (13 meters, 42.6 feet) and all had to be transcribed even if not specifically addressed to their own boat. Much of a radioman's rating depended on how many messages he missed on his watch, as revealed by the sequential serial number for each communication.

From their small compartment just forward of the central control room, the radiomen monitored the hydrophones mounted on the submarine's bow, maintaining contact with pursuing Allied escort vessels above. Their radio duties and proximity to the commander's stateroom—where they could overhear the skipper dressing down a subordinate—kept them the best-informed of crewmen and valued by comrades as sources of information and speculation. They also looked after the boat's collection of phonograph records, a selection of which would be played at specific times during the day. Later, as radar-equipped Allied aircraft became a greater threat, U-boat radiomen also manned the radar detectors and primitive radar sets employed as stopgap countermeasures. By 1944, most U-boats had added a fifth radioman to help with these extra duties.[24]

The *Zentrale* constituted the nerve center of a submarine and was manned by its own mix of specialists, most of them *Techniker* whose performance had earned them the right to this important post. The captain, L.I., and *Obersteuermann* spent most of their time here or close by as a matter of course. A machinist's mate served as the *Zentralemaat* (control room mate), whose prime responsibility, assisted by one or two enlisted men (each designated a *Zentralegast*), concerned maintaining the boat's trim while submerged, alternately pumping or flooding small amounts of seawater into or out of the trim tanks. This in turn required precise data—daily updated in a separate logbook—on the weight distribution of fuel and foodstuffs on board. Other duties included managing the air supply while submerged (for example, pumping air from the engine room spaces to the more crowded forward torpedo compartment); maintaining the periscopes; and checking underwater salinity and temperature levels.

While submerged, an electrician's mate serviced the all-important battery that supplied necessary electrical power, a helmsman operated the rudder, and two planesmen (*Rudergänger*) from the seamen's division manned the hydroplane controls that kept the boat steady, sent it deeper, or brought it to the surface by means of hydroplanes located on the bow and stern of the submarine's hull. When the boat submerged, a petty officer and a lookout from the bridge watch immediately manned the hydroplane controls; but when at "battle stations" in a convoy action or evading surface pursuit, the hydroplanes might be manned by *Gefechtsrudergänger*, planesmen who had demonstrated the best ability and "touch" for the controls and maneuvering the vessel with the L.I. crouched over their shoulders.

In the crowded bow torpedo compartment or *Bugraum*, where more than twenty men and as many as six 23-foot-long reserve torpedoes shared a space of about seventy-five square feet, an *Obermechanikersmaat* (torpedoman's mate, second class) supervised the maintenance and loading of the U-boat's primary weapons. During an attack, he made the final adjustments to the torpedo settings as directed from the bridge or conning tower. At the beginning of the war, these functions were often exercised by another senior NCO, an *Obermechaniker (T)* or *Torpedomechaniker,* but here again the submarine fleet's expansion compelled a devolution of authority. The only chief petty officer quartered among enlisted men, the *Obermechanikersmaat* was directly assisted in the forward compartment by one petty officer (*Mechanikersmaat,* equivalent to torpedoman's mate, third class) and by another who served in the small aft torpedo compartment squeezed into the boat's stern. The *Obermechanikersmaat*'s responsibilities sometimes precipitated skirmishes with the L.I. over the exact amounts of water kept in the torpedo tanks, a matter of improvisation for torpedomen but of precise measurement for the chief engineer.

In addition to its service as the boat's weapons center, the *Bugraum* on a Type VIIC submarine constituted the permanent living quarters for most of the crew. As the tiny aft torpedo compartment of a Type VII provided no living quarters, twenty-seven crewmen of all duties shared some or most of their daily routines in the forward compartment. In addition to the three torpedoman's mates, there were ten to thirteen sailors (usually with the rank of *Matrosenobergefreiter* and *Matrosengefreiter,* or seamen, first and second class, respectively) who performed duties throughout the boat; two or three torpedo mechanics (typically at the rank of *Mechanikersgefreiter,* a designation for which the U.S. Navy had no equivalent) who spent all their time in the forward or aft torpedo rooms; and eleven or twelve engine-room personnel, who tramped the boat's length just to eat and sleep in a compartment that held no other meaning for them. This differed on a Type IX submarine, where eight bunks in the aft torpedo compartment (*Hecktorpedoraum*) accommodated sailors and *Techniker* stationed aft.

At the beginning of a patrol, the occupants of the *Bugraum* could not stand or sit normally, as reserve torpedoes rested atop the deck plates—often covered temporarily by wooden boards—and the remaining spaces were crammed full of provisions. Six bunks on either side of the compartment were usually shared by two enlisted men each; the fixed lower bunks were occupied by the mates and senior ratings. Younger sailors often slept in hammocks hung in available spaces. Even after some torpedoes had been expended and sufficient foodstuffs consumed, the torpedo room remained extremely uncomfortable. In rough seas this section experienced the worst pitching, sufficient to throw exhausted men from their bunks, sometimes even into an occupied lower bunk on the opposite side. As the electrical torpedoes loaded in the forward tubes had to be serviced every four or five days to remain effective, each day usually featured the laborious process that involved one torpedo's removal from its tube for examination, testing, lubrication, and recharging of batteries before return. In an attack, the room became a beehive of activity, especially if torpedoes had to be reloaded.[25]

One of a Type VIIC's two toilets lay tucked into the port side between the *Bugraum* and the senior NCOs' quarters; the other stood opposite the galley on the starboard side. On a Type IXC U-boat, one head was located just inside the hatchway of the aft torpedo room on the starboard side, the second at the back of the forward torpedo room on the starboard side. Only one head, however, could be used as such for most of a patrol, as the other provided storage space for provisions. Thus the only usable toilet on board (often referred to as "Tube 7" to supplement the six torpedo tubes in discharging dangerous matter) marked the one place where all the crew were truly equal. In the days when submarines spent most of their time on the surface, a solitary toilet posed few problems, as latrines could be improvised on the main deck, but when underwater the single head was highly inconvenient, as the earliest toilets could not be flushed at depths lower than twenty-five to thirty meters due to external water pressure and were moreover made of porcelain that proved very vulnerable to the shocks produced by depth charges. As U-boats began spending more time submerged and at greater depths, designers installed new high-pressure toilets (dubbed "thunder boxes") that required special training to operate the complex controls in proper sequence. If the wrong levers were pulled, the commode's contents and a stream of seawater punished the hapless operator with a head-to-foot drenching. Here an overbearing or otherwise unpopular watch officer would learn humility, dependent as he was on a trained petty officer or rating to fully instruct or assist him in disposing of his waste.[26]

That this was ultimately not a laughing matter can be seen in the example of *U-1206* (*Kaptlt.* Karl-Adolf Schlitt), lost on Friday the 13th of April 1945 due to a toilet malfunction. While making a submerged approach to a British coastal convoy off northern Scotland, someone—perhaps the captain himself—encountered problems with the cumbersome controls, so the L.I. dispatched a "toilet graduate" to assist him. The reinforcement proved fatal as the botched operating of levers resulted in a rush of waste and water that flooded the head. The leakage was stopped by bringing the submarine up to a shallower depth, but the salt water seeped into the electrical batteries below deck to mix with the sulfuric acid and create chlorine gas. With no choice but to surface to air out the boat, Schlitt brought *U-1206* up and promptly drew the attention of Allied aircraft, whose bombs further damaged the craft. The crew scuttled their U-boat and sheepishly paddled in lifeboats to the Scottish coast, their good fortune to have survived a sinking muted by association with the most embarrassing German submarine casualty of the war.[27]

Quarters for the senior NCOs lay just aft of the head. Reflecting its occupants' significance, the compartment differed little from the officers' wardroom that adjoined it. Each *Oberfeldwebel* enjoyed a private bunk, the ultimate symbol of status on a submarine. But as with the officers, rest in such privileged conditions proved fleeting against the constant interruptions of duty.

The petty officers, as noted, spent most of their time as assistants and understudies to the senior NCOs in their chosen technical fields. In addition they maintained exact listings of everything stowed away in the compartments in which they worked, particularly of the provisions. Before departing on a twelve-week patrol, for example, a Type IXC boat received fourteen to fifteen tons of foodstuffs that were stored in every available corner and overhead (and completely occupying one water closet for most of a patrol, as already noted). As these items were consumed or moved, the weight changed in every compartment in which they had been stored, a matter of utmost importance to the L.I. when trying to trim the submerged submarine. Every day, the petty officers recorded and passed along to the chief engineer precise details of weight changes involved as the boat and its crew gulped down fuel, food, and water.

The petty officers' quarters, located immediately aft of the control room in a Type VIIC boat, offered little off-duty rest for its occupants. Berths, like those of the enlisted men, were shared, but their occupants enjoyed the advantages of permanent fixtures and more headroom. Because the path through their compartment carried the most daily traffic—everyone moving from the *Zentrale* to the galley, the engine rooms, and the aft torpedo room passed through—the space came to be known as the *Leipzigerstrasse* or *Potsdamer Platz,* equivalent to the American idiom "Grand Central Station." Petty officers usually spent their off-duty time lying down, as the narrowness and use of the passageway discouraged dangling legs. Their counterparts aboard Type IXC submarines, by contrast, enjoyed the placement of their quarters in the less-traveled area just behind the *Bugraum.*

Located just aft of the petty officers' quarters on Type VII boats was the galley. By rank an ordinary seaman but by civilian occupation a baker or butcher, the cook (*Smutje* in German nautical parlance) enjoyed a special exemption from other duties because of his work's extraordinary demands. In a floor space that measured only 59 inches by 27.5 inches, he labored ceaselessly to prepare hot meals for fifty men with nothing more than an electric range's three or four hot plates, a small oven, a soup kettle, and a sink. Assisted by general guidelines and consultation with one of the bosun's mates, he planned the menus at least a week in advance to balance relative freshness of food with variety. Yet very rough seas could render even the most determined cook powerless and reduce the crew to a diet of cold sandwiches. "It goes without saying how terribly important the cook is for the well-being of a crew on a long patrol," commented a German naval physician; "The most important crewman on a submarine, including the captain," observed one veteran petty officer. For all his significance, however, when he came off duty, the cook reverted to his nominal rank in a shared bunk in the *Bugraum* with everyone else.[28]

Alone among the enlisted men, the *Smutje* enjoyed the distinction of a unique nickname. The rest bore collective terms that had developed over years of German naval tradition: Enlisted men in general were *Lords,* ordinary sailors might be known as *Tampen-johnnies* ("rope jockeys") or *Decksbullen* (roughly "deck-apes"), a torpedoman was a *Mixer,* and engine-room machinists retained the anachronistic designation *Heizer* (stoker), a lingering tradition from the days of coal-burning ships. A radioman might be called a *Puster* ("blower"), although this term extended as well to any senior *Techniker* NCO. Behind these differences in nomenclature lay significant distinctions in the background characteristics of the men serving in these categories, as we shall see in later chapters.

During the first half of the war, a new submarine commander usually enjoyed the privilege of hand-picking a few of the petty officers for his crew, typically drawing them from the boat on which he had previously served as a watch officer. Yet most crew members were simply assigned as boats and personnel became available. Nor did the crews remain perma-

nent, as the U-boat fleet's expansion involved constant turnover of personnel, especially of *Techniker* promoted to the next rank and rewarded with
shore-side training before reassignment to new boats. Adm. Hans-Georg
von Friedeburg, head of the U-boat Organization Department, allowed
proven captains more latitude in retaining their veteran crewmen, but
eventually fleet personnel needs prevailed. Veterans of *U-515*, for example,
still grouse about promotions lost or delayed under Werner Henke, yet the
crew's turnover proved constant: During the submarine's twenty-month
history (August 1942 to April 1944) a total of approximately one hundred
men served aboard her, of whom only thirty-four served ten months or
more and only nineteen for the entire period.[29] These veterans, however,
served as a mainstay of stability and experience for the newcomers who arrived before every patrol.

The Life

Combat patrols varied greatly in length over the course of the war. A *Feindfahrt* (literally "war cruise") during the conflict's early months lasted perhaps two to three weeks in the North Sea or in British coastal waters. The
most famous patrol of the war, *U-47's* (*Kaptlt.* Günther Prien) epic raid into
Scapa Flow and sinking of the British battleship *Royal Oak,* took only nine
days in October 1939. Patrols grew progressively longer as the focus shifted
to the North Atlantic and more distant waters; the "lone wolf" operations
of Type IXC boats by late 1943 averaged more than a hundred days. After
the war, British analysts who studied 2,700 completed patrols by 814 commerce-raiding U-boats over the course of the war determined that the average completed war cruise lasted thirty-six days.[30] That figure would de-
crease, however, if it took into account the last patrols of submarines,
when their cruises ended abruptly very often a matter of mere days after
departure.

　　U-boat sailors lived a life of mundane routine punctuated by moments
of stark terror. While on patrol, every twenty-four-hour period followed
the rhythm of the watches. The simplest scheme in theory applied to engine-room personnel, divided into port and starboard watches, who stood
an exhausting pace of six-hour shifts on duty and off; as noted, however,
these might be varied with four-hour shifts. Radiomen alternated four-
hour watches during peak periods (between 0800 and 2000 hours) and six-
hour watches in between, averaging twelve hours on duty out of every
twenty-four. Seamen were organized into three four-hour watches, with
eight-hour intervals used either for sleep or for a combination of various

assigned tasks and free time. Thus after four hours' duty on the bridge, a *Matrosengefreiter* might have the next two hours free for breakfast and relaxation; spend four hours swabbing the deck, peeling potatoes, or serving food to comrades; enjoy two hours' freedom for the main midday meal and a game of skat (a favorite cardgame among German submariners); perform four hours' duty back on the bridge; and then have eight hours' sleep or other relaxation. Once "battle stations" sounded, however, all routine ended and every man remained at his designated post until the action ended—or the U-boat was destroyed.[31]

Veteran captains usually attended to their crews' off-duty hours with as much care as for combat drills. To maintain enthusiasm and interest, chess and skat tournaments were organized, birthdays celebrated, and limerick, lying, or singing competitions arranged. At least one commander improvised games of chance—guessing the number of peas in a bag or the revolution count of the propellers at a designated hour—with the prize of the captain standing the winner's watch. Each crewman might have the opportunity to select the music played over the speakers for one evening's entertainment or to choose one day's dessert menu. The watch officers offered instruction in seamanship, navigation, and signaling to help prepare sailors for their next level of promotion. An onboard newsletter and library provided reading diversions, sometimes accompanied by group discussions of specific books. Special occasions such as Christmas or the crossing of the equator became major celebrations for all, with the performance of time-honored rituals that further bonded the crew.[32]

Music occupied a special place as part of a sailor's morale. A U-boat might carry about one hundred phonograph discs, each with two songs or tunes.[33] Most of the records were picked up by the officers while on leave in Germany or France, but crewmen contributed their own favorites as well. Familiar classical music appealed to most and was encouraged by commanders as a means of music appreciation for a largely working-class crew: Beethoven's *Egmont* overture, Mozart's "Eine kleine Nachtmusik," Liszt's "Préludes," songs from German operettas, and the occasional Wagner overture were typical. A few traditional marches were included in the collection for special occasions, but the crew of *U-505* (*Kaptlt.* Axel-Olaf Loewe) had no qualms about replacing the Prussian classic "Yorkscher Marsch" with the romantic "Valencia." Most records represented tangos, foxtrots, waltzes, and hit tunes by such well-known German singers as Teddy Staufer, Zarah Leander, Marika Rökk, Lale Andersen, and Evelyn Kuennecke. The L.I. of *U-612* (*Kaptlt.* Paul Siegmann) possessed a recording of Kuennecke's hit "Sing, Nachtigall, Sing," a tune so popular that other U-boats left a separate berth for Reith's submarine between the others so that all could enjoy the melody drifting out of the hatchways and conning tower. When the album fell and broke, the engineering crew lovingly glued the pieces back together so that at least some of the song could still be enjoyed.[34]

American jazz was also very popular among young German crewmen but very difficult to come by due to the Nazi regime's suppression of such music at home. The fortunate crew of *U-515* benefited from their commander's possession of a wealth of jazz and Cole Porter records acquired during his previous career as a merchant sailor.[35] Although listening to enemy radio broadcasts was officially forbidden, many commanders indulged their men and themselves, as much for a taste for Glenn Miller as for news of comrades who had survived sinkings as prisoners of war (POWs).[36] Less-understanding *Kommandanten* could be circumvented, as one radioman explained:

Night after night when the U-boat was off the American coast the *Funker* would tune in to New York and Washington stations at 11 or 12 o'clock to get American jazz, which is preferred above all other music by German submariners. This listening was done while the captain was asleep and in spite of standing orders which forbade it. . . . When crews returned to port they often talked about "die schöne Jazzmusik" that they had heard.[37]

An American merchant sailor briefly held captive aboard a U-boat in Caribbean waters reported a distinctly Southern flavor to the crew's tastes in their preference for a Texan radio station that featured "Deep in the Heart of Texas" and "hillbilly band music."[38] Even as they fought against the Allies, U-boat crews demonstrated an openness to foreign influences that their own regime sought relentlessly to stamp out.

Even more than music, humor supplied the glue that held crews together. As with soldiers and sailors of any time, German submariners developed a brand of humor at once universal and unique to their own culture. Crewmen typically received nicknames based on their size, qualities, mannerisms, or similarities in name to German public figures. What one novelist identified as "subject number one"—sex—dominated off-duty conversation on German submarines just as it did on American aircraft carriers or Nelson's ships of the line. The use of doggerel verse and elaborate, unofficial "certificates" to commemorate special events especially distinguished the style of the German navy, from yearbook characterizations of prewar officer cadets at the naval academy to variations on the lyrics of "Lili Marlene" applied to snorkels. The strain of mounting losses quieted but did not mute the laughter, albeit altering its accent toward gallows humor.[39]

In keeping with a submarine's defiance of nature, a U-boat's routine followed a clock that kept time unrelated to the conditions surrounding it. Following standard procedure, the chronometer mounted in the *Zentrale* remained set on Berlin time regardless of length of patrol or distances traveled, changing only when Germany switched to and from summer time. Hours and minutes recorded in the submarine's war diary might therefore represent a difference of several hours from local time in the Atlantic; a U-boat's lookouts scanning the sunset horizon off Cape Hatteras, for example, constituted the midnight watch. To maintain some sense of normalcy in these artificial conditions, commanders usually ordered lights dimmed during the "evening hours." The chronometer regulated daily routine and the organization of watches, as noted in table 2. The number designation of the watches followed the standard by which the I.W.O. took the 0400–0800 period to allow him the rest of the morning to attend to torpedo servicing and checking shipboard routine.

The most critical watch involved the lookouts on the bridge, who served as the U-boat's eyes in seeking out targets and spotting potential danger. The bridge watch was maintained so long as the boat remained on the surface, even when running seas threatened to sweep crewmen away to their deaths. Each watch consisted of an officer, a petty officer, and two or three enlisted men, each covering a different quadrant of the horizon with powerful binoculars; sailors with the best vision usually manned the dawn and

---

TABLE 2 **DAILY WATCH ROUTINE OF A U-BOAT CREW**

0000	First Sea Watch, Starboard Engine Room Watch on duty
0400	Second Sea Watch on duty
0545	Breakfast for Port Engine Room Watch
0600	Crew awakens (wash-up), Port Engine Room Watch on duty
0630	Breakfast for crew
0700	Ship cleaning duties for off-duty crewmen
0800	Third Sea Watch on duty; breakfast for Second Sea Watch
0845	Assigned work for off-duty watches
1200	First Sea Watch and Starboard Engine Room Watch on duty; main meal for rest of crew
1300	Assigned work for off-duty watches
1600	Second Sea Watch on duty
1715	Small evening meal for crew
1800	Port Engine Room Watch on duty
2000	Third Sea Watch on duty
2100	Lights out for off-duty crew
2340	First Sea Watch and Starboard Engine Room Watch awaken, prepare to assume duty at 0000

Source: Reference information provided by Kapt.z.S.a.D. Hans-Joachim Krug for the film *Das Boot*, published in *Cinema Programm: "Das Boot,"* ed. Dirk Manthey (1982), 28.

dusk watches, the dangerous twilight periods that made an approaching airplane difficult to spot. As Allied aircraft grew in numbers and effectiveness, U-boat commanders sometimes increased the bridge watch to as many as six lookouts, allowing each to narrow his focus to a smaller sector of the horizon, although this ran the risk of a delay in clearing the bridge if the need for a crash dive arose. An overlap of up to twenty minutes might occur when one watch relieved another, to allow time for the eyes of the new watch to become used to the lighting conditions.

In addition to the regular watch team, the bridge's occupants might include the captain, the *Obersteuermann* obtaining his readings, and individual crewmen taking turns for a cigarette (smoking was forbidden in the boat's interior). The last was strictly regulated to limit the number of on-deck personnel, each boat devising its own system—pegs on a board in the conning tower, a ring with "R" (*Raucher*, smoker) worn around the neck— to identify those indulging. (Late in the war, snorkel boats often simply dispensed with the privilege and banned smoking altogether.) The bridge had to be cleared and the boat submerged as close to within thirty seconds as possible (larger boats' size and bulk necessarily took longer) from the moment "Alarm!" was sounded, a life-or-death law respected by all and practiced while in port to ensure compliance. The watch officer was always the last below, securing the hatch and assuming his post in the *Zentrale*.[40]

While surfaced, a U-boat could travel at speeds of fifteen to sixteen knots when in pursuit of a target or racing to get into an advantageous position for a convoy attack but often maintained a cruising speed of approximately six knots to conserve fuel on long patrols. This was accomplished by using only one of the two diesel engines connected to its adjoining electrical motor, the latter acting as a generator to the opposite motor to drive the propeller shafts. The diesel engines could be alternated every four hours to equalize the wear, or one engine requiring servicing or repairs could be worked on at length. At the same time, the generator motor could be used (or both diesels could be engaged) to recharge the batteries, an essential task that consumed from two to six hours every day and could only be done on the surface.[41]

For the lookouts, standing less than five meters above the ocean's surface, bad weather always signified an ordeal and often a deadly menace. The low bridge structure that conferred near-invisibility to German U-boats on the nighttime surface also subjected the watches to punishing waves in rough seas. In such conditions many commanders shortened bridge watches to two hours, but bitter losses could not be avoided. On at least twenty-five separate occasions during the war, U-boat crewmen were swept overboard to their deaths. The worst incident occurred aboard *U-106* (*Kaptlt.* Hermann Rasch) on 23 October 1941, when the ocean snatched away an entire four-man watch in an unguarded moment; with the hatch closed to prevent water washing down the conning tower, forty-five minutes passed before the helmsman noted their absence. The loss of an entire watch nearly forced cancellation of the patrol, averted only because other crewmen voluntarily assumed the additional duties and Rasch himself took over a regular watch.[42]

With time it became evident that the keenest human vision could not provide adequate warning against the growing numbers of radar-equipped Allied aircraft. As a result, German technology after August 1942 furnished U-boats with a succession of radar detectors, mounted on the bridge and connected by cables running down the conning tower to the radio room, to scan the wavelengths of probing Allied radar. The radio operator monitored the controls and gave the alarm that had once sounded from the sharpest-eyed lookout on the bridge. In addition to the already-noted assignment of a fifth operator, these increased responsibilities of radiomen often led to adjustments in the radio operators' watches. Aboard *U-94* (*Kaptlt.* Otto Ites), for example, the commander altered the normal radio watch of four hours on, four hours off, to combinations of four-, eight-, and two-hour watches. Thus the time of the watch changed each day, allowing an equitable distribution of peak hours of activity.[43]

The watch schedule outlined above applied for that period of the war when U-boats spent most of their time on the surface. The introduction of the *Schnorchel* (snorkel—a tube from a submerged U-boat that could be extended above the surface to allow the intake of air and the exhaust of diesel gases) and the transition to newer submarine models in 1944–45, however, finally transformed the U-boat into a vessel that spent nearly all its time at sea below the waves. This all but eliminated the need for bridge watches and transformed the entire nature of U-boat routines.

While submerged with the snorkel not in operation, nearly all activities, even moving about, had to be sharply curtailed to conserve oxygen. "All hands to their bunks!" became the rule for off-watch crewmen. For possibly the only time during World War II, officers encouraged their men to stay in their beds and sleep. "We became weak-kneed, our backs hurt," reported one bunkridden veteran. The one exception was the L.I., for whom snorkeling demanded painstaking care and constant attention to hold the submerged submarine at precisely the correct depth. When rough seas or a brief submergence swamped the snorkel head, the intake valves closed to prevent water coming in; the still-operating diesel engines, however, absorbed the oxygen from the interior of the boat while deadly carbon monoxide fumes could build up in the engine spaces. The sudden pressure change might cause some ear and eye problems, but carbon monoxide poisoning could kill the crew if not quickly corrected. Several instances occurred of crewmen incapacitated by fumes from a defective or damaged snorkel, and one crewman died of asphyxiation aboard *U-1228* (*Oblt.z.S.* Friedrich-Wilhelm Marienfeld).[44]

Beyond these extreme examples, snorkel use regularly exposed U-boat crewmen to dangerous levels of carbon monoxide. Whenever a surface wave caused the air intake valve to close, the consequent release of diesel exhaust gas spread forward quickly, affecting the vision and breathing of crewmen in the *Zentrale*. The exhaust fumes moreover affected air pressure within the submarine, which in combination with the gas could cause individuals to lose consciousness. Over extended periods, submariners' blood levels revealed significant increases in carbon monoxide content; prolonged exposure to even low concentrations of the gas led in several cases to central nervous system damage.[45]

Sanitary conditions also deteriorated aboard submerged snorkel boats without the opportunity to dispose of trash overboard, as in earlier days. Eventually this was solved by packing accumulated rubbish into one torpedo tube and firing it every few days, a discharge dubbed the *Müllschuss* ("garbage shot"). Although this prevented any regular use for the particular torpedo tube, it removed the presence of trash—if not its lingering odor. A submariner's sense of smell became accustomed to anything during the course of a cruise, but when a snorkel boat returned to base, the dockyard staff would physically recoil from the stench that emanated from an open hatch.[46]

These, however, represented only the most obvious problems of snorkel use. Before war's end U-boat medical specialists discovered more systematic physical consequences. The running of diesel engines underwater, where the onboard air pressure was greater than on the surface, multiplied the already-noted risks of ear damage: Tests indicated that only one-fourth of submariners returning from a snorkel patrol retained their normal hearing. Although auditory impairments for most of the rest lasted only three or four days, some crewmen experienced temporary deafness or severe pain lasting several months. In addition to the risks associated with carbon monoxide, the increased levels of carbon dioxide present on snorkel boats became manifest in decreased attentiveness, sleeping disorders, and proneness to error.[47] But with technical improvements, and as the only means to escape Allied air attacks and stay alive, the snorkel became accepted by U-boat crews, and even celebrated in the traditional manner of German sailors, in doggerel verse.[48]

Regardless of rank or specialization, a distinguishing trait of the U-boat service within the German armed forces concerned the informality of dress. At the beginning of the war, U-boat crews received standard naval issue uniforms, which included leather jackets and trousers designed for deck and engine-room personnel but which quickly became popular throughout the submarine service. In addition, a special U-boat uniform with gray or field-gray blouse and trousers—known as the *U-Boot-Päckchen,* after the parcel in which it was packed—came into early use, accompanied by the replacement of the broad sailor's cap with the more practical board cap (*Bordmütze*). But when U-boats advanced to French bases in the late summer of 1940, they outran their supply depots, causing their crews to improvise with captured stocks of French Navy blue and British Army khaki—the latter becoming a particular favorite among German submariners. Consequently Dönitz's crews represented a mix of all of these styles, together with nonregulation plaid shirts and homeknit sweaters that defined concessions to U-boat living conditions.

Although the cramped intimacy of a submarine precluded most formalities in displays of rank, some standards remained for efficiency's sake. Officers and senior NCOs wore the blue peaked cap (*Schirmmütze*), but only the commander wore the white cap (normal summer wear) in all seasons for easy recognition, although this was a matter of common practice rather than regulation. Blouses of senior NCOs and chief petty officers often carried removable or sewn-in shoulder boards of rank, and petty officers commonly featured gold chevrons on the points of their collars. Often, however, crews wore no distinguishing insignia or markings at all, and in the tropics the only uniform for the entire crew usually consisted of shorts.[49]

Whatever dress a crewman chose might remain on his body for some time, as the possibility of an alarm at any time precluded undressing for sleep. Underwear was rarely changed, resulting in the popular choice of black shorts (dubbed "whore's undies") to conceal what could not be regularly cleaned. Daily morning teeth-brushings with fresh water remained standard when practicable, but any accompanying washing up usually required using heated seawater with a special saltwater soap, which the sailors disliked for the film it left behind on the skin. With only a small supply of fresh water furnished by a distiller in the galley, most captains allowed their crews to neglect shaving and bathing until they returned home. Their consequent appearance sometimes shocked their enemies on those infrequent occasions when they actually became visible: Describing the surface battle between the USS *Borie* and *U-405* (*Freg.Kapt.* Rolf-Heinrich Hopmann), Samuel Eliot Morison wrote, "German sailors swarmed out of the conning tower, some wearing only skivvies, many with long hair and brightly colored bandannas, which offended our bluejackets' sense of propriety and made them the more eager for a kill."[50]

A U-boat crew therefore represented an intimate collective of specialized but interdependent groups, united by a common mission and, ultimately, a shared fate. In the pages that follow we shall meet these men and experience the war they fought. We will observe how the character of the U-boat service changed and evolved over the course of the war. Perhaps we may even understand how the "insignificant and unexciting lot" described by Nicholas Monsarrat caused Winston Churchill to write: "The only thing that ever really frightened me during the war was the U-boat peril."[51]

2 First Generation

On the afternoon of 13 July 1943, the American destroyer *Barker* recovered thirty-one dazed and battered survivors of *U-487* (*Oblt.z.S.* Helmut Metz), a "milch cow" supply submarine sunk in the central Atlantic only a few hours earlier by aircraft from the carrier USS *Core*. Most of the prisoners were in their early twenties, but forty-three-year-old *Obermaschinist* Herbert Rehrock, taken immediately to the sick bay with bullet wounds in his left arm, legs, and back, raised comment among his captors as to his age. The Dresden native astonished them, however, when he revealed that he had served aboard the Kaiser's submarines in the first Battle of the Atlantic.[1]

Rehrock's example was unusual but by no means unique. Among those who commanded World War II training U-boats were *Kapt.z.S.* Bruno Mahn, who ended World War I in command of the coastal submarine *UB-21; Korv.Kapt.* Friedrich Schäfer, watch officer aboard *U-55* in the North Atlantic in 1918; and *Freg.Kapt.* Helmut Brümmer-Patzig, captain of *U-86* in 1918. At the age of twenty-four, Georg von Wilamowitz-Moellendorf went to sea as a watch officer aboard the first of four U-boats in August 1917; at age forty-eight, he returned to the open bridge of *U-459*, commanding the "milch cow" supply submarine for nearly two years before he died with her after an attack by American carrier aircraft.[2]

Other U-boat veterans from the past occupied key positions in the infrastructure of Nazi Germany's submarine service.

Adm. Hans-Georg von Friedeburg, second in significance only to Dönitz as the man responsible for all U-boat organizational and training matters, could draw upon his 1918 experiences as a watch officer aboard *U-114*. One of his staff assistants, *Korv.Kapt.* Gerhard Schacke, had served as a watch officer aboard *U-70* in 1918. Dönitz's original flotilla engineer in 1935, Otto Thedsen, had risen through the ranks since entering the navy in 1905 and served as the senior machinist aboard a front-line U-boat for most of World War I; he ended World War II as a the senior technical officer under von Friedeburg.[3] Occupying key posts in the *U-bootsabnahmekommando* (U-boat Acceptance Command) that tested and confirmed new submarines as fit for service were such Great War veterans as the Kaiser's third-leading U-boat ace, Max Valentiner, former U-boat commanders Robert Bräutigam, Erwin Sachs, and Friedrich Karl Sichart von Sichartshofen, as well as former submarine chief engineer Walter Hülsmann.

Appointed as director of basic U-boat training in 1943 was *Kapt.z.S.* Albrecht Schmidt, who captained *UB-121* in 1917–18; *Korv.Kapt.* Ernst Hashagen, another First World War ace, commanded one of the U-boat training flotillas in the Baltic. In teaching courses on submarine warfare at the German naval academy in Flensburg, Adm. Otto Schultze garnished his 1940 lectures with anecdotes from his experiences as a U-boat captain in 1915–16 and later as staff officer for the U-boat command in the Mediterranean. *Kapt.z.S.* Hans Rose, whose World War I exploits included the destruction of over 200,000 tons of shipping and a surprise visit to Newport, Rhode Island, in 1916 aboard *U-53*, served in the U-boat Training Command before reassignment to Norway.[4] Many other First World War submariners, reactivated as reservists, served anonymously throughout the training establishment.[5]

The very rebirth of the German U-boat service, a clandestine and uneven process over the general period 1927–35, owed its greatest debt to such First World War veterans as *Oblt.z.S.* Hans Schottky (former watch officer on *UB-19* and *UB-117* in 1918), *Korv.Kapt.* Kurt Slevogt (commander of *U-71* in 1918), and *Kaptlt.* Werner Fürbringer (commander of six separate U-boats, 1915–18). These men laid the foundation for the future campaign of 1939–45, from the selection and development of basic submarine designs to the earliest tactical training in fleet and commerce operations. During World War II all three continued on active duty, but removed from the service whose resurrection they had brought about.[6]

The younger officers who represented the future of the *U-Boot-Waffe* in the 1930s regarded the senior generation as "old men with the crowns on their badges," worthy ancestors but essentially irrelevant for the reborn submarine force. Many of the old aces were not recalled to active service until June 1940, and then they filled administrative or rear-area posts far removed from U-boat operations.[7] Indeed, one of Dönitz's first tasks as operational chief was to counteract the tactical lessons taught by Great War veterans at the U-boat school established by Fürbringer.[8] Yet at a much more fundamental level these veterans imparted to new U-boat crews many of their own attitudes, values, and methods. If they could not offer advice on the best night attack approach against a convoy, they passed along hard-earned knowledge of the sea and submarine life, the meaning of German naval tradition, and an appreciation of the need for flexibility and improvisation. And as will be seen, several procedures and policies survived intact between U-boat generations.

Beyond the demonstrable continuity of these individual careers lay a host of personal connections that can never be quantified but which greatly influenced submariner recruitment in World War II: those whose fathers or uncles had served in the same capacity in World War I. Not less than ten families contributed U-boat commanders from different generations in both world wars. For example, from 1914 to 1916 Georg-Günther Freiherr (Baron) von Forstner sank nearly 100,000 tons of shipping while commanding *U-28;* his nephew, Siegfried Freiherr von Forstner, earned the Knight's Cross of the Iron Cross in 1943 in command of *U-402*. Nor were such traditions limited to officers. When radioman Ludwig Becker joined the crew of *U-1164* (*Kaptlt.* Fokko Schlömer) in September 1943, he followed the course taken by his father twenty-seven years earlier aboard a torpedo boat in the Baltic. These links continue today, as demonstrated by a radioman aboard the new *U-17* who in June 1997 represented the third out of four generations to serve aboard Germany's submarines.[9]

But the direct link between the U-boat wars is the dynamic figure of Karl Dönitz. The man who held the successive World War II posts of *Befehlshaber der Unterseeboote* (commander, submarines—more commonly known simply as BdU), *Oberbefehlshaber der Kriegsmarine* (commander-in-chief of the navy), and finally Hitler's designated successor as Führer began his career in the Imperial Navy in 1910. After serving aboard the cruiser *Breslau* in the Black Sea, Dönitz was transferred to the submarine service, joining the *U-39* as a watch officer in January 1917. Operating in the Mediterranean, Dönitz subsequently commanded the *UC-25* and the *UB-68* until the latter's loss and his capture in October 1918. Dönitz would later attribute the development of "wolf pack" tactics during the 1939–45 conflict to the lessons learned in his final action in World War I (although this ignores other evidence, as will be seen).

But beyond his operational experiences in that conflict, Dönitz embodied the submarine service's character and values, which served as the later foundation for his charismatic leadership under Hitler. In his first war, Dönitz learned boldness in combat, responsibility as a commander, and comradeship as one of a crew; in his second, he infused a new generation of captains with these attributes. Building on a continuity of infrastructure and a firm foundation of lessons learned in organization, personnel selection, and the maintenance of morale, Dönitz maintained intact the distinctive identity of a submarine service born under a monarchy, hidden away under a republic, and put to the ultimate test by a dictatorship. The U-boat crew became a metaphor for the entire *U-Boot-Waffe*, with Dönitz as its captain supreme.

Yet such continuity and dedication exacted a price when required to start again. In the late 1930s Germany's was a small navy that could only begin to rebuild a submarine fleet instead of allowing an existing force to evolve. Inevitably, perhaps, the influence of a previous generation with U-boat experience predominated. That the lessons learned in 1917 would have difficulty meeting the challenges posed in 1943 could have been predicted. To understand the context in how this developed requires a review of the past, with the sudden emergence of a long-neglected weapon and the gradual irrelevance of a once-proud fleet.

Tirpitz's Navy

Germany's first submarine, the invention of Bavarian-born Wilhelm Bauer, resulted from the inconclusive war between the German confederation and Denmark over Schleswig-Holstein, 1848–51. Bauer designed a submersible vessel capable of placing explosive charges on the hulls of blockading Danish warships, but the army of Schleswig-Holstein could not fully fund Bauer's designs. Its specifications weakened to meet budget limitations, Bauer's *Brandtaucher* ("diving incendiary") sank to the bottom during an operational trial outside Kiel on 1 February 1851, although Bauer and his two crewmen escaped to the surface. The conflict's end terminated further German interest in Bauer's projects, but he eventually found employment for his projects in Great Britain and Russia.[10]

Sixty-three years later, at war's outbreak in August 1914, Germany possessed exactly twenty-eight commissioned submarines, barely one-third the number available to Great Britain (seventy-five), less than half those for France (sixty-two), and fewer even than those for Russia (thirty-six). The war interrupted prewar plans for a gradual expansion of the U-boat force to about seventy submarines by 1920, most of which were intended to defend the North Sea and Baltic approaches to German ports; a flotilla of twelve boats would be held for offensive use against enemy blockading forces in the North Sea, with ten more in general reserve. The same naval budget, however, underscored the secondary status of the U-boat with proposed increases in the German High Seas Fleet to a total of forty-one battleships, twenty battle cruisers, and forty light cruisers by 1920.[11]

These conditions reflected the beliefs of the founder of the modern German Navy, Grand Adm. Alfred von Tirpitz (1849–1930). From his assumption of the head of the Imperial Navy Office in 1897, Tirpitz dedicated his efforts to the construction of a large and modern battle fleet that would confirm Germany's status as a global power. Heavily influenced by American naval strategist Alfred Thayer Mahan, Tirpitz embraced the battleship as the key to naval power and rejected the commerce-raiding strategies held by his predecessors and advocated by the *jeune école* ("young school") of the French navy. In his view, submarines could only serve as auxiliaries to the fleet, limited to reconnaissance and harbor defense functions. Not content to simply overrule submarine enthusiasts in the German navy, Tirpitz actively worked to shorten or shelve their careers, for the stakes involved more than mere naval strategy.

Tirpitz's ambitious plans necessarily involved a political dimension in the Reichstag's funding of such a costly program of battleship construction. It has been argued that Tirpitz's scheme above all represented a domestic political strategy for integrating the interests of the German business and agrarian elites as a ruling coalition.[12] For Reichstag deputies skeptical of Tirpitz's budgets and concerned about the advanced submarine development of rival powers, the idea of the submarine as a revolutionary and relatively inexpensive offensive weapon gained increasing support. With this potential threat to battleship construction in mind, Tirpitz dismissed the U-boat as "an expensive fad," limited at best to "specific local and secondary purposes." That German taxpayers in 1912 spent more than forty-three million marks for each dreadnought battleship, while the construction of four U-boats cost them less than six million marks, testifies to Tirpitz's political influence and strategic rigidity.

As a concession to domestic pressure to keep abreast of new naval technologies, however, Tirpitz agreed to invest a modest amount in submarine research and development. In April 1904 Tirpitz issued the first order for the construction of a submarine. The result, launched on 4 August 1906, was formally designated *U-1* in November and commissioned into service on 14 December 1906. By the end of 1909, however, only three other submarines had joined her. Not until 1912 did production rise to five boats, increasing to six in 1913.

The 1910–14 period also witnessed significant qualitative returns on Tirpitz's small investment. The installation of the diesel engine as the main propulsion system after 1910 marked a major advance, greatly expanding a U-boat's operational range and facilitating its use as an offensive weapon, although most German submarines in 1914 remained equipped with less efficient petrol engines. Beginning in 1913, radio equipment became a standard feature on new U-boats at a time when many British submarines still relied on messenger pigeons. German submarines also enjoyed a significant advantage in the quality of periscopes, employing optical equipment superior to that of her rivals.

More significant was the kaiser's approval in December 1913 of an independent Submarine Inspectorate within the Imperial Navy. The new office, which became operational in March 1914, assumed responsibility for submarine development, construction, and maintenance, as well as the training of U-boat personnel.[13]

But the final bill for Tirpitz's long-term neglect of the submarine ultimately fell due after the coming of war in August 1914. No clear U-boat strategy existed, and the few shipyards involved in submarine construction precluded a rapid expansion of the U-boat fleet. Moreover, Tirpitz had never bothered to coordinate his construction of a vast battle fleet with the procurement of adequately trained personnel, especially officers. This factor would later play a critical role in the manning of Germany's submarines and the personnel implications for the surface forces.

When Tirpitz became state secretary of the Navy Office in 1897, the total strength of Imperial German Navy amounted to about twenty-six thousand officers and men. By August 1914 that number had increased to approximately eighty thousand—a tremendous expansion, yet one which could not keep pace with the frantic construction of new warships. As early as November 1912, German admirals commented on the exhaustion of fleet personnel in the performance of multiple duties. Machinists undergoing training, for example, doubled for garrison guard duty at night. The navy estimated that not until two years after the completion of the fleet would an adequate number of engineering personnel be available.[14]

Where these men came from, and how the strongest land power in Europe mobilized its resources to man a modern navy, provides both a prelude to World War I and a legacy for World War II.

The Kaiser's Sailors

As navies grew and modernized at the beginning of the twentieth century, the question of manpower recruitment gained in significance. The U.S. Navy, for example, chose to rely entirely on volunteers. The Americans, however, did not have to compete with universal military conscription, as did their German counterparts, and in any case the U.S. Navy mustered only 51,500 men in 1914. A significant aspect of volunteer recruitment in the United States involved a geographical bias against coastal areas; Navy recruiters favored the "better class of men" believed to be found in the rural Midwest over the "transients" of the waterfront, and "city boys, who are less desirable material."[15]

By contrast, Germany had long accepted the need for conscription to man her warships, for which she relied upon completely different sectors of the population. The Imperial Constitution of 1871 specifically exempted the "entire seafaring population of the empire" between the ages of seventeen and forty-five from army conscription but reserved them for possible naval service. In November 1894, a special naval order established specific population categories for recruiting needs: (1) seafaring men from Germany's coastal and river ports (merchant sailors, fishermen, and coastal and harbor boatmen with at least one year's professional experience); (2) "semi-seafaring" men (from the same occupations, but with less than a year's experience); and (3) non-seafaring men, drawn either from outdoor occupations in coastal and island districts, or machinists, metalworkers, and artisans, and craftsmen from the interior. The latter categories represented apprentices rather than experienced workers, but with basic training in skills vital to the maintenance of an increasingly technological navy. Volunteers could sign on for variable periods of service; draftees served three years' active duty and four years in the reserves.

In practice the navy, lacking the army's conscription apparatus, forwarded its personnel requirements to the Prussian War Ministry for apportioning among the Reich's military districts. Because of the specific categories and occupations reserved for navy use, this meant that the majority of naval conscripts came from northern Germany, the Rhineland, and key industrial centers. Thus, at roughly the same time Tirpitz achieved prominence, the basic personnel patterns of the navy assumed the form they would retain through 1945.[16]

Until Tirpitz's arrival, conscription did not figure prominently in navy recruitment. The new state secretary's ambitious programs quickly changed that policy. Available data for 1913 reveal that volunteers—almost certainly from the same occupational groups selected by the navy—numbered only about 28 percent of the year's intake of recruits. An additional 21 percent represented draftees from the seafaring and semi-seafaring occupations. These, together with most of the volunteers, constituted the Seaman and Torpedo Divisions of the German naval establishment, which furnished the sailors who carried out the nautical and military functions on board warships. The remaining 51 percent consisted of conscripts from the inland population—metalworkers, machinists, artisans, and electricians, drawn predominantly from the industrial centers of western and central Germany to staff ships' engine and radio rooms.

The result, as described by German naval officer and historian Rolf Güth, was the emergence of a dual character of Navy personnel: "Beside the quiet North German seaman and fisherman stood the animated mechanic and industrial worker from western and central Germany. The former was a conservative individualist, the latter organized on a mass basis for both work and politics." This unlikely combination would serve as the foundation of the German navy, and thus of the U-boat service, through two world wars.[17]

Naval officers represented the German middle class, particularly the upper middle class. A statistical study of the professions of fathers of German naval officer cadets in 1907 revealed that nearly half (90 of 197, 46 percent) were academics and more than a quarter (26 percent) were military or naval officers. In sharp contrast to the Prussian army, where members of the nobility still wielded disproportionate influence, only 11 percent of the cadets came from noble families. At the other end of the social scale, only two or three cadets claimed petit bourgeois backgrounds (artisans, lower-level civil servants), a selection policy designed to limit representation to the "better" classes. The cadets were also heavily Protestant and north German; nearly 70 percent originated from the coastal regions of the North and Baltic Seas, while less than 13 percent came from parts of Germany south of the Main River. For the most part, these proportions would not greatly change from their counterparts twenty-seven years later, but some evolution would occur.

Most cadets would progress to the status of *Seeoffizier*, executive or line officers who could expect to eventually command their own warships. Engineering officers, on the other hand, presented a different picture: More typically drawn from the lower middle class, they were never granted equal status with executive officers, with more limited opportunities for advancement. The identity of class background with officer function was expressed in 1913 by one German naval writer:

The faculty of leadership, engendered by tradition and education, may be found with greater probability in the sons of certain classes than in those of others, so that it is a duty to bring such young men into the profession of executive leaders, while actual experience tells us that youths coming from the practical professions of the middle classes make quite excellent engineers.[18]

Organizational aspects of the first U-boats fell under the administration of the Navy's Torpedo Divisions, which also provided the nontechnical crew members. The establishment of the Submarine Inspectorate granted submariners organizational independence. Volunteers now applied directly for U-boat service, with the added inducements of special pay and privileges. By August 1914 the U-boat service numbered just under 1,400 officers and men, of whom 747 constituted the operational crews. The remainder were attending the three-month submarine training courses or performing training, administrative, or other support tasks for the Submarine Inspectorate.[19]

Test of Arms

When war came, neither Tirpitz nor the High Seas Fleet had any plans for using submarines to attack merchant shipping. But within the Submarine Inspectorate staff, *Kaptlt.* Ulrich-Eberhard Blum drafted a study in May 1914 on Germany's submarine requirements in a possible war against England. From the premise that the U-boat should be used in a trade war strategy to strangle British commerce, Blum reckoned that 222 submarines would be necessary, on rotating station at forty-eight key blockade positions around the British isles. Blum's superiors mentioned this study to Tirpitz in June, but even they did not request an acceleration of submarine production.

Considering that only a handful of U-boats were then capable of operating west of Britain, Blum's effort reflects an optimal feasibility study rather than a plan. The Imperial Navy Office demonstrated its continued disinterest in submarines in June and July 1914 when it allowed a German shipyard to proceed with the projected sale of five completed submarines to Greece, negated only by the outbreak of hostilities. Blum's memorandum, however, reveals much of the mentality of Germany's U-boat pioneers: faith in an unproven weapon, belief in a radical strategy, and intellectual independence from the establishment.[20]

Finally, Blum's study foreshadowed, and possibly directly influenced, Dönitz's own 1939 assessment that a minimum of three hundred operational U-boats were necessary to win a campaign against Allied convoys in the Atlantic. Blum's and Dönitz's estimates appear oddly linked by fate: Both prognoses, although realistic in requirements, would prove unattainable for much of the conflict that began mere weeks after each was drafted. Even after war broke out, neither proposal became a foundation for planning until strategic developments encouraged their implementation.[21]

For Imperial Germany, two such developments occurred during the Great War's first months. Contrary to Tirpitz's expectations, the British fleet did not steam into German coastal waters to seek battle but maintained a distant blockade at the northern and Channel exits of the North Sea. The outnumbered High Seas Fleet, aware that it could not challenge the British Grand Fleet on even terms with a reasonable chance for success, lacked a strategy for the situation. Consequently it stayed in port, there to remain for most of the war.

The second and more electrifying event would forever alter military and public perceptions of the submarine as a weapon. On the morning of 22 September 1914, *U-9* under *Kaptlt*. Otto Weddigen—who seventeen days earlier had dispatched the British armored cruiser *Pathfinder*—sank three British armored cruisers off the Dutch coast in just over one hour. Weddigen and his twenty-eight men in an obsolescent, petrol-burning submarine had destroyed nearly forty thousand tons of warships and 1,460 British sailors in a nautical version of David and Goliath. Beyond its demonstration of a submarine's lethal potential, the incident fired the German public imagination to an extent that would outlast Weddigen, the war, and the kaiser. Weddigen's death in action six months later generated an outpouring of press features, poems, and popular literature across Germany. The U-boat became fixed in the public mind.[22]

For many junior and petty officers, Weddigen's exploit served as a magnet to the submarine service. The opportunity for fame, independence, and escape from the tedium of an inactive fleet led many to volunteer for U-boat duty. A contemporary described the attitude aboard a capital ship in December 1914:

Our former adjutant joyously departed yesterday for torpedo training. . . . Today one of our engineers is leaving for U-boat duty. How happy they all are, to move to posts where they can actively participate in the war, although they realize they can never be as comfortable as aboard our big "Bobby." But such is not an ambition during a war.

Two weeks later the writer joined the U-boat service himself: "Everyone congratulates me. I'm very lucky."[23]

An institutional practice of the German navy greatly facilitated the easy transfer of officers from one branch to another. In contrast to Britain's Royal Navy, where executive officers often specialized in torpedoes, gunnery, navigation, or signaling, their German counterparts received intensive training in all these fields but did not commit to a particular branch or role. The ability to move a gunnery officer from a cruiser to command of a

U-boat demonstrated the flexibility required of a navy with limited man-power resources.[24]

Part of the price to be paid for these transfers, however, became evident to Seaman Richard Stumpf by March 1915 aboard the battleship *Helgoland:* "The best and most intelligent of our officers have been transferred to cruisers, torpedo boats and submarines. . . . With a few exceptions those who have remained behind don't have much on the ball."[25] The irony of Tirpitz's proud creation being reduced to a replacement depot was not lost on the historian of the U-boat campaign, who remarked: "The fact that it was possible to select the supply of the needed personnel for our sub-marines . . . was largely due to the fact that the German fleet served as a means of training a reserve of personnel from which officers, petty officers and special enlisted ratings could be carefully selected."[26] The cost of this ever-increasing drain on the leadership within the German fleet would be-come apparent in the naval mutinies of 1917–18 that heralded Imperial Germany's ultimate defeat.[27]

A principal motivation to volunteer for submarine duty in 1914 in-volved the prospect of action, especially as the primary targets remained enemy warships. Following Weddigen's exploit, German U-boats sank an-other cruiser, a pre-dreadnought battleship, one submarine, a seaplane car-rier, and a gunboat before year's end—more Allied warships than would be sunk over the remainder of the war. Merchant shipping represented only secondary targets, for during this period a mere three British steamers fell victim to U-boat attacks, all conducted in strict accordance with interna-tional prize rules that required prior warning and provision for the crew's safety.[28]

Yet throughout that autumn U-boat commanders reported on the favor-able prospects for commerce warfare against the heavy and unprotected merchant traffic transiting Britain's ports. Discussions among naval circles culminated with an October proposal for an all-out attack on merchant ships in British coastal waters. Although not immediately endorsed, the concept nevertheless provided the foundation for the unrestricted subma-rine warfare campaign approved by the kaiser in February 1915, a campaign ultimately doomed by a long-range submarine force of only twenty-one U-boats, the lack of a clear strategy, inadequate intelligence, and a costly indif-ference to international reaction—all legacies of Tirpitz. American outrage following the 1915 sinkings of the liners *Lusitania* in May and *Arabic* in Au-gust curtailed the campaign, which was abandoned in September.[29]

But the hopes raised by unrestricted submarine warfare as the best means to sever Britain's economic lifelines and end the deadlock proved too tempting. Pressured by naval and military leaders, the kaiser's government vacillated between this all-out measure and commerce warfare according to prize rules throughout 1916. Finally in January 1917, after the Battle of Jutland demonstrated the surface fleet's slim chances of breaking the blockade and the "turnip winter" of 1916–17 underscored Germany's vulnerability to food shortages, the advocates of submarine sinkings without warning won their case. With the decision to commence unrestricted submarine warfare on 1 February 1917, the neglected stepchild of Tirpitz's navy became Imperial Germany's last hope for victory.

The oft-told chronicle of the 1917–18 campaign need not be detailed here. In three months U-boats sank two million tons of shipping, a rate of destruction that would have crippled the Allies if maintained. But the introduction and gradual expansion of the convoy system ultimately frustrated the submarine offensive, and the entry of the United States into the war as a direct consequence of unrestricted U-boat attacks doomed Germany to defeat. U-boat losses eventually numbered 178 of a total fleet of 374, and the war ended before an ambitious submarine construction program came to fruition.[30]

Hidden behind these familiar strategic outlines, however, lay the nature of the war as experienced by German submariners, and the foundations thereby laid for their successors.

Legacies

In a navy where the bonds between officer and enlisted man steadily unraveled, service aboard a U-boat crew bonded both in mutual dependence for success and survival. The sharing of cramped quarters, common rations, and constant danger combined to forge a camaraderie not found aboard the capital ships tied up in port. "There was really too much good feeling," one officer later recalled. "I in particular had to exert myself to keep the aloof poise of a naval officer and not get too friendly, because inwardly I regarded each man as a pal." This was reinforced by extended personal contacts between U-boat command authorities and the families of submariners, a "U-boat circle" that included the establishment of a relief fund for widows and orphans within the community. The crystallization of these twenty-to-sixty-man crews into a combat elite, analogous to the storm trooper detachments celebrated by German writer Ernst Jünger, defined a major legacy bequeathed to the Kriegsmarine.[31]

Although the submarine types varied between the two world wars, their variety and differing purposes provided continuity. U-boats of 1914–18 ranged in size from the diminutive "UB I" boats (dubbed "sewing machines"),[32] with a surface displacement of a mere 127 tons and a crew of only fourteen, to the 2,000-ton "U-cruisers" that carried two 88mm guns and sixty-six crewmen. Between these extremes stood the type that proved itself best suited to commerce raiding, the 516-ton "UB III" submarine, armed with five torpedo tubes (four bow, one stern), ten torpedoes, and one 88mm gun. Although difficult to control, the UB III model represented an oceangoing attack submarine with strong offensive power that could be constructed fairly quickly. The more than eighty U-boats commissioned of this series (with subsequent variations) proved highly successful (although less effective than the larger fleet U-boats) and collectively served as the direct ancestor to the mainstay of the World War II fleet, the Type VIIC.[33]

One subtype of the *Ms* (*Mobilmachungs*) *-Boote* class of fleet U-boat, consisting of submarines *U-60* through *U-62* launched in July and August 1916 by AG Weser, featured characteristics virtually identical with those of Type VIIC that came into service twenty-four years later (see table 3). The Type VIIC ultimately enjoyed significant advantages over the Ms-boats only in more-powerful diesel engines and greater forward firepower. A larger variant of Ms-boats, reflected in *U-115* and *U-116* built in 1916, provides similar comparisons with the first Type IX submarines that entered service in 1938–39. Similarly, the genealogy of the Type II U-boats in use when Hitler invaded Poland dated back to the "UF" model drafted in 1917 but never completed, and the Type IA submarines of September 1939 originated with the projected "UG" class of 1918. As one historian has noted, measurements of the relative improvements in speed and range for these evolutions in submarine classes are not impressive; those for the Types VIIC and IX over their predecessors, for example, indicate a overall improvement of less than 6 percent.[34]

This reliance on late World War I models illustrates the long-term consequences of losing that conflict for the German navy. After the cessation of hostilities Allied authorities seized all U-boats (including 183 still under construction) for division and study among the victorious powers. The gains in submarine technology proved invaluable. The U.S. Navy, for example, adopted the German gyrocompass, learned lessons from German periscopes and propulsion systems, and incorporated features of U-boat hull designs, machinery, and torpedo tubes into future submarines. Thus Germany's technological edge in the field passed to her recent enemies even as the Versailles Treaty forbade her any new construction of U-boats. That the *Reichsmarine* almost immediately began a covert evasion of this restriction cannot conceal the tremendous cost to Germany in submarine

TABLE 3 **COMPARISON OF MS-BOATS TO TYPE VIIC U-BOATS**

	Ms-boats	Type VIIC
Surface displacement (tons)	768	769
Length (meters)	67	67.1
Beam (meters)	6.3	6.2
Maximum surface speed (knots)	16.5	17.7
Maximum underwater speed (knots)	8.4	7.6
Range (nautical miles/knots)	11,400/8	8,500/10
Torpedo tubes (bow/stern)	2/2	4/1
Fuel capacity (tons)	128	113.5
Diving time (seconds)	30	30

development during the interwar period. As other navies' intact submarine fleets evolved methodically and gradually, Germany's lost almost two decades before resuming production and planning at the stage interrupted in 1918.[35]

During the First World War, the primary tasks of commerce warfare fell to the submarines assigned to the High Seas Fleet under the operational control of *Führer der Unterseeboote Korv.Kapt.* Hermann Bauer, replaced in June 1917 by *Kommodore* Andreas Michelsen with the redesignation *Befehlshaber der Unterseeboote,* the same titles later assumed by Karl Dönitz in June 1935 and September 1939, respectively. Ironically the U-boats operating under this command usually numbered only about half of the total submarine fleet—for example, 46 of the 105 boats in service as of February 1917, 67 of 121 in October 1918. The High Seas Fleet U-boats included small "UC" class minelaying boats that performed their missions in English coastal waters and fleet submarines that operated in the Atlantic approaches to British ports west of Ireland. When war began, a typical patrol lasted no more than five days; by 1917, the average had lengthened to two to four weeks, not far below the typical duration of Type VIIC submarine patrols from French bases in 1940–43.[36]

For most of the war, U-boats operated individually against merchant targets. Yet as early as 1907 a German publication had discussed the possibilities of submarines acting in concert.[37] In April 1917, even before the introduction of convoying, Bauer proposed to use a radio-equipped U-cruiser as a command boat to coordinate the movements and actions of submarines deployed in the area, an approach that Dönitz experimented with during maneuvers in 1936 and in combat with *U-53* during September 1939.[38] As the Allied convoy system sharply reduced targets over the war's last seventeen months, U-boat strategists grappled with group operations as a response. In particular, *Kaptlt.* Hans Rose and *Kaptlt.* Hans von Mellenthin devoted considerable thought and practical experience to assembling submarines for group attacks on convoys, establishing the foundations of *Rudeltaktik* or "wolf pack" tactics that Dönitz would later develop into a tactical doctrine.[39]

Although conditions in the Mediterranean theater differed markedly from those elsewhere, the U-boat perspective that prevailed there may well have exercised undue influence on the future. Despite the presence of many fewer German submarines there than in the Atlantic (23 of 105 commissioned boats in February 1917, 28 of 121 boats in October 1918), the plentiful targets yielded a disproportionate harvest. Confusion in command authority among the British, Italian, and French staffs and inadequate escorts precluded the establishment of an effective convoy system, and U-boat captains needed no recourse to unrestricted warfare to tally incredible scores. Here *Kaptlt.* Lothar von Arnauld de la Perière, ace supreme among submariners of both world wars, achieved most of his record 194 merchant ship sinkings, including one three-week cruise in July–August 1916 that netted fifty-four ships (ninety-one thousand tons) entirely according to prize rules. From the beginning of 1916 to the end of the war, High Seas Fleet U-boats sank a total of 4.45 million tons of shipping in the Atlantic; during the same period the much smaller force of Mediterranean submarines sank 3.32 million tons. Until the last months of the war, the latter also ran fewer risks, with only two losses in 1917 against thirty-two submarines lost with the fleet.[40]

As Dönitz spent his entire World War I submarine duty in the Mediterranean, this inordinate success rate carried significant implications for the World War II U-boat service. First as a watch officer aboard *U-39* (January–October 1917), then as commander of *UC-25* (February–August 1918) and *UB-68* (September–October 1918), Dönitz participated in the destruction of more than forty merchantmen.[41] These experiences, and those shared with him by other Mediterranean aces, probably left Dönitz with an exaggerated perception of U-boat capabilities. Not having served with the fleet boats that bore the brunt of the submarine campaign, the future BdU lacked personal contact with the frustrations and limitations of the main force fighting in the North Atlantic.

One specific legacy of this optimistic perspective can be seen in Dönitz's later adoption of the statistical yardstick used by the *Führer der Unterseeboote im Mittelmeer, Kapt.z.S.* Kurt Grasshoff, to measure the relative performance of his command: By adding the total tonnage of merchant sinkings and dividing by the total number of operational days spent at sea by all

U-boats, the resulting average tonnage sunk per day offered a precise calculation of submarine success over a period of time.[42] This statistical tool, apparently originated by a staff assistant in Berlin, worked well for a fairly small and constant number of boats operating in a specific theater; that Dönitz would later apply it to an ever-changing number of submarines operating throughout the Atlantic suggests expectations of success all but destined to disappointment.

It is revealing that neither Bauer nor Michelsen used this measurement for the High Seas Fleet boats operating under more difficult conditions. Instead they compiled statistical averages for submarines operating in specific areas for selected periods, to identify profitable patrol areas for future deployment of available forces. Thus in June–July 1917, when the average successes of U-boats operating between the Shetland Islands and Norway proved clearly less rewarding than those operating off the western British coast, the data provided a justification for greater concentration in the latter area.[43] Yet, despite their differences, the analytical means applied by both Mediterranean and Atlantic U-boat commands measured success in terms of rates of merchant tonnage sunk, forecasting Dönitz's emphasis on *Tonnagekrieg* in 1942.[44]

In many other ways the general administration and conduct of the U-boat service established precedents for the future, not least in its rapid growth. From the force of 1,400 that began the war, approximately 18,000 men passed through the submarine combat and support services by war's end, of whom perhaps 11,400 actually served aboard U-boats. During the war 5,132 U-boat officers and men were killed or died of wounds, and an additional 729 captured—a loss rate of over 51 percent. Excluding officers, voluntary recruitment remained the standard until 1917, when expansion of the submarine force required an increased reliance on reservists and outright transfers of qualified personnel from the rest of the fleet. The organizational and training infrastructure also had to be improvised, with the consequence that at least 20 percent of the noncommissioned crewmen received no submarine training prior to assignment. Yet morale remained intact and the overall results proved satisfactory, laying the foundation of both practical experience and a reliance on improvisation to cope with unforeseen problems.[45]

An example of the consequent personnel policies can be seen in the constant turnover among U-boat crews to provide veteran cadres for new submarines. Standard practice became the transfer of up to 15 percent of each crew after every two patrols to assure a continuous flow of experienced men for future U-boats. One acting warrant officer from *UC-32*, for example, revealed to his British captors that in less than a year he had already served aboard four U-boats. The demands of rapid expansion would dictate the adoption of similar measures before the end of 1939.[46]

Bauer established another policy precedent for Dönitz in prescribing conditions for recovering survivors from sunken merchantmen as prisoners of war. Preparing unrestricted warfare guidelines for his captains in January 1917, Bauer wrote: "Captains and machinists are to be taken captive when possible. The U-boat must not, however, be exposed to risks by such actions." A virtually identical directive would be issued by the German Naval Staff in June 1942. In both wars, however, U-boat captains made up their own minds in balancing the dictates of humanity against the necessities of unrestricted submarine warfare.[47]

Casualty and success rates also established patterns that would be repeated twenty-five years later. Of 457 U-boat commanders in World War I, 152 were killed and 33 captured, for a total loss of over 40 percent; their World War II successors would suffer 46 percent casualties. More striking are the disproportionate success rates for a small number of U-boat "aces," as twenty-two out of four hundred commanders accounted for more than 60 percent of all Allied merchant sinkings in the Great War and only 4 percent of all U-boats sank 30 percent of all merchant shipping lost. During World War II this phenomenon recurred as thirty U-boat captains (out of approximately thirteen hundred) sank approximately 30 percent of the total Allied merchant tonnage lost during the conflict.[48]

Still another legacy involved the postwar realization of how many Allied resources had been tied down by the U-boat campaign. Drawing on Allied memoirs and histories, German participants defended their accomplishments in occupying the full attention of several times their own numbers of enemy men and materiel. One source carefully calculated that Britain's fight against the U-boats absorbed the efforts of 770,000 men (including naval and merchant crews, shipbuilders, dockyard workers, and naval ordnance manufacturers) and diverted from other use some 13,000 naval guns, 3,700 searchlights, nearly 46,000 tons of munitions, and 16,327 kilometers' worth of wire for antisubmarine nets. Dönitz would later voice exactly the same arguments for continuing his campaign after May 1943—not only in his memoirs, but in exhortations to doomed U-boat crews whom he asked to fight on against similar odds.[49]

Behind these justifications lay the most significant and dubious heritage left by Imperial Germany's U-boats for the future, a critical but unresolved question: Had the U-boats' unrestricted campaign against merchant shipping helped or hindered Germany's war effort? The answers bitterly divided German naval participants. Most U-boat commanders believed they had vindicated the submarine's potential, enthusiastically endorsed unrestricted submarine warfare, and blamed their government's vacillation in 1915–16 or the failure to build enough submarines earlier for the ultimate outcome. For them the United States' declaration of war in April 1917 derived from long-standing Anglo-American business and commercial ties rather than submarine attacks.

On the other hand *Konteradmiral* Arno Spindler, a former U-boat officer and official historian of the submarine war, spoke for many naval and political leaders with his assessment that unrestricted submarine warfare proved premature rather than tardy and failed in its goals while precipitating American entry into the war. He also criticized Bauer and the High Seas Fleet U-boats for neglecting commerce warfare opportunities under prize rules in 1915–16. Naval leaders who endorsed Spindler, however, sometimes carried another agenda from the Great War, anxieties about the overall structure and function of the navy if it gradually evolved into little more than a submarine force. The achievements of the "war of ensigns and lieutenants," as some dubbed the U-boat campaign, brought into question the need for a large and costly battle fleet. As early as 1915 the Navy Office openly expressed its concerns over promotion potential for flag-rank officers if surface forces increasingly became superfluous.[50]

Notwithstanding the vigor of this debate, which continued into the 1950s, the issue as to whose voice carried greater weight was never in doubt. A German naval historian writing in 1944 ruefully remarked on the influence of the U-boat school:

The unquestioned hopes placed on the decisive effects of the U-boat war were grounded in the Great War conception that we would have won if only we'd had enough U-boats and used them in an all-out effort without regard for political restrictions. The historical research of the past 20 years does not support this contention. Nevertheless it was disseminated throughout the postwar navy, supported by an extensive naval literature, and could not be shaken by the doubts raised by the findings of the Naval Research and Historical Division. Doubtless this view dominated the thinking of leading naval figures at the beginning of the current war.[51]

Although heir to this contested legacy, Dönitz was much more a protagonist allied to Bauer and his comrades. After ascertaining the "negative" tone of Spindler's history, Dönitz dispensed with the final volumes and their conclusions.[52] His assumption of command of the submarine force in July 1935, however, yielded to Dönitz neither control of submarine types or production nor of their strategic employment. When war came in 1939, no consensus existed within the navy regarding the strategic role or significance of submarines. Not until his appointment as commander-in-chief of the navy in January 1943 would Dönitz have a free hand in U-boat production and use.

But at least no doubts existed as to the capability and reputation of the first generation of U-boat warriors. From its paltry beginnings the submarine service had matured rapidly until it shouldered Germany's bid for ultimate victory at sea; that the effort had failed did not mean that the U-boats had been mastered. Untarnished by the stigma attached to Germany's inactive and mutinous surface fleet, submarines retained a grip on the popular imagination that guaranteed future recruits. And finally Dönitz's submarine force entered hostilities in 1939 with a confidence derived in large part from combat experiences and practices acquired at great expense twenty-five years earlier, a debt acknowledged in symbolic acts of homage.

On the wet, gray morning of 5 December 1940 in Bremen's Deschimag shipyard, a new Type VIIC U-boat entered service in the German Navy as *U-109*, under the command of *Korv.Kapt.* Hans-Georg Fischer. Present at the commissioning ceremonies, and honored guests at the luncheon that followed, were Carl Keitel and Franz Dompke, the last living survivors of submarine *UB-109*, lost in action twenty-two years earlier.[53] The torch had been passed.

3   The Framework of the U-boat War

The men who manned Germany's U-boats fought their war within a framework that defined both their objectives and the means to attain them. That framework included the following elements: The *U-Boot-Waffe*'s top leadership, whose policies and character gave the service identity; the command staff that directed operations; the strategy and tactics that provided focus to mission, training, and fighting; and the U-boats themselves, whose physical capabilities ultimately meant the difference between life and death. Each of these subjects merits, and has often received, its own book. Here a description of the key elements of each might allow some glimpse of the invisible structures that bound German submariners even as they sailed toward an endless horizon.

The Leadership

Karl Dönitz dominates any study of the U-boat campaign, more so than the limitations of his offices and power would seem to indicate. Certainly Dönitz stamped his command with the dynamism, charisma, and resoluteness that defined his own character. Yet before 1943 he lacked authority to determine U-boat types or overall strategy; traits ascribed to him sometimes reflect shared characteristics among the Kriegsmarine leadership; and the tremendous expansion of the submarine fleet necessarily diluted Dönitz's influence. Any study of Nazi Germany's submarine campaign nevertheless begins with the commander and his small staff most commonly identified by the acronym "BdU" (*Befehlshaber der Unterseeboote*, commander of submarines).[1]

There was little in Dönitz's background to indicate a singular suitability for U-boats. Born 16 September 1891 into an upper-middle-class family in Berlin, Dönitz's ancestors had no history of professional military or maritime service; his adolescent interests in soldiers and exploration led him in 1910 to enter the navy, where he imagined he could satisfy both enthusiasms.[2] Consistently rated highly by his superiors, Dönitz possessed a strong intellect (his IQ was measured at 138 at Nuremberg, among the highest of the war crimes defendants) and a sense of humor that surprised his postwar captors.[3] Yet only a little more than two of the first twenty-five years of his career involved submarine service, and he played no role in the covert second foundation of the U-boat arm in the early 1930s. When he received his appointment as *Führer der Unterseeboote* (FdU, commander or flag officer for submarines) in July 1935, it probably reflected no more than the navy's confidence in his proven organizational skills[4] to mold the newly established U-boat Flotilla into an efficient unit. He had no power to determine submarine types or construction; the timing of his appointment coincided with an internal shakeup of U-boat offices to integrate the control of submarine development and strategy with that of conventional surface forces.[5]

Nevertheless Dönitz "threw myself with all the energy at my command into the task of successfully building up the new U-boat arm," as he later recalled: "Body and soul I was once more a submariner."[6] His enthusiasm and personal commitment stamped the U-boat arm with an intimacy and sense of comradeship that was retained throughout the war. From the beginning, Dönitz broke with military protocol in addressing his officers with the familiar *Du* and occasionally loaned his commanders an automobile or gave them a few hundred marks from his own funds if they were short of cash in Paris. He also assured his crewmen special treatment in pay, leave, awards, and other benefits.[7]

He did not, however, accord special treatment to his two sons, who entered the navy as officer cadets after the war began. The youngest, Peter, joined the U-boat service. A U-boat radioman described a parade formation where Dönitz greeted each officer by name with a handshake; only after the command "at ease" did he go to his son and hug him. "That impressed us mightily," recalled the veteran. *Lt.z.S.* Peter Dönitz took the same risks as others and shared the same fate as most when his submarine, *U-954* (*Kaptlt.* Odo Loewe), was lost with all hands in the North Atlantic on 19 May 1943. His older brother Klaus died a year later aboard an *S-Boot* (similar to an American PT-boat) in the English Channel.[8]

If the leader called "the Lion" bore these tragedies stoically, he displayed his claws when captains and crews produced meager results. In two-hour debriefings of returning commanders early in the war, BdU scrutinized their decisions and actions recorded in their war diaries, criticizing any lack of aggressiveness or procedural errors. Sometimes he didn't wait but offered his critiques on the parade ground, as when *U-109* (*Korv.Kapt.* Hans-Georg Fischer) returned to Lorient in May 1941:

The BdU greeted all the officers with a handshake. . . . Then he placed himself about fif-teen paces from the front rank and folded his arms across his chest. His lips were sud-denly narrow. "Your patrol was crap, and you know it. . . . Your 7,000 tons wasn't much. You'll have to do better." . . . [Then] Dönitz smiled and his voice was conciliatory as he continued, "But at least you brought the boat back. I suppose that's worth something."[9]

To his men Dönitz always displayed optimism and an aggressive "can-do" spirit reflected in his radioed exhortations to commanders. The most famous example, dispatched as losses mounted in the climactic Atlantic battles of May 1943, read in part:

Now if there is anyone who thinks that combatting convoys is therefore no longer possi-ble, he is a weakling and no true U-boat captain. . . . Keep yourselves aware of your high responsibility and do not fail to understand that you must answer for your actions. Do your best with this convoy. You must smash it to bits. . . . Be tough, get ahead and attack. I believe in you.[10]

These and similar messages have been characterized as "whipcrack slo-ganeering" that substituted for careful analysis,[11] although the same style can also be seen in some of Winston Churchill's wartime messages.[12] To the end Dönitz maintained this confident public face, as one commander reported his words after a brief meeting less than a month before Ger-many's capitulation: "My dear Schaeffer, you know very well we shall fight on until victory. We shall win whatever the cost."[13]

Yet privately Dönitz knew the long odds against his men. On 28 August 1939, perhaps drawing on and expanding the study of *Kaptlt.* Blum twenty-five years earlier, he calculated a requirement for three hundred oceango-ing U-boats as necessary for a successful commerce war against Great Britain, of which one hundred would need to be constantly on operations. War's outbreak a few days later instead found Germany with a total of only fifty-seven submarines, the majority of which could not be used effectively be-yond the North Sea.[14] When Britain declared war on 3 September 1939, navy commander-in-chief Grand Adm. Erich Raeder received the news with an acknowledgment that the Kriegsmarine, hopelessly outnumbered and unprepared for global war, "can do no more than show that they know how to die gallantly."[15] Dönitz did not go quite so far, but the assessment he recalls giving to his assembled staff on 4 September was hardly less grim: "Have no illusions about this war, it will last a long time, perhaps seven years, and we can be satisfied if we manage to end it with a draw."[16]

Dönitz's objectivity allowed him to be both adaptable and resourceful in dealing with military problems. As will be seen, he recognized as early as August 1942 that the growth and effectiveness of Allied air power doomed hopes for long-term success with existing U-boat models. He thereafter by-passed navy channels to promote Hellmuth Walter's revolutionary submarine designs directly to Hitler and discuss accelerated U-boat production with Reich armaments minister Albert Speer. Although initially skeptical of sonar and radar, his conversion to the creed of technology is evident in short-term upgrades of radar detection gear and weaponry and in his commitment as early as 1942 to a future fleet based on advanced submarine models.

Yet he could still lapse into World War I modes of thought, as with the ill-advised rearming of *U-441* (*Kaptlt.* Götz von Hartmann) in April–May 1943 as one of a series of "Flak-Traps," a U-boat antiaircraft reversal of the Q-ship, designed to lure Allied aircraft to destruction. Von Hartmann proved fortunate to survive after suffering twenty-three casualties to strafing attacks by British Beaufighters. Dönitz at least abandoned this notion quickly.[17]

Most characteristic of his leadership style, however, was its reliance on "improvisation." Perhaps the lack of resources left little choice, but if so Dönitz accommodated himself perhaps too well to this chronic condition. As discussed below, the BdU command staff remained extremely small throughout the conflict, facilitating a simplified unity of command at the price of overwork to the point of exhaustion and loss of perspective in solving problems. This style of "inspired improvisation" in a hopeless, reactive race with superior Allied resources, technology, and methodology reflects, as described by one historian, a romantic approach to sea warfare, one that exacted a terrible price from those asked to execute it.[18]

In sum Dönitz remained an impatient warrior preoccupied with fighting a battle rather than a careful organizer crafting resources to win a war. Even after becoming navy commander-in-chief, he did not significantly supplement the BdU command staff with qualified officers drawn from other duties, nor did he systematically review the work of technical departments whose expertise in torpedo development or cipher security deserved a second opinion.[19] For both better and worse, however, his became the public identity of the U-boat service.

Yet Karl Dönitz alone did not shape the character of his crews, and arguably exercised less influence here than his all-but-forgotten colleague, Hans-Georg von Friedeburg.[20] Not quite four years junior to his chief and another U-boat officer from the First World War, von Friedeburg held responsibility for the organization and administration of the entire submarine arm. The "perfect gentleman—correct to the last degree," as he was described by colleagues,[21] joined the submarine force in February 1939 as Dönitz's designated successor, a transition scheduled for 1 April 1940 but forestalled by war's outbreak. Instead von Friedeburg—who referred to himself as "Dönitz's box spanner," the term for the gun-bearer and loader who accompanies a hunter in the field—assumed control of U-boat training and personnel in September 1939 and retained those duties throughout the war, in successive posts as *Chef der Organisationsabteilung* (September 1939–September 1941), *2. Admiral der Unterseeboote* (September 1939–January 1943), and *Kommandierender Admiral der Unterseeboote* (February 1943–April 1945).[22] A former U-boat flotilla commander described him as "the greatest organizing genius produced by the navy," who somehow managed to "conjure up everything from bases, schools, the entire training regimen and all personnel administration matters entirely out of thin air."[23] Where Dönitz inspired and directed his men in battle, von Friedeburg selected and trained them in the first place; it was his art to work behind the scenes and allow others the limelight.

Like Dönitz, von Friedeburg added a personal touch to the U-boat service, but one reflected in lively and genial conversations in the mess hall. Officers knew they could turn to him for support, whether for assignment to the *U-Boot-Waffe* or for backing in disputes.[24] By day he labored over personnel and training matters; by night he wrote regularly to U-boat officers in captivity and to the widows and families of those who would never return from their last patrols. The latter did not represent mere notification and condolence letters, but ongoing correspondence to meet the survivors' material needs and provide some psychological comfort.[25]

Described by one of his staff officers as "highly self-assured, very shrewd and tactful, quite different from the blunt Prussian Dönitz,"[26] von Friedeburg also brought to the U-boat arm a well-placed network of political connections from his previous service in Berlin as adjutant to the minister of war, Field Marshal Werner von Blomberg, February 1933–September 1936. Von Friedeburg's Berlin posting reflected his close friendship with the new minister of war that dated from the naval officer's assignment as liaison to von Blomberg's headquarters in Königsberg (now Kaliningrad), East Prussia, in April 1929. Army rivals considered von Friedeburg actively pro-Nazi, a view reinforced by his approval of Hitler's earliest moves to remove Jews from the German military and his influence to establish a working relationship between *Reichsführer-*SS Heinrich Himmler and von Blomberg. Perhaps this revealed his acute political sensitivity and accommodation, for he also understood the deadly power of the SS, as revealed in his remark to a senior naval officer in January 1935: "When one of us goes into an SS building, one does not know whether he will come out again."[27] Ironically, one of von Friedeburg's sons would later become a prominent official within the Social Democratic Party in Hessen.[28]

This keen political sense proved useful in smoothing out conflicts between the navy and the police power in the Reich. When U-boat ace Werner Henke precipitated a fight with the Gestapo in Innsbruck over the mistreatment of some friends, von Friedeburg used his SS contacts to minimize the damage, then apologized directly to Himmler with an assurance of Henke's chastisement; this immediately ended the problem and kept the veteran commander in service without penalty.[29] In like manner, von Friedeburg quashed an Abwehr report critical of then-*Kaptlt.* Reinhard "Teddy" Suhren's social contacts with non-Aryans and others deemed "undesirable," reflecting the near-paternal relationship between von Friedeburg and a maverick commander responsible for the most popular anti-Nazi anecdote in the U-boat service.[30]

Whatever his political beliefs in 1933, von Friedeburg's intellect allowed him to grasp the growing disparity between reality and self-delusion as the war progressed. In late March 1943, after a front-line commander described how his arguments about Allied radar supremacy had been dismissed by the BdU staff, von Friedeburg took the veteran aside and acknowledged that he was probably correct, but advised, "For goodness' sake shut up and keep quiet or someone will come and lock you up. Take my word for it, we are in a difficult position, our leadership has no choice."[31]

In contrast to Dönitz, however, the gradual deterioration of the U-boat war visibly sapped the "box spanner's" strength. When in late August 1944 he visited his friend and colleague Karl-Friedrich Merten, commanding the 24th U-boat Flotilla in Memel, the latter found him lethargic and seemingly resigned to Germany's inevitable defeat. In von Friedeburg's subsequent expansion of torpedo-firing training units and his refusal to grant Merten's request for command of a new Type XXI boat, Merten saw further evidence of his superior's hope to save his and as many other German lives as possible.[32] At the end of April 1945, Erich Topp found him "only a shadow of himself" as he passed along orders to fight on to the last, then shook hands for the final time as his eyes filled with tears. In less than a month he died by his own hand after negotiating Germany's surrender.[33]

U-boat Command Staff

If Dönitz and von Friedeburg constituted the top leadership of the U-boat force, the lives of German submariners also lay in the hands of those who directly conducted the campaign, the BdU operations or command staff. Their role in translating Dönitz's orders into action deserves far more attention than it receives here, but at least some important characteristics might be noted.

Dönitz and his command staff preferred to be close to the front, where they could immediately debrief returning commanders and quickly evaluate combat conditions. For most of the war's first year they were located at Sengwarden near Wilhelmshaven, and after a brief stay in Paris they established themselves in November 1940 in a requisitioned mansion at Kerneval just south of the port of Lorient. There from the brick-and-stone *Sardinenschlösschen* ("sardine chateau"), as headquarters was known, BdU saluted with a flag signal every U-boat of the 2d or 10th U-boat Flotilla as it arrived or departed. The sixteen-month stay at Kerneval set the routines of the command staff in directing operations of a monthly average of fifty-three front-line U-boats, only one-third of which would be on combat station.

At the end of March 1942, after the British commando raid at St. Nazaire revealed the vulnerability to attack of such ports, Hitler ordered Dönitz to transfer his headquarters back to Paris, where it remained for a year. Following his promotion to navy commander-in-chief, Dönitz and his staff moved in March 1943 to Berlin, first to a hotel in Charlottenburg and nine months later—following heavy Allied air raids they had avoided in Paris—to the more protected *Koralle* bunker in the countryside northeast of the city.

Although Dönitz remained BdU, the daily conduct of operations fell increasingly to *Kapt.z.S.* (promoted to *Konteradmiral* on 1 March 1943) Eberhard Godt, head of the Operations Department (BdU/Op), and the small BdU staff. Thus as Dönitz assumed his new post he necessarily became more removed from U-boat operations at precisely the moment of decision in the Atlantic. Moreover he left in place an overburdened command staff to manage a series of convoy battles unprecedented in scale and significance, involving a monthly average of 238 front-line U-boats during the period March–May 1943.[34] The significance of this decision for the Battle of the Atlantic has never been addressed.

For his command staff, Dönitz relied on a small, dedicated group whom he knew and implicitly trusted. This allowed a unified, simplified control of operations that the Allies could never match; for the war's early years BdU held the initiative and left to the Allies the cumbersome tasks of coordinating the efforts of different nations and rival services. Under Godt the BdU operations staff comprised five, then six, former U-boat commanders with distinguished records, who would eventually be relieved by other veteran captains. They were supplemented by one to four engineering officers, various specialists (medical, ordnance, communications), and a handful of aides and secretaries. A separate communications bunker stood nearby, staffed constantly by shifts of fifteen to twenty radiomen. The lean ex-commanders, with an average age in the early thirties, became known as the "staff without paunches" (*Stab ohne Bäuche*), a physical trait precluded by ten-hour workdays throughout the week.[35]

Every day this tiny group bustled about the two situation rooms at headquarters, keeping track of U-boats outward- and homeward-bound and on station, submarines in training in the Baltic, Allied convoy movements, dispositions and strengths of Allied defensive forces, reported attacks, and weather, tidal, and lunar conditions. Some reviewed the war diaries for just-completed patrols of returning U-boats, assessing the commanders' decisions and performance, or prepared instructions and briefings for outbound captains. *Freg.Kapt.* Günter Hessler, Dönitz's son-in-law and former CO of *U-107*, alone conducted over 4,500 debriefings of returning commanders. Others charted the statistical progress of the campaign in graphs along the walls of the "Museum," tabulating reported successes and presumed losses, tracking the ebb and flow of destroyed ships and drowned men with lines and numbers on paper. The same scenes and statistical yardsticks were duplicated at the British counterpart, Western Approaches Headquarters at Derby House, Liverpool, but on a much larger and more comprehensive scale that included representatives of all the services and a total staff of more than one thousand.[36]

The far smaller German staff, increasingly overwhelmed by the day-to-day conduct of operations, lacked the time and resources to test or reexamine their assumptions. The usual assemblage of assistants and aides were all but eliminated by security sweeps of excess personnel with access to codes and ciphers, an unexpected byproduct of ULTRA intelligence whose gain to the Allies has not been appreciated.[37] Those left were combat officers who lacked general staff experience or training, and even their time at the front left them ill-prepared for the rapid improvements in Allied weaponry and tactics. There was no intelligence subsection within the staff and no systematic effort at incorporating intelligence into operational planning: "We were encouraged to consider intelligence matters, everyone had a quick jab at it, whenever time allowed," as one staff officer described the process.[38]

Nor was an attempt made to scientifically analyze military operations, search procedures, or weapons effectiveness as was done by the Allies with "operations research" (O.R., also referred to as "operations analysis"), an advantage which also reflected superior Allied resources. The sixteen staff officers working in the O.R. Section attached to the Royal Air Force's Coastal Command alone, for example, outnumbered the BdU staff by two to one; the U.S. Navy's Antisubmarine Warfare Operational Research Group (AS-WORG) within the Tenth Fleet numbered forty-four scientists in August 1943, a ratio more than five to one.[39]

Operating in such a relative vacuum of information, the BdU staff trusted to their own technology and their submarine commanders' claims, foundations of wishful thinking that further clouded their assessments of the overall situation. A good example of this occurred with the T-5 acoustic torpedo (code-named *Zaunkönig*, "wren," but often referred to by the Allies as Gnat), intended especially for Allied warships. Although tests on this torpedo had not been completed and it was not scheduled for front-line use until early 1944, Dönitz ordered its operational readiness advanced to 1 August 1943. The T-5 packed a tremendous punch (it sank three escorts in its first use, leaving only three survivors from the combined crews),[40] but superior Allied intelligence had discovered the weapon's existence and potential while it was still being tested and developed as a countermeasure the "foxer," a noise-making device towed behind a ship that attracted the torpedo's homing mechanism. Consequently the detonations heard by U-boat captains were not the destructive hits they assumed, but harmless explosions in ships' wakes. By July 1944 the BdU staff had learned of the Allied countermeasure, but still reckoned that the 345 T-5s fired up to that point had scored 175 definite hits and 20 more "probables," causing the sinking of at least 128 destroyers and other escort vessels, 1 cruiser, 3 submarines, and 20 merchantmen, in addition to another twenty-three warships "probably" sunk. In reality Allied losses to the T-5 amounted to no more than one cruiser and twenty-one escort vessels, with fifteen escorts damaged and eight merchant and landing ships sunk.[41]

In other instances the very incompleteness of information contributed to false evaluations. In assessing the catastrophic losses suffered in May 1943, BdU correctly attributed the "decisive role" to radar-equipped Allied aircraft but lacked the data to appreciate their significant contribution in close support of convoy escorts. Dönitz thus underestimated the increased tactical risks of fighting convoy battles.[42]

Even more illustrative of the BdU staff's limitations was their reaction to the revelation of the ULTRA secret. In a report dated 10 August 1943 and noted in the BdU war diary three days later, the German Abwehr office in Switzerland broke the war's greatest intelligence secret: "Over the last few months the enemy has succeeded in decrypting German naval ciphers, including orders to operational U-boats. All orders have been read by the enemy." Although acutely aware of the long history of suspected and investigated cipher compromise, and despite the tabulation that Allied aircraft had struck at twenty-three of thirty-one radio-arranged refueling or other rendezvous since the beginning of June, Godt and his colleagues again deferred to the naval communications experts who pronounced the ciphers inviolable. The BdU himself remained unconvinced about a systematic decryption but approved minor improvements in the key words and cipher settings and once again further restricted the dissemination of classified information.[43]

This vital intelligence, a rare gift-wrapped package that briefly neutralized the German disadvantages in operations research and lack of resources, came at precisely the right moment for a critical reevaluation of the U-boat effort. The heavy losses suffered throughout the period March–August 1943, which forced a U-boat withdrawal from the North Atlantic battle and all but eliminated the tanker fleet necessary for extended operations, together with the drying up of signals intelligence after the change in Allied convoy codes in June, underscored the need for change in strategy and goals. For example, the commitment to equip all boats with snorkels could have been made in the autumn of 1943 instead of six months later, or perhaps prearranged deployment plans that sharply reduced radio use could have been adopted. Instead BdU resolved to renew the convoy battles with nothing new beyond torpedoes, radar search receivers, and flak armament. That the revelation of cipher compromise slipped through the cracks without a closer examination or broader dissemination—there is no indication that Dönitz saw this intelligence—constitutes a serious error in critical judgment. Rather than overconfidence or arrogance (except, perhaps, for the naval communications experts), it suggests the exhaustion of the BdU staff in merely passing along an oft-raised question to presumed experts for a predictable rejection.[44] It also marks an early step in the progressive deterioration of centralized control of U-boat operations.

Thereafter the tenuous threads of command began to unravel. As new Allied weapons and tactics became evident, BdU again avoided a fundamental reexamination of its ways and means in favor of a stream of constantly updated instructions and advisories to submarine commanders on every aspect of equipment, weapons, and procedures. When U-boat captains protested against this increasing volume of reactive advice, BdU radioed a sharp rejoinder on 15 January 1944:

In the race to overtake the enemy's spurt ahead in developing efficient antisubmarine measures, every single experience must be used to discover these new weapons and methods so as to develop our own countermeasures as quickly as possible. *The flood of constantly changing orders and instructions will not cease* until we have achieved a decisive advantage [emphasis added]. Until then boats must deal with it.[45]

With Dönitz himself preoccupied with general naval matters, command issues became increasingly blurred as to their source and authority. Partly this resulted from BdU's relocation to the new *Koralle* bunker outside Berlin, where a psychological barrier accompanied the physical separation from U-boat bases. A former staff officer described the new headquarters in April 1944 as byzantine in nature and recalled the warning of a colleague that he "would have to understand the atmosphere here. . . . A lot of people didn't say what they really thought."[46] Even the implicit trust and understanding of senior U-boat officers suffered under the strain, as became evident when flotilla commanders interpreted orders in a unique or contrary manner to their original intent.

The most serious example of this occurred with *Korv.Kapt.* Karl-Heinz Moehle. A veteran of the U-boat service since March 1936, Moehle commanded *U-20* (September 1939–January 1940) and *U-123* (May 1940–May 1941) and earned the Knight's Cross of the Iron Cross for his credited twenty-two sinkings of merchant ships. After serving with the BdU staff for a month, he assumed command of the 5th U-boat Flotilla in Kiel in June 1941. For the rest of the war he served at this post, where his task involved the final fitting-out of new U-boats that had just completed their training in the Baltic.[47] In this role Moehle personally briefed outbound captains on questions of equipment and procedures, including policy toward survivors of torpedoed ships. For reasons never explained, Moehle chose to interpret Dönitz's September 1942 order to undertake no rescue efforts on behalf of survivors—known as the *Laconia* order, after the ship and incident that led to its issuance—as an encouragement to kill them. In fact, Dönitz had directly opposed Hitler's murderous suggestion to do so, and Moehle admitted that he never asked either Dönitz or Godt for clarification on the order's meaning. What mattered most was that such a misunderstanding could arise among familiar figures in a command structure, and that the subordinate's misreading was what new and impressionable commanders heard.[48]

Another example concerned the sacrificial efforts to be made to stop the Normandy invasion, including the so-called ramming order. In March and April 1944 Dönitz issued general directives to the U-boat arm that enjoined an all-out offensive spirit to meet the anticipated invasion. The April message in particular sounded a note of extreme self-sacrifice: "Every enemy vessel that serves the invasion, even if it only carries 50 men or a single tank to land, is a target demanding the U-boat's full commitment. It is to be attacked even if that risks the loss of the submarine." The wording of this "guidance" alone proved unsettling for U-boat crews, but veterans such as Peter Cremer didn't take it too seriously: "What else was a Commander-in-Chief to say in those days?"[49] The very next month, however, at a conference of fifteen U-boat captains convened at the headquarters of the 1st U-boat Flotilla in Brest, someone—either flotilla commander *Korv.Kapt.* Werner Winter or the *Führer der Unterseeboote West* (flag officer for U-boats, Operations Area West), *Kapt.z.S.* Hans Rudolf Rösing—reiterated the instructions in a manner that suggested the possible ramming of invasion vessels, at the obvious likely cost of their own lives.[50]

There is no evidence that Dönitz ever issued a ramming order. If this impression arose, it doubtless reflected Winter or Rösing simply adding a melodramatic touch to the April instruction, without fully gauging the reaction of those being asked to sacrifice themselves.[51] When the invasion finally occurred, Godt ordered only snorkel boats—i.e., those with a realistic chance of survival—into the Channel and kept the rest on standby. Dönitz then ordered all available submarines to proceed to the invasion area, but Godt effectively ignored this instruction and instead deployed the U-boats across the Bay of Biscay against a "possible" Allied move there. This doubtless saved some German lives, although in the end U-boats still suffered heavy losses in the Channel for minor gains; but at least no one attempted to ram a landing craft.[52]

The actions of Moehle and Winter or Rösing reveal an internal breakdown of U-boat command and control, as none of these individuals exercised operational command at the time. Prewar U-boat commanders all, they knew Dönitz well and obviously felt competent to offer "guidance" on such fundamental issues as the killing of survivors and suicidal attacks, views inconsistent with or even contrary to official policy. This confusion among a relatively small group of long-time associates illustrates both the war's psychological toll on the U-boat leadership and cracks in the foundation of U-boat Command.

The command predicament paralleled and contributed to a mounting crisis in U-boat crews' morale from late 1943 through the spring of 1944. Outmatched by Allied technological and material superiority, and informed by their leadership that their function now consisted in tying down as many Allied forces as possible, the spirit of the U-boat force steadily deteriorated through this period. Problems began to develop, and some drastic measures had already been introduced when the crisis, like the command predicament, was finally averted by the use of the *Schnorchel*. This simple tube, which allowed a submarine to recharge its batteries and even run on diesel power while submerged, restored to individual U-boat crews some sense of power to determine their own fate. Moreover it marked the final abandonment of pack tactics and reduced BdU's command burdens.[53]

The snorkel demonstrated anew a familiar lesson in submarine warfare, that strategy follows in technology's wake. Unfortunately that admonition came late in the evolution of German strategy and tactics.

Strategy and Tactics

The small size of the submarine service in September 1939 dictated a simplified strategy with accordingly consistent tactics. Dönitz both prepared and used his forces in this manner whenever possible, but external demands continually diluted this effort during the period when it could have made a difference. Increasingly, however, rapid developments in technology—whether in the form of aircraft, electronics, new weapons, or new submarines—came to dominate all aspects of the Battle of the Atlantic, crowding out issues of strategy and tactics.

Historians have often characterized Dönitz's wartime strategy as *Tonnagekrieg*, literally "tonnage war" but usually translated as the "integral tonnage strategy," even elevating it to a theoretical model.[54] Yet this mistakes a phase for a general plan. Dönitz and his staff improvised U-boat strategy throughout the war according to available strength, economy of losses, and the need to fulfill other missions. The BdU succinctly described his guiding principle on 5 November 1940: "The highest objective can only be to inflict the greatest possible damage on England."[55]

During the war's first two years BdU's strategy consisted only of sinking as many ships bound for Britain as conditions permitted, whether these involved political restrictions on targets or—more typically—the Naval High Command's own demands on U-boat deployment in support of the Norwegian invasion, long-range missions off the South African coast, or all-out reinforcement of the Mediterranean. These diversions from the Atlantic arena provoked major disagreements with Dönitz, who could never persuade the *Seekriegsleitung* (Skl, or more specifically 1/Skl, the Operations Section of the Naval Staff) that U-boats could provide little strategic support to ground operations or would sacrifice too many potential sinkings in traveling to distant operational areas with no guarantees of success.[56]

Tonnagekrieg represented a practical argument against such secondary operations, or at least for their integration under Dönitz's own authority and in the context of the broader campaign. It became a natural response to the new situation created by the United States' formal entry into the war, followed quickly by that of many of the Latin American republics, and the consequent addition of their merchant marines to the Allied total. The BdU's definition of "tonnage war" was transcribed in a war diary entry on 15 April 1942:

> The enemy's shipping constitutes one single, great entity. It is therefore immaterial where a ship is sunk. Once it has been destroyed, it has to be replaced by a new ship; and that's that. In the long run the result of the war will depend on the result of the race between sinkings and new construction.[57]

But the context of these statements must be noted, for at the time, Dönitz was justifying the continuation of operations off the American east coast and in the Caribbean while the defenses there were weak. On the one hand, American merchant marine tonnage suddenly had to be added to calculations of Allied capabilities; on the other, American unpreparedness and tardiness in developing convoys and effective defenses convinced Dönitz of a chance to strike a major blow. Despite his success—a total of more than 2.9 million tons of merchant shipping sunk from January to July 1942, in return for only twenty-one U-boats lost—higher authority continued to restrict his options by demanding other submarine assignments.[58] Rather than a long-term strategy that had anchored Dönitz's planning from the start, tonnage war constituted a specific opportunity to be exploited before defenses improved; it could serve as strategy only if sufficient numbers of U-boats became available and losses remained low. More immediately, *Tonnagekrieg* represented a domestic tactic in Dönitz's ongoing battles with the Naval High Command for the allocation and deployment of resources, an argument with which he might bypass channels and approach Hitler directly.

On 14 May 1942 Dönitz briefed the Führer on the overall situation and claimed that the sinking of 700,000 tons per month from all causes, and possibly as little as 400,000–500,000 tons per month, should keep pace with Allied ship construction. Conceding that an improvement in defenses was inevitable, Dönitz nevertheless believed—or hoped—he could maintain that tempo through the greater numbers of U-boats then in training and slipping down the quays, allowing more effective engagement of convoys and continued operations in remote areas. Left unsaid, however, was the possibility that American shipbuilding could produce higher totals than expected.[59]

Dönitz's optimistic calculations did not sit well with the Naval Operations Staff, which had estimated only the previous July—that is, five months before America's entry into the war compelled a reassessment—that at least 800,000–1,000,000 tons would have to be sunk monthly "for an extended period" before Britain would be "ready for peace."[60] In early September 1942 the Operations Staff's intelligence branch answered Dönitz's *Tonnagekrieg* rationale with a detailed counterargument. Recalculating Allied shipbuilding capabilities on a higher basis, and assessing U-boat sinkings during 1942 at a monthly average of 400,000 tons during operations off the U.S. eastern coast, analysts concluded that this figure would have to be raised more than threefold, to 1.3 million tons per month in 1943 (!), in order for *Tonnagekrieg* to outstrip production. As this all-but-impossible rate lay beyond German means, the only alternative lay in the return to *Zufuhrkrieg* ("import war"), attacking merchant shipping carrying war supplies and critical raw materials at strategic points—for example, the Arctic convoys to Russia and the Natal/Freetown area off southern Africa—as well as the fully loaded convoys bound for Great Britain. Only by sinking ships laden with valuable cargoes could U-boats "strike the enemy at his most vulnerable point."[61]

In fact, improved Allied defenses in the western Atlantic in the autumn of 1942 compelled the U-boat effort to shift emphasis back to the North Atlantic convoys. That November U-boats attained their highest monthly total in sinkings, but less than one-quarter of those occurred in the North Atlantic.[62] According to his memoirs, Dönitz had accepted the futility of tonnage war by February 1943.[63] As a reaction in early 1942 to the opening of the American theater, tonnage war had presented Dönitz an opportunity to sink large numbers of ships at little cost to his own forces and compel the enemy to stretch his defenses. With the passage of a year these goals had been met or were no longer possible, and the strategy, which ultimately lay beyond Germany's means, fell by the wayside. As a domestic tactic, however, its success may been instrumental in Hitler's nomination of Dönitz to succeed Raeder as navy commander-in-chief on 30 January 1943, finally giving BdU the authority he needed—and rendering *Tonnagekrieg* unnecessary.

The refocused assault on British supply lines lasted into the autumn of 1943, when heavy casualties and minimal results compelled its abandonment as well. Thereafter the primary objective simply lay in the continued tying down of Allied resources until advanced submarine designs arrived in sufficient numbers to resume convoy battles. When U-boats continued to attack shipping in distant areas in 1944–45, this was not a continuation of

Tonnagekrieg but perserverance in tying down Allied defenses over as broad an area as possible.[64]

In tactics, Dönitz has been justly identified with *Rudeltaktik,* literally "group tactics," the concentration of U-boats to attack protected convoys of merchant ships. Its origins can be traced to the end of World War I, but the line is not straight. In the war's last year the Imperial German Navy, thwarted in its commerce warfare campaign by the Allies' introduction of convoys in 1917, finally began to organize loose groups of U-boats to intercept convoys at expected locations but attained little success with too few boats and inadequate reconnaissance.[65] Dönitz himself claimed that his final World War I patrol (October 1918) involved a planned joint night surface attack on a convoy, but he attacked alone when the other U-boat could not make the rendezvous.[66] In the interwar period some veteran submariners strongly endorsed group tactics for the future. *Kaptlt.* Erwin Wassner, a highly decorated commander of several World War I U-boats (known to his colleagues as "*Onkel* Fritz"), wrote in July 1922 that in future conflicts a convoy offered no special protection but remained vulnerable to surface attack by "sizeable numbers of U-boats acting together" through "further increases in signalling techniques."[67]

Others, however, concluded that the solution to convoy defenses lay in technology rather than tactics. A study in September 1927 by *Korv.Kapt.* Heino von Heimburg is particularly revealing for both its findings and forecasts. Von Heimburg, a highly successful World War I U-boat commander, recommended the development of long-range, fast torpedoes (ideally with a range of five thousand meters, a speed of forty knots, and no visible wake) that would allow U-boats to attack convoys from safe distances. Future U-boats should moreover possess greater diving depths and faster diving times to escape depth charges, add sophisticated acoustic gear to detect and elude escorts, eliminate heavy deck guns as superfluous and thereby increase underwater maneuverability, and develop quieter propulsion systems for submerged travel. Most prescient were von Heimburg's observations regarding the future role of air power:

Without question air power will play a much greater role in future wars. . . . U-boats must grasp that in all seas and at any moment they can be spotted and attacked from the air. A U-boat's best defense against this enemy is to travel submerged. U-boats should accept battle on the surface against aircraft only rarely and reluctantly. . . . Air power in the future will increasingly force U-boats to remain submerged by day.[68]

Von Heimburg and Dönitz were not strangers; both not only captained submarines in the Mediterranean during World War I, but successively commanded the same U-boat as well. Less than two years older than his more famous comrade, von Heimburg handed over the captaincy of *UB-68* to his junior comrade in September 1918. The senior officer's record (sinking three submarines, one armored cruiser, a troop transport, and several merchant ships) earned him Imperial Germany's highest decoration, the Order *Pour le Mérite,* and postwar international distinction.[69] It is interesting to speculate what the future of the *U-Boot-Waffe* might have been had von Heimburg instead of Dönitz assumed its direction before World War II. Far more to the point, however, an overworked and chronically understaffed BdU command staff made no use of von Heimburg's critical faculties during the war.[70]

In fact, however, the infant U-boat arm of the early 1930s possessed neither a clear tactical doctrine nor a consistent view of purpose. *Kaptlt.* Werner Fürbringer, a father of the U-boats' rebirth and organizer of the first training classes, believed in cooperative groups of U-boats but trained them for daylight submerged attacks on warships; he also proposed the use of radio- and cable-controlled torpedoes as defensive weapons for submarines. Some still believed in giant U-cruisers capable of fighting surface actions; others shared the views of World War I ace Ernst Hashagen, who advised naval officers in January 1932 that submarines had been overtaken by destroyers and acoustic equipment.[71]

When Dönitz took operational command of the U-boat arm in July 1935, he discovered that training instructors were echoing von Heimburg's precepts about combating convoys with long-range torpedoes while maintaining a safe distance of three thousand meters for protection against the escorts' asdic (sonar) equipment. The main points of the training program Dönitz immediately installed made clear the new tactical approach: (1) optimum firing ranges of six hundred meters; (2) night surface attacks on convoys featuring the combat techniques of torpedo boats; and (3) concentration of force for group attacks on convoys. These provided the focus for intensive exercises over the next several years, culminating in mid-Atlantic maneuvers in May 1939 aimed specifically at practicing cutting British supply routes. Many lessons were learned in the areas of deployment, the transition from reconnaissance to attack, and communications.[72]

But when war came a number of questions remained unresolved and circumstances prevented the full employment of group tactics for some time. Cooperation with the Luftwaffe, which Dönitz had always considered necessary for effective reconnaissance, never approached the levels envisaged or necessary; on the other hand, the U-boat arm's constant demand for officers drained away in transfers many of precisely those naval aviators best suited for the task.[73] Early in the campaign Dönitz experimented with granting tactical command of groups to a senior officers on the scene aboard "command submarines," but these commanders could not escape the problems of being part of the action rather than coordinating it.[74] In any case, restrictions on targets, fleet demands, and the general lack of U-boats precluded group tactics for much of 1940.

The employment of "wolf pack" tactics in fact became standard only in the spring of 1941, when enough submarines had become available; they remained in effect for more than two years. Command rested firmly in the hands of BdU and his staff. A wolf pack attack would begin with BdU deploying a patrol line across a convoy's anticipated path (under optimum conditions, with the assistance of signals intelligence provided by the B-Dienst). When a U-boat spotted the convoy, the commander, rather than attacking, would shadow the formation while radioing details of its course, speed, and composition to headquarters. There Dönitz or his operations chief, Eberhard Godt, estimated the convoy's future moves and dispatched the patrol line's constituent U-boats on an intercept course—an exhausting and frequently fruitless chase, if the convoy changed course and broke contact. The submarines traveled on the surface by day, attempting to establish position ahead of the convoy for a night attack through the heart of the formation. When BdU had completed arrangements for the maximum concentration of U-boats, he would radio: "Attack when darkness falls." Thereafter the submarines operated independently until contact was lost and the hunt began anew. In conducting submerged or night surface torpedo attacks, however, BdU enjoined his commanders to "go in as close as possible" before firing.[75]

The wolf pack thus represented a tactical solution to a tactical problem (escorted convoys), and its emphasis on night surface attacks offset the Allied technological advantage of asdic. But the pack's formation and movements depended completely on the use of radio, rendering it ultimately vulnerable to the Allies' superior technology in the monitoring and decryption of messages (ULTRA) and the detection of transmissions by escorts (with high-frequency/direction-finding, or HF/DF, equipment). Through hard-earned experience convoy escorts gained in expertise and teamwork even before Allied technology furnished them with the radar that negated the submarines' surface attack value; Allied material superiority gradually translated into continuous air cover and better-equipped escort vessels that rendered group tactics obsolete, at least with the submarine models available. The only alternative lay in submerged U-boats firing more sophisticated, longer-range torpedoes into convoys from greater distances—that is, the solution proposed by von Heimburg in 1927 and taught by U-boat instructors before Dönitz assumed command.

Most packs never found their quarry. When postwar British analysts studied the captured U-boat war diaries, they concluded that only 770 out of nearly 2,700 combat patrols—less than 30 percent—resulted in an engagement with an Allied convoy. When U-boats did encounter the enemy, however, they faithfully executed Dönitz's tactical doctrine of "getting in close" before firing. British calculations indicate that 1,441 out of 2,561 successful torpedo attacks (more than 56 percent) and 984 out of 1,788 unsuccessful efforts (55 percent) were delivered at ranges within one thousand meters.[76]

Yet such efforts could not salvage *Rudeltaktik*'s failure to significantly damage the Allied convoy system. Even during the period of peak U-boat success, from January through August 1942, only 30 out of 3,283 convoyed ships bound for Great Britain were sunk. From September 1939 through May 1943, 72 percent of all ships sunk by U-boats consisted of independent ships or stragglers from convoys, and of 620 ships sunk within convoys, only sixteen—less than 1 percent of all sinkings—occurred where convoys enjoyed both naval and air escorts. By contrast, 65 percent of all U-boats lost fell victim to convoy escorts.[77]

In von Heimburg's interwar assessment of submarine warfare, his opening observation on the 1914–18 conflict bears repeating: "Over the course of the war the Allies developed their antisubmarine capabilities from virtually nothing to a very high level. The U-boats, on the other hand, made no such corresponding improvement."[78]

No other lesson from World War I carried greater importance, nor was neglected at greater cost, for the Third Reich's U-boat arm. In large part this can be attributed to German U-boats' physical capabilities, the deadly potential and fatal defects of which shaped the nature of the Atlantic campaign. Before further consideration of the U-boat war, it is therefore necessary to examine the principal submarine models that carried so many men to war and an early death.

The U-boats

During World War II the Kriegsmarine developed several U-boat classes to perform various tasks, but until late in the war all models shared basic physical qualities that limited them as underwater craft. All relied on a dual propulsion system: diesel engines for surface use, where U-boats were expected to spend most of their time, and electrical motors for much slower and more limited submerged travel. Power for the electrical motors, as for the lighting, radio, and all onboard electrical equipment, depended on massive electrical batteries stored below deck in the boat's central sections. The batteries required daily recharging, a process requiring the use of one diesel engine for several hours and, until the arrival of the snorkel, possible only on the surface. A German U-boat, like any contemporary submarine of the Allied powers, might thus be more accurately described as a submersible torpedo-carrier that spent most of its time on the surface, where its daily routine revolved around the required battery recharging.

It has been argued that the German navy fumbled away a tremendous opportunity to develop a revolutionary submarine first handed to it in August 1933 by Prof. Hellmuth Walter, choosing instead to develop familiar models only slightly improved from 1916–18. By not committing itself to Walter's single-system, high-speed propulsion for above and below the surface, "the navy let slip a great chance, in fact the only real chance to revolutionize submarine warfare," according to one historian.[79] This harsh assessment both understates the difficulties of developing revolutionary weapons technologies on limited budgets and overlooks the problems of the Walter system.

Far more significant was the navy's repetition of the World War I penchant for several different submarine models to perform different missions. From the first submarine construction plans of the early 1930s through the massive fleet envisaged in the "Z-Plan" of 1938–39,[80] naval designers eschewed simplification and indulged their memories of specialized U-boats for specific tasks, from coastal defense through minelayers and "U-cruisers" (the precise term used in World War I) equipped with heavy guns and seaplanes. The carryover of this mind-set into an era of strained resources and limited means, combined with the Kriegsmarine's own indecision about the precise role for submarines in a future conflict, exacted an enormous if hidden price in lost U-boat production in the critical years before the war. When Germany attacked Poland the fifty-seven U-boats in service represented four different submarine types, two with different variants, and construction had begun on two larger classes.[81] Germany thus began the war with too few submarines and too many types.

A full analysis of U-boat development and technical aspects lies outside our study. Here we shall limit our concern to the most basic U-boat types with which German submariners fought, or were intended to fight, the war. Their basic characteristics are summarized in table 4.

The small Type II U-boats, nicknamed *Einbäume* ("dugout canoes") and

TABLE 4 **PRINCIPAL U-BOAT CHARACTERISTICS**

	U-boat Type			
	IIB	VIIC	IXC	XXI
Number commissioned	20	568	54	119
Displacement (tons)	279	761	1120	1621
Length (meters)	41	67	77	77
Beam (meters)	4	6	7	7
Draft (meters)	4	5	5	6
Top speed surfaced/submerged (knots)	13/7	17/7.6	18/7.3	16/17
Range (nautical miles)				
• Surfaced (at 12 knots)	1,800	6,500	11,000	11,150
• Submerged (at 4 knots)	43	80	63	400
Diving time (meters/second)	80/25–35	150/30	100/35	135/20
Armament				
• Bow torpedo tubes	3	4	4	6
• Stern tubes	—	1	2	—
• Torpedoes carried	6	14	22	23
• Guns[a]	1x2cm	1x88mm	1x105mm	2x twin
		1x20mm	1x37mm	20mm
			1x20mm	
Crew (officers/men)	3/22	4/40–44	4/44–50	5/52

Sources: Rössler, *U-boat*, 334–40; Herzog, *Deutsche U-Boote*, 194–203; Busch/Röll, *U-Bootbau*, 41, 54–61.
[a]Artillery armament varied greatly after 1942; deck guns were removed and various additional flak pieces added.

Nordsee Enten ("North Sea ducks"), served as the staple of prewar flotillas and wartime training. Intended primarily for coastal defense, Type IIB submarines carried out risky minelaying operations off British harbors in the war's early days. Most then retired to training duties, although six IIBs were subsequently transported by land to the Black Sea in 1942–43, where they successfully operated against Soviet supply ships and naval forces until the last three scuttled themselves on the Turkish coast in September 1944. The final variant of the class, the Type IID, introduced in 1941, included saddle tanks that greatly extended its range, but its limited size and torpedo capacity eventually reduced it too to a training role.[82]

The Type VII U-boat, and in particular the VIIC variant, served as the workhorse of the German submarine fleet and the largest single class in submarine history: this model accounted for 703 of 1,171 commissioned U-boats (60 percent), of which 568 were VIICs and another 91 the modified VIIC/41 version.[83] As noted earlier, the Type VII originated with the successful UB III model of World War I, and its characteristics also bore a striking similarity to the Ms-boats (*U-60* through *U-62*) introduced in 1916.

Its planned original size (500 tons displacement) facilitated maximum production of an oceangoing combat submarine within the terms of the Anglo-German Naval Agreement of 1935.[84] Dönitz championed the Type VIIA over the larger Type IA since it was much better suited to his own planned *Rudeltaktik:* highly maneuverable with a low silhouette for night surfaced attacks, quick diving times, and good handling qualities when submerged and under attack, and small enough to be produced in mass quantities. The evolution to the VIIB, with better range and surface speed, came about by enlarging the signature "saddle" fuel tanks on either side of the pressure hull and adding superchargers to the diesel engines.[85]

The Type VIIB actually proved the most successful variant of the VII series, carrying the brunt of the trade war from 1939 into 1941. Germany's early trio of top aces, Günther Prien (*U-47*), Otto Kretschmer (*U-99*), and Joachim Schepke (*U-100*), accomplished all of their sinkings with VIIBs; the most successful individual German U-boat of the war was *U-48*, a VIIB that sank fifty-four merchant ships totaling 324,131 tons and a sloop under three captains during the twelve patrols of her operational history.[86] Of the twenty-four VIIB submarines, five accounted for more than 180 Allied ships sunk, six others each dispatched eight or more vessels, and five more destroyed four to six ships apiece. As only 131 of all commissioned U-boats successfully attacked six or more Allied ships, the relative contribution of the VIIB is as remarkable as it is obvious.[87]

The VIIC version featured an enlarged control room to accommodate the installation of rudimentary sonar equipment (the *Such-* or "*S*"-*Gerät*, "search apparatus"), plans which were dropped when it was found that the device's use ironically betrayed its user's position far more effectively than it revealed underwater obstacles. Other modifications included additional buoyancy tanks to facilitate diving, enlarged fuel bunkers, and an improved electrical compressor. Wartime needs for greater surface speed and deeper diving capacity resulted in the VIIC/41 variant, which reduced weight through a rationalization of power plant parts and thickened the pressure hull to allow dives to more than two hundred meters (a depth already exceeded in emergencies by some VIIC captains). Still another modification, the VIIC/42, incorporated plans for further thickening of the pressure hull and additional superchargers for greater engine speed; contracts for 174 U-boats of this variant were awarded, but on 30 September 1943 the navy halted all work in preference for newer designs. Construction of VIIC/41s, however, continued to war's end.[88]

The first Type VIIC, *U-93* (*Kaptlt.* Claus Korth), entered service on 30 July 1940 at the Germaniawerft in Kiel and began operating in the Atlantic that October. On 12 April 1945, *Oblt.z.S.d.R.* Ewald Pick commissioned the last VIIC/41, *U-1025,* at Flensburg. During the intervening four and one-half years the majority of all German submariners lived, fought, and died aboard these U-boats, committed to the heaviest action in the North Atlantic, the Arctic, and the Mediterranean. U-boat supply tankers extended the VIIC's range to the coasts of the United States and Brazil, and dockyard workers extended and reconfigured their superstructures to accommodate extensive flak armament to combat the ever-growing Allied air power. But all their durability and versatility could not reverse Allied supremacy at sea.[89]

The history of the VIIC in microcosm can be seen in the fates of twenty-five VIIC and VIIC/41 boats laid down in the shipyard of *Bremer Vulkan-Vegesacker Werft* from January 1942 to March 1943, and commissioned into service as *U-275* through *U-299* from November 1942 through December 1943. Allied forces destroyed fourteen of them—thirteen with all hands, carrying a total of 630 crewmen to their deaths—and the remainder were scuttled or surrendered at war's end. In exchange for this sacrifice, one of their number sank an American destroyer and a British steamer and a second sank an American merchantman. The rest sank nothing, and only five even had the opportunity to fire torpedoes at targets.[90]

By contrast, the larger Type IX boats enjoyed disproportionate success during World War II despite their relatively poor combat qualities. The Type IX's characteristic broad beam and deck added precious seconds to her diving time and reduced her submerged maneuverability, disadvantages compounded by a larger and more visible conning tower. Dönitz emphasized these drawbacks of the *Seekühe* ("sea cows," as their crews dubbed Type IX boats) when he tried to prevent their commitment in the Mediterranean and off Gibraltar: "These boats are easier to locate than the Type VIIs, more complicated and therefore more vulnerable to depth charges and are more difficult to control when submerged."[91] When Dönitz tried to maintain maximum pressure against the North Atlantic lifelines in April 1943, this class revealed its vulnerability to upgraded convoy defenses: Although IXC boats contributed less than one-third of the overall forces, they suffered heavier losses than Type VIICs.[92]

Yet because of their great range and endurance, Type IX U-boats proved themselves superb commerce raiders against weakly escorted convoys early in the war or operating as "lone wolves" against unprotected shipping in distant operational areas. The fourteen Type IXB submarines (all commissioned in 1940) averaged 100,000 tons of merchant vessels sunk in their careers and contributed the third- through fifth-highest-ranked U-boats in total sinkings; the three most successful U-boat patrols of the entire war all belonged to IXB submarines.[93] Type IXC boats, which entered the campaign in 1941–42, demonstrated their capabilities in prolonged operations in the Caribbean, off Capetown, and in the Gulf of Guinea: Although the 141 IXC U-boats amounted to only 12 percent of Germany's submarine force, they accounted for approximately 37 percent of all Allied merchant sinkings.[94]

Such a record could never have been predicted from the IXC's original purpose. Similar to the *U-81* of 1915, and even more so to a planned class of large Ms-boats (*U-115* and *U-116*) not completed before the end of World War I,[95] the Type IX was designed in 1935 for extended operations in the western Mediterranean and long-range patrols in the Central and South Atlantic, including planned escort missions for German merchant vessels (!). As he had earlier with the Type IA, Dönitz in 1937 made clear his preference for the smaller Type VII boats, especially in view of the self-imposed tonnage restrictions of the Anglo-German Naval Agreement. While the Kriegsmarine's 1939 draft plans for the future fleet (the "Z-Plan") called for an equal balance of Type VII and IX submarines, Dönitz desired a ratio of 3:1 in favor of the former.[96]

The BdU's bias against Type IX U-boats intensified as the war continued, for the resources consumed in their production denied him the larger numbers of VIIs he wanted so desperately. In late January 1942 Dönitz's representatives emphasized this point to the Naval Operations Staff, pointing out that every IXC required twice as many construction workers to complete as a VIIC, and that each IXC swallowed up sixty tons of valuable copper, against only thirty-four tons necessary for a VIIC. Thus every one of the larger submarines required effectively the same investment as two of the more combat-worthy Type VIIs.[97] But it was already much too late for a standardization of U-boat models and Dönitz as navy commander-in-chief permitted the IXC's final variant (IXC/40) to remain in production until well into 1944.[98]

Type IXD U-boats represented a hybrid evolution of the Type IX and prewar plans for large, long-range U-cruisers (designated Type XI) and "Fleet" boats (Type XII). With war's outbreak the latter projects were scrapped and some of their intended roles allocated to an enlarged IXC, which eventually became the IXD, yet by the time of its development these submarines fulfilled other roles. In particular the IXD2 boat, with a surface range (23,700 nautical miles) twice that of a IXC, served as the Kriegsmarine's chief representative in the Indian and Pacific Oceans. Operating from a base established with Japanese cooperation at Penang on the Malayan peninsula, these U-boats performed both transport and combat duties in the German navy's most distant theater. If necessary, a IXD2 could carry home an invaluable cargo of over 215 tons of tin, rubber, wolfram, and molybdenum—raw materials unavailable in Europe.[99]

To those IXD2 U-boats that survived belong the German submarine service's endurance records, including the longest submarine patrol of the war: 203 days at sea by *U-181* (*Korv.Kapt.* Wolfgang Lüth), March–October 1943.[100] *U-862* (*Korv.Kapt.* Heinrich Timm) conducted the longest-distance combat patrol from Germany in November 1944–February 1945 when she circumnavigated New Zealand and twice traversed the length of Australia's southern coast.[101] Equally remarkable was the odyssey of *U-861* (*Kaptlt.* Jürgen Oesten). In the course of a 157-day journey from Kiel to Penang, she sank five ships and barely eluded Allied escorts and aircraft; after refitting for more than three months, the boat then sailed for home, escaping an ambush by American submarines and surviving a collision with an iceberg off Greenland to arrive at Trondheim, Norway, ninety-four days later—all without benefit of a snorkel.[102]

Other U-boat models, produced in limited numbers, performed very specific tasks. Most significant were the 1,700-ton Type XIV *milchkuh* (milk cow) supply tankers (or U-tankers), whose ability to reprovision U-boats at sea with fresh fuel, torpedoes, and food greatly extended the range and duration of combat patrols. Approved for construction in December 1939, the appearance of the first six tankers in 1942 facilitated the expansion of long-range operations that anchored Dönitz's *Tonnagekrieg* strategy. Four more entered service in 1943–44, but by then their time was over as Allied air power came to dominate the Atlantic. The XIV's bulk hindered speed, diving time, and maneuverability in evading an air attack, vulnerabilities exploited by U.S. Navy carrier aircraft dispatched to the areas of U-boat refueling rendezvous through signals intelligence: Six tankers were lost from May to August 1943, and only one lasted as late as June 1944.[103]

Type XB boats often ended their careers as refueling tankers as well, but such had not been their intention. Designed as long-range minelayers, XB submarines and their great size (1,760 tons displacement, even more than the XIVs) became pressed into supply and transport duties as replacements for lost supply ships, "milk cows," and blockade-runners. Six of the eight XB boats did not survive the war.[104]

There remain the advanced submarine designs. These began with Professor Walter's revolutionary plans that combined a new, streamlined hull design more suited to underwater travel and the use of single-system propulsion, in which a gas turbine engine broke down highly concentrated hydrogen peroxide (in a form known as Perhydrol) into water, oxygen, and heat, which could be used by the turbine to achieve underwater speeds of up to thirty knots. Experimental models were built by 1940; with Dönitz's support, Walter in late 1942 began developing different variations on these principles under the collective designation Type XVII, of which BdU planned to have twenty-four operational by 1944.

In the end, however, only seven XVII U-boats entered service, principally for testing. The engine remained a source of problems, especially as Perhydrol was volatile; the submarine proved extremely costly to build and operate; it consumed large quantities of a fuel that was not readily available; and finally it provided little offensive power (two torpedo tubes with just four torpedoes) with a very limited range (about three thousand nautical miles). Larger versions of the Walter boat (Types XVIII and XXVI) were not completed before war's end.[105]

If Walter's designs represented a true submarine, then Types XXI and XXIII constituted what one historian describes as a "halfway house" between the older models and the future.[106] Both classes originated at a November 1942 meeting to discuss developmental problems with the Walter boats, when two engineers suggested the interim solution of packing additional electrical batteries into the new hull designs with conventional double-propulsion engines. With improved electrical motors and built-in snorkels, the new "electro-boats" could travel farther, faster, and for longer periods of time underwater than ever before in maritime history.[107] Although put into production after the XXIs, Type XXIII boats became operational first, and over sixty of these small (234-ton) submarines entered service by war's end; one, *U-2336* (*Kaptlt.* Emil Klusmeier, a prewar U-boat *Obersteuermann* risen through the ranks), accomplished the final sinkings of the war by a German U-boat on 7 May 1945. But as coastal boats their maximum range extended only to British coastal waters, with firepower limited to two single-shot torpedo tubes.[108]

It was the Type XXI that represented Germany's claim to the future of submarine technology.[109] In the spring of 1943 Prof. Heinrich Oelfken and other naval construction specialists designed the model by adopting the smooth contours of Walter's Type XVIII hull design and installing lightweight diesels and two sets of electrical motors, one especially adapted for silent running. With an enormous battery capacity—two batteries totaling 372 cells, three times that for Types VII and IX—a XXI boat could travel underwater at a cruising speed of five knots for sixty hours or go all-out at eighteen knots for an hour without recharging. At more economical submerged speeds a XXI might use its built-in snorkel only every other day for recharging. In combat the new submarine enjoyed the latest in radar,

radar-detection, sonar, and acoustic gear, and featured six bow torpedo tubes, which could be reloaded in twenty minutes with a semiautomatic hydraulic system.

For our purposes, the concessions made to crew comforts deserve mention. The cook's galley included a freezer to maintain meats for extended periods; for the first time crewmen enjoyed access to three toilets and a separate washroom with basins and a shower; and the enlisted men, though they still shared bunks, at last had their own crew compartment removed from the *Bugraum* and no longer slept atop torpedoes.

By turning over production to Armaments Minister Speer, the navy accelerated the output of Type XXI U-boats through prefabrication of sections throughout Germany and final assembly at the shipyards (construction man-hours required per ton weight for a XXI at war's end was just 59 percent that for a VIIC in 1943). But teething problems and delays in the installation of new equipment postponed the XXIs' operational debut until it was too late. Of 119 XXI U-boats commissioned in 1944–45, only one had begun a war patrol when Germany surrendered; eleven others had reached their front commands in Norway. Many others, however, came under air attack before scuttling themselves in the war's last days.[110]

Through these many varieties of U-boats approximately fifty thousand German sailors lived, fought, and mostly died during World War II. But as their vessels multiplied and evolved over the course of the war, so too did the numbers and character of the men who manned them.

4   Patterns of the U-boat War, 1939–1945

Participants and historians of the Battle of the Atlantic usually frame the campaign in specific chronological periods that reflect significant operational developments.[1] Such an arrangement, however logical, often overlooks the materiel, organizational, and personnel aspects that frequently determined the availability and deployment of combat forces. This is especially applicable for the Germans, who waged the uneven battle while continually struggling for a larger share of the limited resources available in Hitler's war effort. In this chapter we shall trace the outlines of the U-boat war according to the rhythm of the German submarine branch's internal evolution, matched to the conflict's principal stages.[2] First to consider are the leadership and weapons that shaped much of the *U-Boot-Waffe*'s character.

The Phases of the U-boat War: A New Look

The Battle of the Atlantic seemingly falls into easily defined chronological phases according to the conflict's geographical expansion and the availability of forces and technologies to each of the opposing sides. Solely from the perspective of BdU's conduct of the war, however, there emerges a different pattern that blends stages in U-boat construction, organizational expansion, and shifting strategic priorities, all played out against a constant background of technical problems and the uneasy relationship between the U-boat arm and the navy as a whole.

During the war Dönitz himself established a succession of phases on the basis of the casualties suffered by his forces, reflected in table 5, which provides a framework for our own chronology.

It is important, however, to first establish the overall effectiveness of the U-boat war. Historian Jak Mallmann Showell, after reviewing the final record of U-boat successes tabulated by Jürgen Rohwer, reached the following conclusions: Out of 1,171 commissioned submarines, only 321 successfully attacked (sank or damaged) an Allied ship during the war. Most of those (190) attacked between one and five vessels; only twenty-five U-boats attacked twenty or more ships. A handful of aces, each of whom typically commanded several different U-boats during the war, inflicted a disproportionate amount of damage, as thirty commanders (about 2 percent) sank nearly eight hundred ships, or almost one-third of all Allied losses to German submarines. By contrast, and with allowance for U-boats used only for training or supply duties or commissioned too late to see action, approximately 550 combat U-boats sank nothing during their operational careers.[3] Historian Bodo Herzog, working with a different data source, concludes that 290 front-line U-boats were lost without ever sinking an enemy, 271 of them without ever having fired a torpedo; an additional ninety-five front-line U-boats survived the war without a single success among them.[4]

While this analysis establishes a perspective for the entire U-boat campaign, the major fluctuations over time must also be considered. Table 6 provides the prospective success and loss rates for all front-line U-boats during specific months of the war. The figures reveal both the sharp contrasts and progressive deterioration in combat conditions experienced by U-boat crews over the course of the war. As we shall see, these changes were not experienced by a single if dwindling submarine corps but by successive cohorts of *U-Boot-Fahrer* who knew, fought, and often died in the unique conditions defining one phase of the campaign.

First Phase: September 1939–August 1940

The initial phase covered the first year of the war, which in many ways constituted a reprise of the 1916–18 campaign but at less favorable odds. *Kaptlt.* Günther Prien's (*U-47*) daring raid into Scapa Flow and sinking of the British battleship *Royal Oak* on 14 October 1939 marked a tremendous victory for the prestige of the U-boat arm[5] but disguised technical shortcomings, lost opportunities, and heavy losses. Embarrassed by the sinking of the liner *Athenia* by *U-30* (*Kaptlt.* Fritz-Julius Lemp) on 3 September 1939, the naval leadership and Hitler delayed full implementation of unre-

TABLE 5 **PATTERN OF U-BOAT AND CREW LOSSES, 1939–45**

Period	Number of U-boats Commissioned[a]	Lost[b]	Number Frontboote at End of Period	Losses[c] Killed	Captured	Total	Avg. Monthly Losses	Percentage of Total Losses
1 Sep 39–21 Aug 40 (12 months)	29	29	27	764	427	1,191	99	3.5
22 Aug 40–24 Aug 42 (24 months)	381	80	149	1,891	721	2,612	109	7.7
25 Aug 42–31 Oct 43 (14 months)	329	257	175	11,008	2,027	13,035	931	38.6
Aug–Dec 42	93	45	204	2,230	698	2,928	732	8.7
Jan–Jun 43	139	114	214	5,058	588	5,646	941	16.7
Jul–Oct 43	97	98	175	3,720	741	4,461	1,115	13.2
1 Nov 43–9 May 45 (18+ months)	375	455	126	15,085	1,825	16,910	927	50.1
Totals	1,114	821		28,748	5,000	33,748	494	100

[a]Data from Busch and Röll, *U-Bootbau*, 6ff. (excluded from the first period are the fifty-seven U-boats already commissioned before the war).

[b]Data from Tarrant, *U-boat Offensive*, 88, 116, 128, 165–69, and Tarrant, *Last Year*, 205.

[c]For first period: BdU/Operationsabt., "1 Jahr U-Bootskriegführung," 24 August 1940 (T1022/1724/PG 32011); for second period, Skl/Amtsgruppe U-Bootswesen, "Aufstellung U-Bootsverluste Stand 24.8.42," 3 September 1942 (T1022/1727/PG 32174); for third period, KTB BdU, Anl.z. KTB 31.1.44 (T1022/3981/PG 30339); data for final period derived from the final totals of killed and captured described in appendix 2.

TABLE 6 **VARYING SUCCESS AND LOSS RATES FOR U-BOATS (ALL THEATERS), 1940–44**

	Oct. 1940	May 1942	Mar. 1943	Jan. 1944
Front U-boats	39	124	229	169
Effective strength[a]	20	62	115	85
U-boats making successful attacks	17	39	57	10
Success rate (percent)	85.0	62.9	49.6	11.8
U-boats lost[b]	1	4	14	15
Loss rate (percent)	5.0	6.5	12.2	17.6

Sources: Compiled from data in Tarrant, *U-boat Offensive,* 96, 106, 116, 128; Rohwer, *Axis Submarine Successes,* 31–35, 92–99, 153–60, 176–77, 198, 202, 204–5, 218, 220, 232–33, 244–45, 253–54, 267, 272–73; and Kemp, *U-boats Destroyed,* 67, 81–82, 105–9, 163–66.

[a]U-boats on operations during the month, calculated at 50 percent of total strength.

[b]Excludes non-front U-boats lost in home waters.

stricted submarine warfare until August 1940. The small number of U-boats generally operated singly and by antiquated stop-and-search prize rules in the early days; Type II submarines often carried out minelaying missions in English coastal waters. Dönitz's employment of his forces moreover depended on broader naval concerns, as in April 1940 when most U-boats were diverted to the support of naval operations in the occupation of Norway. The U-boats achieved little there, largely due to the flawed detonator pistols in their torpedoes: From October 1939 through April 1940 the torpedo failure rate averaged 30 percent, in addition to outright misses.[6]

Critical as this problem was, it merely added another dimension to an ineffective commerce campaign. Through the first nine months of the war, Dönitz's handful of submarines managed to sink 215 merchant ships totaling over 850,000 tons, but only twenty-two of these vessels were sunk in convoy. At the same time Allied escorts destroyed eleven U-boats operating near convoys, unacceptable losses as too few boats were available for more than the occasional formation of a wolf pack.[7] Dönitz's *Rudeltaktik* remained unproven.

Even worse was the price paid. Dönitz reported on 24 August 1940 that the first year's fighting cost him twenty-eight out of a total of sixty-one operational U-boats, or 46 percent. Personnel losses were only slightly less. The original submarine force comprised about three thousand carefully selected volunteers, career officers and men whose commanding officers averaged 29.5 years in age, with the vast majority of crewmen aged twenty-one to twenty-five. From this elite, 79 officers and 685 NCOs and enlisted men had been killed, with a further 33 officers and 394 other ranks captured—a total loss of nearly twelve hundred men, or 40 percent of the force that began the war. Replacing the submarines alone proved an agonizingly slow process: For each month from September 1939 through June 1940 German shipyards completed an average of no more than two U-boats, and only thirteen of these twenty were boats capable of Atlantic operations.[8] But how could the men be replaced?

Perhaps most disturbing for BdU, the strain of combat operations on the physical and mental health of his commanders revealed itself quickly. One month after the war began he noted the need to relieve two captains immediately, with the probability of several others soon to follow. Most of those affected had found the transition from several years' experience aboard small Type II boats to a few weeks' combat duty on a larger Type VII or IX too great to handle, at least temporarily.[9] As a result Dönitz had to juggle his commanders, relieving some outright, shifting others to smaller or larger boats according to their abilities. During the war's first five months the COs of twenty submarines changed, more than one out of every three, and in five cases a third commander had taken over by the end of the fourth month.[10] Such rapid and extensive turnover among its captains further impaired U-boat performance in the war's early days.

Favorable developments outside of Dönitz's control gradually improved the overall situation by the end of this first turbulent period. A formal investigation into the torpedo situation, culminating in the court-martial of several senior administrative officials, at least resulted in a decline of the torpedo failure rate to 13 percent for the last half of 1940.[11] Nearly all restrictions on targets bound for Britain were lifted; France's fall and the threat of German invasion of Britain weakened Allied antisubmarine efforts in favor of home defense; and above all the occupation of France opened her Atlantic ports as U-boat bases, eliminating nine hundred nautical miles in the outbound journey to the convoy lanes. The first U-boat (*U-30*) arrived at Lorient on 7 July 1940 and sinkings of Allied ships rose to 157 (nearly 842,000 tons) from June to August, even as the renewal of pack tactics promised still higher returns.[12]

Most significant for the future character of the U-boat force are Dönitz's organizational lessons during this period. The heavy losses suffered did not shake his faith in the creed of more and more submarines and probably inured him to the likelihood of recurrence as part of the cyclical nature of the campaign, painful but temporary setbacks to be redressed by future success. In addition, his crews' battle losses and COs' psychological casualties demonstrated the terrible vulnerability of even hand-picked, well-trained crews in such a unique and dangerous service.

The conclusions he drew are evident in a training memorandum he prepared in November 1939, which also reveals Dönitz's grasp of the long-term nature of the conflict and the associated implications for manning his force. The plan established a training schedule for the crews of forty new U-boats from April to December 1940 and for sixty-four new submarines every six months thereafter, or a total anticipated fleet of 881 U-boats by the autumn of 1943. The accompanying precise tables of personnel requirements for 3,336 officers and 33,120 noncommissioned officers (NCOs) and enlisted men—arranged by specialist career-track (*Laufbahn*), thereunder by rank (senior NCOs, petty officers, enlisted men), and thereunder by six-month period—could never have been covered by purely voluntary means. Thus the document reveals Dönitz's abandonment of voluntary recruitment for Germany's submarine force a mere two months after war broke out.[13] Although German production fell short of the timetable (the 881st commissioned U-boat, *U-1053*, entered service on 12 February 1944), Dönitz accelerated the training of new boats and crews to attain maximum strength in minimum time. The U-boat arm would pay a steep price for this decision before the importance of longer training was appreciated.[14]

With hindsight, the salient characteristic of the first year remains the time and resources lost for the U-boat effort. Twelve months after the beginning of hostilities, Dönitz's forces were no larger than they were at the beginning. In October 1939 Hitler approved a major U-boat building program for an annual delivery of 352 submarines, but shortages in raw materials and qualified workmen led Raeder in March–July 1940 to scale down construction to only twenty-five boats per month. In the end the shipyards averaged only half of this figure in production, partly the fault of prewar shipyard mentalities but ultimately attributable to the conflicting demands of a major war on Germany's limited resources. For the first sixteen months of the war a total of only sixty-two new U-boats entered service, a figure that would be exceeded in two months and ten days at the end of 1943. Responsibility also lay with the Naval High Command's failure to develop a coherent, consistent U-boat strategy; its choice to build several models of submarines with different requirements; and, perhaps, its decision to table development of new submarine designs such as that of Dr. Hellmuth Walter.[15]

The scale of losses, however, also raises the question of the U-boats' employment by BdU, particularly for new U-boats dispatched on missions with too little training. Yet Dönitz here only followed the lead of the Kriegsmarine leadership, who pursued an aggressive and costly strategy throughout the early war. Perhaps because of this he secured his own position, for by July 1940 the post of fleet commander was held by the third man in ten months, due to disagreements over strategy and discretionary power.[16] Dönitz's survival as BdU in spite of conflicts with Raeder may represent the most significant development in the first phase of the U-boat war.

Second Phase: September 1940–August 1942

Over the next two years, the Atlantic battle fluctuated greatly in geographic expanse and fortunes, yet from the perspective of BdU it can be seen as a single entity—an extended period of sustained growth in preparation for the decisive convoy battles, striking at specific weak points in the Allies' shipping patterns while meeting strategic demands dictated by Naval High Command. Again with the benefit of hindsight, the campaign was all but decided during this period by Germany's failure to defeat Britain before the United States' entry into the conflict. Yet this perception was not evident to the participants on either side at the time, only the recognition by both of the struggle's growing urgency.

For Dönitz, the operational conduct of this phase combined his greatest triumphs with exasperating frustration. The first "Happy Time" for his submariners peaked in October 1940, when a force that averaged only thirteen U-boats at sea per day sank sixty-six ships totaling over 363,000 tons, most of which (207,000 tons) represented convoyed vessels, in exchange for only one U-boat lost. The statistical yardstick by which BdU measured success, average tonnage sunk per U-boat per day at sea, attained its highest wartime mark this month with a figure of 976 tons.[17]

Although successes continued through the winter, a gradual increase of British and Canadian escorts and air cover became evident. After losing no submarines in three months, the U-boat force was shocked in March 1941 by the loss of three of its top aces (Prien in *U-47* and *Kaptlt.* Joachim Schepke in *U-100*, both killed, and *Korv.Kapt.* Otto Kretschmer in *U-99*, captured) to convoy escorts. Citing the improvements in Allied defenses and a greater German difficulty in finding convoys, one historian dates the decisive change in U-boat fortunes from this fateful March, two years before the period of the greatest convoy battles.[18]

Certainly the U-boat war in the North Atlantic dwindled throughout the remainder of 1941. In June the British completed the cracking of the German Navy's communications ciphers (known as Enigma, after the encryption machine used, while the decryption product was designated ULTRA) and for the rest of the year read Dönitz's signals to his commanders with only a few days' decryption interval. This allowed the Admiralty to route convoys around U-boats deployed in their path—according to a detailed review by one historian, ULTRA probably saved the Allies 1.6 million tons of shipping that would have otherwise been sunk in 1941.[19] In August the seasick, demoralized crew of *U-570* (*Kaptlt.* Hans-Joachim Rahmlow) surrendered at sea to a British aircraft, demonstrating conclusively the fallacy of an abbreviated training period; new boats thereafter spent more time on trials and exercises in the Baltic, but this necessarily delayed reinforcements for the front.[20] Meanwhile the Naval High Command continued to withdraw U-boats from Atlantic operations for such secondary missions as weather-reporting and escort duty for blockade runners. Finally in late November, in response to the critical situation of Axis forces in North Africa, all Atlantic boats were ordered into the Mediterranean or off the western approaches to Gibraltar. The disastrous year fittingly closed with the virtual suspension of the U-boat war on the convoy lanes. On 25 December 1941, all seventeen U-boats at sea were either outbound or heading home, with not a single submarine on station anywhere in the Atlantic.[21]

Above all this represented the cost of not building more U-boats in 1940, yet it also underscored a growing problem of increased maintenance and repair demands even as the army drafted more and more of the necessary dockyard workers. As U-boats "aged" in service they required longer periods of overhaul and refitting: two to three months for a submarine after fifteen months' front-line duty, six months for a boat after thirty months. At the beginning of 1942 only 5 percent of all U-boats fell into this category but by the end of the year this figure was expected to rise to 15 percent, assuming more of the needed specialist workers were not lost to Wehrmacht drafts. Through the summer of 1942 Dönitz and senior advisors devoted considerable time in addressing these concerns.[22]

Their success in coping with the problem can be attributed in part to the most notable achievement of the U-boat effort in 1941, the construction of massive submarine pens in each of the major French ports. *U-203* (*Kaptlt.* Rolf Mützelberg) became the first U-boat to enter a protected pen at St. Nazaire on 30 June 1941, and from then through October 1941 submarine bunkers were completed in Brest, Lorient, and La Pallice by the Todt Organization, the organization responsible for military construction in the Third Reich. Secure within walls of reinforced concrete 2.5 to 3.5 meters (8.2 to 11.5 feet) thick, staffs of German technicians and French laborers worked wonders in restoring U-boats to operational readiness, often completing overhauls and repairs before the crews had completed their furloughs. Expanding and strengthening these facilities continued into 1944, defying tardy attempts by Allied bombers to strike at submarines when they were most vulnerable.[23]

The operational picture brightened in 1942 with Operation *Pauken-schlag* ("Roll of the Drums"), Dönitz's initial raid on the poorly protected shipping off the American east coast that developed into a sustained offensive. After U.S. defenses finally stiffened, operations shifted in May to the Gulf of Mexico and the Caribbean. Yet this oft-retold tale[24] of the U-boats' second "Happy Time" again involved only a relative handful of submarines while another twenty were detailed in February to shield Norway from a dimly perceived threat of invasion—a diversion BdU later calculated to have cost his force 500,000 tons of potential sinkings.[25]

Ironically, Dönitz enjoyed a rare and significant advantage in the cryptographic war for most of the year as improvements to the Enigma encryption machine again secured his radio communications from Allied cryptanalysts, while the codebreaking activities of the Kriegsmarine's *B-Dienst* provided BdU with decrypts of up to 80 percent of Allied convoy signals. The appearance of Type XIV supply tankers ("milch cows") in the summer also greatly expanded the ability of U-boats to operate for extended periods in distant waters and in North Atlantic convoy operations. Yet Dönitz could not take full advantage of these opportunities until the late summer when greater numbers of U-boats began to arrive from the shipyards and training stations in the Baltic. By August improvements in Allied defenses led to the gradual German withdrawal from American and Caribbean waters and the marshaling of forces for the decisive battles along the North Atlantic convoy routes.[26]

Throughout this period Dönitz devoted as much time to affairs on the domestic front as he did to the battles at sea. Germany's limited resources and multiple demands in a global war frustrated his plans for the grand buildup of the U-boat fleet. In July 1941 he calculated that, even with allowance for increased rates of losses, the U-boat arm should grow to 212 front-line submarines by May 1942, 313 by the end of 1942, and 477 by the beginning of 1944; but only five months later existing production and maintenance problems revealed that 300 boats might not be available even by the end of 1943.[27] Serious copper shortages compelled a cutback in 1942 production until, applying lessons learned from a captured British submarine, steel replaced copper in torpedo tubes and propellers.[28] From January through June 1942, the number of front-line boats rose slowly from 91 to 126, although losses averaged only 3.5 boats per month.[29] In January Dönitz discussed with Professor Walter the stalled progress of the latter's experimental submarine and immediately cabled his support of the project to OKM, with little result.[30] He also met again with *Reichsmarschall* Hermann Göring and other Luftwaffe leaders in July to petition for greater air support, but again with only limited success.[31]

Torpedo ineffectiveness continued to trouble Dönitz. Without reliable magnetic pistols, U-boat torpedoes that employed less-powerful contact detonators lacked punch, and several hits were usually required to sink their targets. The BdU reckoned that 806 torpedo hits had been necessary to sink 404 Allied ships during the first half of 1942, excluding a still-significant number of torpedo failures.[32] Although new torpedoes were being developed, Dönitz had no direct involvement in their development and sometimes discovered only by accident that other German military research stations were working on weapons projects of direct interest to the U-boat war.[33]

Only in the field of organization and personnel did the U-boat arm show a steady and consistent growth during this period, an accomplishment as significant as the highest month's total of tonnage sunk. While a relative handful of veterans fought at sea, a new generation of submariners was taking shape in the training schools in the Baltic. By July 1942 Dönitz's original corps of three thousand volunteers was long gone—dead, captured, retired to training duties, or dispersed throughout the new fleet. A force more than three times that number now stood in their place: younger—much younger; more "volunteered" than voluntary, but more enthusiastic; inexperienced but confident.[34] If less familiar to their commander-in-chief than their predecessors, they were even more dependent on his guidance. Rather than a hand-picked elite, they represented the products of a system committed to transforming the combat navy into a U-boat fleet.

This was not achieved without taking considerable risks and paying the price, especially at the beginning of the period. Training was cut at all levels; the lack of training submarines hindered basic instruction; and from 1940 through mid-1941 new U-boats and their crews generally spent only two months together on trials and exercises before being committed to action. Mounting losses of new U-boats, including the *U-570* surrender described earlier, finally led to a lengthier and more systematic program.[35] At the front, veteran crews were broken up to distribute their maturity and experience among the newcomers. By the time Günther Prien departed on his last patrol with *U-47*, he retained none of the officers and only seven of the crewmen who had accompanied him on the Scapa Flow raid seventeen months earlier. From his last war cruise neither the veterans nor their thirty-seven new shipmates returned, quite possibly victims of the inexperience of so many crewmen.[36]

Yet the gambles seemingly paid off over the next year. After heavy losses in March 1941, U-boat casualties stabilized at a monthly average of 5 percent while sinkings of enemy shipping dramatically increased.[37] Personnel losses for each of these two years proved almost identical to those for the first twelve months (see table 5), but they were absorbed by the submarine branch's rapid growth—testimony to the organizational work accomplished by von Friedeburg. By 1 July 1942 Dönitz commanded a submarine force with a front-line strength of 151 U-boats and 13,115 men (including administrative and dockyard personnel), supported by 32,247 others in home waters manning the training establishments or becoming submariners themselves.[38]

For the approaching test, however, it would not be nearly enough.

Third Phase: August 1942–November 1943

The ensuing fourteen months marked the climax of the Battle of the Atlantic, a period of greatly fluctuating fortunes for both sides before Allied supremacy became evident. The U-boats had their moments. Between July and September 1942 they executed attacks on fifteen Allied convoys with an average participation of thirteen submarines, with varying degrees of success. November 1942 represented their most successful month of the war, with 117 merchant sinkings totaling nearly 758,000 tons, and during the first twenty days of March 1943 they sank ninety-seven ships (over 500,000 tons)—two-thirds of which were convoyed ships—while losing only seven, prompting an Admiralty observation that "the Germans never came so near to disrupting communication between the Old World and the New."[39]

These successes reflected a number of advantages enjoyed by the Germans at the beginning of this period. The signals intelligence success of the *B-Dienst* and the importance of the Type XIV U-tankers in extending operations have already been noted. In addition, November brought the long-overdue improvement of torpedoes with the introduction of a reliable detonator that combined contact with magnetic capabilities, the Pi (or *Pistole*) 2; this was followed shortly thereafter by the development of the FAT (*Federapparat Torpedo,* spring-operated torpedo), an anticonvoy weapon designed to travel in a straight line for a specified distance, then begin zigzagging or looping once it had entered a convoy's columns.[40]

But these temporary successes only strengthened Allied resolve to close the gaps in their defenses. The larger numbers of U-boats braced the Allies to the need to fight the convoys through the wolf packs, rather than evade them as in 1941. The cumulative effect of expanded air coverage, experienced escorts armed with the latest detection and weapons technology, and restored cryptographic insight into German communications led to a crushing defeat of the U-boats in the late spring and summer of 1943.

Aware that he had lost at least thirty-one boats through just the first twenty-two days of May 1943—nearly as many as were lost in all of 1941— Dönitz withdrew his forces from the convoy lanes to Britain and redeployed them to the central Atlantic. There, American "hunter-killer" teams composed of escort aircraft carriers and destroyer escorts pounced on U-boat refueling rendezvous and all but eliminated the fleet of Type XIV supply tankers that had enabled German submarines to operate in distant operational areas. An autumn attempt by Dönitz to renew the North Atlantic convoy battles after arming his boats with new radar search receivers, flak armament, and acoustic torpedoes collapsed after some initial success, and Allied control of the Atlantic was assured.[41]

Dönitz himself defined this period's beginning in late August 1942, when extended air cover for convoys and an alarming increase in losses due to aircraft warned him that the foundations of his U-boat strategy were crumbling. On 21 August BdU formally acknowledged, "If allowed to continue, this handicap to the conduct of operations can only lead to higher and unsustainable losses, fewer successes, and ultimately to reduced chances for a successful U-boat campaign as a whole."[42] A few days later Dönitz also conceded the use of shipborne radar by Allied escorts, a possibility he had rejected only the previous month.[43]

In late September he presented his new assessments to Hitler, petitioning the Führer for approval of increased Luftwaffe support, improved flak armament, the Walter boat, and surface-to-surface rockets for use against escorts.[44] This time, Dönitz's initiative yielded quick results for Walter boat production,[45] but his continued involvement in technical questions further strained his relations with Raeder. The BdU staff officers feared their chief's dismissal; instead it was Raeder who was forced out and Dönitz named as his successor on 30 January 1943.[46]

As navy commander-in-chief he at last possessed the authority to fully organize naval resources and strategy according to his views: "The naval war is the U-boat war," he immediately informed OKM section heads and staffs.[47] Dönitz thereafter became more involved in organizational issues, with considerable success. Discussions with Reich Armaments Minister Albert Speer led in March 1943 to his takeover of U-boat production, although final agreements were not reached until July; negotiations with Luftwaffe authorities in April 1943 improved relations and brought more reconnaissance aircraft to the U-boats' aid.[48] But as already noted, he did not materially increase the staff he left to conduct U-boat operations.

For the new generation of U-boat sailors, the period was defined by a growing ferocity and deadliness. The abrupt, dramatic increase in losses for the last four months of 1942—more men killed or captured than in the previous twenty-four months (see table 5)—foreshadowed the effectiveness of the growing Allied arsenal in convoy defense. During the winter and spring, U-boat crews weathered severe storms in the search for and pursuit of convoys; engaged in exhausting, nerve-wracking duels with Allied escorts to attack merchantmen; and finally ran a gauntlet of aircraft on the passage home—planes equipped with a centimetric radar whose waves could not be detected by U-boat search receivers. The toll in lives rose precipitously, over 5,600 dead or missing in the first six months in 1943; one of those was *Lt.z.S.* Peter Dönitz, son of the commander-in-chief, lost aboard *U-954.* Yet for all Dönitz's subsequent efforts to improve conditions—a temporary withdrawal, installation of new search receivers and upgraded flak armament, new torpedoes, group passages for mutual defense in the Bay of Biscay—the destruction of U-boat crews actually increased over the last four months of the period, a monthly loss rate (1,115 men) equal to that of the entire first year of the conflict.[49]

More than thirteen thousand German submariners were killed or captured in these fourteen months. In effect, the entire force carefully built up over the 1940–42 period had been annihilated. Yet even as they died von Friedeburg's training organization maintained a steady stream of replacement boats and crews to the Atlantic. Despite the heavy casualties of August 1942–April 1943, the U-boat force attained its peak strength in May with a total force (including support personnel) of fifty-eight thousand officers and men, of whom eighteen thousand served in front-line units and probably twelve thousand manned combat U-boats.[50] In November 1943 front-line strength still numbered 162 U-boats, with 267 more submarines on trials or training duty in home waters.[51] Their turn was yet to come.

That the numbers remained so large was the direct result of Dönitz's Fleet Construction Program of 1943, an ambitious project conceived at the height of the convoy battles and maintained through the disastrous defeats of late spring and summer. After first securing Hitler's approval for increases in naval steel allocations and the exemption of skilled shipyard workers from further military call-ups, Dönitz prepared extensive expansion plans in April 1943 for a navy built around submarines and light surface forces. The planned annual production of 360 U-boats included the first Walter (Type XVII) submarines, but two-thirds of the new boats were to be Type VIICs, modified only by stronger steel construction to allow dives to greater depths.[52] As early as April, naval personnel planners drafted schedules for future monthly transfers of forty young ensigns from other naval forces to U-boat duty during the period January–September 1944, thereafter to be increased to forty-five ensigns per month.[53] On 31 May 1943 Dönitz presented his construction program to Hitler but raised the planned production of U-boats from thirty to forty per month. As subsequently developed by naval construction authorities, the planned 1944 fleet of 434 U-boats, though it would have included ninety Walter boats and six of the equally new Type XXI submarines, still depended primarily on 225 Type VIICs and 49 Type IXC and IXD boats.[54] With hindsight this appears almost irrational, in view of the acknowledged effects of Allied air power since the previous August and especially the severe losses in May. In fact it reflected a recurrent dilemma of the German war effort, devoting most industrial production for mass output of dated weapons models (the Me-109 aircraft, the Type VIIC U-boat) in order to buy time for the development of revolutionary weapons designs (the Me-262 jet, the Walter and Type XXI boats) using only limited resources. The sacrificial nature of the new U-boat fleet is revealed in Dönitz's and Hitler's remarks at the 31 May conference:

DÖNITZ: I am nevertheless of the view that, even if the goal of large-scale sinkings is no longer attainable, the U-boat war must continue as it ties down an unusually large amount of enemy forces. . . .

HITLER (interrupting): There can be no question of a let-up in the U-boat war. The Atlantic is my western glacis, and if I have to go over to the defensive there, that is still preferable to the alternative of having to fight on the coast of Europe. Even if great successes cannot be expected, I can't allow the huge enemy resources tied down by the U-boat war to be released for use elsewhere.[55]

To meet the extensive manpower needs demanded by this construction program, Kriegsmarine personnel authorities had drafted plans earlier in May for scraping together nearly 208,000 new personnel from expanded drafts and recruitment, reclassification of draft-exempt occupations, and streamlining the bureaucracy. The ink was not dry on the signatures before Dönitz raised the total personnel required by September 1944 to nearly 438,000, of whom more than 62,000 were allocated to future U-boat crews.[56] Within a few months this program gave way to one built entirely around Type XXI and XXIII submarines, but its first recruits had entered the training schools by the beginning of the final stage of the U-boat war.

Fourth Phase: November 1943–May 1945

The final eighteen months of World War II, despite major changes and developments in the U-boat campaign, are bound together by a bloody thread. Already defeated in the Battle of the Atlantic, the U-boats now began to be hunted down and killed. Dönitz designated as their new mission the "tying down" of large numbers of Allied forces, as well as compelling the continued use of safe but economically inefficient convoys. He intended this as a transition period until advanced submarine models allowed a renewal of the struggle at more equal odds, but in fact it represented the final phase, the great dying. More than half of all deaths among U-boat crewmen occurred during this period (see table 5), as the U-boat force was reconstituted yet again simply to be wiped out.

One operational development involved the opening of a new theater in the Indian Ocean, where a few Type IX boats had achieved nearly half of all merchant sinkings during the summer of 1943; with Japanese cooperation, a U-boat base established at Penang on the Malayan peninsula provided for a permanent presence for German submarines. During the war's final eighteen months, U-boats in the Far East, commonly referred to as *Monsun* ("monsoon") boats after the operational code name for the early transfer of submarines there, sank forty-four merchant ships (over 234,000 tons) and served as blockade runners in the exchange of weapons technology and raw materials between the Axis partners, a noteworthy accomplishment as twenty-two of the forty-one U-boats committed were destroyed before they reached Penang. The handful of survivors occupied the attentions of five Allied escort carriers, ninety escort vessels, and fifteen squadrons of aircraft.[57]

At the beginning of this period U-boats also attempted to renew convoy operations west of Gibraltar and even in the eastern Atlantic with some Luftwaffe support, but attained little success. Long-range patrols by Type IX boats continued in the Caribbean and the Gulf of Guinea and off Canada, reminding the Allies of what might yet befall unescorted merchantmen. But the continual upgrading of radar search receivers, flak armament, and torpedoes after the summer of 1943 failed to stem the hemorrhage of U-boat losses that averaged 20 percent of all boats at sea over the winter of 1943–44. The trading of so many lives to tie down the enemy finally exacted a psychological toll. For the first and only time, a noticeable decline of morale occurred among front-line crews, a problem that approached a crisis in early 1944 until resolved by a technical improvisation.[58]

The introduction of the *Schnorchel* effectively solved the predicament by restoring at least the illusion of U-boat invisibility. The device became known to the Kriegsmarine in May 1940 aboard captured Dutch submarines, intended for ventilation during cruises to the tropical waters surrounding the Dutch East Indies colonies. Professor Walter first proposed its use for current U-boats and his own Type XVII model in March 1943, and the first orders went out to contractors in August. Although installation on newly built submarines began in September–October 1943, modified designs were not available in quantity until early 1944, and the necessary installation with accompanying conning-tower modifications then required an average of two months' time in dock per boat. More time was needed to correct teething problems and allow crews to adapt to a true submarine environment, so that it was not until the summer of 1944 that the snorkel became standard for the U-boat fleet.[59]

With it, U-boat crews finally gained respite from the ceaseless Allied air presence—even postwar tests by radar-equipped aircraft yielded only a 6 percent ability to detect protruding snorkel mast-heads—and the decline in losses surprised even Dönitz.[60] But time was running out. After a disastrous effort to intervene against the Normandy invasion, the U-boats evacuated the French bases that became threatened by Allied ground forces and transferred to Norway. From there they could still operate in the North Atlantic, but now principally for the gathering of meteorological data (which contributed significantly to the initial success of Hitler's Ardennes counteroffensive in December 1944).[61] They also launched close inshore operations off the British coast and the Irish Sea reminiscent of the war's early days and continued occasional forays into Canadian and American waters.[62] All eagerly awaited the appearance of the revolutionary new submarines to turn the tide.

It is easy with hindsight to see through these illusory hopes—the snorkel merely delayed submarines' destruction until they engaged enemy warships, and the delays in production of advanced models assured they would be too late to matter. But at that moment U-boat crews felt renewed in their faith, especially after scoring a number of successes in December and January,[63] a faith as real as the fear it engendered among Allied leaders. On 26 January 1945 Churchill convened a War Cabinet meeting with his senior naval and air commanders to consider the renewed U-boat threat posed by the snorkel, the anticipated arrival of the advanced model submarines, and the "much more offensive spirit" shown by U-boat commanders. The Admiralty estimated that, reinforced by up to eighty Type XXI submarines by the spring, a new U-boat offensive might be expected to sink 200 merchant ships per quarter in spring 1945 (only 183 had been lost in the first quarter of 1943), rising to 270 losses per quarter by the summer.[64]

As before, Allied fears led to decisive action. Plans to send three hundred destroyers and other escort vessels to the Pacific theater were postponed. The Admiralty's subsequent concentration of forces in coastal waters, amounting to 110 destroyers, 326 other escort vessels, and 528 Coastal

Command aircraft, supported by the laying of seventeen thousand mines, resulted in the destruction of thirty-one of fifty-five U-boats dispatched there in February and March.[65] Meanwhile Germany's accelerating collapse preempted any meaningful employment of the long-delayed new U-boats. Only two Type XXIs began operational patrols in the war's last days, but neither had any combat opportunities before Germany's capitulation; one of the boats had moreover experienced an embarrassing accidental flooding of the main engine.[66]

As a final caricature of the lack of Luftwaffe support, the near-annihilation of the German Air Force left Kriegsmarine vessels exposed as easy prey for Allied air power. During the war's last month British aircraft sank at least twenty-six submarines trying to flee their home bases for Norway, at least eight of which were destroyed by rocket-firing Typhoon fighter-bombers flying from captured German airfields; eighteen more U-boats fell victim to bombing raids while still in their home ports.[67]

Yet even in the last months a number of U-boats performed a valuable if nonmilitary task as part of the evacuation fleets that carried German refugees away from the path of the advancing Red Army. Karl-Friedrich Merten, Knight's Cross winner as the former CO of *U-68*, set the tone as commander of the 24th U-boat Flotilla in July–August 1944 by successive evacuations of six thousand teenagers of the Hitler Youth and then the entire civilian population from Memel over the vigorous protests of the district Nazi party leader.[68] In January and February 1945 U-boats in training commands at the ports of Pillau and Hela in Danzig Bay (now Baltiysk and Hel in the Bay of Gdansk) suddenly became refugee vessels, transporting uprooted civilians, Hitler Youth contingents released from defense duties, and wounded soldiers across the central Baltic to the island of Bornholm. A mix of the newest and oldest U-boat models—at least eleven Type XXIs not yet ready for combat, several Type VIICs, and two ancient Type II "canoes" retired to training duties—participated in these operations, each XXI boat typically carrying forty to sixty passengers to safety. *U-721* (*Oblt.z.S.* Ludwig Fabricius), however, brought away more than one hundred, while the tiny quarters aboard *U-56* (*Lt.z.S.* Walter Kaeding, acting CO and a Knight's Cross winner promoted from the ranks) permitted room only for two women and four children, the youngest still in diapers.[69]

Ironically, U-boat production attained its peak in 1944, with as many as 387 submarines completed in contrast to the 270 of 1943. This tardy solution to a chronic problem resulted from Dönitz's close relationship with Speer, whose deputy Otto Merker arranged for German industries in the interior to prefabricate U-boat sections for transportation and final assembly at the shipyards. Included among the 1944 total were sixty-three Type XXI and thirty-one Type XXIII boats, whose monthly production accelerated as the year ended.[70]

As U-boat operations returned to the familiar hunting grounds of the war's early days, so too the number of U-boat personnel contracted to a size not seen since 1939–40. With the collapse of Dönitz's ambitious Fleet Construction Program, the thirst for U-boat manpower slackened as German ground forces claimed priority on all able-bodied males. The newly formed "small battle units" (*Kleinkampfverbände*), formed in 1944 with midget submarines, manned torpedoes, and frogmen, also drained away a number of U-boat personnel, especially junior officers and seaman NCOs.[71] Revised construction plans in October 1944 still aimed at a fleet of 375 modern submarines in 1945, including 188 Type XXIs, 133 Type XXIIIs, and 38 of the new, larger Walter boats (Type XXVI), but as already noted, developmental problems, shortages of labor and materials, constant bombings, and the general deterioration of Germany's situation confined much of this fleet to blueprints.[72] In any case, crews for the new models required extensive training on the vessels themselves and their systems. Had the planned 1945 fleet of Type XXI, XXIII, and XXVI U-boats achieved reality, yet another generation of German submariner—more specialized and more accustomed to the enclosed, submerged environment—would have been needed to man it.

Instead, the character of the U-boat service at war's end in some ways closely resembled that on duty when the conflict began. On 31 August 1939, forty-six U-boats were at sea; on 8 May 1945, the total was forty-three. On both dates the U-boat Command centered its operations around the British Isles, and on both days it looked to the future for the real U-boat war to be waged. Above all, the crews in both periods were neither novices nor teenagers, but men in their early twenties who were familiar with submarines, led by commanders who had paid their dues and knew their business. The one crucial difference was that in 1945 the dying ended.[73]

THUS THE MEN who served aboard Germany's U-boats constituted several successive corps rather than a single force, an evolution in which only a relative handful participated and survived from beginning to end. Each new corps essentially fought a separate campaign that overlapped their successors' combat experience, with distinctive but progressively deteriorating prospects of success and survival. And each corps in turn sailed to annihilation, with its survivors scattered to training duties and new boats. Yet, though the totality of their defeat appears self-evident today, the fact that they continued to sail to the end marked a victory that their enemies were the first to recognize. As expressed in the U.S. Navy's history of signals intelligence operations written shortly after the war: "It should be borne in mind that the U/B arm was not, in May 1945, defeated at sea. The pre-Schnorchel U/B had been decisively swept from the Atlantic in the summer of 1943; but the loss was made good and the U/B reappeared in force."[74]

Who these men were, how they came together, and some aspects of the war they fought constitute the rest of our story.

5 Spirit and Soul

U-boat Officers

The crucial importance of the commander in determining a U-boat's success or failure has been and will continue to be noted in our story. Beyond combat abilities and technical skills, the captain and his officers acted as spiritual leaders for their crews. Before the war, Dönitz wrote, "The boat's soul is its *Komman-dant*. He must be the leader of his men under conditions like no other." One of the most successful of these leaders, Wolfgang Lüth, extended this analogy to all officers aboard a submarine: "The crew's spirit depends largely on the example set by the officers."[1]

Given their significance, several questions immediately arise: Who were these officers? Where did they come from, and what characteristics distinguished them? Before we examine these background issues let us first consider how they were selected.

Forging An Officer Corps

Most officers who served aboard U-boats—like their American counterparts—were career regulars, obliged to twenty-five years' service after receiving their commissions. They represented the products of a rigorous selection process and intensive training and education, a result of the navy's use of the personnel limitations imposed by the Versailles Treaty (a maximum of fifteen hundred officers) to forge a select officer corps. From 1919 to 1934 the number of line officers rose only from 594 to 737, and engineer officers from 142 to 184.[2] Yet the quality of this maturation process came into question over the years as international crises and war remorselessly curtailed training and instruction even as the number of officer candidates continued to grow. In their haste to streamline and accelerate the training of officers, however, naval authorities had little time to critically examine some fundamental shortcomings of their system.

Cadets who entered the navy from the 1920s through the mid-1930s, regardless of their eventual careers as line or specialized (e.g., engineering, weapons, medical) officers, belonged to the special fraternity of their year's "class" of cadets, or "Crew" in German naval parlance, designated by the last digits of the year of entrance into the navy (thus Crew 34's counterpart at Annapolis was the Class of 1938, denoted instead by year of graduation and commissioning). The 124 members of Crew 26 who assembled in Kiel in April of that year, for example, represented the final choices out of six thousand applicants, a ratio of nearly 1:50. By the time of the selection of the much larger Crew 34 (318 cadets), the need for an expanded officer corps had led the navy to loosen entrance requirements, particularly in accepting former merchant marine officers (*Handelsschiffsoffiziere,* colloquially "HSOs"); yet even then the ratio of those accepted to those who applied stood somewhere between 1:25 and 1:30.[3]

To qualify as an officer cadet involved an imposing battery of grueling intellectual, physical, and psychological examinations. The last included a *Mutprobe,* a candidate's "test of courage" in holding up an iron bar through which a painful electric current would be passed. Other tests are described by Wolfgang Ott in the 1956 German novel *Haie und Kleine Fische* (*Sharks and Little Fish*):

> Well, first there's a character who rattles off a list of numbers fast as he can. Every time he said an even number I was supposed to raise my right arm; when it was an uneven number, I was to raise my left arm. If a number was divisible by three, I was supposed to stamp my right foot. When a prime number came up, I was supposed to wag my head. No joking, gentlemen, it was like the bughouse.

Observers from foreign navies shared this critical view of the testing process, especially evaluations based on handwriting analysis and recorded facial expressions under stress. Nevertheless those accepted by such procedures experienced a low washout rate during their four years as officer cadets—less than 5 percent in the case of Crew 34—suggesting its overall effectiveness.[4]

Those chosen each year developed strong mutual bonds of comradeship and the Crew designation became an indelible stamp for each officer thereafter. In these communities every eighteen- to twenty-year-old cadet knew everyone else and values were as readily shared as lessons and meals. Crew yearbooks caricatured traits and memorialized embarrassing moments of individual cadets through doggerel verse; even after graduation, newsletters maintained contact and information about Crew members as they scattered throughout the navy to their eventual wartime fates. Long after the conflict that ended the Reich and the Kriegsmarine, Crew survivors continue their association and renew old friendships. For what they learned and shared as cadets would in turn be imparted to the men they led in the U-boat service.[5]

Unlike their U.S. Navy counterparts at Annapolis, German navy cadets in the early 1930s did not spend four years in a university environment but experienced a varied instructional and training period designed to develop character, practical skills, and experience. After six months' basic training at Stralsund, a *Seekadett* typically served for three and one-half months aboard a full-masted training bark (usually the *Gorch Fock*), followed by a fourteen-month world voyage aboard a cruiser, one year's classroom instruction at the naval academy (*Marineschule Mürwik*) in Flensburg, six months' specialized instruction in ordnance and communications, and another year's duty on various warships at escalating levels of responsibility. His term at the *Marineschule*—more commonly known as "the Castle," after the building's red-brick facade characteristic of the Teutonic Knights' castles—blended intensive classroom instruction (which in 1936 amounted to forty-six hours per week) with athletic competition, horseback riding, and lessons in social etiquette. Superiors continually evaluated a plebe's performance at all of these varied levels, but—borrowing from an ancient Prussian regimental tradition—the officers aboard his final warship assignment actually elected him by majority vote to his commission as *Leutnant zur See* (ensign). An American observer, struck by the many contrasts with the U.S. Navy's program in creating officers, believed that the two navies "could hardly go about it in more different manners."[6]

An important part of their education centered on absorbing the lessons of the 1918 mutinies. To facilitate future officers' ability to lead men from the lower-middle and working classes, the program aimed first at developing the cadets' leadership qualities. During the late 1930s naval instructors even sought to broaden cadets' horizons through exposure to both National Socialist writings and such pacifist literature as Erich Maria Remarque's *All Quiet on the Western Front*. This was one reason why so much emphasis was placed on practical experience, and U-boat commanders later especially recalled the need for submarine experience before feeling comfortable with command situations.[7]

Submarine training for cadets was virtually nonexistent through the mid-1930s, however. Werner Henke, an HSO retroactively assigned to Crew 33, spent the period from 21 May 1935 through 21 January 1936 in various specialized training courses absorbing the latest lessons in naval ordnance, mines, and communications, but during these eight months his entire instruction at the Submarine School in Kiel amounted to six days.[8] Instead, there was an increasing training emphasis on a much different branch of service, the naval air arm. A review of the annually published navy list (*Rangliste*) for November 1937 reveals that only seventeen of Crew 34's 167 line ensigns were serving aboard U-boats at that time, while thirty-one had gone to the Luftwaffe to become naval aviators; of Crew 35's 325 line midshipmen, not one had yet entered the submarine branch but 161 (50 percent!) had been detailed to the air force. One year later, Crew 36 sent thirty-five of its 324 ensigns into submarines, but dispatched 136 to the Luftwaffe, where most would remain for at least four years, if not the duration of the war.[9] The perceived future of the Kriegsmarine as war approached, it appeared, lay over the waves rather than below.

The number and diversification of cadets in 1937 underscores another problem in naval officer development. After Hitler's accession to power and the consequent acceleration of rearmament, both the exclusivity of selection and the length of training and instruction increasingly fell victim to the need for expansion. The naval officer corps on 1 November 1932 numbered 1,109 with a ratio of line officers to NCOs and enlisted men of approximately 1:20; when war came seven years later, the total number of officers had quadrupled to 4,375, but the ratio of line officers to other ranks had fallen behind to only 1:30.[10] To meet the increased demand, the navy accepted former merchant marine officers or HSOs, promoted qualified men from the ranks, and adjusted recruiting standards to bring in more applicants; and to develop the larger numbers of officers, the navy cut corners in training and education—particularly the latter.

These developments can be traced in the size and training period of several Crews during the decade prior to World War II:

	Cadets	Months
Crew 30	78	54
Crew 33	151	42
Crew 34	318	36
Crew 38	578	30

The implications of these figures for a dilution in quality of training are obvious. Even allowing that the *Reichsmarine* had set its original standards too high, the much larger numbers of later cadets simply did not receive the same levels of training and education. The first cuts were made: The oceanic cruise, for example, became reduced to nine, then eight months, and the specialized technical instruction grew shorter through condensing lessons. Practical command experience, however, remained a priority, and for Crew 36 and all thereafter, that experience involved participation in actual combat. The greatest loss occurred at the level of class instruction at the naval academy, which was reduced first to nine months and then to just seven. As 11 percent of a cadet's time at Mürwik was set aside for military drill, this meant a significant curtailment of academic instruction in languages, mathematics, and electronics.[11]

Thus when war began, a majority of German naval officers moved into command positions with less training and education than their older comrades, and with a bias that favored practical experience over academic knowledge. Wartime classes of officer cadets accelerated these trends as little more than a skeleton remained of the original development program. Crews became designated by month and year as two annual classes of twelve hundred plebes each became the new standard. Officer cadets who reported in December 1939 (Crew XII/39), for example, spent three months each in basic training and aboard a training bark, then served six months' combat duty aboard minesweepers, patrol boats, and even U-boats before heading off to five months of classes at "the Castle," now redesignated the *Marinekriegsschule* (Naval War Academy). Completion of their coursework and examinations in late April 1941 brought promotion to ensign and the beginning of active duty after a total of seventeen months.[12]

Yet naval authorities recognized limits to what could be achieved through streamlining. The training period for one engineering officer cadet of Crew 40, for example, lasted two years and three months, including a several-month stint on a front-line U-boat.[13] For the remainder of the war, class instruction for each Crew at the academy stabilized around six months, with some formerly standard courses (e.g., gunnery) dropped entirely. On the other hand, instruction in social etiquette and in the proper choice of a wife—the navy retained the right of approval of an officer's marriage—remained a fixture in an officer's education.

The *U-Boot-Waffe*'s growing power became evident in March 1944 when, after a personal inspection by Dönitz, most of the academy's faculty were sacked and their places taken by young, decorated U-boat commanders; the new instructors were often more unhappy with having been removed from active submarine duty than they were interested in teaching. On 30 August 1944 the process was completed when the reigning U-boat ace, *Korv.Kapt.* Wolfgang Lüth, assumed command of the *Marinekriegs-schule.* In fact little changed in the curriculum and classes, but the act symbolized the triumph of the U-boat arm within the navy.[14]

Two other sources of officers were also tapped during the war. With the reestablishment of reserves as part of the conscription laws of 1935, reserve officers became available after passing through an accelerated training regimen, often accompanied by retroactive assignment to a Crew. Those who distinguished themselves as commanders of minesweepers and patrol craft might be tapped for U-boat duty. Eventually 179 reserve officers rose to command of submarines, particularly during the 1943–45 period.[15] Yet the preference for regular officers remained strong and relatively unaffected by the press of casualties.

A contrast with the German army even before the beginning of the Russian campaign and its attendant massive losses is instructive. In June 1941, the ratio of active to reserve officers in most German infantry divisions was 35:65, and in the panzer, motorized, and mountain divisions the ratio rose to 50:50 (as it was in the Luftwaffe); in July 1942, when the U-boat force finally began to attain its maximum strength, the ratio of active to reserve officers in front-line flotillas stood at 80:20. Among U-boats in training and the U-boat training establishment, the ratio grew to 87:13.[16] The Wehrmacht depended heavily on its reserve officers; the *U-Boot-Waffe* did not.

Another source of officers consisted of qualified NCOs promoted from the ranks, known collectively as *Volksoffiziere* (literally "people's officers") and a policy of increasing significance throughout the German armed forces after 1942. As with reserve officers (the eventual status granted to most promotees), they received intensified instruction and training at the *Marine-schule* and other facilities and demonstrated their abilities at escalating levels of responsibility. Veteran navigators of the *Obersteuermann* career-track for enlisted personnel proved worthy additions as line officers, not less than thirty-five of whom became U-boat commanders. Communications officers drew very heavily from the ranks of petty officer radiomen. And for the U-boat service, machinists manning the engine spaces were increasingly promoted to the post of chief engineering officer.

The desperate need for officers led in 1944 to an order that every naval command, from naval district headquarters to each commissioned U-boat, should surrender 0.5 percent of its personnel as officer candidates. Some commands duly offered those best qualified; others simply rid themselves of troublemakers and deadbeats. U-boat commanders fell into both categories. Some of the "candidates" required additional basic schooling before they could begin officer training. The net result, according to a U-boat personnel officer, left the navy with a "50-50 split, good vs. bad officer material."[17] The navy's officer selection process had come a long way.

Yet there is no evidence of undue haste in advancement from the ranks. The promotions of *Obersteuermänner* to U-boat command were fairly evenly distributed throughout the war, with more in 1941 (seven) than 1944 (six); the earliest occurred in November 1940, and the year with the largest number (1943, with ten) matches the year of the U-boats' maximum strength. One U-boat torpedo mixer recommended for promotion as an officer candidate in October 1943 had to wait six months before he received travel orders to Germany, then spent thirteen months in classrooms and training before passing his final examinations—eleven days before Germany's capitulation.[18]

The gap in the quality of training and education for regular officers that grew after the early 1930s did not escape Dönitz's attention and doubtless reinforced his and Admiral von Friedeburg's preference for commanders from the earlier Crews. Dönitz was almost certainly inclined toward older officers in any case on a personal basis, men whom he knew and on whom he believed he could rely (as commander of the cruiser *Emden* he had become acquainted with many Crew 34 cadets during their eight-month overseas cruise). This trust is evident from a random survey of 443 frontline U-boat *Kommandanten* over the course of the war (table 7).

From the data it can be seen that 71 percent of these commanders entered the navy before the end of 1937 and over half before the end of 1936. Officers from the wartime Crews amounted to only 16 percent of surveyed commanders, although many more doubtless served as watch officers. As will be seen, the charge that the U-boat force deteriorated into a "children's crusade" in 1943–45 is greatly exaggerated; the average age of commanders remained fairly constant at between twenty-six and twenty-eight.[19]

Yet preference for older captains was probably being phased out in the summer of 1942 in favor of a more systematic reliance on youth. As large numbers of U-boats finally became available, the need for a comprehensive plan to provide the necessary officers became more evident. In July 1942, as his force attained a strength of 138 front-line submarines, with 208 more in training, Dönitz finalized plans for a methodical call-up of new officer classes to serve as U-boat watch officers. According to these timetables, a submarine-qualified member of Crew I/41 might assume his post as a II.W.O. in March 1943, with the promise of advancement to I.W.O. six

TABLE 7 **U-BOAT COMMANDERS BY YEAR OF SERVICE ENTRY (CREW)**

Crew	Number	Percentage
21–32	63	14
33	34	8
34	31	7
35	45	10
36	57	13
37–X/37	82	19
38	39	9
39–39b	18	4
IX/39–XII/39	49	11
40–X/40	19	4
41–V/41	6	1
Total	*443*	*100*

Source: Busch/Röll, *U-Bootkommandanten,* 15–117 (all alphabetical entries, A–J).

Note: All individuals are regular navy officers who commanded front-line U-boats.

months later; new officers from Crew V/41 would begin serving as second watch officers in July 1943. Subsequent wartime classes would follow in turn as the best-qualified watch officers advanced to command posts. This plan doubtless survived as one of the foundations for Dönitz's projected expansion of the U-boat fleet in 1943.[20]

But as this ambitious program fell victim to defeat and conflicting priorities, the reliance on older officers continued for the remainder of the war. Studies by one U-boat veteran reveal that captains from Crews 20 through 24 commissioned 41 percent of all new submarines in 1944, their highest rate of the war, the same year that commanders from Crews 25 through 34 declined to their lowest rate, about 52 percent. By contrast, Crews from 1935 and later contributed only about 7 percent of 1944 commanders, a rate equal to their average participation from 1942–45.[21]

The strains that rapid expansion placed on its capabilities thus revealed one of the officer training program's major shortcomings. A second became evident in increasing shortages of specialized and technical officers. The obvious emphasis on developing *Seeoffiziere,* line or executive officers expected to exercise command responsibility, ultimately contradicted the ideal of an integrated but highly selective officer corps with equal treatment and experiences shared by line, engineering, ordnance, administrative, naval construction, and medical officers. In fact specialized officers always remained something of "second-class" officers. Engineers (often referred to as "high seas mechanics"), ordnance, and administrative officers, for example, received classroom instruction while executive cadets took their training voyage aboard the bark *Gorch Fock*.[22] More practically, specialist officers always numbered only a fraction of the *Seeoffiziere;* if the navy could not adequately train a sufficient number of the latter, what did that imply for the rest?

For the U-boat war, qualified engineering officers in particular were critical. While the navy's training program turned out a total of 2,180 line officers in Crews 32 through 38, the number of engineering officers amounted to only 421, or a ratio of 5:1.[23] (Among our sample of U-boat veterans, the ratio of executive to engineering officers was 4:1.) As the typical ratio on a U-boat was 3:1, the inevitability of shortages under the existing system became obvious. The Kriegsmarine tried to improve the situation by broadening its acceptance of applicants from less than 7 percent in 1933 to more than 34 percent in 1939, but even this could not redress the imbalance.[24] The result appears to have been an increasing reliance on promotion from the engineering ranks to fill the gaps, itself a risky proposition in view of the equally serious lack of *Maschinisten* petty officers. According to the historian of Crew 38, the lack of qualified engineering officers represents a major reason why the *U-Boot-Waffe* never regained full effectiveness after the heavy losses suffered in 1943.[25]

To evaluate the U-boat officer corps it is necessary to examine each of the major officer categories. Our sample includes completed questionnaires for 170 former German navy officers who served aboard submarines during World War II. Two of these were naval surgeons, one a torpedo officer promoted from the ranks, and one a war correspondent; seven were communications officers, U-boat radiomen who rose to officer rank after they left submarine service. Thirty-two men served as engineering officers. All the rest—127 officers, or 75 percent—consisted of *Seeoffiziere* (including line officer candidates) in the capacities of commanders and watch officers. Each of these categories will be treated, with of course an emphasis on the executive officers. In addition to the sample, our study will draw upon data from other sources to provide as complete a portrait as possible of Dönitz's officer corps.

Seeoffiziere

In most modern navies, executive officers have dominated the officer corps at the expense of the necessary but specialized technical officers responsible for propulsion, weaponry, and support systems. This proved as true in Nazi Germany's Kriegsmarine as it had previously in the *Kaiserliche Marine* or later in the Bundesmarine. Three of the four officers typically serving on a U-boat were *Seeoffiziere*, as were 68 percent of all officers who passed through the German naval academy from 1930 to 1938.[26] Their even stronger presence among our sample testifies to their current participation in veterans' affairs and continued interest in historical questions. This is only fitting, as they shaped the character and fate of the U-boat service more than any other group or single individual.

The sample, reflecting the demographics of a survey conducted almost fifty years after the end of World War II, is biased toward younger U-boat officers.[27] Omitted for immediate consideration are the data for four *Fähnriche* (midshipmen, grouped with officers as cadets but technically and literally NCOs promoted from the ranks) and four officers who provided insufficient data. The most common rank was *Oberleutnant zur See* (sixty-eight officers), followed by *Leutnant zur See* (twenty), *Kapitänleutnant* (twenty-six), and *Korvettenkapitän* (five). All of those in the last two categories and twenty-nine of those at the *Oberleutnant* rank commanded their own U-boats. The remaining fifty-nine line officers served as watch officers, as had all but five of those who rose to submarine command. Of particular note is their mobility within the U-boat branch. Each *Seeoffizier* served on an average of 2.5 U-boats during his career and three logged time on six different submarines. Of the total of 119 line officers, only twelve were reserve officers, a 9:1 ratio that furnishes further proof that Dönitz relied much less on this source of officer material than the army or air force. The relative youth of our sample, particularly in contrast to U-boat commanders noted in table 7, is demonstrated by their year of entry into the navy in table 8.

That our sample for the most part constitutes the wartime classes of officer cadets (77 of 119, or 65 percent, entered the navy in 1939 or later) provides a unique insight into that rarely studied group of U-boat officers. Their personal data complement, and provide a basis for comparison with, the information already compiled for U-boat commanders and individual Crews. In this way we may also see if the wartime classes reflect a lessening of standards or change in character from the prewar officer corps.

Background characteristics for these latecomers to the U-boat war reveal a distinctive homogeneity. In geographic origins alone, the data in table 9— arranged in part by individual states and in part by specific or consolidated regions—reveal a strong North German accent: When a U-boat bridge watch changed in the morning, the officers would be far more likely to greet each other with "Moin Moin" rather than the southern "Grüss Gott."[28]

The clear emphasis on North Germany—essentially the former state of Prussia—and the unmistakable underrepresentation of southern Germany

TABLE 8 **U-BOAT LINE OFFICERS SURVEYED BY DATE OF ENTRY OR CREW**

Year or Crew[a]	Number	Percentage
30–32	2	2
33	4	3
34	6	5
35	3	3
36	4	3
37–X/37	14	12
38	9	8
39–XII/39	26	22
40–X/40	13	11
41–V/41	32	27
42	6	5
Total	*119*	*100[b]*

Source: Officer questionnaires in sample.

[a]In cases where the crew was not given or inapplicable, the date was used.

[b]Total adds up to over 100 due to rounding.

and Austria are features not limited to officers, as we shall later see. Interesting too is that within North Germany, the former Hanseatic League cities contributed more than their share: The aged commercial ports of Bremen and Hamburg, with a combined population less than half that of Berlin (2.16 million vs. 4.34 million), gave more than twice the number of their sons as did the capital (seventeen vs. seven) to the submarine service. The state of Prussia, which straddled both northern and central Germany (but omitted the two Hanseatic cities as well as Mecklenburg and Oldenburg), contributed a total of 56 percent of the total. These patterns conform to those for Crew 34, 57 percent of whom were born in Prussia and only 9 percent born south of the River Main, and even for the "Grossdeutschland" Crew 38, which despite its inclusion of Austrian officer candidates still consisted of approximately 50 percent North Germans, 37 percent recruits from the western and central regions, and only 12 percent from southern Germany and Austria.[29]

Religion and education also served as indices of the social homogeneity of the naval officer corps. Crew 34 continued a tradition from the Imperial German Navy of keeping approximately seven Protestant officers for each Roman Catholic, an inevitable consequence of the northern geographic bias. The wartime classes of our sample, with ninety-nine Protestants and fifteen Catholics (nine others did not specify their religion), exhibit no departure from this practice.

TABLE 9 **GEOGRAPHIC ORIGINS OF *SEEOFFIZIERE* IN SAMPLE**

Area	Number in Sample
Bremen	5
Hamburg	12
Mecklenburg	3
Oldenburg	2
East Prussia	5
West Prussia	3
Schleswig-Holstein	10
Pomerania	6
Hanover	5
Brandenburg	2
Berlin	7

- Total, North Germany (= 26% of total German population)[a]   60 (= 49% of *Seeoffiziere*)

Rhineland/Ruhr	8
Westphalia	9
Saxony/Thuringia	20
Hesse/Hesse-Kassel	5
Rhineland (rest)	1
Silesia	3
Sudetenland	0

- Total, Central Germany (= 47% of total German population)[a]   46 (= 37% of *Seeoffiziere*)

Baden/Württemburg	5
Bavaria	2
Austria	3

- Total, South Germany (= 27% of total German population)   10 (= 8% of *Seeoffiziere*)

- Total Born Outside of Germany   6 (= 5% of *Seeoffiziere*)

Sources: The population data are that for the German Reich as of May 1939, as furnished in *Statistisches Jahrbuch für das Deutsche Reich 1939/40;* complete population data for the areas cited with definitions of partial or consolidated regions can be found in table 11 in chapter 6. The sample here expands to 123 officers with the background data furnished by the four officers omitted in table 7.

[a]Divisions of North and Central Germany follow geographic rather than administrative boundaries; thus "Saxony" includes both Land Sachsen and the Prussian province of the same name.

In education, the coveted *Abitur* earned by the top 10 percent of German students served as the standard prewar requirement for acceptance as a naval officer candidate, excepting only the HSOs for their nautical experience. Completion of the *Abitur* (the final examinations necessary for university entrance) after studies at the *Gymnasium* concluded a long process of study and selection that precluded the effort by all but the most academically gifted of students. Here the younger classes of our sample indicate only minor concessions to wartime conditions, as 86 of 123 officers (70 percent) held their *Abitur* with nineteen more Gymnasium students denied their final examinations only by the war. Eighteen officers (15 percent) completed the *Mittlere Reife,* the next highest level below the *Abitur* earned by perhaps 20 percent of all German students that usually led to careers in business or in public service.[30]

These educational levels, consistent with those of earlier Crews, conceal an important evolution in the wartime cadets' social backgrounds. From before World War I through the mid-1930s the naval officer corps represented the stronghold of the German upper-middle class, reinforced by a contingent from the Prussian nobility and a handful of petit bourgeoisie. The navy itself proclaimed priority in recruitment to sons of officers, high civil servants, and owners of landed estates, followed by sons of university graduates (i.e., such professionals as doctors, lawyers, educators) and lastly to sons of medium-level public officials and businessmen. The historian of Crew 34 concludes, "Proper social background and 'character' rather than strictly defined and rigorously applied professional requirements continued to serve as crucial criteria for the navy when it selected its cadets."[31]

But what was the German middle class? Sociologists, political analysts, and historians might agree that all of the above categories belonged, but strong disagreements divide them as to precisely who constituted the *Mittelstand* or petit bourgeoisie, the middle- and lower-middle class.[32] This carries an important political dimension, as observers since the 1930s have explained National Socialism's success on the basis of its mass support among this social stratum. The continued defense of this thesis largely rests upon how this class is defined, whether it includes master craftsmen, artisans, and skilled workers.[33] For our purposes this last point has less significance, for—even omitting these categories—the *Mittelstand* contributed nearly half of our officer sample, not characteristic of earlier Crews. Using the categories established by sociologist Detlef Mühlberger and applied as well to naval noncommissioned officers and enlisted men,[34] the fathers of fifty-two (42.6 percent) of our sample represented the *Mittelstand:* nonacademic professionals (eight), civil servants in lower and intermediary grades (thirteen), merchants and small businessmen (fourteen), salaried white-collar workers (twelve), and propertied farmers (five).

A majority (55 percent) of line officers still came from upper-middle- and upper-class families, the traditional wellspring of naval officers. These cadets' fathers included academic professionals (twenty), higher civil servants (thirteen), career military or naval officers (fourteen), managers (fifteen, of whom three were merchant marine captains), and entrepreneurs (five). Among these upper-class backgrounds are five members of the nobility (distinguished by the use of "von" with the surname). Only three line officer cadets claimed working-class origins, sons of a gardener, a brewery worker, and a turner (lathe operator).

The growth in *Mittelstand* contributions of line officers matches similar changes in the German army's officer corps. An examination of the social backgrounds for officer cadets during the 1928–30 period, for example, reveals that 62.9 percent came from the upper and upper-middle classes against 36.7 percent from the *Mittelstand* and 0.4 percent from the working class. But by the end of 1942, the proportion of middle- and lower-middle class backgrounds of new cadets had grown to 51 percent, and that from the working class to 28 percent.[35] These developments did not remain confined to the war but represented long-term trends in German society. Available data for Prussian and West German higher civil servants, for example, indicate a consistently increasing recruitment from lower-middle-class backgrounds from Weimar through the early Bundesrepublik.[36]

The key factor in social advancement was education. Thirty-four of the fifty-two cadets with middle- and lower-middle-class backgrounds had completed their *Abitur*, as had two of the three working-class representatives. These cadets' academic ability doubtless played a significant—if not decisive—role in their selection by the navy. The opportunity to acquire this formal education, however, represents a development unimaginable for an earlier generation but conventional for the postwar period. Civil servants like teachers, policemen, and railway officials who had never qualified for university admittance themselves, increasingly sent their sons to institutions of higher learning: In the early 1960s over one-third of all university students were sons or daughters of state employees, who amounted to only 6 percent of the total population.[37]

This shift in social backgrounds, of course, illustrates a gradual evolution rather than a dramatic change. Other characteristics of naval executive officers remained remarkably constant over an extended period. Table 10 traces selected traits of officers from Crew 07, Crew 34, and our sample as relative indices of change and continuity within the naval officer corps from Wilhelm II to Hitler.

As is evident, certain characteristics remained constant while the areas of change were gradual. *Seeoffiziere* represented a singularly homogeneous social group, heavily North German, Protestant, and middle class in nature. The strength of these bonds doubtless contributed to their ability to endure what was demanded of them.

TABLE 10 **CONTINUITY AND CHANGE IN GERMAN *SEEOFFIZIER* CADETS, 1907–42**

	Crew 07	Crew 34	Sample (84% Crews 37–42)
Geographic origin			
• Prussia	65.9%	57.3%	56.3%
• Hamburg	3.3	4.9	9.8
• South of Main River	12.7	9.1	8.4
Religion (Protestants:Catholics)	9:1	7:1	7:1
Education (percentage with *Abitur*)	58.9%	87.7%	70.05%
Fathers' backgrounds			
• Nobles	11.2%	5.0%	4.1%
• Army/Navy officers	26.4	25.0	12.3
• *Mittelstand*	>20.0	>30.0	42.6

Sources: Herwig, *Elitekorps*, 39–40; Rust, *Crew 34*, 20–24; officer questionnaires from sample.

Engineering and Other Officers

Engineering officers have been less systematically studied than executive officers, reflecting the natural preference to study those who command men over those responsible for machines. Our sample of thirty-two engineering officers is too small to permit general conclusions but furnishes some interesting comparisons with their higher-profile comrades.

Although the divisions between the *Ingenieur* and *Seeoffizier* career-tracks reveal themselves in many ways, in rank structure and service they largely parallel the younger profile of their executive counterparts. Eighteen had achieved the rank of *Oberleutnant (I)*, eight others *Leutnant (I)*, and one *Fähnrich (I)*; senior officers included three *Kapitänleutnante (I)*, one *Korvettenkapitän (I)*, and one *Fregattenkapitän (I)*. Like their comrades, they also moved around within the U-boat fleet, though at a somewhat reduced scale, each averaging service aboard two submarines during their careers. Of particular note, however, is the promotion of five from the ranks during the war, or nearly 16 percent of the total.

It is in their backgrounds that engineering officers begin to differ from line officers. Ten of thirty-two (31 percent) come from northern Germany, but eighteen (56 percent) from the central states. Representation from southern Germany constitutes an even smaller rate (two officers, or 6 percent) than that for line officers, equivalent to that of officers born outside of Germany's borders. The bias here, not surprisingly, is toward industrial areas. Six officers originated in the area of Saxony and Thuringia, a region of diversified but extensive industries (textiles, machinery and metallurgy, chemicals), while the iron and steel strongholds of the Ruhr and Westphalia provided seven more. The strongest northern contingent (three) came from Berlin, one of Germany's industrial centers before the end of World War II. Each of these industrial areas also served as the homeland for engineering cadets drowned aboard the training bark *Niobe* when it foundered during a storm in the Baltic in July 1932.[38]

In other differences between engineering and executive officers, the former's 3.3:1 ratio between Protestants (twenty-three) and Roman Catholics (seven) is less than half that for line officers (two officers gave no religious affiliation). Levels of academic education are also more varied: Twenty officers had completed their *Abitur* and five others had their *Gymnasium* studies cut short by the war, three had earned the *Mittlere Reife*, and one had attended an engineering school. For three, however, their academic education was limited to the eight years of the *Volksschule* mandatory for all, followed by the instruction and training of an industrial apprenticeship.

In sharp contrast to the social backgrounds of the majority of line officers, twenty-one of thirty engineering officers (70 percent) came from the *Mittelstand* that had begun to furnish increasing numbers of executive officers as well.[39] They were sons of businessmen, schoolteachers, railway officials, and professional engineers. The remaining nine were drawn from the upper classes, with fathers in occupations as managers, higher civil servants, academics, and entrepreneurs. None of the engineering officers claimed working-class origins.

How far these traits of our sample can be extended to the broad field of U-boat engineering officers is unclear. Shortages in qualified technical cadets led to deliberate changes in cadet recruitment policy: Whereas no engineering officers were recruited with working-class, artisan, or lower-level official backgrounds for Crew 33, the same social strata supplied 40 percent of the accepted engineer candidates in 1939.[40] Yet, as already noted, the German navy's emphasis on *Seeoffiziere* in its officer development program resulted in a chronic shortage of engineer officers.

Yet these deficits characterized the whole of the German economy as well. The navy learned in March 1939 that German private industry counted seventeen thousand unfilled positions for qualified engineers.[41] When war came, competition for such precious skills among the armed forces generally left the Kriegsmarine short of its needs. To compensate, a significant number of noncommissioned officers from the *Maschinen* career-tracks were promoted to officer rank. The term *Volksoffiziere* ("officers from the ranks") technically applied to all risen to executive or other technical officer rank but came to be especially associated with engineering officers. Evidence from interrogations of captured U-boat personnel suggests that one-fifth to one-quarter of chief engineers during the 1942–44 period qualified as *Volksoffiziere*.[42] Nothing suggests that their performance fell below that of regular officers, but promotion itself sometimes brought intense psychological pressures that were revealed in behavioral changes.

How this could affect a successful U-boat crew was illustrated by a year-long antagonism between *U-515*'s chief engineer and the diesel *Obermaschinist*. Former friends as machinists, the two grew apart after the promotion; major disagreements over technical aspects of the submarine's machinery disguised some natural jealousy by the *Obermaschinist*, but to most of the engine-room staff the key issue involved the L.I.'s professional insecurity. That most of *Techniker* usually found themselves more in agreement with their NCO than with him did not help the L.I.'s disposition. The chief engineer finally seized on an aborted refueling operation at sea to accuse his rival of active sabotage and, backed by the captain, had the machinist arrested and transferred to a "milch cow" supply U-boat—his hands bound with rope—to be sent home for trial in Germany. Following *U-515*'s own return, the entire engine room staff attended the court-martial in Torgau, where their support failed to prevent a guilty verdict and penal service for the NCO. That the chief engineer was himself relieved shortly thereafter perhaps balanced the books, but the veteran machinists were shaken by the experience: "Everything we believed or had been taught was contradicted by this affair," one recalled sadly after fifty years.[43]

For executive officers, even those engineering officers who had shared the careful selection process and the *Marineschule* as Crew comrades remained somewhat second-class citizens. The obvious preference shown to line officers in command assignments, even for shore-based commands, and grievances in their treatment and formal status led engineers to complain openly to naval authorities in the mid-1930s. These ultimately commanded Raeder's personal attention, which—despite an insensitive speech in January 1936 that merely aggravated the situation—ultimately led to a gradual improvement in the engineers' situation.[44] Individuals might still feel slighted, but others considered disparaging remarks of line officers as normal joking and paid little heed.[45]

In this area the U-boat service stood somewhere between tradition and innovation, as demonstrated by the radical proposals of a senior engineering officer within the training establishment. *Kaptlt.* (later *Korv.Kapt. [I]*) Hans Müller, director of the grueling technical training exercises of the *Agru-Front,* argued in 1942 for the promotion of chief engineering officers to submarine command. Not only were they the best qualified in handling U-boats, he reasoned, but they could more efficiently train new L.I.s for U-boat duty. The shortage of qualified engineer officers was enough to defeat Müller's suggestion, but the iconoclastic engineer further proposed the postwar abandonment of all classification of naval officers into executive, engineering, or other technical specialists in favor of a general education and training for all officer cadets; after commissioning officers could then be assigned to posts according to need instead of predetermined career-tracks. Most interesting for this revolutionary proposal was its endorsement by Dönitz's closest associate, Admiral von Friedeburg, who presented it to the head of the Naval Personnel Department. The war ended, however, without any further action on this idea.[46]

The need for specialization, however, can be seen in other officer categories that demanded technical or highly trained skills. Communications specialists, for example, first acquired officer status only in October 1936 and then only as reserve officers; active officers remained excluded until October 1944, despite the tremendous growth in importance of radio communications and related fields of cryptography (the German naval signals intelligence staff alone expanded tenfold after September 1939).[47] All seven communications officers and officer candidates from our sample were former U-boat radiomen promoted from the ranks and then, except for one, transferred to shore installations. The highest-ranking, after extensive shore and U-boat radio duties, accepted an appointment as an *Oberleutnant z.S.* and returned to submarine duty as a II.W.O., the only one of the seven still serving aboard a U-boat at war's end. Four others rose to the rank of *Leutnant* (*Marinenachrichtenwesen,* or MN) and the others were still midshipmen in May 1945. The navy's need for such specialists is revealed by the irrelevance of seniority: Two of the seven enlisted in the Kriegsmarine as late as April 1942, yet rose to officer rank in less than three years.

These officers' backgrounds match those of the enlisted radiomen (see chapter 6). They came from the same petit bourgeois families that were increasingly providing more regular officers, and in geographic origins central Germany again predominated (five of seven). Moreover they demonstrated strong academic skills: Two had completed their *Abitur,* three others had already received extensive secondary schooling, and a sixth had attended a technical academy.

In addition to *Funker* from their ranks, U-boat crews occasionally included communications specialists from the naval signals intelligence service, the *B-Dienst* (*Beobachtungsdienst*, literally "Observation Service"), to monitor and decrypt Allied naval and merchant ciphers. One submarine, *U-664* (*Oblt.z.S.* Adolf Graef), carried *B-Dienst* operatives on successive patrols in the North Atlantic, April–August 1943. Their true identities, however, were concealed from the crew, who believed them to be additional *Artilleriemechaniker* (gunnery mates).[48]

Far more specialized in skills and training were naval surgeons, who entered the navy as either regular officer cadets or reserve officers serving for the war's duration. The two surgeons in our sample were already university-trained physicians when they joined the Kriegsmarine in 1939 at the ages of twenty-seven and twenty-six, respectively; both eventually attained the rank of *Marinestabsarzt* (equivalent to lieutenant commander). Both came from well-to-do families in central Germany (Saxony and West-phalia).

Submarine duty for surgeons was not a general practice but reflected the evolution of the U-boat war. During the conflict's early years, few surgeons accompanied submarines on patrol, although the first surgeon battle casualty died with the crew of *U-40* (*Korv.Kapt.* Wolfgang Barten) on 13 October 1939 just one month after the war started. Outside of rudimentary medical training furnished to officers as part of their training, medical duties usually became the additional responsibility of a designated petty officer, usually a radioman, who received a thirty-six-hour medical crash course. Serious injuries or wounds to crewmen generally required a rendezvous with a homeward-bound submarine for transfer and later treatment in a naval hospital. Sometimes even this was not possible: it is reported that one commander performed an emergency amputation of a wounded crewman's foot while a shore-based surgeon directed the operation by radio.[49]

With the extension of U-boat operations to American, Caribbean, and South Atlantic waters, naval surgeons joined the new Type XIV milch cow supply tankers as part of the services they offered, providing assistance as needed to combat boats during refueling operations. In 1943, however, as U-boats tried to fight it out on the surface against the increasing Allied air attacks, submarine crews began suffering increasing combat casualties. On 23 May 1943, Dönitz ordered the assignment of a surgeon to every second front-line U-boat. To the degree that this represented a tactical response to conditions, it miscarried in the same manner as the continually upgraded flak armament failed to protect submarines from aircraft. Of 243 naval surgeons who embarked on U-boat missions, 117 lost their lives, the majority of them before the end of 1943; others were fortunate enough to survive as POWs. The drain of such skills from a small corps of surgeons could not be tolerated, and protests from senior medical authorities compelled Dönitz in 1944 to abandon their further use except for boats bound for Asian waters. Their places were taken by specially trained medics (*Sanitätsunteroffiziere mit Sonderausbildung*, or pharmacist's mates), whose story is told in chapter 6.[50]

Beyond their medical duties aboard U-boats, however, naval surgeons studied submariners' living conditions and long-term effects of U-boat duty on crewmen. For example, Dr. Jobst Schaefer used his extensive personal experiences of several war patrols to detail the dietary and nutritional needs of submariners and offer guidelines to every *Smutje* for the types and storage of various foodstuffs, even recommendations for each day's mess during extended patrols.[51]

At a research facility near Carnac on the Brittany peninsula, a staff of twenty physicians investigated various aspects of submarine medicine, including temperature and carbon dioxide levels aboard U-boats, effects of long-term exposure to engine vibrations and noise, problems associated with snorkel use, and psychological stress that accompanied extended service. U-boat ventilation systems were altered, for example, after tests confirmed higher levels of carbon dioxide at eye- rather than foot-level in U-boat compartments. The results contributed to a broader understanding of submarine medicine long after the war.[52]

Conclusion

The naval officers who led Germany's submarine fleet tended to be a socially homogeneous group, north German, Protestant, and solidly middle to upper-middle class in origin. Although open to promotion from below—especially for technical officers—their ranks stood as testament to a highly selective and intensive program taxed to the limit by the demands of wartime expansion. That this system held together as well as it did, in the face of casualty rates unequaled in modern military history, demonstrates its resilience and strength in producing front-line officers.

Our study has shed some light on their collective characteristics and shared backgrounds, but what determined their selection as officers remained assessments of their individual character. This distinguishing quality of the entire German military permitted a wide range of personalities and even ideological attitudes, as will emerge in subsequent chapters. For the navy in particular it also implied an ability to learn more than what

was taught. Beyond the mastery of tactics, navigation, and gunnery, officers had to develop both an understanding of the unique traditions of a
navy with a troubled past, and a capacity for leadership in unfavorable
conditions.

There remained, however, vast differences among them as to their ability to command. Some fit the image of "mavericks" popularized in movies
then as now, others proved "by-the-book" disciplinarians. Some would develop into outstanding submarine captains, others would fall short; a great
many, however, would not live long enough to reveal what their individual capabilities were.

As part of their education, German naval officers, like their counterparts
in all navies, assimilated attitudes and values about their service branch
and the nature of their duty. For the Crews that passed through the *Marineschule* Mürwik, however, this heritage did not rest upon an established
navy with centuries of tradition. German cadets instead stood in the long
shadows cast by the legacy of the Imperial Navy's inactivity and mutinies
in World War I, gazing out beyond the handful of light warships and antiquated battleships left by the Versailles Treaty to an imaginary future fleet
and the dream of global seapower. German U-boat officers would wage
their war with a professionalism and technical expertise that testified to
their training; yet elements of insecurity, fatalism, and exaggerated self-
sacrifice always tinged the edges, vulnerabilities that invited exploitation
by the national socialist state.[53] But before we further examine how German officers met Raeder's dictum of "dying gallantly," we must first consider the character of the NCOs and enlisted men who accompanied them.

6   The Right Man in the Right Place

The propaganda image of U-boat crewmen presented to the German public not only emphasized the submariners' heroism, prowess, and self-sacrifice but their reflection of the whole of German society as well. The Sunday edition of *Hamburger Illustrierte* for 13 February 1943, for example, profiled eleven members of the crew of *U-203* (*Kaptlt.* Hermann Kottmann) from different regions and varied backgrounds, each performing a specific onboard function at a different level. "So should it be for all Germany," concluded the article. "As with this U-boat crew, so the entire nation fights in a common struggle."[1]

Allowing for poetic license, the article did not err in stating that German submariners came from diverse backgrounds representing all parts of the Reich. But was this typical of the U-boat service or did submariners reveal specific patterns of shared characteristics? How did the Kriegsmarine find and insert "the right man in the right place," as described by one naval psychologist?[2] The issue has never been systematically studied, and the evidence available has proved inconclusive.

During the war, for example, U-boat ace Wolfgang Lüth estimated that 20 percent of his crew came from the Rhineland area and that each of Germany's other major regions equally contributed perhaps 10 percent.[3] In 1944 British intelligence studies of German POWs indicated that out of every group of ten U-boat petty officers and enlisted men, four came from North Germany, three from the Rhineland or Westphalia, and the remaining three proportionately divided between central Germany and all other parts of the Reich combined. Moreover, the British found their U-boat captives shared working-class origins and an academic education largely restricted to primary and vocational schools, in sharp contrast to middle-class and more formally educated Luftwaffe aircrewmen.[4] The author's own study of U-boat POWs in the United States supports these findings, but an American historian recently concluded that the majority of German submariners came from the central and southern regions, as North Germans better understood the risks of U-boat service and avoided them.[5]

To test these results was a major purpose in studying this sample of U-boat veterans. German officers have already been treated in the previous chapter; here we shall examine the personal backgrounds of the 937 U-boat NCOs and enlisted men who participated in our survey, first collectively and then by each naval career-track (*Laufbahn*).

The geographic distribution of birthplaces of our sample's enlisted population is provided in table 11, arranged (like table 9) in part by individual states and in part by specific or consolidated regions. The 1939 population is also provided for each region so that a proportional representation per every block of 250,000 inhabitants can be seen as a further index of a region's participation aboard Germany's U-boats during World War II. The percentages that follow the totals for each major division pertain to the total German population and the total number in the U-boat sample.

The results reveal distinctive patterns of regional recruitment, with both northern and central Germany proportionately overrepresented and southern Germany trailing far behind—identical to the pattern already seen with the naval officer corps. This largely supports the wartime British findings: with Berlin omitted, the proportionate representation per 250,000 inhabitants rises to 3.59 for northern Germany, exceeding that for the central regions. Among the coastal regions, those on the North Sea sent relatively more of their sons into U-boats than their counterparts on the Baltic. While refuting the notion that Germans born in states with shorelines deliberately avoided submarine service, the data do confirm an enthusiasm among young Germans from the inland industrial centers for U-boat duty.

No pattern emerges, however, in the sample's distribution between big cities and less-populated areas. Strongly represented are the port cities and the industrial centers; much less so is Berlin, while Munich and Vienna are virtually absent. The rural interior seemingly offered barren ground for recruiters with the curious exceptions of Hanover and the Saarland/ Rhineland-Pfalz. Also noteworthy are the differences between the industrial regions that furnished so many crewmen: The Ruhr (a largely Catholic

TABLE 11   **GEOGRAPHIC DISTRIBUTION OF SAMPLE'S BIRTHPLACES (NCOs/ENLISTED MEN)**

Area	Population (millions)	No. in Sample	Per 250,000 inhabitants
Bremen	0.45	13	7.22
Hamburg	1.71	27	3.95
Mecklenburg	0.90	11	3.06
Oldenburg	0.58	10	4.31
East Prussia	2.19	25	2.85
Schleswig-Holstein	1.59	27	4.25
Pomerania	2.39	31	3.24
Hanover	3.48	55	3.95
Brandenburg	3.01	35	2.91
Berlin	4.34	31	1.79
• Total, North Germany	20.64 (26%)	265 (28%)	3.21
Rhineland: Ruhr cities[a]	4.18	56	3.35
Westphalia	5.21	80	3.84
Saxony/Thuringia[b]	11.61	191	4.11
Silesia	4.87	59	3.03
Hesse[c]	4.14	49	2.96
Rhineland (rest)	3.80	33	2.17
Sudetenland	2.94	21	1.79
• Total, Central Germany	36.75 (47%)	489 (52%)	3.33
Saar/Pfalz	1.89	32	4.23
Baden/Württemburg	5.40	51	2.36
Bavaria	7.17	50	1.74
Austria	6.97	15	0.54
• Total, South Germany	21.43 (27%)	148 (16%)	1.73

- Born outside of Germany = 18 (2%) (13 born in Danzig and Poland)
- No data = 17 (2%)

Source: Population data (as of May 1939) taken from the *Statistisches Jahrbuch für das Deutsche Reich 1939/40* (Berlin, 1940).

[a]*Regierungsbezirk* Düsseldorf of the Prussian *Rheinprovinz.*

[b]The Prussian province of Saxony and the States of Saxony, Thuringia, Brunswick, and Anhalt.

[c]The State of Hesse and the Prussian province of Hesse-Nassau.

region) and Westphalia constituted the stronghold of the coal, iron, steel, and chemical corporations that drove twentieth-century German industry, while Protestant Saxony and Thuringia featured many smaller manufacturers in more diverse industries, including light metals, machines, and optics.[6] The recent annexations of Austria and the Sudetenland in 1938 doubtless accounts in part for the very low totals for those areas.

The extent to which these sharp regional differences highlight popular interest in U-boat service or the navy's selectivity of recruits remains unclear. In all probability both factors acted in combination, although the specific interests of naval recruitment predominated. As we shall see in the next chapter, the term "volunteer"—technically applicable to most of those who served in the Kriegsmarine—must be used with caution and in the context of German conscription regulations.

A salient point remains the regional mix of each U-boat crew. Although uneven, the geographic distribution contributed a national character on every submarine, bringing together Germans from every region to rely for their lives upon each other in that most intimate type of combat unit. The navy shared this organizational pattern with the Luftwaffe and Waffen-SS. The German army, by contrast, maintained its trust in regional formations, that is, units essentially composed of Prussians, Saxons, Bavarians, or Austrians, based on the belief that unit cohesion depended on common social backgrounds. Ironically, both systems worked, perhaps reflecting modern German society in transition: One cemented a mass army through the traditional means of regional and cultural identification, the other molded a select and specialized force by the bonds of technological skills.[7]

Returning to the U-boat sample, another characteristic that emerges from a comparison between the Ruhr and Saxony/Thuringia concerns the religious preferences of U-boat crews. Data for our sample are compared with that for 1938 (pre-Anschluss) Germany and 1939 Germany (including Austria and the Sudetenland) in table 12.

In religion, at least, the U-boat crews approximated the national averages for Germany during the 1933–38 period. An obviously modern bias can be seen in the increase of "other/no religion" responses, presumably a contemporary statement by German veterans preferring not to record the

TABLE 12 **RELIGION OF SAMPLE MEMBERS (NCOs/ENLISTED MEN)**

	Germany		Sample
	1938	1939	
Protestant	62.1%	54.3%	59.2%
Roman Catholic	33.1%	41.0%	27.6%
Other/no religion	4.8%	4.7%	13.1%

Sources: Statistisches Jahrbuch für das Deutsche Reich 1939/40, 25; data from sample.

TABLE 13 **FORMAL EDUCATION COMPLETED AMONG SAMPLE MEMBERS (NCOs/ENLISTED MEN)**

	Number	**Percentage**
Elementary (*Volksschule*)[a]	613	65.4
Elementary plus trade school (*Volksschule + Berufsschule*)[a]	156	16.7
Secondary/Middle school (*Mittel-* or *Realschule*)	108	11.5
Technical/engineering schools	31	3.3
University entrance qualification (*Abitur*)	24	2.6
University	1	0.1
No data = 4 (0.4%)		

[a]The first two categories might well be combined, as most of those in the first would have entered vocational schools but not completed their work prior to entering service.

faith taught in their youth. There is little reason to suppose that Catholics subsequently lost their faith in greater numbers than did Lutherans, or vice versa, and therefore the adjustments probably balance both percentages in the same proportions.

By contrast, the average level of academic education serves as a distinctive feature of U-boat crewmen. British intelligence analysts in late 1943 determined that only 5 percent of their 351 captive U-boat NCOs and enlisted men had received a secondary education beyond the obligatory eight years of the *Volksschule*. This figure represented less than half of the German national average and only a fraction of the 34-percent rate of Luftwaffe enlisted men.[8] The data from our sample, reproduced in table 13, more than verify these conditions.

For these data to be comprehensible, however, one must understand the German educational system as it has functioned for most of this century. Primary schooling there compensated in intensity for what other national systems provided in duration. An American observer in 1914 favorably contrasted the national educational standards, longer school year, and greater number of classroom hours per week in Germany with prevailing conditions in the United States. For those who entered the work force after eight years' schooling, there remained obligatory attendance at continuation schools for a variable number of hours per week through age eighteen, added on to the specialized vocational training (with examinations) expected of a young apprentice in the workplace. As late as 1962, 82 percent of all Germans completed "only" a primary education (by then extended to nine years)—identical to that of our sample.[9]

Interestingly, naval noncommissioned officers enjoyed no educational advantages over their subordinates, as only 22 percent graduated from secondary or technical schools and 61 percent completed only the *Volks-schule*. This indicates that promotion within the ranks was not generally tied to academic credentials, with the exception of certain career-tracks we shall soon examine.

More significant for initial recruitment was the vocational training U-boat men received, for in addition to the 20 percent who formally attended trade schools and technical institutes, the average crewman had already entered his occupation as an apprentice before enlisting. Those occupations proved not to be random but of direct interest to the navy.

When the British studied their U-boat POWs, they found that 55 percent of the noncommissioned personnel had been previously employed as skilled or semiskilled labor, but they did not examine the matter in more detail.[10] The evidence from our sample, presented in table 14, uses a different classification of occupations that permits grouping by socioeconomic status, one that has already been used in social profiles of Nazi Party membership.[11] Moreover it provides comparable data on the veterans' fathers to indicate their status within German society.

As is evident, U-boat crewmen came almost equally from working-class and *Mittelstand* families. Upper-class backgrounds were virtually negligible, as were career military or merchant marine fathers. At least seven sample members, however, noted that their fathers had served in the *Kaiserliche Marine* during World War I, all of them aboard such smaller vessels as torpedo boats and submarines. One other individual also claimed a naval father but with the singular distinction that he wore U.S. Navy blue.[12] Especially interesting is the concentration of fathers as skilled workers and craftsmen straddling the boundary between the working and lower-middle classes: Their ranks included bakers, butchers, plumbers, watch- and shoemakers, tailors, locksmiths, riveters, molders, turners, fitters, machinists, and various categories of mechanics. Most important, this group—although it constituted only 40 percent of submariner fathers—set the vocational pattern for the vast majority of those who would eventually enter the U-boat service.

Continuity of this pattern throughout the navy's enlisted ranks can be seen in a study of the backgrounds of personnel serving in the 1931 *Reichsmarine*. Among 13,436 NCOs and enlisted men, 49 percent came from industrial or technical jobs and 16 percent were former craftsmen. Nine percent had been involved in private enterprise, and only 3 percent had been farmers; the very small size of the German merchant marine was reflected in the mere 2 percent who claimed that profession.[13]

The occupations chosen by the future submariners reveal significant

TABLE 14 **PREWAR CIVILIAN OCCUPATIONS (FATHERS AND U-BOAT SONS)**

Occupational Subgroup	U-boat Sample	
	Fathers	Veterans
Working class		
1. Agricultural workers	1.3%	1.1%
2. Unskilled, semiskilled workers	17.7	6.7
3. Skilled (craft) workers	22.1	66.6
4. Other skilled workers[a]	5.6	11.4
5. Domestic workers	0.2	—
Subtotal	*46.9*	*85.8*
Lower- and middle-middle class (*Mittelstand*)		
1. Master craftsmen	11.6	0.1
2. Nonacademic professionals	4.1	2.6
3. Low/Midgrade white-collar employees	5.9	3.5
4. Merchant marine	1.0	2.5
5. Career military	0.6	0.6
6. Low/Midgrade civil service positions	14.1	0.4
7. Merchants	3.6	1.6
8. Independent farmers	5.0	0.3
Subtotal	*45.9*	*11.6*
Upper class		
1. Managers, higher civil servants	0.3	—
2. Career officers, academic professionals	0.6	—
3. Entrepreneurs	0.7	—
4. Students	—	1.9
Subtotal	*1.6*	*1.9*

No data = 5.5% (Fathers), 0.5% (Sons)

---

[a]Skilled blue-collar workers in the "newer" industries, including auto and airplane mechanics, electricians, and welders.

patterns for both civilian career opportunities and naval recruitment. Although most had not progressed beyond the apprentice stage before they entered the navy, their selected vocations would have largely determined the course of their futures. The evidence indicates that the skilled labor jobs they had begun to fill were neither random nor traditional, but an opportunity for social advancement in a changing world.

In an earlier study the author examined the listed occupations of over six hundred U-boat POWs in American custody for the 1942–44 period. The disproportionate representation of vocations far surpassed that of the geographic distribution. Agriculture, for example, employed more than 28 percent of the German work force in May 1939 but supplied only 3 percent of those captured by American forces. Most striking was the predominance of metalworkers among the POWs, a field that engaged less than 10 percent of the 1939 German labor force but which contributed 56 percent of the total number studied. The general category defined by German vocational classifiers actually embraced a wide range of occupations, from machinists, electricians, and mechanical engineers through plumbers, blacksmiths, and the apprentice *Schlosser* (a term usually translated as "locksmith" but which more commonly defines nonspecialized metalworkers).[14]

In the sample used in our study, metalworker occupations again constitute the majority and to a similar degree (59 percent), representing nearly all of those future U-boat crewmen employed in prewar skilled labor positions. As will be seen, they are not equally distributed but concentrated in specific naval career-tracks; of more immediate concern is the explanation of why so many young men chose the metalworking field and how it became a doorway into the U-boat service.

Given the wide variety of metalworking occupations, firm conclusions are difficult to draw. Long-term trends do not indicate significant improvements in status: For example, among the different categories of skilled labor (e.g., coal mining, construction, woodworking), metalworkers consistently rated below average in increase of hourly wage rates from 1913 to 1939.[15] Yet such trends remained hidden behind popular perceptions that the field offered good pay and future opportunities—beliefs fortified by such interim realities as the ability of a veteran metalworker to earn as much as one hundred *Reichsmarks* per week with overtime and performance bonuses at a time when the average weekly industrial wage amounted to only twenty-seven marks.

During the late 1930s, as the need for metalworkers grew with the rise in priority of armaments industries, the government established a national vocational training program aimed especially at increasing the number of metalworkers, who had been in short supply and great demand during World War I. Apprenticeship programs for all metalworking and construction firms employing more than ten persons became mandatory in December 1936. Less than two years later, a school law required all youths leaving school after the completion of *Volksschule* to enter industrial education programs.

Policy and the perceived benefits together brought new recruits to metalworking, where the work force increased by 250 percent between 1933 and 1937. So many apprentices were entering the field by 1941 that the government tried to close it off, but with only limited success. Instead of a planned ceiling of 105,000 apprentice metalworkers in 1943, some 149,000 entered; even in 1945, the number decreased only to 134,000.[16]

The men who held these jobs represented invaluable assets to the German war effort. Older, skilled metalworkers (43 percent of the total employed in the field as of May 1942) enjoyed the highest exemption rate from military service save the transportation sector in recognition of their significance in the construction of aircraft, tanks, vehicles, ships, and weapons.[17] Younger metalworkers on the other hand represented a boon to the military services, who thereby saved much time and expense in training skills already acquired in the workplace. Thus apprentice mechanics, craftsmen, electricians, welders, plumbers, and lathe operators drew the special interest of the German army, which valued such backgrounds to man and maintain its tanks and armored vehicles. With such career background data recorded on its draft registration card indexes, the army could conscript to fill its needs.[18]

The Kriegsmarine, of course, relied mostly on volunteers, including those volunteering precisely to avoid army conscription. The navy also placed a premium on metalworkers for shipboard work and weaponry, as expressed in a 1935 handbook: "Particularly desired are seamen, sea and bay fishermen, those with technical training in the metals industries and craftsmen of all types."[19] A 1938 publication went further: "Especially desired are craftsmen of all types, above all from the metal industries, such as *Schlosser,* electricians, precision mechanics, smiths, coppersmiths, plumbers, fitters (and) molders. . . . The need for those lacking prior technical or craftsmanship training is very limited."[20] Recruiting publications strongly promoted these trades: For example, the January 1939 edition of *Die Kriegsmarine* observed, "Above all a fleet today requires professional men. . . . Previous manual training as a mechanic, locksmith, cabinetmaker, tinsmith, etc. should precede, if possible, service in the fleet."[21] The 1939 edition of an annual naval handbook even provided the correlation of previous occupations with specific career-tracks in the navy.[22] Only the press of wartime manpower needs made the navy slightly lower its standards, evident in the following excerpt of a recruiting advertisement that appeared in all German newspapers on 17 May 1941: "Men from 17 to 25 years of age who can pass or who have passed the apprentice examination for technical training are especially needed. But skilled and unskilled workers between these ages will also be accepted."[23]

Such appeals proved generally successful when German males enjoyed the option of volunteering for a service of choice after receiving their draft notice. The navy's recruiting drives thus generated interest among targeted groups and preserved their own selectivity in accepting recruits. Recruiting commissions composed of regular officers, physicians, and psychologists traveled throughout Germany to evaluate volunteers' applications, recommending both the acceptance and specialized career-track for those they judged qualified for naval service. Naval psychologists claimed their assessments reduced the washout rate among recruits in specialized training by 30 to 40 percent.[24] Given the variety of specialized naval personnel, however, adjustments became necessary and recruitment had to be accommodated to fulfilling needs regardless of recruits' backgrounds. The result, as demonstrated by the data from our sample, proved an interesting mix in the social character of each naval *Laufbahn* or career-track, identified in table 15 by its numerical and official designation; the table also identifies the number of sample members in each career-track, thereunder broken down (in percentages) by rank.

A recruit who joined the navy usually remained in the *Laufbahn* to which he was assigned for the remainder of his service (one exception was the *Obersteuermann* career-track, discussed below). Within his *Laufbahn* he became eligible for promotion after specified minimum periods—for example, one year (later nine months) from *Matrose* to *Gefreiter,* one year from *Gefreiter* to *Obergefreiter,* three years (later reduced to two) from *Maat* to *Obermaat)*—but mere time in grade alone did not replace individual performance evaluations in securing advancement. The promotion to *Unteroffizier* (noncommissioned officer) status required formal nomination by one's superiors and successful completion of higher technical and disciplinary/command courses. Although the principle of individual determination remained the nominal basis for promotion, the obviously rapid advancement within some career-tracks underscores the overriding demands in specific technical skills.[25]

Seamen

The seaman's career-track (*Laufbahn I,* formally designated the *Bootsmannslaufbahn* after April 1938 but often simply known as *Matrosen*),[26] the most basic of career-tracks, involved the performance of general duties aboard ship, as described in chapter 1. Promotion to *Bootsmann* or *Oberbootsmann* (boatswain, or bosun) represented the culmination of an enlisted man's service here. The career insignia or trade badge for enlisted men was a star, and for petty officers a fouled anchor (for all other career-tracks, the insignia that denoted that *Laufbahn* for the enlisted men was simply super-

TABLE 15 **DISTRIBUTION OF SAMPLE BY NAVAL CAREER-TRACK (*LAUFBAHN*) AND RANK**

Laufbahn (No. in Sample)	Noncommissioned Officers			Enlisted Men			
	Senior NCOs	CPOs	POs	Hauptgefreite	Obergefreite	Gefreite	Matrosen
I Bootsmanns- (229)	Oberbootsmann/ Bootsmann (1%)	Oberboots- mannsmaat (13%)	Bootsmanns- maat (18%)	Matrosenhaupt- gefreiter (9%)	Matrosenober- gefreiter (50%)	Matrosenge- freiter (8%)	Matrose (2%)
II Maschinen- (395)	Stabsober-/Ober- maschinist (13%)	Obermaschin- enmaat (11%)	Maschinen- maat (29%)	Maschinen- hauptgefreiter (4%)	Maschinen- obergefreiter (36%)	Maschinen- gefreiter (6%)	Matrose (0.5%)
III Boots- steuermanns- (46)	Stabsober-/Ober- steuermann (89%)	Obersteuer- mannsmaat (9%)	Steuermanns- maat (2%)	—	—	—	—
IV Fk Funk- (139)	Oberfunk-/Funk- meister (7%)	Oberfunkmaat (27%)	Funkmaat (22%)	Funkhaupt- gefreiter (2%)	Funkober- gefreiter (36%)	Funkgefreiter (6%)	Matrose (0%)
VII Torp./Art. Mechaniker- (117)	Stabsober-/Ober- mechaniker (9%)	Obermechan- ikersmaat (15%)	Mechanikers- maat (20%)	Mechanikers- hauptgefreiter (0.8%)	Mechanikers- obergefreiter (38%)	Mechanikers- gefreiter (18%)	Matrose (0%)
XI Sani- (9)	Sanitätsober- feldwebel (0%)	Sanitäts- obermaat (22%)	Sanitätsmaat (78%)	—	—	—	—

Note: Data on percentage of each career-track who ended the war holding these ranks compiled from sample of 937 naval NCOs and enlisted men. Two sample members belonged to Laufbahn IX (*Verpflegungs-*) and are omitted from the above categories. CPOs = Chief Petty Officers (*Ober-maate*) and POs = Petty Officers (*-maate*), both included among the general category of *Unteroffiziere*.

imposed on an anchor for petty officers). In the past, seamen constituted the majority of a warship's crew, but the growth of technology progressively narrowed their ranks. As indicated in chapter 1, they typically comprised approximately half of each U-boat crew, a ratio essentially duplicated even at the level of the battleship *Bismarck*.[27] However, among 937 NCOs and enlisted men who responded to survey questionnaires, only 229 (24 percent) came from this career-track, making it the most underrepresented in our sample.

In their geographic origins, *Matrosen* tended to more closely follow the national patterns (23 percent northern, 55 percent central, 18 percent southern, and 4 percent outside Germany—the national averages are indicated in table 11) than other career-tracks. The singular exception is the complete absence of Berliners from the group, perhaps reflecting the preference of Kriegsmarine personnel officials to avoid the capital city if desired skills were not involved. Seamen also possessed the least amount of academic education—78 percent received only eight years of primary schooling, the highest rate of any group. The reasons for this had far less to do with socioeconomic status than with their relative youth and wartime enthusiasm to enlist. Seamen tended to enter the navy at an earlier age than others, 38 percent at seventeen and 2 percent at sixteen (again the highest rates), and they represented an almost exclusively wartime cohort, as fully two-thirds joined the navy only in 1941 or later.

Their fathers conformed to the general socioeconomic pattern noted in table 14 (54 percent working class, 45 percent *Mittelstand*, 1 percent upper or upper-middle class), although the ratio of unskilled workers among them is the highest among career-tracks. In the range of occupations they had begun themselves, however, they exhibited a diversity more characteristic of German society. A majority represented traditional skilled crafts, especially bakers (many of whom served as cooks on board U-boats), butchers, brewers, barbers, tailors, and carpenters; others came from farms, the coal mines, and private business. Metalworkers are least represented here (9 percent), but the strongest concentration of former merchant marine men belong to this career (of only twenty-three men with such backgrounds in our survey, eighteen were former sailors), as well as the already-cited individual with a U.S. Navy father.

Details of their collective naval experience indicate that *Laufbahn* I did not represent the fast track to promotion or movement. Although their period of submarine duty averaged well over two years (28.4 months), 60 percent spent that time aboard a single U-boat, the least mobility of any career-track. And as *Matrosen* entered service at an earlier age, so also they qualified as the youngest U-boat crewmen: 68 percent began their submarine service before reaching the age of twenty (including the only sixteen-year-old).

Chances for promotion within this category proved elusive: Only seventy-four men (32 percent) rose to petty officer rank and just three to senior NCO status, rating them at the bottom of our groups. In part, however, this masks the transfer of many of the best and brightest ordinary seamen to a career-track designed to reward those best qualified.

Helmsmen/Navigators

Laufbahn III, (*Steuermannslaufbahn*), the helmsman/navigator's career-track, represented the elite of naval noncommissioned personnel, generally existing only at the rank of chief petty officer and above. As described in chapter 1, the *Obersteuermann's* responsibilities aboard a U-boat included all matters affecting navigation and provisions; as noted in the previous chapter, these duties opened the door to promotion to submarine command, the only noncommissioned career-track where this was possible. Unavailable to recruits, entry into this *Laufbahn* usually occurred only after an individual had already acquired petty officer rank in another career-track (in 1941 entry became possible for outstanding enlisted men as well). Most probably "graduated" from the *Bootsmann* group, although some came from the signalman's career-track as well. Those so selected attended special training and educational courses at Gotenhafen (Gdynia), Tönning, or Wüstrow before they donned the distinctive insignia of two crossed anchors (for qualified enlisted personnel after 1941, a sextant).[28]

Forty-six men of our sample fell into this group, all but five of whom attained the senior NCO ranks of *Obersteuermann* or *Stabsobersteuermann*. As nearly all originated as *Matrosen*, their backgrounds and characteristics complement the data for that group and should perhaps be combined as a single group; their singular status, however, provides a glimpse into the character of a microelite.

Navigators were first of all more heavily northern in origin (41 percent) and least representative of central Germany (also 41 percent) than any other career-track. As with seamen, however, not one claimed Berlin as his birthplace. They came from more affluent homes as well, 65 percent from *Mittelstand* families and 9 percent from the upper-middle and upper classes; and a higher rate (37 percent) completed secondary schooling than any other group. (As navigation required a good grasp of mathematics, the only surprise is that the percentage remained so low.) In their choice of vocations they duplicated the seamen's diversity, although more entered the service straight out of middle or high school; as with *Matrosen,* few were metalworkers. Some chose the navy as a career, others had entered the civil service when war came.

What most distinguished the *Obersteuermann* in his naval service was age and longevity. One-third joined the navy before the end of 1935 (the oldest in 1927), and twelve more enlisted during the 1936–37 period. Most did not enter the U-boat service until age twenty-three or later, and many first saw combat while in their early thirties. If navigators enjoyed childhood advantages in education, they also earned their status through service seniority.

As valued commodities, navigators tended to move around within the navy. Only fourteen served on just one submarine during the war; twenty served on three or more, often eventually transferring to training duties in the Baltic. The convoluted wartime career of Heinz Theen, an *Obersteuermann* who enlisted in 1934 and served on only one combat submarine, deserves mention to demonstrate how much an individual's activities could be shaped by both plan and circumstance:

July 1934: enlisted in navy (seaman's career-track), age twenty
1939–40: *Oberbootsmannmaat* on light cruiser *Karlsruhe*
April 1940: survived sinking of *Karlsruhe,* volunteered for U-boat service (otherwise liable for assignment to battleship *Bismarck*)
May 1940: transferred to helmsman/navigator career; began U-boat training
May 1941–Oct 1943: *Obersteuermann* on board *U-653*
Jan 1944–Feb 1945: Flotilla-*Obersteuermann* for the 27th U.-Flottille in Travemünde
Feb–May 1945: Flotilla-*Obersteuermann* for the 26th U.-Flottille in Warnemünde, barely escaped Russian captivity[29]

Taken together, the seamen and navigators probably represent the navy's optimum ability to select recruits from a pool of volunteers and advance those deemed worthy. Duties rested on the basis of training; learned skills counted less than individual character and background. Those who proved themselves moved onto a special track for promotion; the rest remained more or less frozen in place. But for necessary technical functions, the navy had to seek out and reward those on whom it depended.

Engine Personnel

U-boat engine personnel enjoyed several advantages over the *Matrosen.* Although commonly referred to during the war as *Heizer* ("stoker," from the

early days of steamship travel requiring constant fueling of coal into the
boilers), this group's status gained with the navy's formal redesignation of
their classification as "engine personnel" in 1938 (accompanied by the
renumbering of their career-track (*Maschinenlaufbahn*) from *Laufbahn* XIII
to II), at a time when the Royal Navy still relied on the anachronistic "stok-
ers" and the U.S. Navy continued to classify engine personnel as "firemen." Most important, a raw but capable *Matrose* who wore the cogwheel
insignia on his sleeve could expect to advance to petty officer rank and receive more specialized training and instruction than his seaman comrades.[30]

This promotion opportunity was due to the chronic shortages in qualified engineering personnel throughout the navy. The pressure to accelerate
promotions of enlisted machinists to NCO rank had begun even before the
war: Where a *Reichsmarine* enlisted man was expected to serve three years'
sea duty before qualifying as an NCO candidate, this requirement had
fallen to one year by 1938, thus qualifying 48 percent of all enlisted engineering personnel.[31] Even these drastic measures could not meet the voracious demand for NCOs following the outbreak of the war. A November
1940 memorandum described the situation in the *Maschinenlaufbahn* as
"very strained," especially with regard to noncommissioned officers: Of
410 vacancies of senior NCOs that needed to be filled, only 232 qualified
applicants were available, and for nearly 1,300 open positions among *Unteroffiziere* a mere 455 met the requirements.[32] Inevitably this meant accelerated promotions and reductions in training that continued over the
course of the war. Early in the war the machinists' training school at
Gotenhafen offered U-boat engineering personnel a five-month course in
both diesels and electrical motors; in 1942 the course was shortened to
three months and limited to either diesels or electrical motors instead of
both. By 1943 continued demands led to a further reduction in both courses
to six weeks.[33]

The navy's hastened development of engine personnel is reflected in
that group's size, the largest for a *Laufbahn* among our sample (395 men, or
42 percent of the total). Their most striking characteristic is their shared occupational experience as metalworkers, applicable to 91 percent (360) of
the group. The navy's constant appeals for these specific categories of recruits obviously bore fruit, without which Dönitz could not have achieved
the vast expansion of his submarine fleet in 1941–43. A breakdown of the
principal individual occupations and numbers, including *Schlosser* at all
levels from apprentices to experienced locksmiths, mechanics, and fitters,
reveals the following:

Schlosser	167
Turners/lathe operators	33
Plumbers/sheet-metal workers	33
Copper- and tinsmiths	32
Mechanical engineers	26
Specialized mechanics	21
Toolmakers	20
Electricians	18

By geographic region of origin, engine personnel largely conformed to the sample's overall pattern: 30 percent northern, 52 percent central, and 15 percent southern (the final 3 percent were either born outside Germany or furnished no data). In sharp contrast to seamen and navigators, eighteen engineers came from Berlin. One result was the intriguing mix of homogeneous vocational skills with heterogeneous geography, the opportunity to "talk shop" and learn of working conditions elsewhere in Germany. While off watch on a U-boat, an apprentice *Schlosser* from Dresden could compare notes with a Rhineland machine-mechanic or a plumber from Hamburg. Improvising makeshift repairs to diesel engines or welding cracks in depth-charge-damaged pressure hulls invoked a professional challenge as well as military necessity.

It is important to note that engine personnel differed little from *Matrosen* in education levels and family backgrounds. Seventy-one percent of their number concluded their academic education with the *Volksschule,* very close to the seamen's rate of 79 percent; relatively more, however, completed supplemental trade, technical, or engineering schools (21 vs. 13 percent). A breakdown of fathers' occupations by class virtually duplicates that of the seamen, with only a slight difference in the greater presence of white-collar and civil service employees (20 vs. 13 percent). The only significant difference between the groups centers on the engineers' overwhelming choice of metalworking as a career.

The implications of this background and the navy's personnel shortages, however, loom large when the two career-tracks are compared. While only 32 percent of the *Matrosen* attained petty officer rank, 53 percent of engine personnel did so; only three of the former achieved the rank of *Bootsmann,* but fifty-one of their counterparts became an *Obermaschinist* or higher. They also tended to begin their submarine service at a later age (see table 21) and served less average time on U-boats (26.0 vs. 28.4 months). Finally they experienced greater movement within the submarine fleet, as 48 percent (vs. 40 percent among seamen) served on two or more boats.

But if naval needs dictated more rapid promotion, considerable atten-

TABLE 16 *MASCHINISTEN* **PETTY OFFICERS IN 1945: YEAR OF ENTRY INTO SERVICE**

Date of Service Entry	*Maschinenobermaat*	*Maschinenmaat*
1938 and earlier	8	0
Jan–Sep 1939	6	2
Oct–Dec 1939	8	8
Jan–May 1940	10	5
Jun–Dec 1940	5	23
Jan–May 1941	6	37
Jun–Dec 1941	0	27
1942	0	11

Source: Data from sample.

tion was paid to individual performance and qualifications. This is confirmed by the data for our sample's *Maschinisten* petty officers, whose date of entry into the service is compared with their ultimate rank achieved as of 1945 in table 16. Standard time-in-grade qualifications obviously remained the largest factor in promotion, but the range of dates reveals a considerable variation according to a machinist's capabilities: If a machinist inducted in the autumn of 1940 rose to *-obermaat* rank ahead of some inducted a year before him, then individual merit also counted.

Thus German naval practices suggest a bias favoring engine personnel to address manpower shortages, but which still relied on individual evaluations of merit for advancement. This becomes even more evident with the other specialized career-tracks.

Torpedo and Artillery Mechanics

The weapons specialist career-track (*Laufbahn* VII, *Mechanikerlaufbahn*), which for other types of warships included mechanics in minelaying and net barrages, generally applied only to two to four men on any submarine, but they were often the key to its success or failure. The *Torpedomechaniker,* as noted in chapter 1, maintained a U-boat's primary offensive weapons; the *Artilleriemechaniker* operated either the main deck gun that initially counted for so many U-boat successes or the flak guns that later defended against deadly Allied air attacks. The "mixers" typically received their training at the Flensburg *Torpedoschule* and torpedoman instructional courses at Kiel and Kolberg, while artillerymen learned their craft at one of several gunnery schools in Germany or in occupied territory. The career insignia consisted of a torpedo or two crossed cannon superimposed on a cogwheel (for petty officers, superimposed again on an anchor).[34]

Of our sample, 117 belonged to the *Mechanikerlaufbahn,* ninety-nine as torpedo and eighteen as artillery specialists. Their background characteristics tend to be more distinctive than the rest, again indicating a navy-generated profile of needed skills that shaped the career's character. As with *Maschinisten,* the outstanding characteristic remains previous skills acquired as metalworkers—in this case exceeding even that of engine personnel (95 vs. 91 percent). Again *Schlosser* predominate as an occupation (fifty-six men), followed by specialized mechanics (eighteen), toolmakers (thirteen), and turners/lathe operators (ten).[35] The few remaining occupations ranged from draftsmen to postal employees.

In contrast to engine personnel, however, *Mechaniker* were more northern in character, both by geographic origin (40 vs. 31 percent) and religion (69 percent Protestant, more so than any other group), drawing least from southern Germany (10 percent). Their fathers' occupations were slightly more upscale than the general pattern (49 percent working class, 49 percent *Mittelstand,* 2 percent upper classes), but with a majority (53 percent) serving as skilled workers or master craftsmen. Mechanics tended to be better educated, as 18 percent completed *Mittel-* or *Realschule* or more, a trait shared by less than 8 percent of *Maschinisten.*

Ironically, these background advantages over engine personnel did not translate into the same levels of military advancement. By war's end the navy had promoted only 43 percent of our sample's mechanics to petty officers, and only ten attained the ultimate ranks of *Obermechaniker* or *Stabsobermechaniker,* although their ages of entry into U-boat service virtually duplicate those in the *Maschinenlaufbahn.* In all probability this merely underscores the significance of the shortages in engineering personnel, leading to extraordinary measures not duplicated in other career-tracks. On the other hand *Mechaniker* were more likely to serve aboard more than one submarine (46 percent listed two or more U-boats), although their period of duty averaged just over twenty-two months, the least among the major sample categories.

Radio Operators

Most specialized of the career-tracks was that for radiomen (*Laufbahn* IV Fk, *Funklaufbahn*), whose rapid evolution could be traced by their administrative history. Prior to 1938 they did not share the signalmen's career-track but were grouped in *Laufbahn* XIII with engine personnel; the general reorganization of 1 April 1938 combined them with signalmen but as still-separate subdivisions. Later in the war new subdivisions would be added to the career-track for signals intelligence, telephone operator, and telephone mechanic. The importance of radio communications, including their encryption and decryption, underscored the navy's dependence on men who possessed the requisite physical and intellectual skills associated with competent telegraphy. Those who wore the downward-pointing lightning bolt as a career insignia carried a disproportionate burden of work and responsibility.[36]

This significance broadened the character of the *Funker* to a degree unique among our sample. The 139 radiomen differ significantly in their backgrounds, beginning with their geographic origins. Only 20 percent came from the north, with 58 percent from central and 20 percent from southern Germany, the largest proportional representation for both those regions. Reflecting these origins, radiomen included a higher rate of Roman Catholics (32 percent) and lower rate of Protestants (55 percent) than any other. They were more likely to come from petit bourgeois rather than working-class homes, with 57 percent of their fathers holding *Mittelstand* occupations. And in formal education, they stand second only to the *Obersteuermänner* with 35 percent having completed secondary schooling; their ranks include the lone university student among 937 sample members, who served as an *Oberfunkmaat*. That three former U-boat radiomen have published accounts of their experiences should therefore come as no surprise.[37]

In their own vocational choices radiomen exhibited much more balance than the extremes of other careers. Metalworkers again predominated, but only with 51 percent of the total (seventeen of whom were specialized mechanics, fifteen *Schlosser,* fourteen plumbers, and eight electricians or electrical workers). The remainder included twenty white-collar employees or salesmen; six full-time students; six civil service employees; four draftsmen; three coal miners; and various traditional craftsmen, whose manual skills as typesetters, barbers, butchers, and weavers doubtless facilitated the working of telegraphy keys.

Those who possessed these skills received ample rewards from the navy. Fifty-five percent of our sample's radiomen advanced to petty officer rank and 34 percent to chief petty officer or senior NCO status, in addition to those promoted from the ranks to officers, as noted in the previous chapter. Such practices gain in importance when it is recalled that the group barely existed before the war, as three-quarters of our radiomen enlisted only after 1 January 1940. The price exacted, however, involved constant risks and job insecurity. One radioman discovered he had been "volunteered" for the *U-Boot-Waffe* in May 1940, served aboard a U-boat from December 1940 to October 1942, gained a promotion to warrant officer on training duties, then found he had been reassigned to submarine duty in January 1944.[38] The majority of our sample, however, spent their submarine service aboard a single boat, averaging 22.6 months per tour of duty. Of particular note is the fact that twenty-seven *Funker* (almost 20 percent) did not begin their U-boat service until after September 1943.

Medical Personnel

The medical career-track (*Laufbahn* XI, *Sanitätslaufbahn*) group, almost insignificant in absolute numbers, commands attention as the final evolution of a specific personnel policy for the general health of U-boat crewmen. As noted in the previous chapter, the assignment of specially trained naval medics (*Sanitätsunteroffiziere mit Sonderausbildung,* abbreviated in military slang to *Sani*), equivalent to the U.S. Navy's pharmacist's mates, reflected a specific attempt to provide quality medical and dental care to German submariners while sparing full surgeons from the extreme hazards of U-boat duty. Wearing the insignia of a single-snake caduceus (superimposed on a left-leaning anchor for petty officers), they appeared in increasing numbers aboard U-boats after the summer of 1943. By 1944 the Kiel-based 5th U-boat Flotilla, which was responsible for outfitting front-bound submarines as they completed Baltic training, began receiving thirty such medics every month for submarine assignment. Yet bureaucratic regulations did not keep pace with the risks and significance of their work, prohibiting these *Sanitätsunteroffiziere* from attaining senior NCO status. Proposals to convert medics to the seamen's career-track to facilitate their promotion were still under discussion when the war ended.[39]

Some characteristics of the nine medics among our sample mirror these administrative developments. The highest rank achieved was *Sanitätsober-maat;* none commenced their U-boat service before 1943, and four not until 1944; and only two served on more than one boat. For such a small group, no analysis of background data can be reliable. Except for the complete absence of metalworkers their previous occupations are unremarkable (two salesmen, two barbers, a pharmacist, a local boatman, a roofer, a factory worker, and one career navy man). Barbers and pharmacists, however, were often allocated to the medical career-track.[40] Medical training did not imply extensive prior formal schooling, as only one *Sani* received a secondary education.

FROM THE EXAMPLES of our sample, one leitmotif of naval personnel policy becomes clear: a dependence on previously acquired skills to perform vital technical functions. Metalworkers in particular were actively recruited and culled from the available manpower pool, a policy preserved at least through the Bundesmarine of the 1950s.[41] The evidence indicates that these men were thereafter promoted in a manner that both met urgent specialist needs and rewarded personal qualifications. By contrast, those who filled the ordinary seamen's ranks appear more carefully selected on an individual basis rather than by acquired skills, yet promoted at a slower pace. The latter perhaps indicates the Kriegsmarine's ideal in recruitment and personnel policy, but a strategy that had to be drastically revised for technical services to meet the demands of total war.

As a by-product of such administrative practices, U-boat crews represented a composite of both heterogeneous and homogeneous backgrounds. *Matrosen* and *Obersteuermann* constituted the pick of volunteers from various backgrounds, and the *Techniker* embodied the best special-skilled men recruited from targeted if narrow occupations. If they did not precisely match the geographical distribution of the German population in representation, they nevertheless matched the general regional patterns. For the specialists, acquired skills and the competent performance of their duties opened doors to rewards and advancement much less accessible in civilian life. Finally, regardless of career-track or previous occupation, crewmen also shared distinctive family backgrounds as part of the working class or *Mittelstand* stratum of society.

The contrast between their social backgrounds and those of their officers, noted in the previous chapter, commands attention for the transformation that occurred in less than twenty-five years. The social character of the German navy changed little from World War I, officered mostly by men from the upper and upper-middle classes who commanded lower-middle- and working-class crewmen. But where the High Seas Fleet mutinies in 1917–18 revealed the volatile tensions within this hierarchy, the U-boat service of 1939–45 demonstrated its amazing capacity for cohesion under the horrific strain of a 70 percent casualty rate. A small part of this cement could be attributed to the entrance of *Mittelstand* sons into the officer corps during the war, the first mingling of common backgrounds for officers and men.

Far more significant than class characteristics, however, U-boat crews were held together in part by shared attitudes about themselves and their society, but above all by shared wartime experiences. Self-conscious of their elite status, commanded by officers who had absorbed the painful First World War lessons of leadership, German submariners could draw additional strength from common professional interests and social backgrounds. If not always proportionately representative, the officers and men of Dönitz's U-boats nevertheless more truly characterized the full spectrum of German society than ever imagined by the 1943 editors of *Hamburger Illustrierte*.

Adolf Hitler, accompanied by Grand Adm. Erich Raeder (*extreme left*) and
Kaptlt. Günther Prien (*second from left*), receives the crew of *U-47* at the
Berlin Chancellery on 18 October 1939, four days after their daring sinking of the British battleship *Royal Oak* in Scapa Flow. NATIONAL ARCHIVES,
131-2A-66

Grand Adm. Karl Dönitz greets a *Maschinengefreiter* from one of his crews at a formal ceremony
in France, May 1942. NATIONAL ARCHIVES, 242-PKA-2-127

The last moments of *U-378* (*Kaptlt.* Erich Mader), 20 October 1943, under attack north of the Azores by aircraft from the USS *Core*. Just visible on the conning tower (enlarged to accommodate the latest radar detection gear) is the boat's emblem; none of her fifty-two-man crew survived.
NATIONAL ARCHIVES, 80-G-207651

Rare photograph of the final duel between destroyer escort and U-boat: *U-515* (*Kaptlt.* Werner Henke) has just been forced to the surface after an extended submerged hunt and is being raked by fire from USS *Chatelain*, 9 April 1944.   NATIONAL ARCHIVES, 80-G-227192

Interior view of the captain's cabin aboard *U-505* (*Oblt.z.S.d.R.* Harald Lange) shortly after her capture by U.S. Navy forces, 4 June 1944. The personal bunk and coffeepot marked the singular luxuries afforded a U-boat commander.

Quarters for *Unteroffiziere* (NCOs) aboard *U-505*. The curtains at left provided some privacy in the shared bunks and protected open shelves (*center*) for the storage of manuals, books, and belongings.

In the beginning: *Kapt.z.S.* Robert Bräutigam (*second from right*) and three of his officers from the U-boat Acceptance Command talk shop sometime in the summer of 1939, attired in prewar gray leather jackets. Bräutigam, a World War I U-boat commander, died of natural causes in October 1944.

NATIONAL ARCHIVES, 306-NT-1291-A-10

At the end: *Kaptlt.d.R.* Uwe Kock (in white cap) and his officers ponder the future on the bridge of *U-249*, the first U-boat to arrive at Weymouth Bay, England, after Germany's surrender, 10 May 1945. NATIONAL ARCHIVES, 306-NT-1342B-2

Final muster: The crew of *U-249* display a variety of U-boat uniforms as they break ranks and disembark for the last time under the watchful eyes of Royal Navy guards, 10 May 1945. NATIONAL ARCHIVES, 306-NT-1342B-4

A view of the conning tower of newly commissioned *U-566* (*Kaptlt.* Dietrich Borchert) in the summer of 1941, preparing for operations in Arctic waters. Emblazoned on the conning tower is the city coat of arms for Lindau, Borchert's birthplace; the two crewmen on deck may be commiserating on their hair loss, a not-infrequent occurrence among submariners.

COURTESY OF INGE MOLZAHN

The features of an early-war Type VIIC boat are evident in this photograph of *U-566* off Norway, circa July 1941: the upward-slanting bow flooding slots, forward 8.8-cm gun, and small aft bridge. The mottled camouflage scheme was probably distinctive for U-boats operating along the Norwegian coast. COURTESY OF INGE MOLZAHN

A common view for U-boat sailors: The bow of a Type VIIC slicing through the waves toward an endless Atlantic horizon. COURTESY OF INGE MOLZAHN

Generaladmiral Hans-Georg von Friedeburg, the number-two man in Germany's U-boat arm during World War II. Originally scheduled to replace Dönitz in 1939, he instead took over the U-boat Organization Department and cobbled together the entire training establishment. He died by his own hand at war's end. COURTESY OF THE U-BOOT-ARCHIV, CUXHAVEN

U-boat recruits about to undergo underwater escape exercises as part of their training at the *1. Ubootlehrdivision,* Neustadt. Except for the kimono-clad instructor, each is wearing the *Dräger* apparatus, a combination breathing device and life vest. COURTESY OF THE U-BOOT-ARCHIV, CUXHAVEN

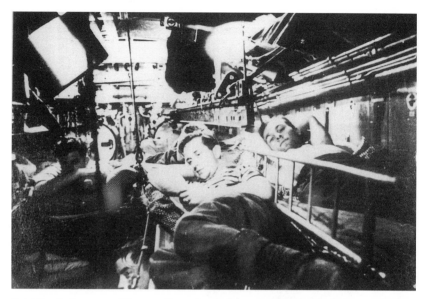

Quiet time in the cramped *Bugraum* (forward torpedo room) of *U-552* at the beginning of a patrol, with memories of leave still fresh for the clean-shaven *Lords*. COURTESY OF THE U-BOOT-ARCHIV, CUXHAVEN

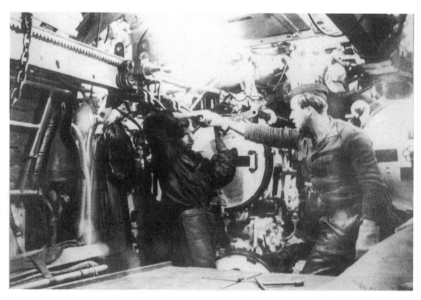

At right, a *Bootsmaat* (bosun's mate) lends a hand to a young seaman in sealing the port bow torpedo tube of *U-376* before seeking out some additional storage space. COURTESY OF THE U-BOOT-ARCHIV, CUXHAVEN

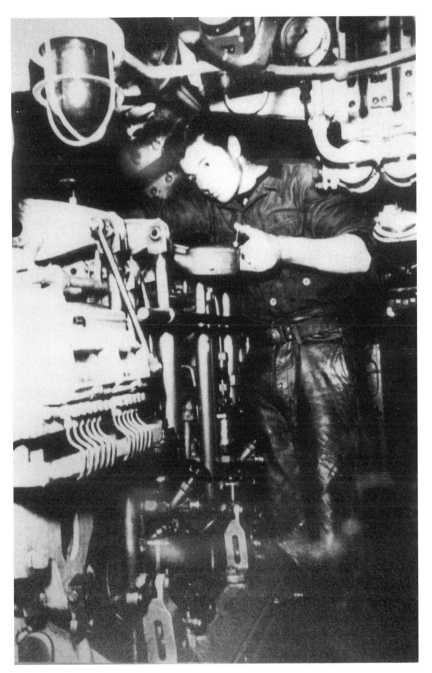

A *Maschinenobergefreiter* oils the diesel engines aboard *U-376*. COURTESY OF THE U-BOOT-ARCHIV, CUXHAVEN

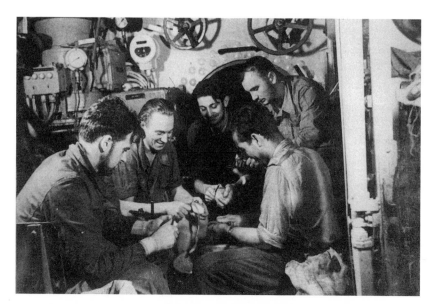

KP duty for five seamen aboard *U-431* just inside the forward hatch of the central control room (*Zentrale*). Potatoes constituted a staple of every U-boat crew's diet. COURTESY OF THE U-BOOT-ARCHIV, CUXHAVEN

The *Smutje* (cook) hard at work in *U-376*'s galley, using some tins to bake bread in the oven. Above him is his rudimentary cooking ware and the locked pantry. COURTESY OF THE U-BOOT-ARCHIV, CUXHAVEN

The canteen is open for business in the officers' wardroom aboard *U-124*, selling packaged sweets, cigarettes, and other treats. COURTESY OF THE U-BOOT-ARCHIV, CUXHAVEN

Horsing around: Two crewmen enjoying a joke at a third's expense aboard supply tanker *U-461*, probably during the milch cow's resupply operations west of the Cape Verde Islands in early 1943. COURTESY OF THE U-BOOT-ARCHIV, CUXHAVEN

"Neptune" baptizes the neophytes of *U-459* when the Type XIV supply tanker crosses the equator, 11 September 1942. The commander, World War I veteran *Korv.Kapt.z.V.* Georg von Wilamowitz-Moellendorf (in the white cap), observes at far right. COURTESY OF THE U-BOOT-ARCHIV, CUXHAVEN

New submarines, old habits: Just aft of the streamlined conning tower of the Type XXI boat *U-3037*, a crewman enjoys a smoke. The photo probably depicts the U-boat in the Weser River in March 1945, less than two months before war's end. COURTESY OF THE U-BOOT-ARCHIV, CUXHAVEN

This is an example of the humorous "certificates" that were constantly being awarded in the German navy. The text reads, "Diving Master Diploma. We Masters of the Guild of Trim Tamers and Chief Engineer Torturers herewith make known that the most worshipful Lieutenant (Eng.) Hirschmann today before the undersigned took a submarine of medium size undamaged below the surface without danger for the galley and the nap of the training officer and moved same in moderate oscillations up and down so that now he has been found worthy to be admitted into the brotherhood of the glorious diving boat people. Given this day 26.2. in the year 1943." The certificate is signed by "The Chief Engineer Training Officers of the Agru-Front."

Quality before Quantity

The Making of U-boat Men

In the last two chapters we have reviewed the backgrounds and characteristics of the various types of Kriegsmarine officers and enlisted men who manned the U-boats. But what distinguished them as submariners? What transformed them into the *Freikorps Dönitz*? And did their training match Dönitz's own dictum of "quality over quantity"? We shall seek answers to these questions here, beginning with the important question of an all-volunteer elite.

Defining a Combat Elite

As reviewed in appendix 2, the often-accepted figure of approximately forty-one thousand U-boat officers and crewmen appears to be at least 10 percent less than the actual number who served at some point during the war. A larger final total of between forty-five and fifty thousand *U-Boot-Fahrer*, however, does not significantly affect the issue of the "elite" character of the submarine force. The service's continued operations in the face of horrific losses in killed and captured of nearly thirty-four thousand men—a permanent casualty rate of more than 70 percent—alone qualifies Germany's submariners as an extraordinary group in military history.

Yet serious questions remain about the nature of this nearly annihilated elite. The traditional portrait of a hand-picked, all-volunteer force implied by Dönitz's prewar comment, "The navy represents the cream of the armed forces, and the U-boat arm represents the cream of the navy,"[1] has recently been challenged by a nearly opposite view, that "it was German policy to send conscripts (draftees) into the submarines" and "the majority were conscripts drafted to the U-boat arm."[2] Which assessment is valid?

Dönitz's ideal doubtless stood as the standard when war broke out in September 1939. A true hand-picked elite of three thousand front-line submariners represented only 8 to 10 percent of those who applied for U-boat service during the prewar period.[3] One of those, who somehow survived tours of duty aboard three U-boats and surrendered to the British at war's end near his native Hamburg, later recalled that more than one tooth cavity would be enough to disqualify a U-boat recruit. Of 150 applicants in his 1938 class, only fifty met the strict physical qualifications, of whom a mere twenty passed the rigorous written examinations.[4]

As we have seen, this elite force suffered 40 percent losses in killed and missing during the war's first year, a painful reality that carried major implications. The heavy casualties first of all demonstrated submarine warfare's lethal indifference to intensity of training or painstaking selectivity of crews. Moreover, merely replacing these losses in a brief period would have proven difficult enough, but war with Britain entailed a massive expansion of the submarine fleet in 1940–42. To man such a growing fleet required more than a mere relaxation of prewar standards. Dönitz understood this by no later than November 1939, when he drafted plans for training more than four thousand submariners before the end of the next year and more than twenty-six thousand before the end of 1943, sufficient to man an envisioned fleet of 881 U-boats. The program's requirements in specific categories of technical personnel (e.g., 3,538 petty officers and 6,220 enlisted men from the engineering career-track, nearly 3,900 radiomen, and almost 3,000 torpedo mechanics) precluded faith in the appropriate numbers of qualified volunteers stepping forth in time.[5]

Thus, just as the *Kaiserliche Marine* had abandoned voluntarism for manning its U-boats before the end of 1917,[6] Dönitz recognized the same necessity mere months after the outbreak of the Second World War. The reliance on volunteers continued through the end of 1940, but by the middle of 1941 the assignment of needed personnel to submarine duty had become common practice.[7]

Officers felt the first effects of the change. *Oblt.z.S.* Siegfried Koitschka, who eventually won the Knight's Cross as commander of *U-616*, lost his

hopes for a torpedo boat posting in 1939 when medical examiners qualified him for submarine duty, where he would serve until his capture in
1944. Naval authorities simply designated Werner Henke for U-boat training in March 1940 without regard for his disinterest in the service. *Oblt.(I)*
Rudi Töpfer received orders to report to submarine training after his destroyer, *Erich Giese,* was sunk at Narvik in April 1940. In October 1940 the
German destroyers *Friedrich Ihn* and *Friedrich Eckholdt* lost their torpedo
and gunnery officers to submarine assignment.[8] That same month Grand
Admiral Raeder emphatically rejected wholesale transfers of junior officers
to the submarine branch—transfers that would have delayed the commissioning of the battleship *Tirpitz*—yet it merely postponed the inevitable.[9]
One year later this practice had advanced to the stage where the flag officer
for destroyers wrote that he "considered one of his tasks to be the training
and release of officers for U-boat duty," even at the cost of removing two of
his destroyers from operational readiness due to personnel transfers.[10]

U-boat needs also bled German destroyers and torpedo boats of many
engineering officers. One of the latter described his own selection for U-
boat service:

At the end of 1941 all destroyers had three engineering officers and the "Thirds" were all
taken out and put into U-boats. I had mixed feelings; on the one hand I was sorry to lose
the large and powerful machinery on the destroyer but on the other I was pleased to get
a position as "L.I." so quickly. Also at that time the U-boats were going well and there
was much prestige to be with them.[11]

Personnel authorities within *Marineoberkommando Ost* (Naval Chief
Command East), the principal regional command for the Baltic, released
for U-boat service all medically qualified officers who had been evaluated
as "suited for small vessels."[12] The naval pilots who had transferred to the
Luftwaffe in the 1930s also proved a rich source of U-boat officers: Many
came voluntarily to the submarine service, but one group simply received
orders in mid-December 1940 to report for U-boat training.[13] Such mass
transfers continued through Dönitz's promotion to commander-in-chief of
the navy in January 1943, when, for example, 125 officers and midshipmen training as pilots for the nascent Naval Air Service suddenly found
themselves transferred to submarine duty.[14]

These personnel movements brought about a transformation of the U-
boat officer corps. Dönitz's commanders at the beginning of the war have
been described as a "submarine culture" within the navy, officers whose
limited perspective separated them from their fleet comrades.[15] Both the
validity and limitations of this interpretation can be seen in the previous

TABLE 17 **PREVIOUS NAVAL SERVICE OF 1,152 U-BOAT COMMANDERS**

	Number	**Percentage**
U-boat only	422	37
Light surface units[a]	294	25
Destroyers	48	4
Cruisers, battleships	135	12
Luftwaffe	99	9
Coastal artillery/shore unit	114	10
Command staffs	40	3
Total	1,152	100

Source: Compiled from Lohmann and Hildebrand, *Die Deutsche Kriegsmarine (Personalien).*
[a]Minesweepers, patrol vessels, torpedo and motor torpedo boats.

naval service of 1,152 U-boat commanders over the course of the war, re-produced in table 17.

The data reveal that, while many submarine captains knew no other employment, a majority actually came from other naval duties. The relative contributions by light vs. heavy surface forces most probably reflect the large number of naval personnel involved in coastal tasks against the relatively small size of the surface fleet. If the U-boat service never became fully integrated with the rest of the German navy, the latter found itself increasingly absorbed within the *U-Boot-Waffe.*

But officers were not the only ones for whom U-boat needs exceeded qualified volunteers. Technical specialists—diesel and electrical engine machinists, radiomen, and torpedo mechanics—also had to be fed into the growing U-boat fleet without regard for personal preference, and the first transfers began in the spring of 1940. *Funkmaat* Wolfgang Hirschfeld, a 1936 enlistee and former torpedo boat radioman, learned in April 1940 that he had simply been assigned to U-boat duty, with the only choice left him that between service aboard a Type VII or a Type IX boat.[16] On at least one occasion all medically qualified members of a graduating class of *Obermaschinisten* (chief diesel and electrical machinists) at Kiel were immediately assigned to outbound U-boats.[17]

A torpedo mechanic recalled how career-track promotions for his specialty developed into a U-boat recruitment tactic. After completing the April–June 1941 instructional course at the *Torpedoschule* Mürwik, his class was told they would not receive the expected promotion to *Mechanikersmaat* until they first completed basic submarine training—and hence became eligible for U-boat duty.[18] Shortages of senior bosun's mates also caused the reassignment of qualified chief petty officers, even when they lacked submarine experience, as with a forty-two-year-old *Stabsoberboots-*

mann assigned to *U-233* (*Kaptlt.* Hans Steen) in 1944, his first U-boat duty since entering the navy in 1921.[19] When more manpower was needed for the Mediterranean fleet of U-boats in 1943, all enlisted personnel of the 2d Landing Flotilla based at Castellammare, Sicily, were ordered to report for examination for suitability of transfer to submarine duty.[20]

Beyond outright assignment, peer pressure also played a role in securing less-than-enthusiastic volunteers. A *Maschinenmaat* who survived *U-464's* (*Kaptlt.* Otto Harms) sinking by British forces in August 1942 described his recruitment earlier that year in a monitored discussion with a comrade:

At Kiel they were doing all they could to popularize U-boats. I had promised at home that I wouldn't join the U-boat arm. Then they asked us: "Who will join the *U-Boot-Waffe?*" I thought—no, I won't do that. Then they put up their hands one after the other and my friend said: "Put up your hand. Let's stick together." I thought—no. Then he pushed my arm up when it came to our turn and they took down our names. Then I thought, "Perhaps I shall be lucky in the examination," but I was taken on.[21]

Thus many *Freiwillige* for submarine service did so unwillingly or with little choice. Yet this often mirrored the nominal "volunteer" status of most of those who served in the navy. Even before the war, men who knew they would be drafted into the army opted for the Kriegsmarine as a preferable alternative. "I didn't like the idea of marching or freezing in Russia, so I volunteered for the navy," explained one U-boat veteran.[22] Thus naval commissions had their pick of recruits who passed the qualifications, possessed the skills needed by the navy, and preferred what looked to be a better life. That these men and the old hands who had enlisted for twelve-year stints in the early 1930s counted equally as "volunteers" should not disguise the difference between them.

Still, even these motivations could not produce sufficient numbers of qualified recruits. At the beginning of June 1941 the navy reported serious manpower shortages and especially inadequate numbers of volunteers for combat units, with even worse prospects for the immediate future.[23] This situation illustrated the shortcomings of the remaining category of naval recruits: draftees.

During the prewar period those liable to naval conscription consisted of annual intakes of about twelve thousand to fourteen thousand men between the ages of eighteen and forty-five from the "seafaring and semi-seafaring" population who served for two years and then entered the naval reserves; when war came they and their fishing or other private boats typically entered the navy for patrol and minesweeping duties or performed coastal defense duties.[24] How broadly "semi-seafaring" could be interpreted, however, became the subject of a popular joke during the abortive preparations for the invasion of England in 1940: Desperately searching for anyone qualifying as a *Binnenschiffer* (inland waterman), a naval press-gang leader asks a Bavarian vagrant his occupation and on receiving the heavily accented reply *"Bienenzüchter"* (beekeeper) orders his immediate conscription.[25]

Because of its ever-expanding role and responsibilities the navy sought to expand its share of conscripts but the German Armed Forces High Command strictly regulated the available manpower pool, juggling the services' rival claims according to the most pressing demands. With priority accorded the army and Luftwaffe, the navy obtained only 9 percent of the total replacement pool (volunteers and draftees) in September 1939, a figure reduced to 4.4 percent one year later. In October 1941 this quota rose to 10.2 percent, the apogee of naval recruitment before the voracious maw of the Eastern Front clamped down on German manpower needs.

By November 1942 German authorities had fixed the annual naval quota at thirty thousand volunteers/draftees. Following his appointment as naval commander-in-chief, however, Dönitz approached Hitler for approval of a massive expansion program in men and submarines. Plans drafted by the Naval Personnel Department in May 1943 proposed increasing the year's quota of volunteers to seventy thousand for those born in 1926, as well as a broadened definition of the seafaring population to include several thousand newly qualified youths of the *Marine-Hitler-Jugend,* the naval division of the "Hitler Youth" organization. More than thirty-one thousand of this greater manpower pool—whether drafted or enlisted—were designated for assignment as U-boat crewmen.[26] In his meeting with Hitler on 15 June, Dönitz pushed these figures even higher.[27]

The program and statistics are illustrated in the experience of a single man. Eduard Vogt had been employed as a boilermaker at the naval shipyard in his native Wilhelmshaven for three years when, in August 1943 and one month shy of his eighteenth birthday, he received his draft notice into the navy. He hadn't realized that his service in the *Marine-Hitler-Jugend* and an administrative reclassification had suddenly altered his draft eligibility. Passing his physical examination with flying colors, Vogt was pronounced "U-boat qualified" and entered the *Mechaniker* career-track. In early 1944 he began his submarine training aboard the old passenger liner *Robert Ley,* seemingly destined for front-line duty and a less than 50 percent chance of survival. But as will be seen in the next chapter, the planned expansion of early 1944 never approached its goals and the U-boat fleet in fact contracted as the focus shifted to new submarine models. Vogt joined the reserve personnel pool at Kiel, where he spent the rest of the war working out of the U-boat repair shop. That he was never assigned to a submarine might represent mere fortune or a deliberate decision to avoid further use of draftees, especially as the introduction of the new, advanced submarine models strengthened a reliance on submariners already trained and experienced.[28]

The assignment of conscripts to U-boats remained a rarity; most of those who claimed that status appear among U-boat POWs only in 1943–44, reinforcing its link to the partially implemented fleet expansion program of that period. Several claimed mixed Polish parentage, but Polish surnames were not uncommon throughout the Wehrmacht. Four survivors of *U-505,* captured at sea in June 1944, told their captors they had been drafted, but this might represent a misinterpretation of their involuntary assignment to U-boat duty.[29] There is moreover no evidence to indicate that individuals were compelled to remain aboard submarines, a condition as undesirable to the rest of the crew as to the individual affected.

Thus, although submarine duty in the German navy proved less voluntary than proclaimed at the time, too much should not be made of this. Anyone unsuited for U-boat service did not stay long, if only for the safety of the rest of his crew. How many true volunteers remained? "I estimate that 80 percent were genuine volunteers but from the end of 1942 . . . there weren't so many," recalled one *Bootsmaat,* adding, "I remember an almost complete absence of married volunteers after this time."[30] On the other hand, a shortage of volunteers for submarine service never existed. Studies by the U-Boot-Archiv indicate that only 37 percent of those who applied for U-boat duty in 1944 were accepted.[31] If many who served aboard U-boats did not do so voluntarily, a considerable number who volunteered did not meet the standards.

Moreover, the policy of drawing upon the entire navy for personnel helped integrate the U-boat arm into the Kriegsmarine as a whole. From a select but sequestered service, the *U-Boot-Fahrer* evolved into just one more hazardous branch of the navy at large. Self-awareness of elite status gradually moved toward a more detached and professional stoicism. A U-boat officer who served at sea during the 1942–45 period expressed this attitude: "We felt we were just doing our job like everyone else, that everyone in the navy had to shoulder a heavy burden and ours was no worse than anyone else's."[32] If indeed a significant number did not choose submarine duty voluntarily, more than the prestige of U-boat service is necessary to account for their ability to endure the losses they did. For an explanation we must examine the process that turned them into submariners.

Patrolling with Barkow

The voracious appetite for submarine recruits, voluntary or otherwise, imposed tremendous strains on the U-boat training establishment as they strove to square the circle of replacing losses, multiplying the size of the operational fleet, and creating an experienced training cadre. That a force of three thousand men in September 1939 with a 40 percent casualty rate in the first year could rise to a front-line strength of over thirteen thousand by July 1942 testifies to the overall achievement.

This could only be accomplished by cutting corners in various ways. Many newly commissioned officers, for example, were assigned directly to U-boats as watch officers and thereby required only abbreviated training to complete their promotions to command. Overriding personnel requirements occasionally led to the direct funneling of new recruits straight from boot camp onto combat submarines without preliminary U-boat training, as was claimed by POWs recovered from three U-boats sunk by U.S. forces. The same also occurred to sample member Günter Koch, who found himself commandeered as a cook aboard *U-66* (*Kaptlt.* Friedrich Markworth) in December 1942.[33] Most U-boat sailors, however, passed through a more regular, two-phase training process that first taught them the basics and later molded them into effective crews. Both the extent and quality of this training, however, varied over the course of the war.

The earliest prewar training occurred covertly under the auspices of what was designated the *Unterseebootsabwehrschule* (UAS, "Antisubmarine Warfare School") established on 1 October 1933 at Kiel. Over the next year only one class of seven line and two engineering officers and about seventy to eighty enlisted men passed through the course, reflecting political concerns and the temporary suspension of planned submarine construction.[34] Through 1935 new training remained subject to the uneven tempo of U-boat production as students received classroom instruction in technical aspects of submarine design, propulsion systems, underwater trimming and movement, and underwater escape procedures: "We were crammed with theory up to our collars," wrote Günther Prien, who began his six-month training in October 1935. Prien's class, which also included future aces Joachim Schepke and Viktor Schütze, became the first to train aboard Germany's initial U-boats in early 1936.[35]

With the establishment of the U-boat Flotilla "Weddigen" in late September 1935 under *Kapt.z.S.* Karl Dönitz, a regular six-month training program emerged. Six submarines (*U-1* through *U-6*) became the Training Unit

(*Schulverband*), in which every trainee spent between four and twenty days at sea (varying by trainee career-track) in practical instruction of onboard realities, in addition to classroom lessons. Combat exercises and torpedo attacks, however, were conducted with the operational boats of the flotilla (initially *U-7* through *U-12*), with as much time spent at sea as possible. Each U-boat conducted sixty-six simulated torpedo firings (with "slugs" of compressed air, as torpedoes were few and costly) from both surfaced and submerged positions before proceeding to detailed tactical training. The latter included day and night tactical operations, the conduct of surfaced and submerged attacks, escape maneuvers, and submerged handling of boats. As additional U-boats were commissioned they were first tested by the newly established U-boat Trials Acceptance Committee (*Erprobungsausschuss für U-boote*, or EAU), later designated the U-boat Acceptance Command (*Unterseebootsabnahmekommando*, or UAK), both to test the boats' machinery and hulls and their crews' ability to handle them. In May 1937 the growth of the submarine force compelled the relocation of the *U-bootschule* (the fictional "UAS" designation long since discarded) to Neustadt on the Holstein coast; by August 1939 the Training Unit had expanded to a flotilla of twelve U-boats.[36]

Thorough as the training was, it also embodied a spirit of "can-do" optimism in the face of supposedly superior Allied technology. Dönitz specifically sought to debunk the widespread belief that sonar (or asdic, the British designation) stripped away the submarine's cloak of invisibility, a conviction furthered by World War I U-boat commanders in their training lectures given at the *U-bootschule* in 1934–35.[37] As proof of his success in this regard he later quoted one of his commanders' postwar comments:

The salient feature of this training year, 1935–36, was the fact that it eradicated from the minds of all the commanders and their crews the inferiority complex, which had undoubtedly been prevalent among them, and the idea that the U-boat had been mastered and rendered impotent as an instrument of war by recent highly developed anti-submarine devices.[38]

Yet this proof had not come easily. The first tactical exercise involving U-boats operating against a sonar-equipped escort vessel, conducted in the spring of 1939 in Kiel Bay, failed utterly: To Dönitz's chagrin, the submarines were detected before they could launch a torpedo. In subsequent exercises in the central Baltic and the Skagerrak during May and June he reversed that verdict with successful simulated U-boat attacks that evaded sonar detection. In the opinion of a naval officer involved in the antisubmarine defense during these exercises, sonar ineffectiveness here reflected less of superior tactics and more of warming trends in Baltic waters.[39] To the new commander of U-boats, assuring his crews of their own capabilities mattered more than technology. Before the end of April 1940, however, Dönitz would press for effective antisonar measures or devices as "the most urgent task," "decisive for success in the coming U-boat war."[40]

Dönitz had revealed a similar antipathy toward radar at the end of the 1938 autumn maneuvers. *Oblt.z.S.* Otto Köhler, radio officer on the *Königsberg* and liaison to Dönitz and his staff quartered on board the light cruiser, correctly pointed out that radar developments would soon possess the capability of detecting objects as small as marker buoys on the surface and in darkness. The unimpressed U-boat officers ridiculed the idea. Köhler had occasion to remember the discussion in 1943 when, as commander of *U-377*, he barely eluded radar-directed British attacks to return home.[41]

These examples illustrate the attitude of the U-boat command toward antisubmarine technologies when the war began. They believed that human ingenuity and resoluteness could overcome or negate the technical capabilities of detection devices, that technology ultimately bowed to the human spirit. However laudable Dönitz's effort to instill confidence in his men, it was not accompanied by a search for long-term answers to the technological problems posed by sonar and radar for a submarine campaign. Together with routine lessons in buoyancy and submerged trimming, this mind-set became part of the training program imparted to submariners. During the early war years such lessons doubtless contributed to the aggressiveness and success of U-boat commanders; but from 1943 advances in Allied detection technology and weaponry rendered these attitudes dangerous for survival.

The coming of war immediately began to affect U-boat training. The entire Training Flotilla had to be committed to operations (albeit defensive in nature) throughout the Polish campaign, a task repeated during the Norwegian invasion the following April.[42] Heavy losses and the need to maintain maximum combat strength compelled the abandonment of the prewar policy of using watch officers and senior NCOs to train new crews.[43] In outlining his expansion plans in November 1939, Dönitz paid lip service to the principle of "quality over quantity" in wartime training even as he conceded that every trainee could no longer expect to receive onboard submarine experience. The same document projected the establishment of a second U-boat training school at Gotenhafen by 1 July 1940.[44]

Over the course of 1940 the organizational structure for U-boat training assumed its basic wartime form. Dönitz first had to fend off the Naval High Command's proposal to commit the training units to combat after the fall of France, then win an intense administrative battle to retain control of training, which Raeder wished to place under the *Kommandierender Admiral Ostsee*. With his prerogatives secure, Dönitz combined the administrative and training functions of his command under then-*Kapt.z.S.* von Friedeburg as *Befehlshaber der Unterseeboote/Organisationsabteilung*, or *BdU/Org*. As we have seen, von Friedeburg furnished continuity in this capacity and his subsequent positions as 2d admiral, U-boats, and commanding admiral, U-boats, throughout the war. And it was solely to von Friedeburg's organizing genius, in the opinion of a former flotilla commander, that Dönitz owed everything in setting up a training establishment and program to feed new U-boats and crews to the front.

Von Friedeburg had to make one of his earliest critical decisions in April 1940, when Allied mining of the waters around Kiel forced the U-boat School to move to the East Prussian port of Pillau (now Baltiysk, Poland), where it was redesignated the 1st U-boat Instructional Division (*1. Unterseebootslehrdivision*, or 1. ULD) under *Freg.Kapt.* Hans Ibbeken. The new U-boat school at Gotenhafen, delayed in construction, opened in November 1940 as the 2d U-boat Instructional Division under *Freg.Kapt.* Werner Hartmann, who as commander of *U-37* sank over 100,000 tons of shipping during the war's first seven months.[45] (An overview of the training commands as of July 1942 is provided in appendix 3.)

Each ULD numbered between two thousand and four thousand trainees and was divided into two sections, the larger one for enlisted men and the other for officers and NCOs. The sections were in turn organized into companies ranging in size from 90 to 250 men according to rank and career-track, with separate sections for potential commanders, chief engineers, and watch officers. Trainees lived aboard former cruise liners converted into training depot ships or were quartered ashore, and divided their time between classroom instruction and physical drills. The severest tests featured underwater escape exercises (repeated several times) with and without an artificial lung (known as the *Dräger* apparatus) in a diving tank filled with eight meters of water. One percent of the trainees tested in these exercises suffered severe middle ear injuries, including ruptures of the ear drum, leading to a reduction in the number of tests. In the end the swiftness of destruction and the ocean's depths rendered most of these exercises academic, yet the *Dräger* apparatus would save the lives of survivors from at least twelve U-boats and provide the deepest recorded escapes of the war, 230 feet by a survivor of *U-767* (*Oblt.z.S.* Walter Dankleff) off the Isle of Wight in June 1944 and 240 feet by *Obersteuermann* Klaussen of *U-1199* (*Kaptlt.* Rolf Nollmann) in the English Channel in January 1945.[46]

Attached to each ULD for seagoing exercises was a training flotilla of approximately twenty U-boats of different types: the 21st U-boat Flotilla (the original *Schulverband*) for Pillau and the 22d U-boat Flotilla for Gotenhafen. Originally intended to accommodate all trainees for practical submarine experience, however, the flotillas came increasingly to be reserved to train officers and NCOs. At the end of 1941, as the rapid expansion of the U-boat fleet placed its maximum demands on the training program, only the five highest-rated trainees from the enlisted seamen companies at Pillau earned the privilege of training aboard a U-boat at sea; the rest had to make do with exercises on minesweepers and quick evening visits aboard berthed submarines in port. Even with the establishment of the 3. ULD (in September 1943, intended principally for technical personnel) and the 4. ULD (in February 1944, intended primarily for technical personnel of advanced submarine models), this situation did not significantly improve as emphasis turned to the new Type XXI boats, for which no instruction models were available.[47]

Enlisted men initially completed their ULD training in six months, later reduced to three months and then eight weeks; radio-and torpedomen found their specialized training time decreased to only five weeks. As with officers, the number of personnel increased proportionally as training was cut back. Between September 1942 and December 1943 approximately fifteen thousand recruits passed through the 2. ULD at Gotenhafen alone. Some then immediately joined U-boats, particularly technical personnel required to fill vacancies due to illness or reassignment. Most were held in readiness as a manpower reserve at a Submarine Training Detachment (*Unterseebootsausbildungsabteilung*, or UAA) situated close to each ULD. There they and some veteran submariners who had rotated home received additional training or refresher courses in cooking, antiaircraft gunnery, or propulsion systems, but they had to be ready for submarine assignment at a moment's notice.

Among the members of our sample who joined the U-boat force in 1941, training periods varied greatly. Two men found themselves aboard U-boats five months after entering the service; three others spent less than three months in U-boat training, one of whom passed through in less than seven weeks. Others, however, experienced more standard submarine training periods lasting five or six months. That such variations can be found in a single calendar year suggests that, as with U-boat commanding officers, personal evaluations of an individual's capabilities determined the amount of training he received.[48]

For line officers, practical training on submarines generally alternated with theoretical instruction on a weekly basis, averaging a total of seventeen to eighteen days at sea during an eight-week course. The classrooms themselves offered practical demonstrations and training on elaborate simulators. One, for example, consisted of a mock-up of a U-boat bridge with mounted binoculars through which the officers peered at model ships to determine distance and bow angle for a surfaced torpedo attack. More complex was the *F-Gerät* (*Fahrt-Gerät*, Patrol Apparatus) used at Neustadt: a full-sized, rotating conning tower suspended over a large tank of water on the surface of which miniature ships moved singly and in convoy formation. The trainees sat in the conning tower and peered through the lens of the periscope that extended down toward the water. The ship models, mounted on metal rods manipulated by a civilian operator, could simulate different speeds by moving them toward or away from the periscope. Lighting and water conditions could be altered to replicate day or night attacks on convoys in rough or calm seas. Trainees were expected to complete fifteen successful "submerged" attacks on convoys with this device, after which they could say they had "patrolled with Barkow"—the name of the civilian who operated the model ship controls.[49]

Executive officers' training also included the mastery of simpler devices. One of their onboard duties consisted of pumping out the contents of a U-boat toilet at a depth of twenty meters, a relatively simple task compared to that of the high-pressure heads used late in the war, but one which earned each his own humorous "water closet certificate" (*W.C. Schein*). Beyond their practical value such exercises helped to acquaint officers with the intimacies of submarine life and loosen the barriers between officers and men.[50]

Although wartime necessities shortened the ULD training sessions for line officers from three months to eight weeks, future commanders still averaged six months in overall training. After specialized instruction in torpedoes and communications, they concluded their internship with a four- to six-week "Commanders' Course" (*Kommandantenlehrgang*) with the 24th U-boat Flotilla in Memel (later supplemented by the 23d Flotilla in Danzig), the course also required for U-boat watch officers who bypassed the rest of the training program. Here a monthly average of eighteen to twenty future COs learned the fine points of surfaced and submerged torpedo marksmanship under the tutelage of such Atlantic veterans as Karl-Friedrich Merten, and received practical experience in coping with sonar. The *Schulboote* were themselves led by former watch officers, not yet old enough for combat command. The course culminated in several days of exhaustive torpedo firing drills, a demanding daily schedule that included attack exercises from 7:00 A.M. to 3:00 P.M., followed by reloading of torpedoes and night shooting practice from 8:00 P.M. until midnight or as late as 2:00 A.M., again followed by torpedo reloading for the next day. Each prospective commander typically fired thirty-five to fifty torpedoes over twenty to thirty separate attack exercises under differing simulations of combat conditions. These exercises continued without letup, the training personnel themselves receiving only every fourth weekend off on leave.[51]

With the completion of this final course the graduate advanced to command of his own submarine, relieving a front-line commander (especially true for an experienced watch officer), taking over a training U-boat, or—most commonly—receiving a new submarine. With the last, a second phase in training commenced.

Frontreif

The commander assigned to a new boat proceeded to one of the U-boat shipyards where his submarine entered the last stages of construction. There he would meet his L.I. and possibly the first watch officer and senior NCOs and begin the *Baubelehrung* (literally "construction acquaintance") process. This four- to six-week period allowed the boat's officers to examine the new vessel, discuss its capabilities and limitations with the shipyard's experts and workers (designated *Werftgrandis*), and perhaps make suggestions for minor alterations. No less important, *Baubelehrung* allowed the officers to become acquainted with one another. During the final weeks, the rest of the crew also assembled at the shipyard, usually a mix of experienced and newly promoted petty officers with raw enlisted men fresh from the ULD or UAA. In a formal commissioning ceremony, often attended by local dignitaries and World War I U-boat veterans, the boat and her crew then entered the service of the Kriegsmarine. Each crewman often received a small memento from the shipyard firm—a coffee mixer or photo album, perhaps—which he stored away with his dress uniform as ceremony yielded to sea trials and exhaustive training.

First stop was Kiel for two or more weeks of hull and engine trials under the U-boat Acceptance Command (UAK). These featured tests in the Kiel pressure dock at simulated depths of up to ninety meters (nearly three hundred feet) to detect the minor leaks that invariably occurred in new boats, as well as engine tests of the propulsion systems at various speeds, both surfaced and submerged. Diving and trimming trials probed the crew's—and especially the officers'—capabilities in handling a submerged boat as much as the submarine's seaworthiness. The operation of the torpedo tubes, deck guns, wireless, and antiaircraft artillery was also evaluated. Finally, the boat's hull was "wiped" (depermed, reducing the permanent magnetism of the metallic hull to render it less vulnerable to magnetic mines or torpedoes).

Next came silent-running trials, generally conducted off Rönne on Bornholm Island, where shore-based listeners measured the boat's underwater noises as it lay still on the bottom or glided beneath the waves. In tests conducted over a couple of days, audible evidence of the submarine's electrical motors, onboard machinery, trimming procedures, movement of gear, and passing of orders was collected and the submarine's optimum silent-running speed determined.

Thereafter the training course varied according to the period and circumstances. If the boat had a veteran captain, it might participate in just a few weeks of torpedo firing and tactical exercises before returning to Kiel to outfit for the first combat patrol. For inexperienced captains and crews, a more extensive and standard regimen had emerged by 1942, beginning with a visit to the *U-bootsausbildungsgruppe* (UAG, U-boat Training Group) at Danzig for eight days of additional engine tests and speed trials. Then the submarine proceeded to Gotenhafen for two or three days of torpedo tests, for the first time employing real torpedoes to proof the firing mechanisms. With the conclusion of these tests, the crew's easy training days ended as they headed toward Hela (now Hel) and the feared *Agru-Front*.

The *Technische Ausbildungsgruppe für Front-U-Boote* (literally Technical Training Group for Combat U-boats, abbreviated *Agru-Front*) grew from its establishment in the autumn of 1941 into an unorthodox but highly realistic means of testing submariners' skills and mettle. The original two-week course gradually lengthened to five weeks of grueling and dangerous tests of simulated emergency situations in deep waters, relieved periodically by additional classroom instruction. A training officer with extensive combat experience—on occasion even *Kaptlt.(I)* Gerd Suhren, the first U-boat chief engineer to win the *Ritterkreuz* and brother of ace commander Reinhard "Teddy" Suhren—would come aboard and stage difficulties during maneuvers. He might disable controls during a full-speed crash dive or compel the crew to repair simulated damages by flashlight while he ignited a smoke bomb. Such exercises tested the crew's ability to cope with emergencies without panicking and prepared them for the realities of Atlantic warfare, even to the extent of taking serious training risks: Suhren himself had to regain control of a plummeting *U-512* to avoid destruction during an April 1942 test. Other exercises dealt specifically with mastering depth-charge attacks and, beginning in 1944, the use of the snorkel.

Little wonder that these nerve-wracking tests earned the *Agru-Front* its nickname as "The Fifth Column" among German submariners. On completion of this course, however, the U-boat crew could proudly paint on its conning tower a red chevron beneath a diving U-boat encircled by oak leaves, the *Agru-Front* emblem that proclaimed the submarine *Frontreif:* ready for combat.[52]

In fact this marked the transition to the final training phases, the first of which involved torpedo target practice (*Schiessausbildung*) at Pillau. Requiring about ten days, these exercises tested the commander's marksmanship with practice torpedoes fired at variable ranges against target vessels. *Oblt.z.S.* Günter Leupold of *U-1059* allegedly set the standard in November 1943 with fifty-seven hits in fifty-eight shots, including more than forty amidships. Early in the war, four days' gunnery practice supplemented the torpedo firings, but as U-boats increasingly lost the opportunity to sink merchantmen by shellfire this exercise was replaced by antiaircraft gunnery drills.

Last came sophisticated training in group exercises and convoy attacks, usually conducted off Pillau or Danzig with the 20th U-boat Flotilla. These maneuvers lasted ten to fourteen days, during which the submarines remained at sea and simulated combat operations by day and night. Experienced instructors taught U-boat crews the appropriate procedures to maintain contact with a convoy while a wolf pack assembled; the optimum courses in pursuing, approaching, and attacking targets; escape maneuvers to elude attack by convoy escorts; and effective defense against aircraft attack. Refueling operations (using water instead of oil) were also practiced. Submarines that failed to impress during these exercises could be made to repeat them, although U-boat Command set limits on that practice: One training commander's orders prevented him from holding back more than two boats when he wanted to fail his entire group.[53]

In 1943 German authorities upgraded and restructured the final training phases to improve performance in convoy operations. After completing its *Agru-Front* term, a U-boat crew received ten days' preliminary tactical training in maneuvers and attacks. This was followed by attack and torpedo firing drills over fourteen to sixteen days, involving six to nine U-boats operating against convoys composed of three or four target ships with escorts. Finally came the group exercises, five tactical problems over a ten-day and -night period that featured an average of eight submarines attacking a simulated convoy of three to five merchantmen protected by four or five escorts and Luftwaffe-supplied air cover. Combat conditions were simulated as closely as possible, including a mass of radio signals and responses to be recorded, decrypted or encrypted, and entered into the radio logs by the *Funker*.[54]

With training complete, a U-boat then went into drydock for its final overhaul. The engines and equipment received their final tune-up and the boat was painted while the crew took their final home leave. The submarine then returned to Kiel, where the first trials had begun, to load live torpedoes, ammunition, provisions, fuel, and operational orders for the first patrol, sometimes straight to an operational area but usually a passage through the Skagerrak into the North Sea and around Great Britain to their future French base. In all, a U-boat spent about six months in trials and training, although delays or technical problems might push this back: *U-512* (*Kaptlt.* Wolfgang Schultze), for example, spent more than eight months from commissioning to departure on her first patrol due to engine problems and minor damage suffered in a collision.[55]

U-boat training proved hazardous, both for the novices and for those employed in the training units. To the major risks inherent to submarine handling by inexperienced crews, the Royal Air Force added an extensive minelaying campaign in the Gulf of Danzig in 1944–45. A total of thirty U-boats with 856 officers and men met their ends in the course of trials and training exercises in the Baltic: Six foundered in diving accidents, sixteen sank in collisions, and eight were lost after striking mines. Twenty of those represented new boats in training, the remainder *Schulboote* from the training establishment. More intriguing is the chronological progression of losses, from two U-boats in 1942 to eight in 1943 and eighteen from February 1944 through March 1945.[56]

IN VIEW OF THE steep price paid and the enormous demands for rapid expansion, the key question of U-boat training remains: How well did it work? The answer depends on the period considered.

From the beginning of the war until the autumn of 1941, von Friedeburg gambled on intensified but abbreviated training to increase combat strength as quickly as possible. At the beginning of the war, training periods were extremely short, with dire consequences: Of the eight new submarines commissioned into service between September 1939 and January 1940, six were lost by mid-April 1940. *U-55* (*Kaptlt.* Werner Heidel), commissioned 21 November 1939, departed on her first patrol less than two months later and was lost after thirteen days; the small Type IIC boat *U-63* (*Oblt.z.S.* Günther Lorentz), commissioned on 18 January 1940, underwent a mere twenty-nine days' training (!) before leaving on her first mission, which ended eight days later with her destruction.[57]

Thereafter individual U-boat workup and training periods became more standardized around three months, and for the remainder of 1940 newly commissioned submarines enjoyed longer life spans. Improvements in Allied defenses in the spring of 1941, however, again lowered the life expectancy of green captains and crews. First to pay was *U-70* (*Kaptlt.* Joachim Matz), dispatched to the front less than three months after commissioning and sunk on 7 March, only fifteen days after departing Kiel. Seven more U-boats that entered service between February and June 1941 were lost in action less than five months from their date of commissioning, one (*U-452, Kaptlt.* Jürgen March) sunk with all hands a mere eighty-eight days after she had raised her flag.[58] The most damaging single loss, however, involved *U-570*. Three months and one week after commissioning she departed on her first patrol from Trondheim; after four days the crew was seasick, the boat had gone off course and nearly run aground, and discipline had begun to break down. When damaged by attacking aircraft, *U-570* surrendered to the astonished British airmen and remained obligingly on the surface for several hours until trawlers arrived to take the captive in tow. Recommissioned as HMS *Graph,* the U-boat yielded invaluable technical intelligence to the Allies, a direct result of that particular's crew unpreparedness for combat duty.[59]

It has been alleged that *U-570*'s loss led to longer training periods,[60] and doubtless it contributed to that result. Yet in fact the extension of U-boat training to a minimum of four months was due to shortages in dockyard repair personnel and the lack of adequate torpedo-recovery craft among the training units, as von Friedeburg informed Dönitz on 24 October 1941.[61] These delays however, probably proved beneficial, as more resources were allocated to U-boat training even as the number of new boats and crews increased dramatically. In the last quarter of 1940, an average of only seven new boats per month entered service; one year later that figure had tripled.[62] Throughout 1942 the training system met these challenges and produced ever-growing numbers of qualified submarines and crews, leading to a peak combat strength of 105 in October with an annual loss rate that fell well below percentages for any previous year.[63] The training reflected a familiarity with Allied antisubmarine warfare measures and tactics then current and marks the high point of German submarine training. No one anticipated how quickly Allied technological and material superiority would alter the balance.

In early 1943, with Dönitz now commander-in-chief of the navy and committed to a new fleet construction program, von Friedeburg accordingly reorganized and expanded the training establishment. Basic training of submariners in the ULD and UAA organizations came under the direction of a newly established *Höhere Kommando der U-Bootausbildung* (HKU, or High Command for U-boat Training), directed by *Kapt.z.S.* Albrecht Schmidt, another World War I veteran; working up the new U-boat crews now became the responsibility of the *Führer der U-Boote—Ausbildung* (flag officer for U-boats, training) under *Kapt.z.S.* Viktor Schütze, one of the war's top aces. Many older Type VIIC submarines were retired from combat to training duty, replacing the outmoded Type II boats heretofore used and raising the overall total of *Schulboote* from sixty-two in November 1942 to ninety by December 1943.[64]

In addition to the expanded and improved tactical exercises already noted, these training authorities learned from the mistakes of 1941 and refused to rush new boats and their crews to the front. *U-1059*, the first of the Type VIIF class submarine, spent a total of nine months in trials and tests after her commissioning on 1 May 1943 before departing for combat duty. The steady deterioration of Germany's situation throughout 1944 did not translate into an overly hasty commitment of new submarines to action, as illustrated by the following examples that indicate the intervals between date of commissioning and completion of operational outfitting:

U-995: 16 September 1943–24 April 1944 (7 months)
U-1002: 30 November 1943–23 January 1945 (14 months)
U-1229: 13 January–12 July 1944 (6 months)
U-1169: 9 February 1944–7 February 1945 (12 months)
U-1273: 16 February 1944–10 February 1945 (12 months)
U-1051: 4 March–18 December 1944 (9.5 months)
U-1209: 13 April–13 November 1944 (7 months)
U-1172: 20 April–6 December 1944 (7.5 months)
U-327: 18 July 1944–19 January 1945 (6 months)[65]

The same patience could be seen in the training of new submarine models and their crews. To expedite the employment of Type XXI boats, for example, the navy originally planned for no more than a seventeen-week trials and training period, but technical problems gradually forced authorities to cancel such ambitious ideas and settle for an average of four to six months.[66] Patience, however, did not imply a lack of either intensity or risk, as indicated by the loss of eight U-boats in training during 1943 and eighteen more in the period February 1944–March 1945, representing 4.3 percent of the six hundred submarines commissioned during this time.

Yet all this effort, patience, and intensity proved wasted. The U-boat training establishment, like the Kriegsmarine in general, simply lacked the technological means to adequately prepare their men for combat in the Atlantic. The handful of German sub-chasers and other escort vessels that participated in tactical exercises lacked the weaponry, radar, HF/DF, and more advanced sonar equipment of the Allied warships they nominally represented and thus could never duplicate the disadvantages under which U-boats operated after the spring of 1943. The aces of 1940–42 who taught the classes and commanded the training flotillas could offer little advice on conditions they had never experienced. Prolonged training therefore counted little for a U-boat's ability to survive: Of the ten submarines listed above, eight were lost in combat during the final stages of the war.[67]

The very totality of loss that characterized submarine warfare moreover hindered the learning of any lessons. Without the capacity to interview survivors as to how their boats had been hunted down, naval authorities lacked essential information to improve the limited training methods available to them. *Freg.Kapt.* Karl-Friedrich Merten, who trained future commanders in torpedo marksmanship, noted:

The war diaries of front-line boats, from which we drew lessons for the training of young commanders, were often too old to portray the actual situation. Thus our teaching, so important for these youngsters and by no means limited just to torpedo firings, limped along weeks behind combat realities.[68]

Results became evident in operational performance. Errors in navigation and torpedo firings and questionable decisions by commanders (including highly decorated veterans) have been ultimately traced to the failure of training to impart mastery of submarines, especially to men assigned rather than carefully selected for the task.[69] Ace Teddy Suhren, who served with Erich Topp in a training flotilla from March 1943 to May 1944, especially criticized the ten days allotted to tactical exercises as far too few: "That was the discrepancy: We advised 'Better training, better training.' On the other side the command was: 'Boats to the front, boats to the front!' The results show how unprepared they were."[70]

Critics of the system award the final word on the overall training program to *Korv.Kapt.* Hans Müller, former head of the *Agru-Front,* in his post-war assessment: "The U-boat schools and training flotillas certainly did not earn their laurels. . . . What U-boat men did *not* know and could *not* do was horrifying."[71]

Yet it must be remembered that all the above represent recollections after the fact, with the implied conclusion that extended training would have improved performance and saved lives. The notion that new U-boat crews were technically incompetent is challenged by a postwar survey of 115 U-boat captains who operated during the 1943–45 period, 87 percent of whom found no complaints with the technical or psychological preparedness of their crews. Whether the remaining 13 percent marks a significant increase over the experiences of 1939–42 commanders is unknown, but the overall rating would appear to be satisfactory.[72]

Moreover the question of crew preparedness overlooks the more general vulnerability of German submarines to new Allied technology and weapons during the second half of the war. If the same training program resulted in loss rates of only 3.9 percent from January to June 1942 but 39.3 percent in July 1943, then the problem lay less in its curriculum than its capacity to keep pace with developments in the Battle of the Atlantic. Doubtless influenced by the heavy casualties to his forces in 1939–40, Dönitz himself believed that training could not substitute for combat experience, as noted in his war diary on 25 July 1942: "We cannot alter the fact that the difficult school of convoy attack cannot be completed at home, but ultimately only when in direct contact with the enemy."[73] A U-boat chief engineer echoed these sentiments in commenting on the importance of training:

All the training in the world, with few exceptions, didn't help the earlier COs to survive unless they, like Topp, were withdrawn from the front early in the game. . . . In 1944/45 the level of training of the COs was of relatively little importance. Well-trained as well as "young" newcomers fell by the wayside at equal rates, and survival was to a far greater extent a matter of simple luck: If you were found at all, there was hardly a chance for survival, no matter what your skills were.[74]

But if U-boat training was not ultimately related to combat success, its accomplishments were nevertheless real.

Conclusion

The end of training, of course, merely marked another stage in the learning process for German submariners as they absorbed the harsh lessons of combat. In sharp contrast to the British "Western Approaches Tactical Unit," no system existed for further operational training once the boats arrived at their front-line bases.[75] The experience of the first patrol—if they were fortunate enough to survive—proved a far more effective teacher than anything in the ULD curriculum. At the other end of the spectrum, senior U-boat commanders huddled over drinks in a Parisian hotel to exchange ideas on submerged evasive maneuvers during depth-charge attacks.[76] Throughout the 1942–44 period, a U-boat crew's interval in port grew increasingly preoccupied with mastering new forms of radar search gear, flak guns, and torpedoes. U-boat Command, as the only center to collect and evaluate intelligence data on Allied antisubmarine capabilities, issued a constant stream of radioed admonitions and advisories to commanders on tactics, countermeasures, and the use of equipment—all of which, of course, were duly intercepted, decrypted, and read by Allied intelligence.[77]

But the training received in a U-boat's workup period had served another, more basic purpose. It had converted sailors into submariners and molded men into crews. Through their training, German seamen not only learned how to operate submarines but came to understand how much they relied on one another for success and survival. The bonds of mutual dependence proved more durable in comradeship than nationality or ideology. They learned the names, faces, voices, and smells of the men with whom they would share laborious watches, drinks on leave, and—for most of them—death.

For officers, or at least the best officers, U-boat training underscored the unique leadership skills demanded by submarine warfare. They learned to lead rather than simply command, to blend modesty with decisiveness, and to pass on these values to their successors. American interrogators, for example, were astounded to learn in May 1943 that aboard *U-128* (*Oblt.z.S.* Hermann Steinert), the I.W.O. (*Kaptlt.* Siegfried Sterzing) outranked the captain yet accepted his subordination without question because of Steinert's greater submarine experience.[78]

Another example of the process could be seen with *Fähnrich* Horst Bredow, who reported in September 1943 to *U-288* (*Oblt.z.S.* Willy Meyer) as the boat ended her training exercises in the Baltic. The captain offered the young midshipman the choice to play at being an officer or to learn the truths of U-boat life. Bredow opted for the latter, whereupon Meyer placed him anonymously among the ordinary seamen for six weeks to share the conditions and menial tasks of the *Lords,* as well as absorb invaluable practical lessons in navigation and torpedo characteristics. His brief tour completed, Bredow then attended formal training courses as a U-boat watch officer and awaited his first combat assignment as *Lt.z.S.* To his surprise and delight, Meyer requested him to serve as *U-288's* new second watch officer. To Bredow, "This was the greatest and most meaningful distinction I ever received throughout my naval career."[79]

These relationships and attitudes, while not uniformly shared in the U-boat service, nevertheless reveal much of its character and appeal. The training program performed a fundamental role in creating German submariners, although it would prove to be outmatched as an insurance for survival. The question remains, did factors such as age and experience operate in such a way as to offer some protection for U-boat captains and crews?

A Children's Crusade?

Age and Experience of U-boat Crews

In his writings, Lothar-Günther Buchheim, author of the ac-claimed account of life aboard a World War II U-boat *Das Boot*, always emphasized the extreme youth of German submariners he considered sacrificed by Dönitz: "The majority of crews in the later war years consisted of little more than children," he wrote, pointing to the specific example of a sixteen-year-old aboard *U-96* (*Kaptlt*. Heinrich Lehmann-Willenbrock).[1] German naval historian Michael Salewski accepted this verdict for offi-cers as well, stating that during the 1943–45 years—when the U-boat service allegedly became an "empire of the dead"—the sub-marine commanders were only twenty-one or twenty-two years old and the watch officers only nineteen or twenty.[2] Former U-boat ace Erich Topp endorsed this view with the comment that "after 1943 . . . commanding officers were usually 23."[3]

Neither Buchheim nor Salewski cited sources for their data, but they might have relied upon a speech by Dönitz himself in December 1943, when he informed his subordinates that the Kriegsmarine's manpower needs necessitated a greater reliance on youth, citing examples of twenty-one-year-old submarine commanders and twenty-year-old chief engineers.[4] More spe-cific evidence might seem superfluous, as any American veteran who entered Germany remembers the teenagers and old men who filled out the Wehrmacht's ranks in 1945. The logic of ever-younger and inexperienced crews sustaining ever-growing losses appears inescapable. Logic and truth, however, are not always the same.

U-boat Commanders

In considering ages of U-boat captains, it is noteworthy to consider the comparative experience of the Royal Navy, as described by British submarine ace Rear Adm. Ben Bryant:

> During the war we had COs of 22. But I think, on an average, probably the best years of a submarine CO's life are 25 to 30—old enough to have experience, self confidence, and judgment; young enough not to think too much.[5]

Although German navy personnel records are not generally open for public research, biographical data for U-boat commanders are available in standard reference works.[6] Using this data, former *Kapt.z.S.* Rolf Güth and Jochen Brennecke refuted Salewski's conclusions with yearly summaries of the ages of German submarine commanders throughout the war (table 18). The data confirm that the German navy and Admiral Bryant shared the same views regarding optimum ages of commanders. Although younger captains do appear in the ranks, the average age remains remarkably constant throughout the peak years of 1942–44 and actually rises in 1945.

Güth and Brennecke found that during the years 1943–45, the number of twenty-one-year-olds who received U-boat commands amounted to exactly twenty-three. Even if one adds the sixty-two twenty-two-year-olds who also obtained submarine commands, the total still comprises less than

TABLE 18 **AGES OF U-BOAT COMMANDERS AT TIME OF FIRST COMMAND**

Ages	1939/40	1941	1942	1943	1944	1945
20–21	0	0	0	9	14	1
22–24	6	14	59	115	115	20
25–27	34	78	129	122	80	20
28–30	29	38	41	49	33	10
31–35	36	53	27	44	49	20
36+	10	20	15	19	15	6
Totals	115	203	271	368	304	77
Avg. Age	29.5	29.5	26.7	26.8	26.7	28.8
Pct. KIA	16.5%	32.5%	33.2%	29.0%	20.8%	4.0%

Source: Güth and Brennecke, "Hier irrte," 43–47.

Note: Ages for commanders' second and subsequent commands are omitted.

12 percent of the total number (549) of new submarine captains during this period and only 9 percent of the U-boats placed in commission. A further analysis of one hundred captains below the age of twenty-five who rose to command during the period December 1943–December 1944 revealed that ninety had previously served as U-boat watch officers, seventy-five of them for periods of eleven months or more. Thus, neither extreme youth nor inexperience was characteristic of U-boat commanders in the late war years.[7]

More intriguing are the casualty rates. Far from a death sentence, those who first commanded submarines in 1943 suffered proportionately lower losses than did their comrades from 1941 and 1942; the new commanders of 1944 suffered even less. If commanders' youth and inexperience do not account for the catastrophic losses of the U-boat service in 1943–45, what does? The high casualty rates of 1941–42 suggest that, whatever the final answer, experience did not help.

The impression that younger commanders suffered disproportionately in the second half of the war draws strength from the association of U-boat aces with age and experience. Jak Mallmann Showell described this handful of overachievers as follows:

Just under 800 [Allied] ships were sunk by 30 commanders. . . . Eight of these commanders joined the navy before 1927, 19 of the men joined in the period 1930–34 and three belonged to the 1935 class. Therefore almost 33 percent of all Allied shipping was sunk by 30 older men who joined the navy before Hitler reintroduced national conscription in 1935.[8]

This observation is confirmed by the individual data for the thirty-two commanders who sank at least 100,000 tons of Allied shipping, listed in table 19 ranked not by tonnage sunk but by age at date of first sinking. The implication that these aces opened the submarine campaign or achieved their totals early in the war is counterbalanced by the inclusion of the date of the first sinking. Although all entered the navy before 1936, many became U-boat commanders only during the vast expansion of 1940–42. To further establish the context of their accomplishment, the type of submarine used by each ace to accomplish most of his sinkings is also indicated.

In reviewing the information in the table, some patterns become clear. Only eight of the thirty-two were active in the war's initial months, joined by five more after the first full year of war. Ten did not accomplish their first sinking until at least August 1941, every one of whom—significantly—earned their ranking with Type IX submarines. This applies as well to twenty of the group as a whole, in addition to two others who split their

TABLE 19 AGES OF TOP 32 U-BOAT ACES AT TIME OF FIRST SINKING

Name	Age[a]	Date[b]	Type UB[c]
Jochen Mohr	25,3	9/41	IXB
Erich Topp	25,11	6/40	VIIC
Harald Gelhaus	26,1	8/41	IXC
Wolfgang Lüth	26,2	12/39	IXA, IXD2
Jürgen Oesten	26,3	1/40	IXB
Hans Jenisch	26,5	3/40	VIIA
Georg Lassen	26,10	3/42	IXC
Günther Krech	26,11	8/41	VIIC
Helmut Witte	27,1	5/42	IXC
Carl Emmermann	27,2	5/42	IXC
Otto Kretschmer	27,4	9/39	VIIB
Ernst Bauer	27,5	7/41	IXC
Joachim Schepke	27,6	9/39	VIIB
Reinhard Hardegen	27,9	12/40	IXB
H. Lehmann-Willenbrock	29,0	12/40	VIIC
Engelbert Endrass	29,3	6/40	VIIB, VIIC
Herbert Schultze	30,1	9/39	VIIB
Robert Gysae	30,2	3/41	VIIC, IXD2
Heinrich Bleichrodt	30,11	9/40	VIIB, IXB
Günther Hessler	31,4	10/40	IXB
Adolf Piening	31,5	2/42	VIIB
Günther Prien	31,8	9/39	VIIB
Heinrich Liebe	31,8	9/39	IXA
Hans-Ludwig Witt	32,6	6/42	IXC
Victor Oehrn	32,7	5/40	IXA
Klaus Scholtz	32,11	2/41	IXB
Karl-F. Merten	33,1	9/41	IXC
Victor Schütze	33,8	10/39	IXB
Werner Henke	34,4	9/42	IXC
Ernst Kals	36,4	12/41	IXC
Werner Hartmann	36,9	9/39	IXA, IXD2
Richard Zapp	37,2	6/41	IXC

Sources: Herzog, Deutsche U-Boote, 255, and "Ritterkreuz und U-Bootwaffe," 248–49, supplemented by data in Busch and Röll, U-Boot-Kommandanten and U-Bootbau, and Rohwer, Submarine Successes. Additional biographical data on these aces can be found in Dörr, Ritterkreuzträger, passim.

[a]Expressed in years, months (and rounded off to month to match date of sinking).

[b]Expressed in month/year.

[c]Denotes the principal type of U-boat during the ace's career; Gelhaus, Topp, Lüth, Kretschmer, Schepke, and Hardegen accomplished their first sinkings with Type II submarines, Schütze his first with a Type IA.

time between Types VII and IX boats. Exactly half of the group did not sink their first vessel until they were thirty or older, most of whom rode the bridge of a Type IX to fame.

The association of this class of U-boat with high-ranking aces is not co-incidental. As noted in chapter 3, these submarines, capable of operating at great distances for extended periods, proved especially effective in stalking unescorted, independently routed single ships in such distant operational areas as the Caribbean, West African, and southern African waters. If Type VII submarines demanded the advantages of youth in their commanders—energy, aggressiveness, quick reactions, optimism—for convoy battles, Type IX boats required the virtues of maturity exemplified by veteran officers—patience, endurance, insight, coolness under pressure, and discretion—while operating in remote areas on patrols that averaged more than a hundred days. Of the commanders for the forty new IXC submarines commissioned into service during 1941, for example, twenty-seven were thirty-one years old or older. Regardless of precise age, however, the captains of these 1941 Type IXs took full advantage of the vulnerable shipping in remote, weakly defended areas: Of the forty, eighteen earned the Knight's Cross with their sinkings and eight ended among the top thirty aces, despite their relatively late entry into the campaign.[9]

Thus the age of a commander had less connection with success than the good fortune to command a Type IX submarine before Allied defenses in distant operational areas improved. That this U-boat was more commonly captained by an older man, however, does not imply that age alone brought a commander greater chances of success or survival, as shall be seen.

It is in the measurement of casualties versus survival that the relationship of age and performance might be more firmly determined. Our sample of German navy officers offers little assistance in this analysis, as it is too small in overall numbers and pertains only to those who survived. Of 167 officers surveyed, 97 continued to hold posts with the submarine fleet at war's end, 46 of them aboard advanced Type XXI or XXIII U-boats. Included among these were twenty *Seeoffiziere* still serving as U-boat watch officers: The average span of their operational submarine service accumulated by that date amounted to twenty months. No haste in promoting officers to command is evident here.

To determine if specific experience levels or other characteristics can be correlated to losses requires a review of all U-boat commanding officers' backgrounds. Using the data compiled by the U-Boot-Archiv (which differ slightly from those used by Güth and Brennecke), we may isolate and analyze some of the key background characteristics of 1,386 German U-boat commanders and their commands during World War II.[10]

Of these 1,386, some 530 were killed in action and 104 captured, for a casualty total of 634 (46 percent). Twenty-eight others died in accidents or of other causes; seventeen lost their commands in accidents or other causes but survived and were recovered by German forces. Neither of the latter categories is included in our considerations of casualties. Of the remainder, 369 served as U-boat commanders during the war but no longer commanded operational submarines at war's end, a status limited to 338 captains on 8 May 1945—numbers that provide another indication that submarine officers were not in short supply.

The first factor to examine is Admiral Dönitz's selection of his commanders, a highly subjective process that ultimately relied on an assessment of an individual's capabilities. "The ability of the commander will always be the decisive factor," wrote Dönitz,[11] and in recognition of this he held to no fixed formula by which an officer automatically qualified for command. Based on observation, experience, and a battery of tests, senior U-boat officers evaluated a candidate's character and abilities to determine his fitness for the unique task of submarine captain. As a result, U-boat commanders displayed a wide range of prior submarine service and personal qualifications. Can any of these varied characteristics be isolated to identify an area of vulnerability?

For example, 873 commanders had previously served as U-boat watch officers. The average junior experience amounted to just under a year (11.3 months), but with considerable variations. The largest numbers are clustered around six to eight months and fourteen to eighteen months, but many others spent only one month in this capacity. In many cases, the I.W.O. inherited command of a U-boat when his commander departed for other duties. The total casualties for the 873 officers numbered 403 (46 percent)—exactly the same as the overall loss rate. As with the casualties among U-boat COs from 1941–42 noted in table 18, previous experience apparently counted for little if anything. Those with fourteen months or less watch officer's experience suffered higher losses (52 percent) than those with fifteen months or more (32 percent), but this may merely confirm that the latter required (and received) additional maturation before meriting submarine command.

By contrast, 412 commanders had no prior experience as watch officers. Their casualties numbered 189—again, 46 percent, exactly the same rate as for former watch officers. Seventy (including some with watch officer experience) enjoyed the advantage of a "confirmation" cruise as a commander-in-training aboard a combat submarine with a veteran skipper; casualties among this group after attaining their own commands numbered thirty-one, or a nearly identical 44 percent. (Excluded here are at least twenty-seven other *Kommandantenschüler*, who were killed or captured aboard front-line U-boats while still in their training stage.) Still others had no previous submarine experience whatsoever before being entrusted with commands. Most successful of these was *Kapt.z.S.* Kurt Dobratz, who came directly from the Luftwaffe and assumed command of *U-1232* in March 1944 with only the U-boat commander's course behind him, yet at the age of forty he earned the Knight's Cross of the Iron Cross by sinking three ships and damaging two in January 1945.[12]

A separate question concerns U-boat commander ineffectiveness. The unique pressures of submarine command exacted a demanding daily toll in stamina and mental agility, rendered increasingly acute by steady increases in Allied antisubmarine effectiveness. Some commanders never performed according to expectations; others did well but then experienced "burnout" from too many decisions or too much strain. Despite officer shortages, Dönitz had to begin relieving prewar commanders for "health reasons" one month after the commencement of hostilities.[13] The painful lessons he learned in the spring of 1941 through shortcuts in CO training have already been noted; some questionable decisions, bad luck, and hostile subordinates could also end a commander's career.[14]

But even proven veterans might eventually crack under the pressure: *Korv.Kapt.* Heinrich ("Ajax") Bleichrodt, winner of the Oak Leaves to the Knight's Cross aboard *U-109*, had to abort a mission in the Caribbean in January 1943, and *U-505's Kaptlt.* Peter Zschech, with a year's command experience and a previous year as a watch officer behind him, committed suicide during a depth-charge attack in October 1943.[15] Other notable incidents included the relief and demotion to the ranks of *U-3's Kaptlt.* Helmut Franzke in November 1940 and the relief, court-martial, and execution of *Kaptlt.* Heinz Hirsacker, CO of *U-572* from May 1941 to December 1942, for cowardice in the face of the enemy.[16] Still other psychological breakdowns occurred without official documentation, as recalled by the chief engineer of one of the U-boats that surrendered at war's end, with a potential mutiny averted only by Germany's capitulation.[17]

Still, these examples hardly constitute evidence of a general failure in the commander selection process developed by Dönitz and von Friedeburg. The U.S. Navy in the Pacific, waging a successful undersea campaign with many fewer casualties, relied on more conventional practices in personnel assignments but still relieved 30 percent of its submarine commanders for nonproductivity in 1942 and 14 percent in each of the succeeding two years.[18] If German commanders with different backgrounds experienced the same losses and successes, and did not suffer a general psychological breakdown, then the selection process worked. An explanation for the unacceptably high losses lies elsewhere.

In addition to age and the selection process, length of command service can be reviewed to attempt to correlate casualties with relative experience. Using the date of a CO's assumption of command as a base, the amount of operational experience until death or capture is given in table 20. At first glance these data confirm the vulnerability of commanders with less than a year's experience, especially as the initial four to six months usually involved only training in the Baltic. Yet this figure also includes captains who had already seen a moderate amount of action. The high losses for those with more than a year's sea duty—over 40 percent of the total—extends this further and indicates a critical reality for German submariners: Allied combat effectiveness improved both dramatically and quickly, rendering useless those lessons learned in earlier, less hazardous times.

Here Dönitz proved ill-served by his policy of promoting his aces from U-boat bridges to command of front-line flotillas, training units, and staff positions. In 1941 this offered an ideal solution to limit commander burnout, preserve and transmit these veterans' knowledge and experience to new COs, and furnish the small BdU staff with needed perspective and advice—indeed, no other solution made sense at the time. But by 1943 the new technology, greater resources, and revised tactics of the Allies changed the ground rules by which the veterans had fought, rendering their experience virtually meaningless.

Dönitz and his small command staff never maintained adequate pace with the rapid developments in Allied weapons and technology. Unsupported by an independent body of scientific advisers, compelled to rely upon the Kriegsmarine's overmatched technical departments, BdU operated for much of the war in a technological vacuum. Not until June 1942 did the navy's Communications Department conclude that Allied aircraft

TABLE 20 **LOSSES BY COMMAND EXPERIENCE**

Months of Experience	Number	Percentage
6 or fewer	71	11
6–12	268	42
13–20	169	27
21–30	72	11
31+	16	3

Note: Omitted from the above are 38 casualties (6 percent) among prewar and September 1939 commanders. Average U-boat command experience among all COs = 13.5 months.

were using radar to locate surfaced U-boats. In September of that year the U-boats' own primitive radar detectors revealed that Allied warships were radar-equipped, a possibility rejected in an official inquiry only a few months earlier. And the Allies' use of shipborne high-frequency direction-finding (HF/DF) radio equipment remained unknown until June 1944.[19] U-boat training exercises could never catch up with such tardy recognition of Allied technical capabilities. The otherwise sound practice of promoting U-boat veterans to flotilla commands and key staff and training positions (applicable to twenty of the thirty top aces noted earlier)[20] to share their experiences with younger subordinates accomplished little when Allied warships employed improved weapons and tactics never encountered by the aces.

The facility with which Allied improvements in tactics and technology overtook the Germans' learning curve is demonstrated in the collective fate of the largest "class" of U-boat commanders, the 448 men who took command of their vessels in 1941. The training corners cut during that year of the submarine fleet's tremendous expansion did not exact an excessive price, with only twenty-four casualties (about 5 percent) suffered during the first six months of operational experience. But with seven to twenty months' experience, 1941 commanders lost 184 of their comrades to death or capture, a severe 41 percent loss rate that mostly occurred from autumn 1942 to summer 1943. Among the forty Type IXC commanders noted earlier, good fortune proved fleeting—they suffered an even higher casualty rate, losing twenty-one of their number to death or capture. This was the true "empire of the dead."[21]

Yet the high mortality in the submarine service was not simply a product of Allied supremacy in weaponry and numbers of escorts. The seventy U-boat captains trained in the prewar period constituted Dönitz's original elite, as proven by their contribution of nineteen of the top thirty-five submarine aces produced by Germany during the war. But they paid a steep price, as thirty-eight of their number (54 percent) became casualties before the remainder retired to flotilla commands, training duties, or staff posts. During the war's first nine months, twenty-four U-boats were destroyed of the fifty-seven on hand when hostilities commenced. Their counterparts in the Royal Navy suffered equally, losing twenty-six of fifty-two submarines up to December 1940. Occurring in an era of relatively primitive antisubmarine weapons and forces, these losses underscore the inherent dangers and potential risks of submarine warfare even under favorable conditions.[22]

Two smaller categories of specialized officers also deserve mention. Reserve naval officers frequently commanded submarines for specific tasks or periods, such as U-boats retired from active duty to home waters; in these capacities they still suffered substantial casualties (65 of 179, 36 percent). The lowest loss rate was turned in by former *Obersteuermänner* promoted from the ranks: Of thirty-five who received submarine commands, only nine became casualties (26 percent). Most of these commands involved training rather than front-line boats, but their selection for advancement appears more than confirmed by their unique ability to defy the odds.

For all the other categories of U-boat commanders, however, Allied firepower and numbers scythed through their ranks with an indiscriminate lethality. The ages, previous experiences, and characteristics of U-boat commanders mattered little against rapid and effective improvements in Allied weaponry, equipment, and tactics, redoubled in their effect by more numerous escorts and aircraft. The German navy's inability to keep pace with these developments, reflective of the materiel and technological shortcomings of the entire German war effort, doomed U-boat crews more effectively than any limitations in CO personnel policies.

But the accusation remains that U-boat crews' relative youth played a factor in the disaster, that the campaign represented a children's crusade against hopeless odds. For this accusation to stand requires an examination of German submariners' ages.

U-boat Crewmen: The Evolution of Personnel Policy

The numbers of NCOs and enlisted men who manned Germany's U-boats preclude a similar analysis of their personal characteristics and submarine experience. Nevertheless our sample of 937 crewmen provides some general data regarding year of service entry and age, reflected in tables 21 and 22.

Most revealing is the relationship of prewar versus wartime recruits. Our sample indicates that 16 percent of U-boat crewmen enlisted prior to January 1939, men who planned a career in the navy before the war became a factor. That proportion remains approximately consistent throughout the technical careers, but it is noteworthy that this small group contributed 78 percent of all navigator NCOs and only 8 percent of ordinary seamen. Thus the *Steuermannslaufbahn* remained almost exclusively the preserve of prewar enlistees, while the most common career-track of ordinary seamen consisted overwhelmingly of wartime recruits. The *Maschinisten, Funker,* and *Mechaniker* career-tracks all reveal an interesting balance of recruitment throughout the prewar and war years, indicating the navy's recognition of its dependence on skilled technical personnel regardless of the international situation.

TABLE 21 **YEAR OF ENTRY INTO NAVY FOR SAMPLE MEMBERS (NCOs/ENLISTED MEN)**

	Seamen	Navig.	Engine	Mech.	Radio	Medic	Total Sample
			Career-Track				
Before 1936	2	16	27	5	4	0	54
1936–37	4	12	12	5	10	1	44
1938	12	8	19	4	9	1	53
1939	16	5	33	8	12	1	75
1940	41	5	48	13	26	4	137
1941	67	0	124	29	33	4	257
1942	59	0	95	33	34	0	221
1943	25	0	33	20	11	0	89
1944	2	0	2	0	0	0	4

Note: No data provided by three survey respondents.

TABLE 22 **AGES AT ENTRY INTO NAVY AND INTO U-BOAT SERVICE FOR SAMPLE MEMBERS (NCOs/ENLISTED MEN)**

Age	Into Navy	Into U-boats
16 or younger	10	1
17	281	40
18	350	268
19	202	240
20	69	143
21	14	83
22 or older	7	156

Note: No data provided for entry into navy by four survey respondents; no data provided for entry into U-boats by six survey respondents.

The age data support the image of a youthful submarine service but confirm that some interval of time separated a recruit's joining the Kriegsmarine and subsequent service aboard a submarine. That 41 percent of the total joined the U-boat service at age twenty or later also contradicts the view of an excessive reliance on teenagers.

More intriguing is the chronological breakdown of service entry, with nearly a quarter of our sample enlisting by the end of 1939 and a majority (51 percent) joining up during the critical years 1941–42; the years 1943–44, by contrast, constitute only 10 percent of the total. Such variations indicate that the study of crewmen's characteristics at different periods of the war might illuminate the evolution and role of U-boat personnel policy in the campaign.

His hand-picked crews that began the war represented the best blend of age and training that Dönitz could accomplish in the four years after his appointment as commander, submarines. During that period the number of *U-Boot-Fahrer* had grown from approximately 850 to 3,000.[23] A majority of the commanding officers, as we have seen, were between the ages of twenty-seven and thirty-one. Erich Topp, then a watch officer aboard *U-46*, later recalled the average age of U-boat sailors during this period as twenty-three or twenty-four.[24] An emphasis on the mid- to late twenties is also evident for the 129 petty officers and enlisted men recovered as U-boat prisoners by British forces during the war's first four months:[25]

Age twenty or younger: 9 (7 percent)
Ages twenty-one through twenty-five: 94 (73 percent)
Ages twenty-six through twenty-nine: 14 (11 percent)
Age thirty or older: 12 (9 percent)

Among the 937 members of our sample, 144 had joined the navy before war's outbreak, but only forty-eight of these were serving aboard submarines in September 1939. Significantly, their average age at that point was 23.0 years; their ninety-six comrades who had not yet joined the U-boat force were distinctly younger, with an average age of 21.6. There can be little doubt that in September 1939 Dönitz preferred his crewmen to possess the maturity of their mid-twenties rather than the enthusiasm of their late teens. One probable reason for this, of course, may have been the establishment of a mature nucleus of future petty officers to allow large-scale expansion in the event of war.

But when that conflict came, the best training and optimum ages did not prevent Dönitz's crews from suffering severe losses during the war's first year. For the period that historians continue to describe as the "grey wolves' first happy time," U-boat personnel casualties in killed and missing during the initial twelve months totaled nearly twelve hundred, equivalent to an astonishing 40 percent of the original force.[26]

The scale of these early losses is significant for two future developments. First they provide some perspective of Dönitz's acceptance of devastating casualties in 1943–44: That he had seen his force absorb similar punishment in 1939–40 doubtless influenced his decision to maintain the campaign. Of more immediate importance, however, the experience and training lost with these men so early in the war contributed to the stunted expansion of the U-boat fleet. From fifty-seven U-boats in September 1939, the total number of submarines in service did not amount to one hundred until February 1941, and an average strength of thirty U-boats at sea was not attained until June 1941. Dönitz himself would later attribute this to misplaced priorities in the allocation of resources,[27] but in truth BdU lacked both the manpower—especially in qualified noncommissioned officers—to provide crews for the expanded U-boat force he envisaged, and the organizational infrastructure necessary to train them.

The new crisis compelled improvisation, the dilution of standards, and a return to old measures. Dönitz's struggles to expand his submarine training establishment have already been noted. In November 1939 he reaffirmed the importance of "quality over quantity" in preparing his crews for war but abandoned the principle that every future crewman would actually receive training aboard a submarine. That same month, the German navy Fleet Command reinstituted the First World War practice of withdrawing 15 percent of each U-boat crew after the completion of two war patrols for the nucleus of a new crew.[28]

As the specter of a protracted naval conflict assumed reality, German naval authorities pondered with deep concern the vexing questions of manpower requirements and available resources. The conquests of Denmark, Norway, the Low Countries, and France made the navy responsible for the security of vast stretches of coastline; Italian naval defeats compelled the detachment of scant resources to the Mediterranean; and the prosecution of a naval conflict with Great Britain involved an oceanic struggle with attendant demands for production and logistical support. From an all-volunteer, highly selective force that numbered seventy-eight thousand at war's outbreak, the Kriegsmarine's growth to 370,000 by June 1941 threatened to overload its ability to both adequately train its recruits and provide effective leadership in officers and NCOs. The ratio of officers to enlisted men in August 1939, for example, was 1:16; by March 1941, despite a 250 percent increase in the size of the officer corps, the ratio had grown to 1:28. Yet still more men were needed to meet the multiple demands.[29]

These requirements imposed severe limitations on Dönitz's options. During the autumn of 1940 the Naval High Command concluded that Dönitz's planned expansion of the submarine force could only be done by stripping the surface fleet of junior officers and forcing delays in the commissioning of the battleship *Tirpitz* and recommissioning of the light cruiser *Leipzig*, options firmly rejected by Navy Commander-in-Chief Raeder.[30] One year later the need to replace the German army's heavy casualties in the Russian campaign claimed priority in the allocation of manpower and reduced the Kriegsmarine's previous allotment of 10 percent of new recruits into the armed forces to a mere 4.4 percent.[31]

For replacements and expansion, the U-boat fleet inevitably turned to youth and relative inexperience. The change could be seen among the survivors recovered as prisoners-of-war by the British in 1940, of whom 25 percent were twenty years old or younger, a category that rose to more than 32 percent in 1941.[32] The average age of 269 crewmen (excluding officers) who died aboard eight submarines in 1941 was only 22.7.[33] Buchheim's reference to a sixteen-year-old he knew aboard *U-96*, it should be noted, most probably occurred during the artist's detail aboard that submarine from October to December 1941.[34]

Significantly, neither the increased reliance on youth nor the corners cut in training caused undue losses as the U-boat fleet multiplied. From December 1940 through November 1941, a total of 185 U-boats entered active service against only twenty-five lost. During the first half of 1942, the number of front-line U-boats increased from 91 in January to 138 in July, while only twenty-one submarines fell victim to Allied forces—a loss rate of less than 4 percent of the submarines at sea each month. Dönitz moreover did not hesitate to commit his new boats and crews to convoy battles: "Very often three-quarters of the U-boats attacking a convoy were commanded by young officers who, together with their crews, were in action for the first time."[35]

The enlarged submarine force that fought the crucial battles of 1942–44 in the Atlantic retained a youthful character, but included more (and older) reservists. *Korv.Kapt.* Wolfgang Lüth later characterized the ages of the crews he commanded during this period as twenty to twenty-two for enlisted men and twenty-three to twenty-five for petty officers.[36] A detailed study of the personal characteristics of 619 German U-boat crewmen (again excluding officers) captured by American forces from May 1942 to August 1944 confirms Lüth's observation. At the time of their capture nearly half (307) belonged to the 20–22 age group and 19 percent to ages 23–25, with the remainder divided between ages 18–19 (18 percent) and age 26 or older (14 percent). Of particular significance is the continuation of this pattern among prisoners recovered in the summer of 1944, when one might expect to find evidence of younger crewmen. Instead, the proportion of crewmen less than twenty years old declines to 7 percent and those twenty-six or older rises to 19 percent.[37]

Had Dönitz's 1943 original plans worked out, German eighteen- and nineteen-year-olds might well have figured more prominently among submarine crews. With his appointment as navy commander-in-chief on 30

January 1943, Dönitz at last enjoyed both the authority within the service and the influence with Hitler to implement his own agenda. Having learned in November 1942 that new models of submarines with high underwater speeds and endurances would not be ready for mass production until late 1943,[38] he resolved to build as large a fleet of existing submersible types as possible. As noted in chapter 4, Dönitz had begun planning for a massive expansion of the U-boat fleet in April 1943, implicitly accepting a war of attrition in the Atlantic until the new generation of submarines was ready. It was a gamble whose costs would soon become evident.

In May 1943 Allied forces inflicted their heaviest losses of the war—forty-one submarines destroyed, more than were sunk during the first nineteen months of the war. Yet this catastrophe did not alter but merely interrupted Dönitz's plans. In conferences with Hitler in late May and June he won approval for an increase in production to forty U-boats per month and additional light surface forces. The personnel required for this program through September 1944 numbered nearly 440,000, of whom 62,000 would man the 634 U-boats scheduled for production; Dönitz acknowledged that new U-boat officers would have to be transferred from the army and the Luftwaffe. Such fantastic numbers exceeded existing manpower allocations by over 300 percent and prompted an astounded Hitler to plead, "I don't have these forces." The Kriegsmarine's own administrative offices calculated that fulfilling these personnel needs would mean manning future U-boat crews with "45-year-old reservists, Alsatians, ethnic Germans from foreign states, and prisoners-of-war."[39]

Nevertheless Dönitz continued to push his program through November 1943, when the shortfalls in necessary manpower—especially for *Techniker*—could no longer be evaded. The Armed Forces High Command (*Oberkommando der Wehrmacht,* OKW) tried to accommodate him, even to the extent of transferring several thousand men from the army, but the desired numbers could never be met. As Field Marshal Wilhelm Keitel, chief of the OKW, responded, "These requirements . . . will probably not be filled, in particular the demands for technical personnel of recent annual drafts, who simply don't exist."[40]

In the end the program never approached fulfillment, with only a fraction of the requested personnel ultimately allocated. The character of the U-boat crews, with some individual exceptions, remained basically unchanged and Dönitz never had to confront the dire predictions for the future. By August 1943 Dönitz conceded the obsolescence of the Type VII and IX submarines, which had borne the brunt of the Atlantic battles for four years, and reorganized the construction program—still optimistically set at forty boats per month—around the new Type XXI and XIII models. The teething problems of such advanced designs, however, inevitably delayed large-scale construction until late 1944 and beyond.[41]

Until then, the Atlantic war would continue to be fought with outmoded submarines designed in the interwar period. Improved torpedoes, expanded flak armament, and constantly upgraded radar search receivers served as stopgaps in the losing race with Allied technology. In anticipation of Dönitz's plans for a greatly enlarged U-boat fleet, however, the crews experienced accelerated turnover in personnel as veterans moved on to qualifying training, promotions, and new assignments. In their places came raw recruits. The experience of *U-172* during its layover in Lorient in November 1943 provides one example:

> Eighteen men of the old crew were gone, including the captain, chief engineer, II.W.O., Bosun, torpedo mechanic's mate, and five petty officers. Replacing them were 28 new officers and men, the latter with an average age of 20, some of whom had neither been through U-boat School nor had ever gone to sea. . . . With the transfer of our old hands we were no longer the old battleworthy crew. A catastrophe for our boat. . . .

U-172, under its new twenty-two-year-old commander *Oblt.z.S.* Hermann Hoffmann, was lost on its next patrol.[42]

The fate of this U-boat offers support to the image of inexperienced, too-young crews committed to action late in the war against overwhelming odds. Similarly BdU's characterization of *U-377* (*Oblt.z.S.* Gerhard Kluth) as an "experienced and proven boat" when it was lost—probably to its own acoustic torpedo—in January 1944 belied the fact that its commander was only on his second patrol and the chief engineer, radioman, diesel machinist, and one torpedo mechanic all lacked experience.[43] As will be seen in the following chapter, such experiences during this period contributed to a crisis in morale in the U-boat service. Yet this pattern of crew turnover represents a line of continuity in personnel policy stretching back to the hasty expansion of the submarine fleet in 1940–42. In those early days, Dönitz's gamble with his crews' lives to build up his force succeeded; in 1943–44, taking the same risk to replace losses while awaiting new submarines failed.

At tremendous cost, the U-boats withdrew from the convoy battles in the Atlantic, then yielded the Channel to Allied invasion forces bound for Normandy. Forced to abandon their French bases and eventually German home waters as well, the U-boats transferred to Norwegian ports, constantly savaged by omnipresent Allied aircraft. Active U-boat operations returned to their initial hunting grounds, English coastal waters. That the

Kriegsmarine had lost the Battle of the Atlantic by May 1943 is now universally recognized; often overlooked are the enormous losses incurred after that decision had been reached. Many more U-boats were lost during the last twenty-three months of the war (396) than were sunk from September 1939 through May 1943 (234); as noted in chapter 4, more than half of all U-boat personnel losses occurred after October 1943.[44]

The significance of these losses can be seen in just a four-month period in 1944. After February, Dönitz attempted to conserve strength by dropping convoy attacks altogether as too costly, yet his submarines proved unable even to elude Allied forces. In April and May, in return for sinking a total of only thirteen merchant ships, the U-boat arm lost as many or more men killed in action in each month (790 and 757, respectively) as it had for the entire first year of the war (764). Losses rose dramatically the next month in the aftermath of the Normandy invasion, with over twelve hundred permanent casualties (killed and captured) in return for a meager sixteen sinkings. In July another 713 *U-Boot-Fahrer* died as the U-boats began evacuating the French ports that had been home for four years. Altogether Dönitz lost 3,222 men killed and 785 captured in these four months—the dead alone nearly equaled the total number of U.S. submariners lost throughout World War II (3,506).[45]

In view of these losses, what then was the character of the U-boat crews at the very end of the war? In sharp contrast to the youths and old men thrown into combat by the army in the final days, the U-boat service's personnel had not noticeably changed from that of two years earlier. Compiled birth dates for 611 U-boat NCOs and enlisted men who were killed, captured, or surrendered during the last week of the war in Europe in May 1945 reveal an age structure consistent with that of their 1942–44 counterparts, but with less reliance on teenagers; even more interesting is the comparison with ages of U.S. Navy enlisted personnel in 1945 (table 23).

An excessive reliance on enlisted men less than twenty years old in 1945 is thus *less* characteristic of the U-boat fleet than of the United States Navy in general. If the argument is made that many young American sailors served in logistical rather than combat functions, the equivalent data for enlisted men of the U.S. Marine Corps in 1945—21.1 percent of whom had not yet attained their twentieth birthday—allow no such room for doubt.[46]

The U-boat crews of 1945 probably retained this age structure because of a side-benefit of the expanded submarine program Dönitz secured in June 1943. Although the original construction and manpower goals never approached fruition, the U-boat training infrastructure, reorganized in January 1943 under the overall command of Admiral von Friedeburg, had ex-

TABLE 23 **AGES OF U-BOAT CREWS, 1942–44 AND 1945, AND U.S. NAVY, 1945**

| Ages | U-boat Crews | | U.S. Navy |
	1942–44	1945	1945
18–19	17.8%	11.0%	24.9%
20–24	65.2	73.2	41.0
25–29	13.8	14.0	17.3
30+	3.2	1.8	16.8

Note: Data for the 1942–44 U-boat crewmen from Mulligan, "German U-boat Crews," 270–71; the 611 crewmen for May 1945 represent casualties and POWs recovered for fifteen U-boats sunk or surrendered/interned at war's end, from the same sources as used by Mulligan for 1942–44; and U.S. Navy data from chief of the Bureau of Medicine and Surgery, Navy Department, *Annual Report of the Surgeon General, U.S. Navy, to the Secretary of the Navy Concerning Statistics of Diseases and Injuries in the U.S. Navy for Calendar Year 1945*, 16. The German data for 1945 are biased *toward* a younger profile, as they omit sixteen married petty officers (certainly over 20) put ashore by *U-977* in Norway before the submarine's subsequent voyage to internment in Argentina (see Schaeffer, *U-boat 977*, 147–50).

panded its resources and streamlined its procedures to produce as many submariners as possible. Although, as we have seen, the quality of training aroused concern, the mere output of 616 new U-boat crews in 1943–45 marked an amazing accomplishment in the light of previous experience. It is perhaps problematical whether this program would have met the requirements of the submarine fleet originally planned, but it served well enough the needs of a force totaling approximately four hundred U-boats on 1 May 1945. With most of the older U-boats out of service and the newer models just coming off the quays, there were more qualified U-boat sailors than there were submarines to man.

These included large numbers of individual machinists, radiomen, and other technical specialists who were also trained and kept available for future duty. But in contrast to the great expansion of personnel in 1940–42, when recruits passed through an abbreviated training course and then joined the "flotilla reserves" in France for individual assignment, their counterparts in 1944–45 remained together at U-boat training facilities as a personnel pool, drilling and exercising, until their services were needed. In the spring of 1945, for example, nearly three hundred fully trained petty officers with the *1. Unterseebootsausbildungsabteilung* at Plön engaged in sports and sailing while awaiting assignment, and surplus commanders and watch officers were reassigned to other duties.[47]

Thus, the German U-boat service did not end the war in the desperate manpower and training situation that characterized the rest of the 1945 Wehrmacht. To the extent that the U-boat campaign constituted a "children's crusade," that description most applies to the great expansion of the submarine fleet in 1940–42, when losses remained low. Many Allied successes and German shortcomings determined the outcome of the Battle of the Atlantic; the ages and relative experience of Germany's U-boat crews did not figure in the decision.

But sheep need not be lambs to be slaughtered. Periods of heavy casualties formed part of the rhythm of the Atlantic campaign from 1939 through 1943, and in that context Dönitz's read of May 1943 as a setback rather than a irreversible catastrophe can be understood. Similarly, the sacrifice of lives to buy time sometimes represents a military necessity, and the U-boats certainly tied down a disproportionate amount of Allied forces in 1944–45.[48] But whether that mission justified the massive bloodletting of a technologically and tactically outmatched U-boat force after the summer of 1943 must weigh heavily in the final assessment of Dönitz.

9   More One Cannot Be

The Morale of an Involuntary Elite

More than fifty years after the U-boat war the most compelling question remains: How could German submariners retain their morale and fighting spirit in the face of such horrific casualties? No less an implacable foe than Winston Churchill paid tribute to "the persistence of Germany's effort and the fortitude of the U-boat service" that fought to the last day.[1] Yet little has been done to evaluate the basis for this unmatched morale beyond studying the attributes of Dönitz's leadership and the German navy's own development of "Innere Führung" ("leadership from within").[2] On the other hand, some historians argue that the victory of Allied convoy escorts alone constitutes proof that they had "outlasted the will-power of the U-boat crews," or that the root cause of Dönitz's defeat in May 1943 "lay with the U-boat crews. . . . They had lost heart."[3] Perhaps an understanding of the motivation of U-boat crewmen simply lies beyond the grasp of outsiders, as suggested by one German submariner shortly before his death in the war's early days: "We were just doing our duty; but you do not understand what that means, because you simply do not know."[4]

This may be true, for the morale of the U-boat service—as

with any particular combat force at a specific moment in time—involved an intricate mosaic of cultural, military, specialty branch or arm, and operational factors that varied over time and individual unit. As discussed at the beginning of chapter 7, U-boat crews ceased to represent an all-volunteer, hand-picked force within a year after the beginning of the war. How the navy and Dönitz preserved their crews' self-consciousness of elite status offers one focus to our efforts, but only in the general context of how that morale could be maintained while the "elite" was being annihilated.

General Factors in U-boat Crews' Morale

Before treating the specifics of combat morale for Kriegsmarine personnel and U-boat crewmen, we must first consider the foundations laid long before they entered the service.

The German national character has provided a subject of much international comment in the twentieth century, particularly with regard to exaggerated martial virtues and authoritarian values. Stereotypes and half-truths have substituted for analysis in much of this, attributing to genetic or cultural causes that which at heart is the product of an effective military establishment, one that first demonstrated a capacity for operational excellence in the nineteenth century. National "traits" therefore do not figure in our considerations,[5] but there can be no doubt that those who manned U-boats drew heavily on the elements of patriotism, idealism, and hard work common to all national cultures.

The conditions that prevailed in Nazi Germany, however, have direct bearing on the development of future submariners. Participation in the Hitler Youth, compulsory for everyone ten or older after December 1936, prepared all German males for military service through physical conditioning, formation drills, and combat exercises. Ideological indoctrination there also reinforced the strains of nationalism, self-sacrifice, and loyalty to the regime already taught in the schools and home. Most men also served a stint in the Reich Labor Service that furthered their physical conditioning. Ace Karl-Friedrich Merten praised the qualities brought by younger recruits in contrast to older sailors:

After the reintroduction of general military service (in 1935) the crewmen of all career-tracks brought much enthusiasm with them. They had nearly all served in the Hitler Youth and already had the hard school of the Labor Service behind them, were very idealistic, and performed their tasks happily. This contrasted noticeably against the old career sailors of the Reichsmarine, whose limited opportunities for promotion . . . dulled their military ambition and often led to disciplinary problems.[6]

The role of National Socialism and its relationship to the navy will be discussed in chapter 11.

Above all, future *U-Boot-Fahrer* absorbed as youths the notion of an elite submarine service that had distinguished itself in action, embodying qualities of courage, competence, patriotism, and selflessness that captured the public imagination. Popular interest generated during World War I continued throughout the interwar period in the dedication of such public monuments as the U-boat Memorial at Kiel-Möltenort, published memoirs, syndicated newspaper articles, movies, and lectures by U-boat veterans. The submarine blended public interest in the "modern marvel of technology" with the appeal of adventure. Werner Fürbringer, a successful former commander, described his efforts to transmit the values of his generation of U-boat men to the next during a series of lectures in the spring of 1932:

> I explain for many hours. . . . I note how a bridge is gradually built between my listeners and myself, and feel that the relationship between us becomes ever stronger the more I explain how our U-boat men fought for the highest good, fought on even when the struggle appeared hopeless, yet through an unshakeable faith in Germany they kept the strength to hang on and offer their last lifeblood for the Fatherland.[7]

Fürbringer's rhetoric would prove to be convincing and prophetic for the audience of his time. The morale of Dönitz's U-boat crews rested upon a foundation of the cultural values they absorbed as children and adolescents. Yet the strength of this basis varied according to the individual and would be tested by capture and exposure to different cultures. For those raised on National Socialist teachings of German superiority and self-righteousness, the test of combat could prove to be a shock.

Privileges and Pay: Navy Rewards for U-boat Service

Acceptance into the Kriegsmarine alone carried the prestige of exclusivity. The navy's prewar policy in this regard survived its wartime use on draftees, as even at peak strength (810,000 in 1944) it amounted to less than 9 percent of the total manpower serving in the Wehrmacht. In 1941, the relative proportion amounted to less than 6 percent and in 1940 to only 4 percent.[8] As noted in chapter 6, naval recruiting commissions during the first half of the war thoroughly reviewed volunteers' applications before accepting them into the service, a form of screening more advanced than—although not fundamentally different from—that employed by the army in calling up much larger numbers of German males.[9]

Yet as we have also seen, naval recruitment strategy did not select according to the best available talent but rather with a view toward matching civilian skills with specific service needs. The heavy reliance on metalworkers to serve as technical specialists especially illustrates an often-overlooked by-product for morale, the striking homogeneity of backgrounds and occupations that characterized German naval combat personnel in general and U-boat crewmen in particular. The opportunity to share common experiences and "talk shop" about occupational skills served as part of the cement that bonded crewmen living together in confined spaces and confronting long periods of inactivity.

Building morale began in boot camp, as it did for everyone who served in the German armed forces. Beyond basic training and physical conditioning, the transition to military life also imparted values of duty and discipline that transcended mere obedience to authority. Near the completion of this initial stage of service recruits participated in a ritual-laden ceremony as they swore their oath of loyalty, a long-standing German military tradition appropriated by Hitler to serve his own agenda. A semiofficial Kriegsmarine publication describes its recruits as being "inspired as if by a sacred calling" as they vowed: "I swear by Almighty God this sacred oath: I will render unconditional obedience to the Führer of the German Reich and people, Adolf Hitler, Supreme Commander of the Wehrmacht, and, as a brave soldier, I will be ready at any time to stake my life for this oath." With this the recruits finally earned the right to stand beneath the war flag and be addressed as "soldiers."[10] The strong influence of this tradition can be seen in the comment by a U-boat veteran in 1982:

We only knew what we were told: Our duty. We got the feeling that someday we would die together from the Americans and the Russians. But we had given our oath. That's a bad soldier, who forgets he put up his three fingers. Everywhere in the world, in every force, soldiers have to think the same way.[11]

Death in combat, however, constituted more of an abstract than a daily reality due to the nature of modern naval warfare. Until it overtook them, the ultimate fate of so many German submariners remained in their imagination rather than their experiences. In part, this reflected the phenomenon observed in all navies during both world wars, the near-absence of psychiatric casualties: As improved weapons technology increased the ranges at which naval combat took place, the greater distances emotionally removed sailors from the act of killing. Opposing targets were ships and planes, rather than human beings. U-boat crews celebrated the sinking of individual vessels and total tonnage, rather than the destruction of lives on board. The fate of survivors of torpedoed ships was a subject generally avoided in shipboard discussions. As will be seen, Dönitz specifically refused Hitler's suggestion of killing survivors of sunken ships because of the effect it would have on his crews' morale.[12]

At the same time, U-boat sailors—unlike their comrades on the Eastern Front—did not have to become accustomed to mud, blood, death, and crippling wounds as everyday expressions of warfare. Except for the limited period when U-boats remained on the surface to battle attacking aircraft, submariners suffered few casualties that did not involve the loss of their boats as well. When friends and comrades were lost on other submarines, they simply disappeared, without need of identification or burial. By the circumstances of submarine warfare, perhaps as the trick of a laughing Fate, a U-boat crewman's usual encounter with death was only his own. So long as he eluded this destiny, he enjoyed the unusual privilege of belonging to a designated combat elite that was usually spared the sight of casualties.

Among specific measures to maintain morale, food and pay served as direct indices of the navy's preferential treatment of its own. As a direct legacy of World War I, the navy implemented changes to upgrade the quality of food served to enlisted personnel. This was paid for by a mess allowance included in each sailor's pay, a portion of which was deducted from the base pay of all ranks on active duty. U-boat crews always received plentiful supplies of meat, potatoes, bread, and vegetables, with fresh fruit for the beginning of each voyage and vitamin supplements for the remainder. The fourteen tons of foodstuffs typically carried by a Type IXC boat for a twelve-week patrol included 1,728 pounds of milk, 441 pounds of fruit juices, 359 pounds of coffee, tea, and hot cocoa, and 108 pounds of chocolates. So long as weather and combat conditions permitted the use of the stove, German submariners enjoyed three daily meals that catered to the appetite rather than a balanced diet. Careful studies of U-boat crews' weight changes while on operations in the Atlantic over the winter of 1942–43 revealed that more men gained weight (and by an average of approximately nine pounds) than lost; only on extended war cruises in the North Atlantic, where severe weather inhibited hot food preparation, did the pattern reverse (and again by the same average weight). U-boat sailors also enjoyed the privilege of a special furlough parcel (known as the *Führerpakete*) containing valued flour, butter, sugar, coffee, and sausage to take home on leave. Good food in quantity provided tangible proof of special status.[13]

But then as now pay remained the true test of professional appreciation. Basic pay scales were fairly uniform throughout the Wehrmacht as a *Ma-*

trosengefreiter's annual base pay of 1,080 *Reichsmarks* (RM), equivalent to about $432, approximately matched that of his army counterpart. Beyond this, however, navy personnel benefited from both a broader set of allowances and generally faster promotion with a more elaborate structure of noncommissioned officer grades. In addition to the family, field duty, and combat service allowances paid all Wehrmacht personnel, U-boat crewmen received several special allowances. For each day spent at sea while on combat operations, for example, ordinary seamen drew a *Raumbeschränkungszulage* (literally "confined space allowance"), varying according to rank, with higher allowances for each category of technical specialist (*Maschinenzulage, Mechanikerzulage,* and *Funkerzulage,* according to career-track). Moreover, while in training in home waters, submariners received a special allowance (*Tauchzulage,* diving allowance), again paid according to rank, each day the U-boat submerged. During the war these allowances were simplified and somewhat expanded: In March 1941, the *Tauchzulage* grew from 1.5 RM to 2.5 RM per day for petty officers, and in November 1944 the differentiated allowances while on patrol were consolidated into flat 2 RM per day earnings for every crew member regardless of rank.[14]

As many allowances were pegged to rank, the importance of promotion within the enlisted and noncommissioned ranks loomed ever larger, and during the war rapid advancement became more common. Prior to the outbreak of World War II, promotion was slow. Standards prescribed one-year minimum promotion intervals from *Matrose* to *Gefreiter* and thence to *Obergefreiter* and *Maat;* the latter then spent three years before qualifying for *Obermaat.*[15] In December 1941—precisely as the expansion of the U-boat fleet hit full stride—navy regulations loosened these time standards in favor of performance. A recruit might now become a *Gefreiter* within nine months, and a *Maat* could advance to *Obermaat* after two years. Above all, no time limitation existed for promotion to petty officer status, thus encouraging merit as the prime qualification. Promotion also provided a welcome albeit temporary break from active service as the candidate transferred off his submarine to attend a four- to six-week instructional course and pass the necessary examination; he would then usually join a newly commissioned boat with his new rank and a fresh start. The gradual opening of the elite officer corps to the lower decks, as described in chapter 5, offered further proof of the service's recognition of merit over credentials.[16]

Rapid promotions and higher allowances thus allowed submariners to accumulate considerable pay. Many, especially officers, lived on their field allowances and banked the rest at home. Others made more immediate use of their funds: "We had a lot of money paid to us for the four months at sea," recalled veteran Peter Petersen of *U-518* (*Kaptlt.* Friedrich-Wilhelm Wissmann). "They paid us high wages and we got lots of bonuses, so we were rich, and we blew it on girls, beer, and presents."[17]

The additional pay complemented yet another advantage of the U-boat service, home leave. As a general policy, submarine crews received ten to twelve days' home leave by turns after the completion of each combat patrol, half of the crew departing within forty-eight hours after arrival. They did not have to depend on routine means of transportation, but took an express train (known as the *BdU-Zug*) home to Germany. In the war's early days, a furlough meant carefree enjoyment and relaxation with family, friends, and girls. Idolized at home, they often enjoyed free drinks, meals, and other amenities. By 1943, however, home leave assumed a different tone as Allied bombing raids on German cities steadily increased, and the focus shifted from recreation to caring for loved ones. For so many U-boat crewmen with families living in the exposed port cities and industrial Ruhr, leave provided the opportunity to attend to family needs. The lucky ones could arrange for the relocating of family with relatives living in less-exposed areas; the less fortunate arranged for burials.[18]

Such furlough experiences in 1943–44 carried a double edge for morale. On a number of occasions embittered crewmen ended their leaves early to return to action as soon as possible: "At least here everything was in its place, I knew where fore and aft lay," recorded one veteran. Their families' vulnerability to air attack drove home Germany's precarious situation more effectively than their own experiences. A U-boat commander on home leave in devastated Hamburg described his feelings: "Out [at sea] is bad enough, but if someone starts attacking me, at least I can fight back. . . . But here you can only sit tight and hope for the best—a sitting duck to shoot at. And to think that, whatever we do out there, we cannot prevent this!"[19] That most submariners understood the need to continue in action and tie down Allied aircraft could not relieve the depressing presentiment of German defeat.[20]

Yet the furlough privilege enjoyed by U-boat crews cannot be overemphasized in its significance with regard to the rest of the German armed forces. The average German soldier was entitled only to fourteen days' leave per year (plus two days' travel), always subject to wartime developments: It was not unusual for a soldier on the Eastern Front to go a year or more without a furlough. When polled for the best single means to increase their fighting power, German infantry commanders strongly but futilely argued for extending home leave to at least fifteen days every six months. Precisely this average was written into navy regulations for U-boat crewmen in 1944.[21]

In addition to furloughs, U-boat crewmen spent an equivalent amount of time laying over in port. While half the crew enjoyed home leave, the remainder cleaned and painted the submarine, worked on repairs, over-hauled the engines and motors, installed and tested new equipment, and received instruction in the latest models of torpedoes, radar search re-ceivers, and flak guns. These activities occurred at close to regular work hours, with evenings free to enjoy the bars and brothels in town. Subse-quent Allied air raids devastated the cities but rarely affected the U-boats, safe in their massive concrete pens, or their crews, whose quarters were moved to newly built camps well outside the ports in early 1943. (Far from being "terrorised by bombs in [sic] their Biscay bases," as postulated by one writer, U-515's crew in Lorient used to send out their designated "scrounger" in the aftermath of air raids to scavenge for usable goods in the ruins be-fore the military police arrived.[22]) From these quarters—furnished with athletic facilities and cinemas—crewmen commuted by bus to port for their work, which almost resembled peacetime conditions. In all, a German submariner spent perhaps one-third of his active duty in port or on home leave, away from the tedium and terror that defined U-boat warfare.[23]

It was when he returned from leave that a U-boat crewman came to the foundation of his morale.

His Boat and Mates

Since World War II a substantial number of studies have indicated that the glue that binds men together in combat is primary group cohesion, the loyalty shared among the immediate comrades of their squad or section. Fi-delity to nation or ideology takes second place to reliance on those around you for survival. Two American psychologists provided much of the foun-dation for this thesis with their wartime investigation of German POWs' attitudes and motivations, which revealed the significance of these traits: "For the German soldier in particular, the demands of his group, reinforced by officially prescribed rules, had the effect of an external authority."[24] A submarine crew differed from an infantry squad in the frequency and in-tensity of combat exposure, but the principles remained the same. More-over, the absolute dependence of each man on the entire submarine crew necessarily extended the concept to a double primary group, the immedi-ate crewmates of one's career-track (seamen, engineering personnel, ra-diomen) with whom one shared specific shipboard responsibilities, and the broader group of the crew itself. A *Matrosengefreiter* in the forward tor-pedo room need not know the name of the *Maschinenmaat* manning the electrical motors to understand the latter's significance during a crash dive.

On the other hand, the confines of a fifty-man submarine bestowed a familiarity and intimacy impossible on a larger warship or in the impersonal relationship of an infantry squad with its division artillery. The experiences—and especially successes—shared by a crew provided each boat its own esprit to distinguish its achievement from that of each identical submarine berthed next to it. Belonging to the designated elite of the *U-Boot-Waffe* conferred status and privileges, but membership in a U-boat crew required entrusting your life to others as they vouchsafed theirs to you.

Symbolic of crew identification, individual U-boats and flotillas made liberal use of distinctive conning-tower insignia and cap badges. These insignia, often accompanied by epigrams, reflected a wide range of unique experiences, sentiments, functions, and backgrounds in the histories of specific U-boats and could be supplemented or replaced over the course of time with new commanders and occurrences. The navy recognized the significance of such emblems for morale and tacitly accepted them, despite the intelligence risks they posed for easy identification of individual submarines and crewmen in occupied France and Norway. After the heavy losses suffered in 1943 Dönitz officially prohibited their further display as fixed symbols, leading to their placement on wooden placards that could be mounted and removed at the time of departure and return from patrols. Their use continued throughout the war, even among the advanced Types XXI and XXIII submarines that never carried out an operational mission.[25]

Inspirations for insignia derived from every conceivable source. A U-boat commander might supply his Crew symbol from his graduating class of naval officers, for example, the five joined Olympic rings for officers belonging to Crew 36 (the year Germany hosted the Olympic Games), which appeared on at least thirty-six U-boats. Another common device employed the city coat of arms (*Stadtwappen*) of the commander's birthplace, which would itself become the boat's sponsor-city (*Patenstadt*). Other familiar figures predictably included devils (used for fourteen boats), fish (fourteen), dogs (thirteen) and wolves (ten), but the most popular animal escutcheon was the elephant, appearing on the conning towers of not less than sixteen U-boats. Others used or added their flotilla insignia, such as the "laughing swordfish" of the *9. U-Flottille* (itself borrowed from the emblem of *U-96*, flotilla commander *Korv.Kapt.* Heinrich Lehmann-Willenbrock's original boat) or the "snorting bull" motif of the 7th U-boat Flotilla, a tribute to Günther Prien's personal emblem aboard *U-47* and adopted after his loss at sea in March 1941. Whatever the design or motif, each represented its own story and significance for its crew.[26]

Association with a *Patenstadt* also reinforced both a U-boat's distinctiveness and its relationship with the German civilian population. For those so linked, the sponsor-city would often invite the crew of "their" U-boat to be fêted with speeches, banquets, and gifts. Following her return from a second successful patrol off the American coast, *U-123* (*Kaptlt.* Reinhard Hardegen) had to proceed to Kiel for needed repairs. While there the crew traveled to Hardegen's native Bremen for a two-day celebration: "Only with great difficulty could our completely disrupted formation arrive at the Ratskeller, the sea of flowers and crowds of people were worse than anything in the Atlantic," observed Hardegen. While there, the crew almost certainly visited "Mutti" Rosiefski, owner of a Bremen coffeehouse and a foster mother to many U-boat crews.[27] The smaller city of Plauen, nestled in the Vogtland of western Saxony, similarly hosted their native son *Kaptlt.* Werner Hartenstein and the crew of his boat, *U-156,* and maintained an ongoing contact that furnished the adopted sailors fifty harmonicas, a guitar, and a piano accordion for onboard musical entertainment.[28]

U-boat crewmen thus enjoyed numerous collective benefits as members of the navy, of the *U-Boot-Waffe,* and of their own extended primary groups of comrades. To all these could be added the individual perquisites of awards and decorations.

Decorations and Recognition

To supplement the pay and promotions accorded its men, the navy provided a generous quantity of war badges and decorations to its combat personnel. For his submariners Dönitz moreover saw to it that these were awarded as quickly as possible:

I also made it a practice of presenting at once, in the name of the Commander-in-Chief, any decorations which the captains of the boats had recommended and of which, bearing in mind the need of equal treatment for all U-boat crews, I had approved. Where decorations were concerned, there was no correspondence and no red tape in U-boat Command. . . . I regard this practice of immediate awards to those engaged upon operations as psychologically important.[29]

Privately, Dönitz appears to have been more skeptical of decorations' value. According to a staff officer BdU once jokingly suggested that every possible medal be awarded to each man in the U-boat service at the start, then for each act of heroism a decoration would be taken away until "whoever ends up with an empty chest first would obviously be the best man."[30]

The most fundamental of these awards was the U-boat Badge (*U-boots-kriegsabzeichen*)—a resurrection of a World War I award featuring an emblem of a submarine superimposed on an oval laurel wreath, but with the imperial crown replaced by a swastika—awarded to submariners once they completed two operational patrols. In May 1944 the navy instituted a bronze clasp (*Ubootsfrontspange*) for crewmen who had already received the badge and who demonstrated continued meritorious service (although Dönitz had to approve each award); in November 1944 this was followed by provisions for a silver clasp under similar conditions.[31]

No strict rules governed the awarding of Germany's most traditional decoration, the Iron Cross (*Eisernes Kreuz*) First or Second Class (usually abbreviated E.K. I and E.K. II in German military parlance), and no statistics are available to indicate how many submariners received either version. The medals were cumulative—the E.K. II had to be earned first—but could apply either to a single heroic act or to continued meritorious service. During the war the German army and Waffen-SS together awarded 2.3 million E.K. IIs and 300,000 E.K. Is throughout a total of perhaps 11 million men, or approximate ratios of 1:5 and 1:37, respectively. The Kriegsmarine doubtless maintained at least similar rates, and the U-boat crews probably received higher proportions. Nevertheless, the available evidence indicates that the Iron Cross remained a decoration that had to be earned and could never be taken for granted.[32]

Success usually guaranteed a supply of medals for all. Günther Prien's exploit in sinking the *Royal Oak* in October 1939 immediately earned him the Iron Cross First Class and his entire crew the E.K. II; Jost Metzler's receipt of the Knight's Cross of the Iron Cross in July 1941 carried with it the E.K. II for all the crew of *U-69*, or the E.K. I for those already so decorated.[33] As sinkings increasingly grew more difficult, however, conditions for the award became a subject of debate. The commander of *U-953*, *Kaptlt*. Karl-Heinz Marbach, recommended ten of his crew for the Iron Cross First Class after some hazardous snorkel missions in 1944, but received approval only for three; strong protests from Marbach finally won one more, but that rested more on the basis of time at sea than heroic conduct. Even Lüth acknowledged that controversy existed over the decoration and suggested its award, as a pragmatic compromise, to deserving individuals who remained on board and did not transfer off for promotion.

As a consequence of the uncertainties governing its award, the distribution of Iron Crosses varied greatly from one submarine to the next according to the relative experience of their crews. Thus, of fifty-seven officers and crewmen aboard Werner Henke's veteran *U-515* at the beginning of her fifth patrol, forty-three had received the Iron Cross Second Class, but only sixteen wore the E.K. I; after completing that very dangerous and difficult war cruise, Henke recommended eight more of his crew in each category for their bravery and performance. By contrast, when the inexperienced crew of *U-1059* departed on its first mission in February 1944, only nine E.K. II medals could be counted among fifty-five officers and men and only two Iron Crosses First Class.[34]

For U-boat commanders, the *Ritterkreuz* (Knight's Cross of the Iron Cross), supposedly awarded for the sinking of 100,000 tons of merchant shipping, served as the benchmark of achievement for the first half of the war. Although only thirty-two commanders actually attained this total, the navy awarded 145 Knight's Crosses to members of the *U-Boot-Waffe,* or nearly half of all Knight's Crosses given to Kriegsmarine personnel (318) throughout the war. Of U-boat recipients, the vast majority (124) represented executive officers: 121 submarine commanders, two watch officers, and Dönitz himself. Fourteen engineering officers also qualified for the award, as did seven NCOs (the navigator career-track predominant with four). Apparently, the Knight's Cross remained the exclusive preserve of commanders until late October 1940, when *Kaptlt.* Heinrich "Ajax" Bleichrodt, commander of *U-48,* refused to accept the award until his I.W.O., *Oblt.z.S.* Reinhard "Teddy" Suhren, received one also. The more liberal award of this decoration reflected the need to maintain morale in difficult times. Thus Dönitz rewarded his late-war commanders equally for their efforts as he had decorated their predecessors for results: In 1944, seventeen captains received the *Ritterkreuz,* as opposed to eighteen in 1940 and twenty in 1941. U-boat commanders also dominated the higher grades of the Knight's Cross awarded within the navy: twenty-eight of fifty-three Oak Leaves (*Eichenlaub*) to the Knight's Cross, and all five of those decorated with Swords and Oak Leaves (*Eichenlaub mit Schwerten zum Ritterkreuz des Eisernen Kreuzes*).[35]

In September 1941 a new decoration, the German Cross (*Deutsches Kreuz*), was introduced throughout the Wehrmacht to recognize continued outstanding service that exceeded the Iron Cross but fell short of consideration for the Knight's Cross. Known as the "fried egg" after the appearance of its sunburst star centerpiece, the medal could be awarded in either gold or silver, the latter usually reserved for senior officers serving in support commands. For the navy the gold version served especially as a means for honoring officers, NCOs, and enlisted men who would not usually be eligible for the *Ritterkreuz.* Among the 1,381 naval recipients of the *Deutsches Kreuz in Gold,* approximately 12 percent were given to U-boat officers (often engineering officers) and 26 percent to U-boat noncommissioned officers and men; the remainder were divided between other operational and staff officers (51 percent) and enlisted ranks (11 percent) serving in combat commands.[36]

With respect to their numbers, U-boat personnel thus received more than their share of medals and decorations. Some historians criticize Dönitz's abandonment of previous standards in favor of exaggerated U-boat claims as proof of his capitulation to propaganda.[37] They appear to miss the point that the ultimate purpose of medals is to acknowledge superior effort and thereby maintain men's morale rather than to uphold abstract measurements of performance. The grand admiral's flexibility in adjusting standards to reward the efforts of his 1943–44 crews as he had earlier honored the achievements of his 1939–42 submariners demonstrates his understanding of this principle.

But beyond medals, Dönitz recognized his men in other ways. He kept individual crewmen at sea informed by radio as to the births of children (for example, "a U-boat with periscope arrived today" denoted a boy, "a U-boat without periscope" a girl) and allowed proxy-marriages by the same medium.[38] He also maintained close contact with U-boat POWs in North America, even plotting two prison breakouts from camps in New Brunswick and Ontario, Canada, to be capped by daring rendezvous and rescues of the escapees by *U-262* (*Oblt.z.S.* Heinz Franke) and *U-536* (*Kaptlt.* Rolf Schauenburg) at different points along the New Brunswick coast in April and September 1943. In the end, the plans failed and *U-536* was sunk, but the effort alone reveals Dönitz's commitment to his men even in captivity.[39]

Discipline and Leadership

Military cohesion ultimately rests on the means of discipline used to hold men together. The Kriegsmarine had educated its officers to lead rather than merely command, but as with every military service it had to establish and enforce boundaries of conduct by its personnel. The process was complicated by both the navy's own legacy of mutiny and the ideological nature of the regime it served. On average the navy successfully instilled self-discipline among its U-boat crews based on mutual trust and respect. Former U-boat commanders surveyed after the war recalled such specific measures to maintain their crews' confidence as direct personal discussions, the sharing of vital information, and crew participation in organizing the boat's routine and in some operational decisions.[40] When necessary, the exertion of authority proved a complex and paradoxical mixture of understanding and uncompromising harshness. Most crewmen grasped the boundaries, even when they changed, and held together even as combat conditions began to erode the foundations.

Discipline while ashore could serve as a means of bonding a crew, especially when submariners had problems with an external authority such as the German military police. Dönitz and his subordinates employed a common-sense approach of leniency to allow his men to "let off steam," at least so long as no serious damage was done. For example, when crewmen of his *U-515* fell afoul of the authorities, Henke always secured their release; later, when Henke himself became embroiled with Nazi party and Gestapo officials in Innsbruck, Dönitz and von Friedeburg intervened directly with Heinrich Himmler to smooth out matters without a court-martial. In October 1943 some of *U-518's* crew celebrated too exuberantly with their firearms outside Lorient, bringing out the army garrison in search of French partisans; the culprits received a dressing-down from their captain but the threat of an all-night drill turned into a rest in a cornfield. And during an air raid on Lorient on 3 June 1942, as the watch officer of the 2d U-boat Flotilla reported:

The crews of *U-154* [*Korv.Kapt.* Walther Kölle] and *U-505* [*Kaptlt.* Axel-Olaf Loewe] could not be awakened for 30 minutes after the air raid alarm had sounded. The men were in such a vomiting-sick drunken stupor that they could not move to the air raid shelters and did not react to strenuous efforts to arouse them. For this the flotilla commander denied both crews shore leave and canteen privileges for two days, probably the minimum time needed in any case for the men to recover from their hangovers.[41]

But discipline at sea required a different touch that tested morale aboard every submarine, demanding special skills of every captain at all times and extraordinary capabilities as defeat loomed larger. The best elevated the handling of discipline to an art form, and none exceeded Wolfgang Lüth, the ace who concluded his outstanding operational career with an incredible 203-day patrol aboard *U-181*. Decades after the war his former crewmen still idolized him to the extent that an American biographer did not hear a bad word said against him.

In a 1943 lecture to younger commanders, the captain who had dispatched nearly 230,000 tons of Allied merchant shipping to the bottom passed along his secrets, which began with the observation that the first factor in a crew's morale was the onboard discipline. "Generally I had the tendency to punish as little as possible . . . by taking particularly good care of one's men, by truly leading and educating them, and by issuing clear orders to make obedience easier." Specific examples of punishments followed: A man impertinent to his superior was deprived of use of his bunk for three days; one who stole food received the silent treatment from his comrades for two weeks. Once Lüth confronted a chronic complainer before the entire crew, promising that the sailor would return from the patrol either as his friend or to an Eastern Front penal battalion: Two weeks' extra duty in peeling potatoes, cleaning bilges, and shifting supplies worked its charm and the grumbler later won the Iron Cross. After noting the many daily means to maintain and boost morale, Lüth returned to his fundamental theme: "It is the duty of every captain to have faith in his men, even if they have disappointed him at one time or another. . . . We must only show them respect and like them."[42]

Another who exemplified this approach was *Kapt.z.S.* Kurt Freiwald, who at thirty-seven years of age succeeded Lüth as commander of *U-181* in November 1943. Freiwald, who had not commanded a submarine since the prewar period, now confronted an extended patrol to Indonesian waters while replacing a legend as captain. Yet Freiwald possessed the assurance of command to take the crew into his confidence by creating the onboard role of a "coward on duty" (*Feigling vom Dienst*)—having his officers take daily turns in criticizing the commander, grumbling, or expressing worries and concerns of the crew that might not otherwise reach the captain's ear. Freiwald would then respond to the issues raised and make changes if he thought them necessary. As one of his officers observed, Freiwald thus created "something like a democratic command on our U-boat."[43]

Punishment administered to a crewman always had to reflect the general context rather than match the offense. When a bored seaman standing watch on the bridge of *U-518* accidentally discharged a flare pistol through the conning tower and into the *Zentrale,* he earned himself the uneviable duty as *Backschafter* (steward or waiter) to the petty officers' quarters for the rest of the patrol, bringing them their meals and cleaning their dishes. By contrast, an eighteen-year-old aboard *U-505* nearly caused the loss of the boat when he was late opening the aft vents during a dive. Before control could be regained the U-boat's bow lay submerged and the stern had raised out of the water, leaving her helpless to any patrolling Allied aircraft. But none flew by, and *U-505* escaped unobserved and unharmed. *Kaptlt.* Loewe confronted the sobbing sailor responsible for the error and merely asked for his assurance that it wouldn't happen again. It didn't, and Loewe's calm handling of the case cemented the relations between captain and crew.[44]

Some individuals just never fit into the character of the U-boat service and either lacked the needed touch of an outstanding captain or simply couldn't be reached. A hapless crewman aboard *U-1221* (*Oblt.z.S.* Paul Ackermann), disliked by his shipmates and a chronic offender in sleeping on duty, one day ended his misery by leaping off the bridge into the sea three hundred miles southwest of Nova Scotia. An onboard investigation rejected a verdict of suicide in favor of desertion, with death an accidental consequence.[45] Such incidents, however, remained extremely rare among U-boat crews, with only about a half-dozen recorded cases.[46]

Of greater damage to morale, however, was the routine rotation of veteran commanders to staff and training posts against the background of the continued expansion of the U-boat fleet, which inevitably meant that younger, less experienced, and less self-assured individuals became more common among the U-boat officer corps. Worse, those assuming command in 1942–43 expected to repeat the success of their predecessors, and the risks they took that were once rewarded now brought destruction.

First to see the results were the veteran U-boat petty officers, sensitive to the need for mutual confidence between captain and crew on a submarine and at the same time aware of improvements in Allied weaponry. Their observations were quickly picked up by Allied interrogators. Survivors of *U-606* (*Oblt.z.S* Hans Dohler), sunk 22 February 1943 in the North Atlantic, described the last of their three commanders as a "weak character completely dominated by the executive officer," the L.I. as "an ignoramus," and the I.W.O. as someone who delighted in meting out severe punishments for relatively minor infractions. Summarizing the "unusually poor morale" of the crew, a petty officer rhetorically asked, "What sins have I committed in my life that I should have been assigned to such a boat?"[47]

Although he was *U-664*'s only commander in her thirteen-month history, *Kaptlt.* Adolf Graef never won over his crew, who considered him a "martinet . . . a man lacking all the skills necessary for a U-boat skipper . . . totally unable to understand any of the problems of his crew."[48] Through six patrols the crew of *U-591* (*Oblt.z.S.* Reimar Ziesmer) counted itself successful and happy, but in late June 1943 the commander, I.W.O., and chief engineer were all replaced. Their successors, according to the boat's survivors taken prisoner on 30 July,

indicated a decline in the U-boat arm. The more experienced petty officers in particular were dissatisfied, feeling that the young officers not only were ill-equipped to handle a front boat under the present dangerous conditions, but were also unwilling to accept advice tendered with good intentions.

One chief petty officer among the survivors extended this assessment to the entire U-boat arm, observing that the new officers were either "too cautious . . . or are foolhardy. . . . Green crews react badly to either attitude." He and other older hands had become "fatalistic," and "many of the crew felt the U-boat arm has already lost the war."[49]

These views naturally reflected the consequences of the defeats suffered from May through July 1943. Although never aware of the details, U-boat crews gradually became aware of the scope of the disaster. They experienced the improvements in Allied countermeasures and weapons for themselves; the inability of radar search receivers to detect Allied centimetric radar and provide adequate warning of air attacks proved especially unnerving. Radiomen meanwhile monitored the repeated but unanswered calls from U-boat Headquarters to submarines no longer capable of reply. Crews fortunate enough to return to base observed the empty berths for U-boats that had departed before their own patrol had begun and could only hope that friends had survived as POWs. Dönitz, sensitive to the effects on his men, admonished his commanders by radio on 6 August: "Do not report too much bad news, so as not to depress the other boats; every radio message goes the rounds of the crew in every boat. If necessary report matters which ratings do not need to know by officer's cipher."[50]

But it was too late.

The Crisis of Morale: Autumn 1943–Spring 1944

In his memoirs Dönitz described the crisis in confidence of the U-boat service in the spring of 1940 caused by defective torpedoes.[51] The grand admiral omitted reference to another plunge in morale that began in the autumn of 1943 and continued well into the spring of 1944, rooted in the technological shortcoming of German submarines' demonstrated obsolescence. This time, however, there would be no formal acknowledgment of a crisis, much less an official investigation into the cause; rather, recognition came at different levels in distinctive ways. The gravity of this crisis is evident in some of the countermeasures applied, in which Germans paid not with their professional reputations but their lives.

U-boat Headquarters' confession of a morale problem coincided with its only solution at the time, a prayer of self-sacrifice. On 13 November 1943, after the attempt to renew the Atlantic convoy battles had collapsed with heavy losses, BdU cabled a lengthy message to its submarine crews that closed with this passage: "Your actions have tied down significant enemy air and naval forces. These forces must not be freed for use against the homeland. Thus you are protecting your homes even though the struggle appears hopeless to you."[52] Dönitz himself spread this gospel through the U-boat flotillas in visits to the French ports.[53] Even for those who accepted this thesis, it offered little comfort to be told that to save others, one must accept crucifixion.

Among the general ranks, signals of discontent could be read in a shift of criminal cases brought before navy courts-martial in 1944. In a random sample of four thousand cases heard by naval courts during the war, which included proceedings against 375 U-boat personnel, certain patterns of disciplinary problems emerged. Until 1942, charges brought against submariners were too few to draw conclusions, testifying to the excellent morale of U-boat crews during that period. In 1943, military theft displaced insubordination as the leading disciplinary action, but morale problems begin to materialize in desertion and unauthorized absences that numbered 16 of 153 cases (10 percent), including five cases of *Wehrkraftzersetzung* (literally "undermining of fighting power," manifest in defeatism or rumormongering). For 1944 a further decline of morale can be seen in the rise of desertion and absences to 20 of 121 cases (17 percent) with seven cases of *Wehrkraftzersetzung* or outright treason. This occurred despite the repeated dissemination of regulations and Dönitz's personal pledge that "Desertion costs your head."[54]

Moreover, these problems were not confined to the U-boat rank and file. Beginning in the summer of 1943, submarine officers in the Atlantic theater attended compulsory lectures that, beyond promises of new weapons and equipment in the future, attempted to whip up enthusiasm and generate more animosity toward the foe. Slogans such as "Victory at all costs!" and "Who has the better morale shall win!" echoed hollowly among veterans of prolonged depth-charge attacks, prompting whispered responses of "They would do better to give us decent weapons, we'll do the fighting without this talk." One Knight's Cross winner exclaimed to his wife,

This is really the limit! We are called to a briefing to be told that we should hate and despise the enemy, otherwise we cannot do our duty. . . . The mere suggestion is an outrage. Why should I hate the enemy? They are standing by their country as I am by mine. Despise them? What for? None of us out there in his right senses would dream of underestimating what we are up against. . . . How very stupid it would be, belittling the enemy but detracts from one's own achievement.[55]

The ineffectiveness of these speeches is also revealed in the comments of surviving officers of *U-231* (*Kaptlt*. Wolfgang Wenzel), sunk 13 January 1944 in the North Atlantic, who characterized such pep talks as "the usual Dönitz crap" ("*Dönitz-scheisse*") to their captors—direct objects of the intensified "hate" campaign.[56]

Although these expressions proved the ineffectiveness of Dönitz's pep-talk treatment, they represented nothing more than symptoms of a deeper malady. Beneath the surface, a disease was gradually but steadily spreading, eating away at the links that held the U-boat service together even as it steadily shrank, from a monthly average of 111 *Frontboote* through the first half of 1943 to a mere sixty-seven from November 1943 through April 1944.[57] It was easy to mistake the signs for exhaustion, especially in the aftermath of the summer's heavy losses: "Burnout" of submarine commanders and crews, as noted earlier, was not an unusual phenomenon. But in 1943's last months, the cumulative effects of the losing U-boat campaign for the first time began to break the will of those expected to lead the fight.

The first clear evidence came when *Kaptlt.* Peter Zschech, commander of *U-505*, shot himself during a depth-charge attack on the evening of 25 October 1943. The only known suicide by a U-boat captain whose boat did not sink,[58] Zschech's action could only be attributed to his psychological state. The depth-charge attack was neither prolonged nor very damaging, merely unnerving. Zschech, although only twenty-five, came to *U-505* with a year's experience as a watch officer aboard *U-124*, but in thirteen months he sank only a single vessel. His I.W.O. brought *U-505* back to Lorient, where nothing more was said about the incident.[59]

Just over a month later, *U-154* tied up at the same port, empty-handed after completing her second patrol under *Oblt.z.S.* Oskar-Heinz Kusch. Before the I.W.O., *Oblt.z.S.d.R.* Dr. Ulrich Abel, departed Lorient for submarine commander training, he denounced his captain for *Wehrkraftzersetzung*. Abel, supported by the naval surgeon detailed to serve on *U-154*, testified to Kusch's repeated anti-Nazi and anti-Hitler remarks and criticism of the obsolescence of German U-boats in front of the crew. On 12 January 1944 Kusch was arrested and, in another occurrence unique among the ranks of submarine commanders, court-martialed and convicted of sedition; the deciding factor concerned such conduct before the men of his crew. On 12 May 1944 he died before a firing squad outside Kiel—ironically, two weeks after Abel met his own death at sea in command of *U-193*. This case is described in more detail in chapter 11 in terms of its political significance, but it deserves mention here both as evidence of a U-boat commander who broke faith with the regime and the navy's willingness to deal ruthlessly with anything that smacked of rebellion.[60]

But Kusch was not alone. At the same moment that Abel was preparing his denunciation of Kusch, the I.W.O. of *U-172*, *Oblt.z.S.* Max Coreth, made his personal decision to break ranks and assist American naval intelligence in the interrogation of his erstwhile comrades. Coreth joined at least four other U-boat survivors from submarines sunk in June and August 1943 who had been persuaded to serve as "stool pigeons" at the secret interrogation center located at Ft. Hunt, Virginia, a few miles south of Washington, D.C. (The British employed willing U-boat POWs along similar lines but details have not yet been made available.[61]) Coreth, captured when *U-172* was sunk on 13 December 1943 and a fixture at Ft. Hunt after his arrival there on 8 January 1944, shared "bugged" quarters with other captured U-boat officers to engage in friendly conversation and glean as much military information as possible.

Beyond the intelligence value of whatever he revealed or cajoled from others, Coreth stands out as the only front-line U-boat officer in American captivity to offer his services to the enemy. At least three additional U-boat enlisted men, captured in May–June 1944, joined him and the four others at Ft. Hunt to act as informants among their former comrades.[62] Less actively cooperative but no less treasonous were the actions of another U-boat officer and two radiomen (all from separate U-boats) in furnishing information on radio cipher procedures and the Enigma machine during the period December 1943–March 1944.[63]

Still other POWs dissociated themselves from the regime and the U-boat service. Among these was *Oblt.z.S.* Günter Leupold, commander and one of the few survivors of *U-1059*, bound for Indonesia when she was surprised and sunk west of the Cape Verde Islands on 19 March 1944. Leupold, in defiance of the image of the young German officer (only twenty-three when he was captured) heavily indoctrinated with National Socialist ideology, cooperated fully with his captors, who rated him as an anti-Nazi with "an enthusiasm for America that knows no bounds." When he was sent to a POW camp for anti-Nazis he actually embarrassed American authorities by antagonizing other German captives. A U.S. naval intelligence officer considered him "a fanatic, that is to say, he is so vicious against not only the Nazis, but apparently all Germany, and so sold on America, that he does not use good judgment."[64]

The price for such collaboration, however, could be steep. *Mechanikersobergefreiter* Werner Drechsler was one of the earliest "stool pigeons" employed at Ft. Hunt after his recovery from the wreckage of *U-118* (*Korv. Kapt.* Werner Czygan) on 12 June 1943, probably based on his father's three-year incarceration in a concentration camp as a political opponent. After several months in the guise of "Obermaat Limmer," Drechsler asked to be relieved and sent to an anti-Nazi POW camp. Through bureaucratic error, Drechsler instead wound up at Papago Park, Arizona, where he was immediately recognized by crewmen of *U-615* as the "plant" who tried to engage them in military conversations. Less than seven hours after his arrival at Papago Park on 12 March 1944, Drechsler died in a shower stall at the hands of his erstwhile comrades. Dönitz, informed long after the event by covert mail, approved the action and instituted measures to have the U-boat crewmen involved promoted. Instead, American authorities identified, tried, convicted, and executed seven of them in August 1945.[65]

The examples of Zschech, Kusch, Coreth, Leupold, Drechsler, and the deserters bear a significance that belie their number, evidence of an erosion in the self-consciousness of a neither voluntary nor hand-picked elite that was being bled to death. This is not a surprise in view of the acknowledged defeats and continued bleeding from May 1943 through the spring of 1944; that it did not spread testifies to the naval leadership's reaction to the problem.

The Crisis Mastered: Spring–Summer 1944

If Dönitz and his subordinates never admitted that a morale crisis developed in 1943–44, they nevertheless acted to resolve it. Pep talks continued with new references to the tangible evidence of long-promised new types of U-boats that finally began appearing in 1944. Dönitz regularly made the rounds of the training flotillas in the Baltic at that time to promise that these and other secret weapons would eventually turn the tide. With some physical basis for hope, the commander-in-chief's optimism proved infectious: "Whenever he visited us he left us feeling better, and despite the gloomy present we looked forward hopefully to the future," recorded one commander and veteran of the 1942–43 battles.[66]

It is also within the context of morale problems that Lüth's famous lecture on "Problems of Leadership in a Submarine," presented to an assembly of officers in Weimar on 17 December 1943, should be placed. The speech and its subsequent widespread dissemination and use in classroom instruction reflects some attention paid to the same complaints aired by captured U-boat petty officers to their American interrogators earlier in 1943.[67]

For those who had broken ranks, on the other hand, punishment was swift, severe, and publicized. Records of naval judicial actions indicate that from July to December 1944 alone, at least 139 men of the Kriegsmarine were executed for various offenses, of which desertion and sedition accounted for nearly 80 percent. Most cases involved land-based personnel, but the U-boat crewmen noted earlier who fell into these categories were doubtless included in this number.[68] The fates of Kusch and Drechsler further testified to the severity with which the navy could deal with its own. According to British assessments in March 1944, "U-boat prisoners show much higher security consciousness than six months ago. There is a general belief that those who divulge information will be punished after the war."[69]

At the same time, more carrots accompanied the threat of the stick. On

30 November 1943 Rear Admiral Godt, chief of U-boat operations, advised his commanders: "In the present situation the prospects of sinking ships are slight. When considering decorations therefore I shall attach all the more weight to determination and perseverance in operations even if they do not lead to success." The result was an immediate increase in awards of the German Cross in Gold, especially to U-boat personnel. Official announcements of the decoration's award to individuals for four months in July–October 1943 totaled 138, of whom 49 (36 percent) were submariners; but for just the three-month period December 1943–February 1944, however, the totals rose to 197 awards, with U-boat officers and men garnering 120 (61 percent).[70]

Whatever its corrosive potential, the morale crisis of 1943–44 had not significantly penetrated the rank and file. Allied propagandists in September 1943 hoped that the heavy U-boat losses inflicted during the summer and an adroit radio propaganda policy would produce "the complete breakdown of morale . . . specifically, of the German naval forces."[71] An assessment of U-boat POWs by the British Admiralty in March 1944, however, punctured this balloon: Conceding that crews had grown younger, less efficient, and more convinced of eventual Allied victory, the study nevertheless found "no marked deterioration in the fighting spirit of either officers or men while still engaged in war," nor "any proven cases of refusal to carry out orders."[72]

Necessary as all of these personnel measures may have been, the morale crisis derived from the technological inferiority of German submarines, and its mastery ultimately required technological solutions. These began in March 1944 with the introduction of a combination radar/radar-detection set, code-named *Hohentwiel,* and more-effective radar-detection equipment (*Mücke* and *Fliege*) that at last allowed U-boats to detect the shortwave radar used by the Allies. Above all, the gradual installation of the *Schnorchel* on all remaining boats that began in early 1944 and continued throughout the autumn dramatically improved U-boats' ability to escape detection. Troublesome as it was, the snorkel at least permitted U-boats a good chance to arrive at, and return from, their operational areas (although the superiority of Allied technology usually asserted itself once the snorkel boat entered combat). After crews learned to cope with the technical problems and adapt to a true submarine environment, morale improved significantly. *Kaptlt.* Rolf Nollmann, after completing an entirely submerged fifty-day patrol off the Scottish east coast in October 1944 with *U-1199,* reported his crew "convinced that the U-boat arm is again superior to the enemy."[73]

U-boat morale remained stable for the rest of the war, apparently unaffected by Germany's physical collapse in 1945. In a 1981 survey of 115 U-boat captains from the 1943–45 period, 87 percent stated they had no memories of problems with the morale or technical proficiency among their crews.[74] U-boat POWs at Papago Park organized and effected the largest mass escape in the United States at the end of December 1944.[75] The submarine crews in Norway, physically removed from the devastation in their homeland, could look to their U-boats for psychological escape, or what one contemporary commander describes as a "flight from reality," continuing what they had been trained to do and were capable of doing while Germany's fate lay beyond their ability to influence. "More than a U-boat sailor one cannot be," read a hand-painted slogan on a naval barracks wall in late January 1945.[76] However representative that sentiment may be for the entire service, it reflects a faith in themselves as submariners that transcended loyalty to the regime. A British witness to the arrival of eight surrendered U-boats at Londonderry on 14 May 1945 described the crews as

mostly very young men. Some were sullen and many were arrogant. . . . An officer on [Adm. Sir Max] Horton's staff says that the morale of the commanding officers was unbroken. . . . Their first question was "When do we start fighting the Russians?"[77]

Fortunately for them, their fight was over.

10 Humanity vs. Necessity

U-boats and Unrestricted Submarine Warfare

"My humanity I'll prove even in war
But it's something I won't take a beating for."
Schiller, *Wallenstein*

Since the sinking of the *Lusitania* in 1915, the Allied public image of U-boats has been fixed as cold-blooded killers of women and children, their captains and crews as fanatical as they were determined, as ruthless as they were capable. One British account published in 1943, for example, described U-boats blasting lifeboats to pieces with torpedoes.[1] Through postwar perpetuation in film and television, these propaganda images have left an indelible mark on British and American popular culture.[2]

Moreover, several historians continue to maintain this perspective. Steven Roskill, author of the British official history *The War at Sea*, wrote a decade after the war:

Although we British are notoriously bad haters . . . there is no doubt that the German U-boats did finally arouse feelings of the strongest loathing in [British sailors'] minds. . . . It is sheer casuistry for German apologists to claim that their methods of waging war were justifiable, or even humanitarian.[3]

In a scathing biography of Dönitz, British naval historian Peter Padfield concluded that in September 1942 BdU issued secret oral instructions to his submarine commanders to kill all survivors of sunken ships. John Terraine concurs that only a "small difference" existed between Hitler and Dönitz in the killing of merchant crewmen.[4] Another historian suggests that a more complete understanding of the navy's acceptance of National Socialism's murderous program will be gained by future study of "firing on survivors of U-boat attacks."[5]

There remains, however, the matter of evidence.

The use of unrestricted submarine warfare in World War II was not limited to Germany. On trial before the International Military Tribunal at Nuremberg, Dönitz drew support from affidavits submitted by the British Admiralty and U.S. Navy Adm. Chester Nimitz that acknowledged the adoption of the same policy by the Allies. American submarines in the Pacific made no provision for the rescue or safety of Japanese merchant crews, and in one incident in January 1943, Capt. Dudley "Mush" Morton, commander of USS *Wahoo*, surfaced and killed the survivors of a Japanese troop transport he had torpedoed.[6] Lt. Cmdr. Anthony Miers, captain of the British submarine *Torbay*, machine-gunned German soldiers who survived the sinking of their caïque proceeding from Crete to the Greek mainland on 9 July 1941, an incident very similar to an earlier action by the British submarine *Rorqual*.[7] Beyond individual events and their circumstances, the dictates and technological developments of total war inevitably eroded international law and morality: The growth and capabilities of air power alone exposed surfaced submarines to intolerable risks the longer they dallied at the site of an attack.

Yet the German navy served the particular goals of the Third Reich, and its members grew up under the influence of National Socialist teachings and doctrine. A contemporary historian argues that the adoption of Nazi racial ideology throughout the German army facilitated their committing war crimes in the USSR and parenthetically notes that the Kriegsmarine was also "deeply permeated by Nazi indoctrination." In support of this argument, Padfield hypothesizes that any independently routed ships lost to U-boat attack with all hands reflects a deliberate policy of annihilating merchant crews.[8]

An opposite view was recorded by ace Otto Kretschmer as "Standing Order No. 4" aboard *U-99*: "Survivors are to be assisted if there is time and by so doing the submarine is not exposed to undue danger. The crew of *U-99* . . . would expect to be rescued by the enemy, and that is precisely what the enemy have the right to expect from us."[9] Former U-boat commander Peter "Ali" Cremer echoed this sentiment: "For us U-boat commanders, nonetheless, the humane treatment of shipwrecked seamen of the enemy powers was a matter of course. They were not enemies any more, but simply shipwrecked and had to be helped as far as possible."[10] Can such differing perspectives be reconciled?

This requires an examination of the course of German U-boat policy, how it evolved over time, and whether it ultimately depended on the directives—secret or otherwise—of Karl Dönitz.

The Early War Period

As already noted, the war's first ten months saw a return to the conditions of 1914–18. The mistaken sinking of the *Athenia* notwithstanding, German U-boats operated within a complex set of policy restrictions and international prize regulations in the war's early days. Despite charges that the German "submarine culture" pushed for an all-out war against commerce from the start,[11] Dönitz's commanders adhered to international prize rules during this period. When *Kaptlt.* Günther Prien sank his first victim, the British cargo vessel *Bosnia,* on 5 September 1939, he recovered the crew and turned them over to a passing Norwegian steamer.[12] Before the end of the month, five merchant ships were sunk by scuttling charges after being stopped and searched, and three others brought into German harbors by U-boat prize crews; none of the original crewmen suffered a scratch.

During this period several future U-boat aces recovered survivors of sunken ships and turned them over to neutral or even British ships for safe passage home: Examples included *Kaptlt.* Herbert Schultze of *U-48* (survivors of *Royal Sceptre,* 5 September), *Kaptlt.* Heinrich Liebe of *U-38* (survivors of *Inverliffy,* 11 September), and *Kaptlt.* Joachim Schepke of *U-3* (survivors of *Vendia,* 30 September). Schultze later displayed a mixture of bravado and humanity after sinking *Firby* on 11 September, when he issued a radio message *en clair* announcing the position of the sinking and requesting the Royal Navy to pick up the survivors. On 7 September, *Kaptlt.* Hans-Wilhelm von Dresky (*U-33*) stopped and sank the British freighter *Olivegrove* after allowing the crew to take to the lifeboats; von Dresky then stood by the boats for nine hours until he radioed an approaching American passenger liner to recover the Englishmen.[13]

The remarkable patrol of *U-35* (*Kaptlt.* Werner Lott) in September–October 1939 provides the clearest demonstration of humanity in sea warfare. Lott allowed the first British steam trawler he encountered in the North Atlantic to pass when he recognized that the thirteen-man crew could never have reached land in the available lifeboat; in return, the grateful British captain warned Lott of the aircraft carrier *Ark Royal's* presence in the general area. Later that day *U-35* sank two of a group of three trawlers—the third he spared to carry home the crews of all three. On 30 September, Lott measured the blacked-out, forty-five-thousand-ton passenger liner *Aquitania* in his sights at a range of only five hundred meters, but respected the restriction on attacking such vessels (which, ironically, had already been lifted, though this had not yet been communicated to *U-35*) and allowed her to proceed unmolested. Three days later he sank the Britain-bound Greek steamer *Diamantis* but took aboard her entire crew, putting them ashore the next day in neutral Ireland's Dingle Bay.[14]

This limited and sometimes chivalrous campaign, however, had already begun to erode into a more destructive and general struggle. Operating by prize rules often left the advantage to the merchantmen, as *U-53* (*Korv.Kapt.* Ernst Sobe) discovered when two British steamers ignored his signals to stop for searches and radioed the U-boat's position before speeding away. Dönitz especially feared a resurrection of the Q-ship, the "submarine trap" disguised as a harmless merchantman but carrying hidden guns manned by regular navy crews hoping to lure an unsuspecting U-boat to her doom. The threat posed by these vessels, which had destroyed at least fifteen German submarines in World War I, figured prominently in a 1939 Kriegsmarine manual with cautionaries and lessons learned from 1914–18. Yet when he read his commanders' war diary comments on actions taken on behalf of merchant crews, Dönitz realized he had not made his point. As U-boat losses rose from one in September to six in October 1939, he became convinced (erroneously, as we know today) that the restrictions placed on his submarines were primarily responsible for these casualties.[15]

Hitler partially alleviated the situation on 23 September when he approved BdU's proposals for expanding the shipping categories subject to attack, including torpedoings without warning of clearly identified enemy merchant ships.[16] But this was not enough, as Dönitz made clear in late November when he issued new tactical guidelines to his commanders in Standing Operational Order No. 154. In addition to combat recommendations, he stressed:

Do not rescue people and take them along. Do not worry about lifeboats. Weather conditions and proximity of land are of no consequence. Concern yourself only with your own boat and the effort to achieve the next success as quickly as possible. We must be hard in this war.

On trial at Nuremberg, Dönitz specifically justified this admonition on the basis of the youth and inexperience of many of his commanders, whose "very unselfish deeds of rescue" reflected their humanity but jeopardized the safety of their submarines. He was convinced, although he could not prove, that some of his losses in this early period were due to such misguided rescue efforts—a belief not disproven until after the war. The former BdU moreover pointed out that the order was intended for upcoming operations in English coastal waters, and by the next year the order had been rescinded.[17]

With most Allied merchant ships now armed and traveling in convoy, U-boat captains adhered to the directive but often undertook humanitarian measures on their own. From February through November 1940, *Kaptlt.* Heinz Scheringer (*U-26*), *Kaptlt.* Fritz-Julius Lemp (*U-30*), *Korv.Kapt.* Hans-Gerrit von Stockhausen (*U-65*), and *Kaptlt.* Otto Kretschmer (*U-23*) all provided water, liquor, cigarettes, navigational directions, and when necessary medical supplies to the survivors of vessels they sank. On one occasion in September 1940, Kretschmer retrieved a stunned British merchant sailor from the sea, revived and clothed him, then transferred him to a lifeboat with his comrades—over the protestations of the sailor, who believed he had been rescued by a British submarine. In May 1940, Lemp rescued thirteen survivors of the neutral Swedish vessel *Hagar,* sunk by a British mine.[18]

Circumstances in any case wrought major changes in the nature of the submarine war by summer 1940. The collapse of France shifted the campaign's focus to the North Atlantic as Hitler dropped most restrictions on commerce warfare in August. At the same time the U-boat fleet accelerated its expansion, bringing into the service officers and crews who had no memory of the early war's more limited campaign. The new phase of the U-boat war thus carried moral as well as strategic implications.

Era of Choice: Summer 1940–September 1942

Without regard for the different strategic phases, the period from the fall of France to September 1942 can be seen as a single era for humanitarian aspects of U-boat warfare. In contrast to his tight control of operations, Dönitz issued no detailed directives on rescue or nonrescue of survivors but left these matters to the judgment of each commander. The shift of operations from English coastal waters and the North Sea to the Atlantic's open seas itself changed the character of the struggle to a more general, impersonal, and destructive confrontation of convoys versus wolf packs. British statistics revealed that the ratio of torpedo to gunfire attacks by U-boats on merchant ships rose from less than 3:1 over the first year of the war to 8:1 during the six months after September 1940.[19] Moreover Allied merchantmen were now armed with deck guns manned by navy regulars who, when circumstances permitted, gave a good accounting when incautious submarines approached too close on the surface.[20] The greater difficulty in attacking merchant targets and the increased risks posed by Allied escorts often rendered the question of U-boat rescues academic. Yet with some categories of sinkings, and with Allied air power not yet an omnipotent presence, German submarine commanders confronted the dilemma of choice.

Convoy actions exposed the most ruthless aspects of submarine warfare. During this period of 1940–41, convoys sailed with few escorts and only occasionally with designated vessels to act as rescue ships for torpedoed victims, conditions that contributed significantly in the well-publicized tragedy of the sinking of the *City of Benares* by *U-48* (now under *Kaptlt.* Heinrich Bleichrodt) on 17 September 1940 with the loss of 256 lives, among them seventy-seven children. Through March 1943, convoy escorts were ordered not to stop to recover survivors until contact with attacking U-boats had been broken. The giant passenger liners that served as troopships likewise followed instructions to ignore survivors, as demonstrated by the *Queen Mary* when in May 1942 she sped past five packed lifeboats from a sunken Canadian liner. Casualty rates among the merchant crews of British vessels lost to U-boats rose from 11 percent in 1939 to 30 percent in 1940, and to 39 percent in 1941—the highest annual rate of the war. Not until the outfitting of over thirty specialized Rescue Ships (beginning in late 1941) and the significant increase of convoy escorts (in 1942–43) could merchant crews in convoy expect a better chance of surviving a sinking.[21]

In part, this reflected the choice of many U-boat commanders, whether operating against convoys or single vessels, to follow Dönitz's admonitions and risk nothing to aid survivors, even at the cost of important intelligence. Typical of this attitude was *Kaptlt.* Friedrich Markworth, whose *U-66* sank the unescorted steamer *West Lashaway* on 30 August 1942 southwest of Trinidad. Surfacing briefly in an unsuccessful attempt to identify his victim, Markworth made no attempt to interrogate or assist the nineteen survivors before departing.[22] During one convoy battle in April 1943, *U-631* (*Oblt.z.S.* Jürgen Krüger) approached the survivors of the Dutch vessel *Blitar,* recovered the ship's captain, and after a brief interrogation dropped him back into the water again. Krüger's signal to the lifeboats to recover the individual failed to save the captain, who drowned before his fellow survivors could reach him.[23]

In other circumstances, the need to conserve torpedoes and rely on artillery fire to finish off merchant vessels necessarily risked firing on, and killing, men as they lowered lifeboats. When *Kaptlt.* Victor Oehrn (*U-37*) sank the British freighter *Sheaf Mead* by gunfire on 27 May 1940, he expected neither the cold silence with which survivors answered his questions nor the later inclusion of the incident as a war crime by the Allies.[24] Similar charges in connection with the sinkings of the Brazilian coastal vessel *Antonico* by *U-516* (*Kaptlt.* Gerhard Wiebe) in September 1942 and the British trawler *Noreen Mary* in July 1944 by *U-247* (*Oblt.z.S.* Gerhard Matschulat) likely fall into the same category of firing at the ship interpreted as firing at survivors; as Dönitz noted, the U-boats moved off shortly after the vessels sank and did not linger to finish off those still alive, the most likely course had that been the intent.[25]

Surprisingly, survivors' chances improved if they were sunk on convoy stragglers or independents. On 8 April 1941 *U-124* (*Kaptlt.* Wilhelm Schulz), operating in the convoy-free waters off Freetown, sank the small British steamer *Tweed* about 150 miles from the coast. Schulz observed through his periscope that the larger of the two lifeboats launched by the crew had capsized. Despite the risk of aerial attack in full daylight, Schulz drew up to the lifeboats, took the survivors aboard, righted and set the sail of the larger boat, furnished medical assistance to two wounded crewmen, and gave food, water, and alcohol to the survivors as they reembarked for Freetown. Schulz's actions earned him an invitation seventeen years later to a reunion of the survivors in Poole, England.[26] The next month, *Kaptlt.* Jost Metzler (*U-69*) undertook similar measures for the crew and passengers of the first American merchant ship sunk in the war, the *Robin Moor*, en route from New York to Capetown.[27] In June, *Korv.Kapt.* Klaus Scholtz (*U-108*) provided survivors of the Greek steamer *Dirphys* water, bread, rum, aspirin, and matches.[28]

Pure chance often dictated the opportunity to undertake efforts for survivors. When he sank the Norwegian tanker *Ranja* on 17 March 1942 in the North Atlantic, *Korv.Kapt.* Werner Flachsenberg (*U-71*) did not dally but continued on to his operations area off the American east coast. En route home three weeks later, *U-71's* lookouts spied a lifeboat bearing three skeletal figures. They proved to be the last of eleven survivors of the same *Ranja* that had fallen victim to the U-boat earlier. Moved, Flachsenberg issued the survivors food, water, alcohol, cigarettes, and a chart to assist them to Greenland.[29]

Compassion was not limited to older captains, but required the right circumstances. When rookie skipper Cremer led his *U-333* into the convoy lanes in January 1942, his first victim, the British freighter *Caledonian Monarch*, sank with all hands in rough seas. Four days later, when Cremer sank the straggling *Vassilios A. Polemis,* he provided bandages and dressings for the wounded and food, cigarettes, and directions for the rest. When he next sank the Norwegian *Ringstad,* Cremer approached the lifeboats but slowed when he observed survivors operating a radio transmitter. After a rejected offer of food and water, Cremer hastily departed before his position could be reported—a good demonstration of balancing humanitarian efforts against military necessity.[30]

Between August 1940 and October 1941 German U-boats on several occasions recovered survivors of Allied merchantmen and warships as prisoners. *U-34 (Kaptlt.* Wilhelm Rollmann), for example, rescued the sole survivor of the British submarine *Spearfish* on 1 August 1940; *U-123* and *U-65* each picked up survivors of torpedoed victims on the high seas in October and November 1940; and *U-75 (Kaptlt.* Helmuth Ringelmann) recovered British army personnel from two troop-carrying lighters he sank off the Libyan coast in October 1941.[31]

Perhaps drawing upon these experiences, the *Seekriegsleitung* issued a directive on 5 June 1942 ordering U-boats to recover as prisoners the captains of sunken merchant vessels, when and where such efforts did not endanger or impair the submarine. Tacitly acknowledging the high survival rate among merchant crews, the order intended denying the Allies as many experienced, trained merchant officers as possible and securing some side benefits in intelligence.[32]

Dönitz never thought this policy productive, mistakenly believing even after the war that only ten or twelve merchant captains and engineers had been brought in by his U-boats. In fact, the directive facilitated rescue efforts on a much larger scale by U-boat commanders so inclined. From May through mid-September 1942 alone, German submarines rescued a minimum of twenty-four survivors of sunken Allied ships in seventeen separate incidents. Most of those recovered were merchant marine officers, as specified in the *Skl* directive, but they also included three ordinary seamen of the Dutch *Mendenau* sunk off West Africa and recovered by *U-752 (Oblt.z.S.* Karl-Ernst Schroeter). Nearly all the incidents involved single vessels traveling in areas where convoys had not yet been instituted, as Dönitz expanded operations to new waters.[33]

When a handful of U-boats wrought havoc among unescorted shipping off the American east coast in early 1942, the proximity of U.S. naval and air forces persuaded most submarine commanders not to take chances in assisting survivors. Hardegen and *U-123,* however, once chose not to play it safe while very close to the shore. After he torpedoed the tanker *Gulf America* on 10 April off Jacksonville, Florida, Hardegen determined to finish his victim by shellfire; yet, rather than risk the lives of American civilians on the beaches with overshots, he instead maneuvered precariously into the shallow waters between the stricken tanker and the shore to deliver his artillery fire seaward.

Removed from hazardous coastal waters, Hardegen felt secure enough to attempt greater measures on behalf of merchant crews. In January 1942, he provided food and navigational bearings to the survivors of the British steamer *Culebra*. The next day, after sinking the Norwegian freighter *Pan Norway*, Hardegen intercepted the Swiss vessel *Mount Aetna* and directed her to the recovery of survivors—even to the point of compelling her to complete the rescue work when the Swiss vessel tried to cut short the errand of mercy.[34]

Dönitz's shift of emphasis to Caribbean waters in the summer of 1942 offered more targets to U-boat captains, but the confined area and ever-increasing Allied air power required even greater caution. The proximity of enemy coasts meant that a torpedoed vessel's distress signal could be answered quickly, leaving little margin of safety for a surfaced submarine. Yet such captains as Nicolai Clausen (*U-129*), Karl-Friedrich Merten (*U-68*), Fritz Poske (*U-504*), Ulrich Heyse (*U-128*), Werner Schulte (*U-582*), Walther Kölle (*U-154*), Ulrich Gräf (*U-69*), Axel-Olaf Loewe (*U-505*), and Werner Henke (*U-515*) all furnished survivors with provisions and bearings during this period, as did Heinrich Bleichrodt (now in command of *U-109*), operating off the West African coast. Small sailing schooners, important for the food trade among Caribbean islands, were often stopped by submarines and sunk by gunfire after the crews were allowed to escape. In one case, *Kaptlt.* Albrecht Achilles (*U-161*) took aboard the eight-man crew of a Dominican schooner because their lifeboat was unseaworthy, releasing them the next day to another sailing vessel.[35]

On at least two other occasions in the Caribbean, U-boat commanders rescued American merchant seamen and brought them aboard their vessels for extended periods. On 15 June 1942 *Kaptlt.* Ernst Bauer (*U-126*) recovered thirty-six-year-old Archie Carr Gibbs from the American freighter *Kahuku* after he had torpedoed her; Bauer kept Gibbs aboard for four days, then stopped a Venezuelan motor-skiff and released his prisoner. Revealingly, Bauer made no report and left no official record of his deed, which violated Dönitz's specific orders and every rule of military security—a point amply demonstrated by Gibbs' subsequent fourteen-page account to U.S. naval intelligence of his observations while on board the U-boat. Bauer's actions are especially remarkable in view of his place among the top thirty-two U-boat aces of the war.

Two weeks earlier, *Kaptlt.* Jürgen von Rosenstiel (*U-502*) had torpedoed the American tanker *M. F. Elliott* 150 miles northwest of Trinidad. The sinking vessel capsized her lifeboats, but U.S. Navy planes responding to the SOS dropped life rafts that provided safety for most of the survivors. Two crewmen left swimming without a raft suddenly saw *U-502* rise from the depths and bring them aboard. After three hours' confinement in the forward torpedo room, the Americans were released in a rubber dinghy with provisions, eventually to be picked up by a Brazilian ship. They proved more fortunate than their rescuers, all of whom were lost when Allied aircraft dispatched *U-502* on 5 July in the Bay of Biscay.[36]

Similar actions occurred at the same time in areas far removed from the Caribbean. Several thousand miles to the east, *Kaptlt.* Wilhelm Franken (*U-565*) ceased his artillery attack on a fleet of sailing vessels near the Suez Canal when he realized they were not transporting goods but were only fishing boats; he recovered the crew of one schooner he had sunk, treated a wounded sailor, and turned them over to another of the fishing fleet. *Vizeadmiral* Leo Kreisch, operational commander of Mediterranean U-boats, could not endorse such an action when British aircraft might appear at any moment, but acknowledged, "It pleased me nonetheless."[37]

During the July 1942 massacre of Convoy PQ-17 in Arctic waters, several U-boats provided relief to survivors of sunken merchantmen. After sinking the 6,600-ton *Empire Byron* on 5 July, *Kaptlt.* Heinz Bielfeld (*U-703*) fished an engineer out of the water and gave him to one of the lifeboats, together with bread, biscuits, sausage, and apple juice, while taking the ship's captain along as a prisoner. Later that day Bielfeld sank the *River Afton* and provided water and a large sausage to the survivors, apologizing that he could not take them aboard as he departed. Over the next twenty days, *U-255* (*Kaptlt.* Reinhard Reche) sank the American freighter *John Witherspoon* and furnished the survivors cigarettes, water, and cognac, along with directions to avoid a pack of ice ahead of them; *U-355* (*Kaptlt.* Günter La Baume) provided bread, gin, rum, and directions to survivors of the *Hartlebury;* and *U-376* (*Kaptlt.* Friedrich-Karl Marks) gave water, cigarettes, biscuits, blankets, a compass, and charts—much of which had been recovered by the enterprising Germans from a still-floating wreck—to survivors of the British steamer *Carlton,* sunk nearly three weeks earlier by another submarine.[38]

These incidents, and particularly those in the Caribbean, demonstrate how much initiative remained with U-boat commanders in undertaking rescue measures, even to the neglect of standard security. Inevitably, one such incident on a sufficiently large scale would lead Dönitz to attempt to eliminate such discretion and establish an unequivocal policy.

The *Laconia* Incident

In 1942 as throughout the war, the daily conduct of U-boat operations absorbed Dönitz's attention. The mass of tactical and technical detail in coordinating a global conflict crowded out studies of U-boat rescue efforts. Ironically, the first pressures on BdU to consider policy changes in this area came from above, rather than the conduct of his subordinates.

On 3 January 1942 Adolf Hitler met with Japanese ambassador Hiroshi Oshima in Berlin to discuss the war situation in the aftermath of Pearl Harbor. With regard to the Battle of the Atlantic, Hitler emphasized the importance of killing as many American merchant marine crewmen as possible to discourage enlistment: "I must give the order that since foreign seamen cannot be taken prisoner, and in most cases this is not possible on the open sea, the U-boats are to surface after torpedoing and shoot up the lifeboats." In fact no such order followed, but Hitler had revealed his own position in a characteristically ruthless manner.[39]

The subject next arose in a joint discussion among Hitler, Raeder, and Dönitz on 14 May at Hitler's headquarters in East Prussia. There Hitler asked his submarine commander-in-chief if something might be done to reduce the number of survivors from sunken merchant ships; Dönitz responded only that newer, more powerful torpedoes would increase personnel losses by sinking ships faster. Hitler accepted this answer, and the issue subsided.[40] Possibly this conference prompted the *Skl* directive the next month regarding the capture of ships' officers.

On the evening of 12 September 1942, *U-156* (*Kaptlt.* Werner Hartenstein), proceeding south of the equator with four other submarines en route to operations off the Cape of Good Hope, encountered and sank a northbound passenger liner. Interrogations of survivors revealed the victim as the twenty-thousand-ton British liner *Laconia*, transporting 1,800 Italian prisoners of war and hundreds of Allied military and civilian personnel to England. The dilemma of choice that many U-boat skippers had faced on a small scale now confronted Hartenstein with a life-or-death decision for nearly three thousand human beings: What was he to do?

Hartenstein could be considered typical of many U-boat commanders of 1942. Although he entered the navy as an officer cadet in 1928, his transfer to the U-boat service occurred only in 1941. In command of *U-156* for a year, he had enjoyed success on his previous patrol in the Caribbean, including a daring shelling of oil refineries on the island of Aruba. In particular view of the number of Italian allies he had put at risk, Hartenstein wasted little time on his decision: Consistent with the actions of other U-boat captains, he chose to initiate rescue operations on his own. Given the scale such an operation required, however, he reported the situation to BdU, adding that he had already taken ninety survivors on board.

At his Paris headquarters, Dönitz weighed the various factors and concluded as paramount the need to rescue the Italians. The risk to the boat, loss of operational time, and the impossibility of distinguishing Italian survivors from British all took second place to preserving the Axis alliance. In addition, Dönitz considered the effect on the morale of his men if he were to command them to throw rescued survivors back into the water. Despite directives from both Raeder and Hitler not to endanger his submarines, BdU determined not only to support Hartenstein but to greatly expand the rescue operation. Thus the next day Dönitz ordered the remaining four U-boats destined for Capetown to turn about and join the rescue efforts. Two other boats, *U-506* (*Kaptlt.* Erich Würdemann) and *U-507* (*Kaptlt.* Harro Schacht), and the Italian submarine *Cappellini*, already operating off Freetown, Sierra Leone, were also diverted.

Negotiations with the Vichy French government soon yielded a commitment of French naval vessels from bases in French Equatorial Africa, allowing the four other Capetown-bound submarines to resume their original course. Even without them, however, the diversion of limited U-boat resources to rescue operations remains unequaled in the history of submarine warfare. Over the next three days *U-156*, *U-506*, *U-507*, and *Cappellini* began the Herculean rescue task. Each German submarine took aboard between 110 and 150 survivors and towed several lifeboats carrying hundreds more. The submariners then assumed the role of hosts for the survivors taken on board. An Englishwoman later recalled:

We were given hot tea and coffee, black bread and butter, rusks and jam. . . . The German officers gave up their bunks to us, and many of the crew gave up theirs to our men and to the Italians. . . . The Germans treated us with kindness and respect the whole time; they were really sorry for our plight. One brought us eau-de-Cologne, another cold cream for our sunburn; others gave us lemons from their own lockers, articles of clothing, and tinned fruit. The commandant was particularly charming and helpful.[41]

Their decks crowded with humanity, the U-boats steered northeast toward a linkup with the Vichy French vessels. Hartenstein broadcast messages *en clair* explaining his position and displayed a Red Cross flag on the bridge. But on the afternoon of 16 September a B-24 bomber of the U.S. Army Air Forces' 343d Bombardment Squadron appeared in the sky. Its commander, Lt. James D. Harden, contacted his superiors at the U.S. 1st

Composite Air Squadron on Ascension Island, who ordered him to proceed with the attack. Despite the lifeboats, crowded decks, and Red Cross flag draped over the submarine's forward gun, Harden made a bombing run that led him to claim a U-boat destroyed. In fact the aircraft's bombs inflicted only moderate damage to the submarine but destroyed one lifeboat and killed other survivors in the water. Hartenstein hastily cut the towrope, forced the onboard survivors back into the water, and submerged to avoid further damage.

When Hartenstein radioed news of the attack, Dönitz ordered *U-156* to break off further rescue efforts. A second signal followed to *U-506* and *U-507* with orders to maintain their ability to maneuver and dive and to transfer all but Italian survivors to the lifeboats. Before the U-boats could rendezvous with the Vichy vessels, *U-506* barely escaped destruction from another attacking aircraft. Finally on 17–18 September the U-boats and *Cappellini* sighted the French warships and transferred the remaining survivors.

Thus ended what became known as the *Laconia* incident. Ultimately the intentions behind specific decisions all failed to be realized. Hartenstein's initiative rescued more than a thousand survivors, but only about 450 of the Italians were saved; the American bomber failed to sink or seriously damage *U-156*, instead merely adding more Allied victims to the death toll; and despite Dönitz's efforts on behalf of the alliance, Italy would leave the Axis in less than a year. Finally, BdU's diversion of valuable resources for a humanitarian mission not only failed to score even a token propaganda victory, but the subsequent order he issued landed him in the dock at the Nuremberg war crimes trial.

For the *Laconia* incident had finally convinced Dönitz of the need "to issue orders to preclude the possibility of any recurrence of such a situation and which also left U-boat captains with no authority to use their discretion . . . in attempting a rescue or not." And so on the evening of 17 September he radioed to all submarines the following order:

No attempt of any kind must be made at rescuing the crews of ships sunk. This prohibition applies to the picking up of men in the water and putting them in lifeboats, righting capsized lifeboats, and handing over food and water. Rescue remains contrary to the primary demands of warfare for the destruction of enemy ships and their crews.

The specific references to practices of commanders unrelated to the *Laconia* affair reveal the order's genesis. Dönitz's obvious misgivings about the risks his men had taken since 1940 in assisting survivors appeared fully confirmed by the growth of Allied air power and its ruthless application.

Up to this point he had conceded discretionary powers for humanitarian measures to his commanders, who had reciprocated by not endangering their boats when they had aided survivors. Now as the increasing threat of Allied aircraft reduced a U-boat commander's ability to gauge the safety factor, Dönitz eliminated his discretionary powers altogether: "I did not want to give [a U-boat commander] a chance to act independently, to make his own decision," Dönitz later explained. He left in place, however, the *Skl*'s directive to recover captains when practicable, with an additional provision to "rescue the shipwrecked only if their statements [are] important for your boats."[42]

After the war, Allied war crimes prosecutors would try Dönitz as a war criminal for this message—thereafter known as the *Laconia* order—which they interpreted as an instruction to kill shipwrecked survivors. If so, it failed within a week of its issuance, for on 24 September *U-617* (*Oblt.z.S.* Albrecht Brandi) recovered a survivor of the Belgian steamer *Roumanie* in the North Atlantic.[43]

That Dönitz's message fell far short of an order to murder became a subject of discussion among Hitler, Raeder, and Dönitz in a conference at the Reich Chancellery in Berlin on 28 September. Hitler seized upon the *Laconia* incident to advocate the outright killing of survivors: "It is nonsense to offer provisions to survivors in their lifeboats, or provide sailing instructions for their return home. I hereby order that ships and their crews are to be destroyed, even if the crews are in lifeboats." An eyewitness recorded Dönitz's reaction as follows:

No, *mein Führer*. It goes against the honor of a seaman to shoot at shipwrecked survivors. I cannot issue such an order. My U-boat men are volunteers, waging a costly struggle in the belief they are fighting honorably for a good cause. Their combat morale would be undermined by this order. I must request that you withdraw it.

Hitler, lapsing into a Viennese dialect, backed down: "Do what you want, but no more offering assistance and sailing instructions."[44] Few stood up to Hitler in such a manner; fewer still won their point. For this, Dönitz deserves due credit, but perhaps it is ultimately attributable to his understanding of what his submariners would and would not do.

War to the Death?

Dönitz's order unquestionably had an effect, but probably less so than the facts of the incident. Officers at sea who monitored Hartenstein's transmissions questioned the wisdom of his actions (one termed it "suicide") and predicted the likely outcome.[45] News of the incident doubtless impressed

U-boat commanders with the Allies' determination to kill them at any cost and eliminated inclinations about undertaking rescues, although it did not increase animosity toward survivors of sunken vessels.[46]

To a large extent, however, the issue grew more academic as U-boats encountered fewer and more difficult targets. The increasing effectiveness of Allied air power revealed in the *Laconia* incident also caused Dönitz's withdrawal of most of his forces from the Caribbean. From the autumn of 1942 through the spring of 1943 the U-boat war returned to its focus on the North Atlantic convoy lanes that temporarily lay beyond the range of land-based aircraft. Convoy battles permitted fewer amenities to survivors, and the combined influence of Dönitz's order and the Allies' own actions during the *Laconia* incident doubtless convinced many U-boat commanders of the impracticability of aiding survivors. In this struggle mercy served primarily as a handmaiden to intelligence, yet instances of rescues and humanity remained a part of the pattern.

During this critical period of convoy battles, Allied forces—despite the claims of some postwar historians[47]—concerned themselves with prisoners mostly in terms of risk and convenience. For example, Capt. Frederic John Walker, the Royal Navy's famed hunter of U-boats, refused to bring the survivors of *U-202* (*Kaptlt.* Günter Poser) aboard his sloop *Starling* until they revealed the identities of their boat and commander.[48] Recent studies based on British official records moreover reveal the following incidents:

23 April 1943: A British aircraft sank *U-189* (*Korv.Kapt.* Helmut Kurrer) and observed the crew going into the water. The aircraft's suggestion that convoy escorts pick up the survivors was rejected by the escort commander because of the possible presence of additional U-boats, and none of the crew survived the U-boat's loss.

6 May 1943: The British corvette HMS *Snowflake* rammed and fatally damaged *U-125* (*Kaptlt.* Ulrich Folkers), then requested permission to recover survivors for interrogation. The escort commander refused and the survivors perished.

23 May 1943: After British aircraft mortally wounded *U-752* (Schroeter), the destroyer HMS *Escapade* recovered thirteen German survivors but left behind an estimated twenty to thirty more, only four of whom (eventually rescued by another U-boat) survived.

16 October 1943: When aircraft sank *U-470* (*Oblt.z.S.d.R.* Günter Grave) in the wake of Convoy ON-206, the destroyer HMS *Duncan* was ordered to pick up survivors but elected not to risk a stop and recovered only two men fortunate enough to hang on to grappling nets, leaving approximately fifteen to twenty others to drown.[49]

For their part, German U-boats during this period found it increasingly difficult to fight their way through convoy escorts to sink ships in the first place. Interestingly, the loss rate among merchant crewmen of sunken British vessels in 1943 (29 percent) actually declined from that of 1942 (30 percent), a testament to the convoy rescue ships and further evidence that U-boat captains were not in fact killing survivors. On the contrary, when circumstances permitted, German submarine captains continued to recover survivors of their victims.

From mid-September 1942 through May 1943, twenty-four different U-boats recovered not less than forty-nine survivors from sunken ships. Again most were ships' officers, and in at least one case (*U-632, Kaptlt.* Hans Karpf) the immediate interrogation of a chief engineer furnished valuable intelligence regarding the course of the next convoy.[50] On 28 November 1943, *U-238* (*Oblt.z.S.* Horst Hepp) recovered two British aircrewmen from the sea, survivors from an RAF B-17 shot down earlier by *U-764* (*Oblt.z.S.* Hanskurt von Bremen), and the essential data from their interrogation were entered in the BdU war diary by that evening.[51] In two cases, U-boats rescued and brought aboard entire groups of survivors: *U-753* (*Korv.Kapt.* Alfred Manhardt von Mannstein) picked up six survivors of the Dutch ship *Madoera* on 27 February 1943, and *U-336* (*Kaptlt.* Hans Hunger) recovered six survivors of the American Liberty Ship *Jonathan Sturges* on 5 April 1943. In both instances the U-boats had not attacked the vessels in question but had simply come across the survivors and acted to save lives. The discretion Dönitz had supposedly denied his commanders in fact remained with them. If BdU enjoined his men to "be harsh" and write off enemy survivors of no practical benefit, the examples of these boats demonstrate a widespread adherence to earlier practices.[52]

Additional proof of old habits dying hard could be seen in *Kaptlt.* Harald Gelhaus's (*U-107*) conduct. After sinking the British merchantman *Roxborough Castle* northwest of the Azores on 22 February 1943, Gelhaus approached the survivors, one of whom later recalled:

The U-boat captain then asked us (in perfect English) did we have any injured, did we need any food or water, did we especially need anything at all. We thanked him and answered "no" to his questions. He then apologized for sinking us and told us how far it was [to the closest island], gave us a course to steer by, wished us good luck and left.[53]

Korv.Kapt. Wolfgang Lüth's final patrol with *U-181* in the Indian Ocean, the second-longest (203 days) by any U-boat during the war, provides examples of all the rescue options exercised by a commander, as determined by individual circumstances. On 26 May 1943 he sank the Swedish steamer *Sicilia* according to prize rules, stopping the vessel and examining her papers before allowing the crew to depart safely. On 15 July Lüth sank the British collier *Empire Lake* and left her survivors on some floating wreckage without further ado; when he dispatched the *Clan Macarthur* one month later, however, he treated the wounded survivors and signaled their position to Allied authorities on Mauritius when he achieved a safe distance.[54]

The evidence thus dispels the hypothesis that after the *Laconia* incident Dönitz issued secret instructions to kill survivors. The precise issue of survival of merchant crews, however, occupied an important place in German naval command discussions even as the convoy battles approached their climax. In mid-December 1942 the German Foreign Office, the Abwehr, and the Navy High Command pooled their efforts to calculate Allied merchant crew numbers and losses. They estimated that 190,000 seamen manned the Allies' merchant fleet, of whom 63,000 had been lost up to that point. This proved to be a considerable overestimate, as the total number of combat deaths among Allied and neutral merchant seamen for the entire war amounted to approximately fifty thousand. The miscalculation became evident in early April 1943 when the British Transport Minister remarked that an average of 87 percent of merchant crewmen survived the sinkings of their vessels. This new intelligence was forwarded to the *Skl* for recommendation, with the killing of survivors an implied option.[55]

The Naval Operations Staff did not dodge the issue. "It is in the interest of our conduct of the war to prevent the crews of sunken merchant ships from being used again," noted the *Skl* in its war diary of 4 April, "but we consider it inappropriate to employ special measures to prevent rescues of enemy survivors." If this was not clear enough, the *Skl* continued:

A directive to take action against lifeboats of sunken vessels and crewmen drifting in the sea is for psychological reasons intolerable for U-boat crews, as this is contrary to the innermost feelings of all seamen [emphasis added]. . . . An action by U-boats against the crews of sunken ships, which would quickly become known, would call forth the severest reprisals by the enemy against U-boat crewmen now or in future in their hands. It is irresponsible to adopt a measure of dubious effectiveness but which must also have the direst consequences for our U-boat crews.[56]

Just as Dönitz had deflected Hitler in May, so too the *Seekriegsleitung* proposed that the best way to reduce survivors was to employ more powerful torpedoes. This decision gains in significance when it is remembered that Dönitz had become commander-in-chief of the navy on 30 January 1943. The *Skl* opinion confirms a rejection of killing survivors as a matter of policy as well as the choice of individual captains.

Dönitz nevertheless intensified the campaign's severity in the autumn of 1943. After heavy losses compelled him to temporarily abandon the convoy battles after May, BdU accelerated the rearmament of his submarines with heavier antiaircraft guns, improved radar detectors, and new types of torpedoes. By September he was ready to renew the struggle. As the U-boats returned to the North Atlantic, Dönitz issued a directive on 7 October specifically targeting the rescue ships that now accompanied Allied convoys: "In view of the desired destruction of ships' crews, their sinking is of great value."[57] Allied superiority and the U-boats' inability to mount a sustained threat to Atlantic convoys, however, rendered this order academic.

More than any specific instruction, however, Dönitz's harsh language and tone influenced several of his subordinates. *Korv.Kapt.* Karl-Heinz Moehle, a prewar U-boat skipper who sank twenty-two Allied ships while commanding *U-20* and *U-123* in 1939–41, took command of the 5th U-boat Flotilla in June 1941. This unit, based in Kiel, was one of three involved in the final fitting out of submarines bound for front-line duty in the Atlantic (see the organizational chart in appendix 3), and Moehle handed out the latest standard instructions and standing orders to new captains before they departed for the front. When he received his copy of the *Laconia* order, Moehle considered the ambiguous terminology capable of interpretation as an endorsement of the killing of survivors. After obtaining a seeming confirmation of this impression in a subsequent conversation with one of BdU's staff officers, Moehle began to transmit this view to all outbound U-boat captains in his unit. As late as February 1945, Moehle advised new commanders on Dönitz's "unwritten orders" to kill survivors of sunken Allied ships and downed aircraft, although he also stressed that such a decision ultimately rested on the conscience of each captain.[58]

Neither Dönitz, his operations staff, nor any of the combat flotilla commanders, however, interpreted the *Laconia* order in this way. In January 1946 sixty-seven U-boat captains held in the British POW camp at Featherstone Park signed a petition that they had never been ordered or encouraged to kill survivors. Moehle's supposed confirmation of the murderous intent of the directive rested upon an incident in which a commander was allegedly reprimanded for not killing downed British aviators on a raft in the Bay of Biscay; the documentary evidence in fact proved the opposite—that Dönitz criticized the commander in question (*Oblt.z.S.* Fritz Albrecht of *U-386* in September 1943) for *not* rescuing the fliers for interrogation.[59] Most significantly, none of the young U-boat captains briefed by Moehle—save one—acted on his "suggestion."

Nor did U-boats operating against Soviet forces behave in any different manner. In the Black Sea, *U-23* (*Kaptlt.* Rolf-Birger Wahlen) and *U-24* (*Oblt.z.S.* Klaus Petersen) recovered nine Soviet survivors, some of them wounded, from sunken landing craft as prisoners during the period August–October 1943. Operating in Arctic waters, *U-957* (*Oblt.z.S.* Gerd Schaar) picked up three survivors of a Soviet survey vessel and the four-man crew of a Soviet radio station on Sterligova Island in August–September 1944 and *U-995* (*Oblt.z.S.* Hans-Georg Hess) retrieved the survivor of a Russian fishing vessel off the Soviet Arctic coast in December 1944.[60]

One incident in March 1944 provided the most incriminating example of "ruthless" intensified submarine conflict, the only incontrovertible case of a U-boat firing upon survivors. En route to operations in the Indian Ocean, *U-852* (*Kaptlt.* Heinz Eck) encountered and sank the Greek steamer *Peleus* southwest of Freetown on 13 March. After a brief interrogation of survivors, the U-boat moved off but then turned back and opened fire on the life rafts, killing or mortally wounding all survivors but three, who were recovered twenty-five days later. *U-852* did not survive her patrol, and the captured Eck and his officers were brought back to England for trial as war criminals.

Although this proved to be his only submarine patrol, and *Peleus* his first victim, Eck was no novice. A ten-year Navy veteran, he had commanded minesweepers until joining the *U-Boot-Waffe* in June 1942. Apparently obsessed with the need to eliminate any trace of his boat's presence, Eck justified his action as an attempt to destroy all physical evidence of the sinking to conceal his position, an attempt abandoned only when he realized he could not destroy the rafts. The British interrogators of *U-852's* crew noted, "There appears to have been much criticism and indignation among those of the lower deck about this act." When he later addressed his depressed crew, Eck reiterated familiar phrases of "harshness" and analogies to Allied bombing raids on Germany, but he never defended his unique action as an interpretation of the *Laconia* order. Convicted of war crimes, Eck and two of his officers were executed by the British in November 1945.[61]

It is not accidental that the *Peleus* incident occurred during the crisis of morale that struck the U-boat arm in early 1944. As discussed previously, psychological strains mounted for commanders and their crews as their vessels proved ever more vulnerable to Allied countermeasures. Eck's attempts to destroy the evidence of his victim and justify the action in terms of Allied bombing raids suggest the insecurity of a new commander under the greatly adverse conditions that prevailed in those months. But by the time of Eck's action, U-boats no longer exercised a major influence on the naval war. The submarine force that had claimed 452 British merchant vessels in 1942 alone sank only sixty-seven of the same category in 1944 and a mere thirty in 1945. Merchant crews' survival rates on sunken vessels rose as well, from 71 percent in 1943 to 74 percent in 1944 and 84 percent in 1945. By war's end, the issues of U-boat commanders' choices, selective nonrescue, and more powerful torpedoes had all been rendered meaningless by Allied supremacy at sea.[62]

Conclusion

In August 1945 investigators from both the British Admiralty and the U.S. Navy advised the chief American prosecutor for the Nuremberg tribunal of "insufficient evidence to convict [Dönitz] or to warrant his being tried."[63] During the trial Francis Biddle, the senior American member of the tribunal, commented that "Germany waged a cleaner [naval] war than we did." Yet Dönitz would be prosecuted on three counts (conspiracy, crimes against peace, and war crimes), convicted, and sentenced to ten years' imprisonment, a sentence he fully served. As a historian of the Nuremberg Trial wrote, "The majority of the Court had convicted Dönitz because of submarine warfare but agreed to say he had been convicted on other grounds." His moderate sentence, however, reflected at least a partial vindication of the U-boat service by its opponents, if not a tacit acknowledgment of questionable Allied actions in the war at sea.[64]

The evidence confirms the ruthless nature of unrestricted submarine warfare and a clear division in considerations shown for merchant crews after the first year of war. Yet for the next two years, many U-boat commanders continued to make provision for survivors of vessels they had sunk, extending to measures they did not report to headquarters. Even after the *Laconia* affair and subsequent Dönitz order seemingly settled the issue, and in spite of Moehle's open encouragement of killing survivors, individual captains still exercised their own judgment in rescue matters.

In the Third Reich, where Hitler's musings and fantasies were often translated into murderous reality, Dönitz's refusal to accept the Führer's expressed views on killing shipwrecked survivors commands attention. More striking, however, is the consistency with which a significant number of U-boat commanders chose on their own initiative to preserve some measure of humanity with a weapon that was fundamentally inhumane.

And this, in turn, raises the question of the relationship of U-boat commanders and crews to the means and ends of the National Socialist regime.

Disinterested Service

The Navy and National Socialism

A question that has always intrigued students of the German armed forces is the degree to which ordinary soldiers and seamen served as standard-bearers of National Socialism (NS) and its ideology. The recent studies of Israeli scholar Omer Bartov, who concludes that the Wehrmacht's criminal conduct during the Eastern campaign demonstrates a widespread influence of Nazi racial and ideological views,[1] have brought new focus to this issue. Here we shall consider the significance of this question for World War II German naval officers and U-boat crewmen. We shall weigh the relevance of evidence from our sample, trace the development of navy–NS relations from the 1920s through Dönitz, and examine the place of the navy in the German resistance. First we must note the sharp changes in perception that necessitate this review.

The Evolution of Historiography

As passions cooled after World War II, historians generally accepted the Kriegsmarine's relationship to National Socialism as that allegedly ascribed by Hitler, "I have a reactionary Army, a National Socialist Air Force, and a Christian Navy."[2] The smallest of the three services, geographically restricted to the Atlantic periphery of occupied Europe, the navy escaped participation in the atrocities associated with the war in the East. Hitler's land-oriented strategy left him relatively ignorant of and detached from naval affairs, demonstrated by Raeder's and Dönitz's open defiance of the Führer, at least as recorded in their memoirs. The navy remained "apolitical," claimed Raeder, committed to its "tradition of patriotism and disinterested service to the State."[3]

With time, however, came access to primary-source documentation and a more critical generation to exploit it. Some historians argued that the socially conservative navy facilitated the Nazi takeover and that the navy's leadership encouraged Hitler's plans of global domination to further their own goals of a massive battle fleet with overseas bases. Others found extensive evidence of the navy's internal accommodation to the Nazis' domestic agenda, especially manifest in the absence of naval officers' participation in the German resistance. Karl Dönitz in particular came under harsh scrutiny for his unconditional loyalty to Hitler and unquestioning willingness to sacrifice his crews in a hopeless cause. The Bundesrepublik seemingly confirmed this evaluation when it banned servicemen from appearing in uniform at Dönitz's funeral in 1981.[4]

Inevitably the men of the U-boat branch have come under this new scrutiny, but not in any systematic or convincing manner. For example, Wolfgang Lüth's biographer argues that the U-boat ace was a convinced National Socialist (although acknowledging that Lüth neither joined the party nor forced his views on his crew), but the statement remains an allegation rather than a basis for further study.[5] A 1987 general account of the U-boat war devotes a chapter to the increasing role of "Nazis" among U-boat officers after 1940 but relies simply and uncritically on the wartime remarks of British interrogators. An examination of similar American POW interrogation reports reveals that any German who followed standard procedure in refusing to divulge more than name, rank, and serial number was usually classified as a "fanatic Nazi."[6] Reflecting the Bartov perspective, a 1996 British film documentary comments:

> The sense of being specially chosen for one of the most dangerous and demanding jobs in the armed forces appealed to dedicated young Nazis. As a result, the U-boat arm was more deeply politicized and more driven by ideology than any other branch of the Wehrmacht.

Neither the film's narrative text nor credits, however, provide a source or evidence for this assertion, as remarkable for its extravagance as for its unsubstantiation.[7]

The research in this field thus stands in the early stages and because of its ideological nature remains elusively subjective. We cannot entirely escape such limitations here, but data from our sample of U-boat officers and men might offer some tangible evidence on which to draw more reliable conclusions.

Evidence from the Sample

Political choice remains as always a matter of personal opinion, subject to change over time and circumstances. The fifty thousand men who manned Germany's submarines during World War II thus offer fifty thousand individual answers to the question of their attitudes toward National Socialism, each of which may well have been revised in the course of time. To take but one example, nineteen-year-old Erich Topp became Nazi party (NSDAP) member no. 2,621,078 in May 1933 and by 1934 had joined the *Allgemeine* (General) SS as well. When his application as a naval officer cadet was accepted in March 1934, he had to drop active membership in both organizations because of his new status as a member of the armed forces. After a highly successful wartime career as a U-boat ace, Topp gradually reevaluated his experiences and came to terms with the criminal nature of Hitler's regime. He also became a severe critic of Dönitz, eventually entering in heated debates with former comrades over the cause for which they had fought.[8]

Considerable variation can be seen among other top aces in their attitudes. Neither Otto Kretschmer (born May 1912) nor Joachim Schepke (born March 1912) joined the Nazi party prior to their entry into the navy in 1930, although the latter's wartime memoir reflects NS ideology and anti-Semitism.[9] Günther Prien (born January 1908), on the other hand, became party member no. 1,128,487 in May 1932, a fact noted in his 1940 autobiography, which otherwise ignores Nazi themes.[10] As will be seen, other U-boat aces and commanders proved decidedly anti-Nazi.

These contrasts and Topp's individual course make obvious the limitations of any quantitative study. The data from our sample, oriented toward U-boat veterans' personal background and military service, do not address political issues, which would have been more pertinent in any case for their fathers during the decisive period 1924–33. The extensive recent research in sociological profiles of Nazi party voting patterns and membership caution against generalizations and extrapolation based on geography or occupation.[11]

Among the fathers' occupations, for example, we have already seen that

36.2 percent were skilled laborers and craftsmen, a category traditionally considered a pillar of Nazi support. Yet within this group—which included occupations as diverse as a baker in a family pastry shop, an engine mechanic in the new aviation industry, and a master cobbler who owned his own business—Hitler enjoyed no clear majority. In addition, the most recent research reveals major differences in NSDAP membership patterns among skilled workers according to external factors (religion, region, community size, age) as well as internal considerations (prospects for business independence, degree of unionization, and orientation toward domestic or export goods).[12] Doubtless a number of U-boat crewmen grew up in homes where their fathers were enthusiastic Nazis, but whether this is more true of submariners than members of any other branch of service cannot be determined from the available evidence. There are on the other hand specific examples of men who volunteered for U-boat duty to "clean the slate" for their fathers, whose anti-Nazi views had led to incarceration in concentration camps.[13]

The sample does offer, however, the opportunity to compare the background of the naval officer corps with that of the Praetorian guard of Nazi Germany, the Waffen-SS. Bernd Wegner's recent analysis of the men who served in the latter includes a social profile of 582 officers whose ideological commitment to National Socialism stood beyond question. Did U-boat commanders and Waffen-SS officers share the same or similar characteristics and backgrounds?

A comparison of the data for regional origin, religious affiliation, and education completed (table 24) reveals that the two groups of officers do not merely differ greatly, but almost come from different worlds. The naval officers are disproportionately northern, Protestant, and well-educated in comparison with their Waffen-SS comrades, even more so than indicated in the table. The southern origins for the latter, for example, are actually stronger, as most of the listed as "foreign-born" represent Austrians. Moreover, the educational data apply to all Waffen-SS officers, including generals, whereas our U-boat sample consists almost entirely of lieutenants and lieutenant commanders; if the focus is narrowed only to SS majors and lieutenant colonels (*Sturmbannführer* and *Obersturmbannführer*), the differences become even more pronounced:

Education	SS Majors/Lt. Cols.	U-boat Officers
Elementary school	38.1 percent	0.5 percent
Middle school	29.6 percent	30.0 percent
University-qualified	32.3 percent	69.5 percent

TABLE 24 **BACKGROUNDS OF WAFFEN-SS AND U-BOAT OFFICERS**

	Germany[a]	Waffen-SS	U-boat
Geographic origins			
• North[b]	32.3%	32.8%	44.9%
• Central[c]	46.5	30.9	43.1
• South[d]	17.5	21.0	5.4
• Outside borders[e]		10.3	6.0
• No data		5.0	0.6
Religion[f]			
• Protestant	62.1%	74.1%	77.2%
• Roman Catholic	33.1	25.9	14.4
• Other/none	4.8	—	8.4
Education			
• Elementary school	—[g]	21.3%	0.5%
• Middle school[h]	—	31.4	30.0
• University-qualified	—	47.3	69.5

Sources: U-boat sample for 167 U-boat officers compiled by the author; data for 582 Waffen-SS officers in Wegner, *Hitlers Politische Soldaten,* 217–27; and data in *Statistisches Jahrbuch,* 25.

[a]All adult males within January 1938 German borders.

[b]Includes East and West Prussia, Berlin, Brandenburg, Pomerania, Schleswig-Holstein, Hanover, Mecklenburg, Oldenburg, Hamburg, Bremen, and Lübeck.

[c]Includes Westphalia, the Rhineland, Hessen and Hesse-Nassau, Saxony, the Prussian province of Saxony, Thuringia, and Silesia.

[d]Includes Baden, Württemburg, and Bavaria.

[e]The category for Germany used by Wegner includes data for Alsace-Lorraine, or 3.2% of the total figure for Germany.

[f]For 433 Waffen-SS officers, indicates religious affiliation initially entered in service record, many of which were subsequently canceled; for nearly 150 officers (26%), no data given.

[g]No data available for the general German population.

[h]Includes *Mittel-* and *Realschulen.*

Thus, in the context of backgrounds, Dönitz's officers stood distinctly apart from their comrades who wore runes on black collars. Why then did both groups fight so faithfully for the same cause? The search for an answer must begin with the end of World War I.

Affiliations, 1918–1933

Germany's defeat in 1918 marked the death of the Imperial German Navy and the birth of National Socialism, a common yet neglected genesis that would later bind Hitler and the Kriegsmarine in an unlikely partnership. As a fledgling Nazi party repudiated the verdict of 1918, naval officers contemplated their own responsibility for the debacle. After assuming a disproportionate role in precipitating the conflict by antagonizing Great Britain, the navy had then proved incapable of breaking the Allied blockade that ultimately starved Germany. Its all-out submarine offensive not only failed to accomplish the promised victory but led to American entry into the war; the prolonged inactivity of its battle fleet had culminated in mutinies that ultimately sparked the 1918 revolution, toppling the monarchy and ending the war. Hitler himself passed judgment in *Mein Kampf*:

The navy leadership was itself infected with the spirit of half-heartedness. . . . While the army leadership remained free of false trains of thought, the navy, which unfortunately had better "parliamentary" representation, succumbed to the spirit of parliament. It was organized on the basis of half-baked ideas and was later used in a similar way.[14]

Naval officers who bridged the interval between kaiser and Führer never eluded these specters of the past. "Every superior officer in the navy," wrote Raeder, "silently swore that there should never again be a November 1918 in the navy."[15] Sensitivity to alleged lack of aggressiveness and weak leadership became a legacy for the future and influenced both political attitudes against the Weimar Republic and acceptance of strategic risks, self-sacrifice, and unconditional loyalty in the war to follow.

The first tenuous links of affiliation with the Nazis can be seen in the participation of naval—and especially U-boat—officers in the *Freikorps* (Free Corps), the nationalist military units that battled Poles and Communist groups in the Weimar Republic's formative days. The largest, organized in Kiel as the *III. Marinebrigade* but more commonly known as the *Freikorps von Loewenfeld* after its commander, included many former U-boat captains and crewmen among its ranks. Ace of aces Lothar von Arnauld de la Perière commanded its Assault Battalion, in which Dönitz's friend and academy classmate Heinrich Kukat died fighting pro-Communist forces in the Ruhr in the summer of 1920. Others could be found in the more radical *II. Marinebrigade* (*Freikorps Ehrhardt*) and the *Marine Brigade von Roden* in bitter street fighting in the Ruhr, Berlin, Munich, and Upper Silesia. All of these formations also shared a hostility toward the new republic, evident in their support of the 1920 Kapp Putsch, an abortive right-wing attempt to overthrow the government. One future U-boat ace, Richard Zapp, began his military service with a *Freikorps* in Silesia and as one of Kapp's supporters in the streets of Berlin.

Because many who served in these units later joined the *Sturmabteilung* (SA, more generally known as the Brownshirts) and other Nazi party organizations, the *Freikorps* have become identified as "the vanguard of Nazism."

But here the naval connection, which was limited to only three of more than forty *Freikorps*, strains if stretched too far. One former U-boat commander and *Freikorps* veteran, Wilhelm Canaris, later played a prominent role in the opposition to Hitler that would cost him his life.[16] What was significant, however, was the incorporation of strongly nationalist and antirepublican attitudes in the interwar navy, most evident in the mass integration of 2,500 veterans of *Freikorps von Loewenfeld* among the grand total of 15,000 navy personnel established in 1922, that is, every sixth man in the *Reichsmarine*. The legacy can also be seen in the wartime appellation "*Freikorps Dönitz*" for the entire German submarine service.[17]

Several prominent figures from the Imperial Navy later joined the Nazi party. Former admiral Magnus von Levetzow, released from service after the Kapp Putsch, maintained contact with the NS movement throughout the 1920s, apparently as part of an effort to control Hitler within a coalition of traditional conservative parties; in 1932 he won a seat in the Reichstag as a Nazi party deputy.[18] Two World War I U-boat aces, Hans Rose and Otto Steinbrinck, joined the party and attained officer status in the *Allgemeine* SS; a third, Max Valentiner, became a party member in November 1932.[19] As noted in chapter 2, both Rose and Valentiner returned to active duty with posts in the U-boat training establishment. Steinbrinck, who became an executive with the Friedrich Flick concern, rose to SS-*Brigadeführer* (brigadier general) rank and a close association with Himmler; after the war he was tried and convicted with other Flick industrialists at Nuremberg.

Other former U-boat commanders moved in a very different direction. Martin Niemöller, for example, entered the Lutheran clergy and later emerged as a leader in the German resistance to Hitler. The old ties, however, proved stronger than new politics: Steinbrinck intervened on Niemöller's behalf with Himmler, and the submariner-turned-clergyman reciprocated by supporting Steinbrinck before Allied prosecutors.[20]

In the period immediately preceding Hitler's accession to power, pro-Nazi sympathies within the navy's ranks drew comments from sources as disparate as naval officers, Army General and later Chancellor Kurt von Schleicher, and Nazi propagandist Joseph Goebbels as Germany veered toward economic collapse and political revolution.[21] Hitler's nomination as chancellor in January 1933 thus found a wellspring of support among naval officers and men. Reactions of the next year's class of officer cadets consisted of genuine enthusiasm for the new regime in expectation of national unity, internal stability, and the prospects for rearmament, although these were somewhat tempered by concern for the possible consequences.[22] Karl-Friedrich Merten, already a seven-year navy veteran and future U-boat ace, candidly described the reactions of himself and a comrade as they listened to the radio broadcast of the celebrations of 30 January: "We were overwhelmed, deeply impressed, and accepted the event for what it was, a national upheaval. . . . Never again in my life would I be so swept up as at that moment."[23]

Navy commander-in-chief Grand Adm. Erich Raeder welcomed Hitler's nomination, but far more as an opportunist than a Nazi sympathizer. After his appointment in October 1928 Raeder had tried to distance the navy from reactionary organizations and "political incidents," presenting himself as a friend of the republic while maintaining traditional and conservative values within the service. He believed Hitler's movement might at last provide the broad political foundation for rebuilding a large fleet, one suited to Germany's—and the navy's—aspirations as a global power.[24] Raeder thus embodies the navy's interwar affiliations with National Socialism: skeptical if not hostile to the republic, favorably disposed toward a nationalist mass movement that might restore the navy to its former status and glory, and rather indifferent to any specific political agenda in gratitude for domestic stability and the appearance of national unity. How the navy would accommodate to National Socialism in power provided a different test.

Raeder and the Navy's Accommodations, 1933–1942

Hitler moved quickly in the first months after his nomination as chancellor to consolidate his authority through a process termed *Gleichschaltung* ("bringing into line"), smashing political and labor opposition and purging the civil service. The armed forces escaped immediate attention in return for their noninterference in domestic affairs, but the army, as the most significant and powerful military institution, soon became the focus of a struggle that would endure through the Third Reich's existence. Compromised by its complicity in Hitler's elimination of the SA leadership and other opponents in the Röhm Purge of June 1934, the army found its autonomy increasingly undermined by NS influence; through dismissals and resignations, the leadership gradually became a more pliant tool for Hitler's plans. Yet the army's potential as a center of opposition could still be seen in July 1944, when a handful of conspirators nearly overturned the regime and suggested what might have been accomplished in the preceding years.[25]

In dealing with Hitler, however, the army operated from the disadvantage of a supposed strength that ultimately proved illusory. By contrast, the

navy consciously utilized its relative weakness to negotiate accommodations with Nazism to further its own ends.

The initial adaptations involved the removal of Jews—as defined by the
"race" of one parent or grandparent—from service, mandated in March
1934; by June the navy had released three officers and eleven other ranks
who fell within these definitions. (As noted in chapter 3, the future *Kommandierender Admiral der Unterseeboote* Hans-Georg von Friedeburg endorsed
and facilitated this action.) Raeder apparently protected the officers from
further persecution and even secured their reinstatement as reserve officers
after war broke out. He also effected releases of individual Jews with whom
he was acquainted. Yet these commendable acts—duplicated elsewhere
throughout the Wehrmacht—serve merely to underscore the divorce between personal decency and official conformity. Less than fourteen
months after the Nazi takeover, the armed forces had quietly capitulated
on a key element of Nazi dogma.[26]

The commander-in-chief's ingenuity, however, allowed him to adapt
Nazi ideology to meet his own agenda of social etiquette, a preoccupation
that earned Raeder the sobriquet "The Schoolmaster." In 1935 he banned
officers from carrying briefcases, wearing raincoats, smoking pipes, or sport-
ing monocles because of the negative images conveyed. In the same context
Raeder strongly advised naval personnel attending the 1936 Olympic
Games in Berlin to avoid "visits to Jewish restaurants and Jewish stores" as
this would "damage the public reputation of the Wehrmacht." Later injunc-
tions followed against dancing to American jazz tunes ("negroid music in
hot style") or the English "Lambeth Walk," although the degree of actual
compliance remains problematical.[27]

The navy's acceptance of casual anti-Semitic rhetoric can be seen in
Crew 35's yearbook comments that described the visit to "eastern America,
the center of Jewish world finance."[28] But navy officers reacted strongly
against the regime-sponsored violence toward Jewish businesses, syna-
gogues, and individuals during the "Night of Broken Glass" on 9–10 November 1938, and Raeder protested the violence directly to Hitler.[29]

Yet it was the issue of the navy's internal values that produced Raeder's
strongest disagreements with Hitler and the regime. For example, he re-
sisted the Nazi party's attempts to reduce or control the activities of naval
chaplains and continued to promote traditional Christian values within
the navy, although always as a matter of personal conscience rather than
political activism.[30] Raeder's greatest confrontation with Hitler—a two-hour
shouting match at the Berghof in June 1939—centered on his preoccupation with officers' choices of suitable spouses. The argument involved the

"questionable past" of the wife of Hitler's naval adjutant, with the navy commander-in-chief demanding the adjutant's dismissal and the Führer defending his staff officer's right of choice. The resulting mix of soap opera and farce saw Raeder win his point, although the dismissed officer stayed on as Hitler's personal adjutant; a piqued Raeder long refused to appoint a successor and a petulant Hitler abstained from attending the next ship launching. The marriage meanwhile ended in divorce and the wife returned to her former lover.[31]

Raeder's choice of battlefields with Hitler serves as an index of his priorities. The gradual buildup of the fleet, facilitated by the Anglo-German Naval Agreement of June 1935, provided common ground between regime and navy. Nearly a year before the incident of the naval adjutant's wife, the chief of the German army's General Staff, *Generaloberst* Ludwig Beck, resigned in protest over Hitler's willingness to risk war with Britain, France, Russia, and Czechoslovakia to acquire the Sudetenland. Representing the one service least capable of matching strength with Britain, Raeder might have joined with Beck: Indeed, in a prepared memorandum at that time (July 1938), a Naval High Command staff officer concurred in predicting a disastrous outcome to such a conflict, which would eventually also likely involve the United States.

Yet Raeder abstained from objections, and instead the crisis became the basis for systematic planning for the fleet's expansion to meet a war with England. A blueprint for large-scale cruiser warfare, relying heavily on "pocket battleships" (*Panzerschiffe*), minelayers, and U-boats was drafted in October 1938. The previous month, the fleet commander used the situation to argue for building up the home fleet and four massive task forces on patrol around the globe in anticipation of a future conflict "against one-half to two-thirds of the world's powers." Later Hitler ordered a revision of planning to include more battleships. The end result, approved in January 1939 as the "Z-Plan," envisioned a fleet of 10 battleships, 15 pocket battleships, 29 heavy and light cruisers, 4 aircraft carriers, 68 destroyers, and 249 submarines for use by 1948.[32]

Underpinning all these plans lay the recognition that construction of the scheduled warships would require several years. The concomitant diplomacy thus demanded avoidance of conflict with Britain for as long as possible. Raeder therefore enjoyed a second opportunity to influence Hitler's actions and follow Ludwig Beck's example if unsuccessful. Instead he chose simply to trust Hitler's judgment in risking global war while squabbling with the Führer over the moral character of a subordinate's wife. Some historians offer the explanation that Raeder always intended to build a massive fleet, and had begun considering a naval war with Britain as early as 1934.[33] It is enough to say that Raeder's attempt to accommodate Nazi ambitions with his own designs for a rebuilt fleet backfired.

In manning his future warships and U-boats, Raeder discovered one more means by which the Kriegsmarine might utilize National Socialism. As noted earlier, the specter of the 1917–18 mutinies haunted the postwar naval leadership, who methodically examined and attempted to resolve the problems of leadership and officer–enlisted relations. For example, they turned to their own advantage the provisions of the Versailles Treaty that imposed severe personnel restrictions on the navy, painstakingly screening officer candidates and seaman recruits alike for the best possible physical and character traits. During the years 1926–27 less than 1.5 percent of the annual applicants were accepted into the service, and the number of officers actually declined each year below the 1,500 permitted by Versailles. In part this reflected the deliberate placement of qualified officer candidates within the ranks to learn firsthand the conditions and attitudes below decks before their eventual promotions to command.[34]

In casting about for examples of natural leaders rising through the ranks, the navy needed look no further than the Führer. In 1932 *Kapt.z.S.* Siegfried Sorge drafted a handbook on leadership for naval officers, *Der Marineoffizier als Führer und Erzieher,* without reference to Hitler. When the work finally appeared in early 1937, however, it contained numerous references to Hitler peppered with occasional NS catchphrases and quotations from *Mein Kampf* (as it also included quotations from Julius Caesar, Martin Luther, Goethe, Theodor Storm, and disgruntled World War I seaman Richard Stumpf). Placing Hitler in the Prussian-German tradition of Frederick the Great, Bismarck, and Hindenburg, Sorge's treatment invoked NS ideology to buttress such conventions as the "proper" naval wife and how officers could best lead enlisted men from working-class backgrounds. Sorge specifically recommended National Socialist education for officers to understand the industrial revolution's impact on German workers and to recognize that the "*Volksgenosse* [member of the national community] from a different class and a different political camp was a brave and upstanding German and an unselfish comrade." The handbook also upheld traditional views on the value of religion, and quoted Hitler's disparagement of antireligious activists as "fools or criminals."[35]

Whatever inferences may be drawn today regarding NS influence within the navy, Sorge's and other publications served a practical purpose: They assisted older officers from the upper middle class to effectively command a new generation of working-class crewmen who knew only the NS regime as Germany's government. As noted earlier, the thirty most successful U-boat aces nearly all joined the navy before 1935, testifying to their ability to bond with their crews in achieving success. In this fusion, the discriminating use of an idealized Hitler and selective perceptions of National Socialism provided some of the cement. As an example of this interaction, Wolfgang Lüth delivered Sunday speeches to his crew on the Reich's history and great leaders and spoke directly about Hitler on the Führer's birthday, although he avoided overtly political speeches. Karl-Friedrich Merten displayed the process from a different perspective when he favorably compared the enthusiastic young recruits of 1939, idealistic and eager to serve, against the less-motivated and often more troublesome older career seamen.[36]

Still, this process never implied the navy's integration of Nazi philosophy and principles to contemporary officers, who on the contrary believed their service sheltered them from NS ideology and practices. Veteran officers of Crew 34 later recalled they were "glad the *Reichsmarine* shielded us from the Party and its institutions."[37] Naval officer candidates from the merchant marine specifically sought to escape the growing influence of the SA within Germany's merchant navy, where stewards and cooks with party membership tried to intimidate officers for personal advantage.[38] Most significant are the examples of those officers who actively disliked the Nazi regime and chose service in the navy as a means of escape. One of these was Oskar Kusch, whose case is discussed below; another, an Austrian aristocrat and U-boat officer who later cooperated with his American captors, described the attitudes of his comrades who entered the navy before the war:

It may be said that the beliefs held by naval officers are in many instances not consonant with National Socialist ideas. Thus a definite freedom of expression has survived [especially] in the officers of 1930–38. This freedom of thought extends even to politics and to foreign relations, and is relatively independent of the opinions that appear in the German press. . . . [These] officers, stimulated by the dearth of foreign newspapers, listen to foreign radio broadcasts of both neutral and allied stations.[39]

In sum, Raeder's efforts to accommodate National Socialism recall the attempt by conservative German politicians in January 1933 to contain Hitler by bringing him into the government to "tame" his movement for the manipulative use of traditional elites to maintain their power. While the navy commander-in-chief ultimately proved no more successful than Franz von Papen and his colleagues, he nevertheless retained considerable autonomy for his institution. If Raeder fumbled the opportunity to oppose Hitler's risk-laden diplomacy, it must be remembered that Beck's courageous stand ultimately availed nothing. In return, the navy endorsed or acquiesced in NS policies, even if it did not incorporate them. The final rupture between Raeder and Hitler in January 1943 confirms the gulf that separated them; Raeder's farewell speech paid necessary homage to National Socialism but stressed instead the legacy of inner discipline and obedience to authority he bequeathed his successor.[40]

Dönitz: The Alliance of Navy and National Socialism

Grand Adm. Karl Dönitz's assumption of command marked a clear shift in the navy's relationship with the regime. Where his predecessor accommodated NS ways and means to further naval ends in a largely peacetime environment, Dönitz brought the navy into line with Hitler's requirements for total war. The perceptive American psychiatrist who interviewed both naval commanders at Nuremberg expressed the difference between them as follows: "Raeder was a schemer who planned to use Hitler *for* the navy; Dönitz was a disciple who wanted to serve Hitler *with* the navy" (emphasis in original).[41] Yet the question remains whether this adjustment represented more an extension and exaggeration of the navy's traditions and attributes rather than the service's transformation, whether change signified substance or style.

When Karl Dönitz assumed control of the Kriegsmarine, an NS tone to his leadership became apparent in his initial address:

Our lives belong entirely to the state. Our honor lies in our fulfillment of duty and readiness for action. None of us may claim the right to a private life. All that concerns us is the winning of this war. We must pursue this goal with fanatical devotion and the harshest will to win.[42]

Our study has already noted a similar tenor in Dönitz's exhortations to U-boat commanders, missives that have drawn the attention of historians as further evidence of Dönitz's Nazi sympathies.[43] But as we have also observed, such "pep talks" reflected BdU's primary concern to encourage aggressiveness among inexperienced commanders whom he did not know and thus belong more to military tactics than political ideology.

More specific issues concern Dönitz's personal loyalty to Hitler and the degree to which he stamped this personality trait upon the Kriegsmarine, a question made significant by the navy's relative absence from the German Resistance. That Dönitz fell under Hitler's spell cannot be denied: "The enormous strength which the Führer radiates, his unwavering confidence, and his far-sighted appraisal of the Italian situation have made it clear how very insignificant we all are in comparison with the Führer," he wrote in

August 1943. "Anyone who believes he can do better than the Führer is silly."[44]

In a December 1943 speech to senior naval commanders, he echoed Hitler's views on the need for ideological conviction among military officers:

It is therefore necessary that a soldier fulfills his duty with his soul and all his spiritual strength and willpower. And that includes his conviction, his *Weltanschauung*. . . . It is nonsense to say that the soldier or officer must be nonpolitical. The soldier embodies the state in which he lives, he is its representative, the outspoken advocate of the state. Therefore he has to stand behind this state with all his might.[45]

Dönitz demonstrated this personally in February 1944, when he joined the Nazi party as member no. 9,664,999.[46] According to Reich Armaments Minister Albert Speer, Hitler recognized and appreciated the qualities of his new naval commander-in-chief: "Dönitz is a National Socialist through and through, and he keeps the navy free of all bad influences. The navy will never surrender. He has implanted a National Socialist concept of honor in it."[47]

But if Dönitz planted anything, he took care not to disturb the existing roots. In September 1943, for example, when he issued an "Order against Habitual Criticism and Grumbling" that threatened chronic complainers with swift military justice, the directive specifically recognized the right of front-line personnel to "harmlessly let off steam."[48]

In accordance with a policy instituted throughout the Wehrmacht in late 1943, Dönitz established an NS indoctrination staff (*wehrgeistige Führung*) within the Naval High Command, but the office exerted little influence among operational units. Senior staff officers assigned as "NS leadership officers" were generally men lacking Nazi backgrounds but with regular church affiliations.[49] "Politics was no subject for us," observed one Crew 34 officer, while another commented, "Discussing politics was usually avoided as a most unpleasant subject."[50] These conditions had not changed for those serving at the very end of the war, as recounted by the chief engineer of *U-190* (*Oblt.z.S.* Hans-Edwin Reith) during the period February 1944–May 1945:

Any attempt to introduce political ideology into our lives was met with deep resentment. The very rare young Nazi fanatic who appeared aboard was looked at with benevolent amusement and otherwise ignored. . . . The one thing we bitterly resented after the [July 20th] assassination attempt was the replacement of the military salute with the so-called *Deutscher Grüss*, the raised right arm, but we swallowed that too.[51]

Although the "Hitler salute" became common in the Kriegsmarine—as indeed throughout the German armed forces—after the summer of 1944,

Dönitz otherwise kept the Nazi party at arm's length. As already noted he limited the influence of NS leadership officers, and at no time did he permit the stationing of political commissars aboard his U-boats, an unsubstantiated yet still-repeated allegation.[52] To a significant degree it became unnecessary, for two reasons: (1) considerable latitude existed between the lip service paid to NS ideals and actual practice, and (2) the navy judged its own.

The German Navy and the Jewish Question

The dichotomy between Dönitz's proclaimed rhetoric and actual conduct is demonstrated in his treatment of Jewish policy. In March 1944, the grand admiral stood in for Hitler at the *Heldengedenktag* (Heroes' Memorial Day) parade in Berlin and delivered a rousing speech on the unity of the *Volk* under National Socialism, with references to "degraded Jewish human enslavement" and "the disintegrating poison of Jewry."[53] However, when Adm. Kurt Fricke, commander of naval forces in the Black Sea, proposed the destruction of Jewish refugee transports departing Rumania for Palestine, Dönitz disregarded Fricke's "suggestions" and actually provided naval escorts to the refugee transports for the outbound part of their journey.[54]

Another living example of the contradiction between doctrine and practice was Helmut Schmoeckel, who eagerly joined the navy as an officer candidate in 1936 before discovering that his maternal grandfather was "100 percent Jewish" (*Volljude*), leading to his discharge from the service as a *"Mischling"* (half-Jew). Schmoeckel's father nevertheless petitioned for his reinstatement, which was granted in July 1939. After serving aboard the cruiser *Admiral Hipper*, Schmoeckel entered the U-boat branch in 1942 and in September 1943 as a *Kapitänleutnant* received command of *U-802*. He survived the war's most difficult period and even sank an Allied merchantman on March 1944, and at war's end he was en route to operations off the New York coast.[55] A member of Crew 34 of similar parentage also experienced dismissal from the navy, and although his efforts at reinstatement proved less successful, he did receive a reserve officer's appointment during the war.[56]

Surviving officers of Crew 34 acknowledge awareness of the persecution of German Jews prior to the war but deny knowledge of the genocidal policies that followed.[57] Perhaps the strongest support of this view comes from the interrogation of a twenty-two-year-old U-boat *Maschinenmaat* captured by the Americans in April 1944, who offered these responses to questions about Nazi anti-Semitism:

The injustice toward minorities would have ceased eventually, P/W thinks, just as injustice towards Indians and negroes will eventually stop in this country. Furthermore, there were many deserving Jews and even former Communists who have not been molested by regime, as long as they played ball with it. . . . Even a Germany under Hitler should have no trouble getting along with the U.S. The two peoples would, for instance, get together about the Jewish question and solve it in no time—the German way, preferably, but giving the Jews a better break, nevertheless, as a concession to the U.S.[58]

This U-boat machinist's interpretation of "the German way" to "solve the Jewish question" indicates both the isolation of German submariners from their regime's true nature and the low level of NS racial indoctrination among the fighting men expected to kill and die for it.

Yet some insight into the truth of the "final solution" became available through brothers, uncles, and cousins serving in occupied Poland and Russia, and occasionally from a submariner's own experiences prior to joining the U-boat arm. A crewman of *U-569* who had trained in the Latvian port of Libau (Liepaja) confirmed to his comrades in American captivity the allegations of mass killings of German Jews that had occurred there:

One fellow who was present told me that they drove [the Jews] far outside the city into the woods at three o'clock in the morning. . . . We could hear the shooting at four or five. It was done at that hour so that no one could see it.

One of his listeners responded with a description of an atrocity witnessed by his uncle in Poland: "It was inhuman . . . they beat them to death and did the most horrible things imaginable. Afterwards they don't make any report and go to sleep after these deeds." The concluding exchange probably represented the feelings of many German soldiers toward the Holocaust:

CREWMAN 1: They will certainly pay us back for all we have done, hundreds and thousands of innocent men, women and children have been murdered.
CREWMAN 2: We can't help it, kid.
CREWMAN 1: Could those poor Jews help their being murdered?
CREWMAN 2: No, that's the sad part of it.[59]

Yet officially such damning knowledge remained excluded from the Kriegsmarine, as is evident from a speech of *Reichsführer*-SS Himmler to an assembly of senior naval commanders at Weimar in December 1943. Delivered only two months after he had openly discussed the genocide of European Jews before an assemblage of SS leaders and possibly other officials at Posen,[60] Himmler's December address is revealing for what it concealed.

After an introductory reference to the "current struggle of race against race, the true test of selection to determine which people and blood predominate and which will be exterminated," most of the speech consists of a general description of the SS and its component parts. In its course Himmler informed the naval leaders that the Gestapo relied on "only a couple of dozen" agents to monitor dissension within Germany, instead of the thousands imagined by enemies, and that the majority of those sent to concentration camps to perform useful labor were not political prisoners, but German habitual criminals, although there were "naturally many Poles and Russians" there as well.

Except for a reference to his orders to "kill partisans and Jewish commissars" on the Eastern Front, Himmler's sole comment on the fate of European Jews is placed—and lost—in the context of population movements: "So-and-so many Jews have been brought to the East." The euphemism of "resettlement" had long been used as a cover term for genocide, but Himmler's avoidance of the true program at the time, together with his other distortions of SS operations, is instructive: Navy commanders were formally excluded from the regime's darkest secret.[61]

Political Opposition within the Navy

Although the personal loyalty of Dönitz and von Friedeburg to Hitler cannot be questioned, they also tolerated the independent spirit characteristic of many of the "mavericks" among U-boat commanders, even when the captain's independence assumed a political dimension. In July 1943, for example, Knight's Cross winner *Kaptlt.* Werner Henke added to his independent reputation when he berated members of the Innsbruck Gestapo as "gangsters" for the mistreatment of some friends; only a direct apology from Dönitz to Himmler averted the arrest of the U-boat ace. More fortunate was another free spirit, *Freg.Kapt.* Reinhard "Teddy" Suhren, who gained notoriety throughout the navy for a single comment. Carefully timing his approach to a berth at Brest with *U-564* at the end of a long patrol, he shouted through his megaphone, "Are the Nazis still at the helm?" When those on the dock replied "Yes," the immediate reversing of engines and backing away from the quay provided a laugh to all present.[62]

Such expressions required the sympathetic ears of trusted comrades, however. Suhren, for example, claimed his comment was specifically directed at his friend and comrade *Kaptlt.* Horst Uphoff, successful captain of *U-84* (his sinking of more than twenty-eight thousand tons of shipping earned him the German Cross in Gold) and known throughout the flotilla for caustic jokes at the Nazis' expense. Nothing happened to either captain and Suhren even rose to overall command of submarines in Arctic waters.[63]

Other commanders—how many we will never know—shared their views. *Kaptlt.* Hans-Joachim Brans of *U-801*, who had piloted a Luftwaffe bomber over Britain before transferring back to the navy, was described by his crew as "extremely anti-Nazi"; they added that he "together with the engineer officer endeavored to discourage all interest in the Nazi Party on board." It is interesting to observe that Brans earlier served for three months under Up-hoff on *U-84*.[64] An even stronger example proved to be one of the youngest commanders, twenty-three-year-old *Oblt.z.S.* Günter Leupold, who survived the loss of his *U-1059* in March 1944 and astonished his American captors with the virulence of his anti-Nazi and anti-German attitude.[65]

But if an officer went too far in the wrong company, he might pay the ultimate price. Such was the case of *Oblt.z.S.* Oskar Kusch, whose experiences laid bare the tensions within the navy on the issue of loyalty to Hitler.

Kusch—well-educated, sensitive, reflective, and a devout Catholic—had entered the navy in part because of its nonpolitical reputation. His reservations regarding the Nazi regime grew steadily, unaffected by his rise to command of *U-154* in February 1943. Two long patrols with his Type IXC submarine (March–July and September–December 1943) yielded only one sinking and several ships damaged but featured open feuding between Kusch and his I.W.O., *Oblt.z.S.d.R.* Dr. Ulrich Abel, who in January 1944 denounced his commander for an attitude "strongly opposed to the political and military leadership of Germany." According to Abel, Kusch continuously attacked Hitler and the party, often characterizing the Führer as insane; ordered the radioman to tune in to enemy propaganda broadcasts; criticized the shortcomings of German U-boats and their equipment; and proclaimed his belief in Germany's ultimate defeat. Kusch usually restricted his remarks to the officers' wardroom but occasionally expressed these views before the crew in the *Zentrale*. Alleging that his private efforts to dissuade Kusch had failed, Abel—who had joined the NSDAP in June 1932 and apparently held the post of a party district leader in Hamburg before joining the navy[66]—rejected suggestions from superiors that he drop the charges and forced the issue to a court-martial.

During the three-day trial that followed, other officers who had served aboard *U-154* supported Abel's statements; most important, the court established that a number of petty officers had also heard their captain's remarks. Kusch did not use the court-martial as a forum for anti-Nazi speeches but defended his comments as private. The court instead determined that he had acted publicly in his "seditious remarks . . . some of which bore the character of high treason." The court found Kusch guilty and sentenced him to death, duly carried out by a firing squad in Kiel-Holtenau on 12 May 1944.

Controversy over the case has continued from May 1946 (when Kusch's father unsuccessfully brought charges against the court members and surviving prosecution witnesses) to the present. Dönitz, who rejected Kusch's final clemency appeals, later echoed the sentiments of his judges in arguing that the critical factor involved the undermining of the crew's morale rather than the captain's personal convictions, a perspective always tinted by the 1917–18 mutinies. The event's occurrence during a period of near-crisis in U-boat crews' morale doubtless contributed to the extreme judgment.[67] For our purposes, the critical point concerns the convergence of navy and NS aims: Unswerving loyalty to a military ethic implied unconditional political acquiescence. The navy's willingness to execute dissenters and the presence of convinced Nazis such as Abel within the officer corps dissuaded further expressions of doubt. For the navy, there would be no need of public trials of political opponents before the *Volksgerichtshof* ("people's tribunal").[68]

OSKAR KUSCH'S example underscores the uncertain place of the German navy in the Resistance. Hitler himself offered the initial assessment after the 20 July 1944 assassination attempt against him: "Not a single one of those criminals belonged to the navy. There won't be a Reichpietsch [the German seaman and ringleader of the 1918 mutinies] there!"[69] In fact, three naval staff officers—one of them the older brother of Claus Schenck Graf von Stauffenberg, Hitler's would-be assassin—played active roles in the conspiracy, for which two paid with their lives.[70] Others with navy backgrounds joined the Resistance, most notably Abwehr chief Adm. Wilhelm Canaris, who retained his naval rank until September 1944.[71]

It must always be remembered that, while active opposition in an authoritarian regime begins and remains a matter of individual conscience, the determination by military officers to attempt the overthrow of the government requires unusual associations of shared values, conviction, daring, and trust. A military coup reflects the military culture that produces it, and the July 20th plot cannot be dissociated from the German army and its Prussian heritage. Why the subculture of the Kriegsmarine did not share this experience involves several factors that transcend the personal influence of Karl Dönitz.

First, the size and social homogeneity of the officer corps of the army and navy differed significantly. By 1943 the German army officer corps had expanded to sixty-four times its size ten years earlier, despite losing nearly as many officers killed or captured (102,636) from 1939–44 as were in service when war began (105,394). This evolution inevitably transformed the character of the officer corps, especially after Hitler and the army determined in 1942 to promote qualities of combat skills and leadership over education and seniority. As an example of the changes thus set in motion, an internal army study revealed that 44 percent of new officer candidates from 1939 to 1942 had formerly been Nazi party members.

The conspirators did not reflect the officer corps that emerged in 1942–44 but the much smaller traditional prewar elite, united by friendship and regimental association: Twenty-one officers who participated in the abortive coup had before the war served with the prestigious *Infanterie-Regiment 9* in Potsdam, five others with *Bamberger Reiter-Regiment 17*. Their revolt might be seen as both a defensive reaction to the upheavals within the officer corps they had once dominated and a return to traditions that continued to characterize the army they no longer controlled.[72]

By contrast, the naval officer corps' expansion, while considerable (from 4,500 in August 1939 to 11,000 in March 1941), threatened neither its character nor its social homogeneity, which remained substantially unchanged from World War I. But if naval officers enjoyed the comfort of greater stability and cohesion, they still suffered from the lingering insecurity of the 1918 legacy of mutiny and revolution. In acting against Hitler, the heirs of the Prussian military tradition could draw upon generations of proven service and the actual achievement of a united German state; their naval counterparts, with a much more abbreviated history to draw upon, dared not risk the stigma of responsibility for another internal collapse within twenty-six years. In short, naval officers collectively lacked the self-assurance of their own place in German history to act against Hitler.[73]

In addition, a noticeable insularity of the navy distinguished it from the other services. For the U-boat fleet in particular, this isolation existed in both a physical and an intellectual dimension. When not on patrol, U-boat crewmen spent most of their time in bases on the coastal frontiers of France and Norway, where relatively moderate conditions prevailed under German occupation. These circumstances spared them personal knowledge of the brutal and criminal nature of National Socialism practiced in occupied Poland, Russia, and Yugoslavia. By contrast, many German army officers joined the opposition as a direct result of witnessing atrocities and war crimes that characterized the Eastern Front. One captain, for example, resolved to assassinate Hitler after witnessing the execution of five thousand Jews in the Ukraine in October 1942.[74]

This geographical isolation reinforced an intellectual detachment that reflected the navy's functional approach in training officers. As noted in chapter 5, the navy rejected the army's general staff concept as both a command organization and a means of selecting and educating highly qualified officers to serve in this capacity. Command at sea, the navy felt, itself required a sufficiently broad knowledge of seamanship, ship technology, weapons systems, and leadership. Throughout the interwar period the navy especially stressed the last to improve officer–enlisted relations, the positive results of which could be seen during the war.

But the navy paid a stiff price in sacrificing the broader perspectives gained by the *Generalstab* approach. This became most evident in questionable naval strategy and faulty analysis of operations and tactics. At a deeper level, it also hindered an understanding of the political issues at stake, as front-line officers preoccupied with immediate combat concerns could neither perceive the emerging patterns of enemy supremacy nor recognize the war aims for which they fought. This point is underscored by both the fatal participation of not less than twenty-three army general staff officers in the plot to kill Hitler and the fact that those navy officers who joined the conspiracy did not command combat units but occupied staff positions in higher headquarters.[75]

All of these factors conditioned the navy to obedience to authority and loyalty to the regime. Under Dönitz and the demands of total war, the navy completed its evolution from earlier affiliations and accommodation to an amalgam with National Socialism. In his boundless grasp at unattainable goals, Hitler required combat forces whose fighting spirit and political reliability remained unquestioned in spite of horrific casualties; the navy demanded the same of its own to erase the failure and shame of 1918, to "die gallantly" against impossible odds as a vindication for the future of German seapower. Through Dönitz the navy also came into line with the promotion of officers from the ranks introduced at Hitler's insistence in the army. Moreover the tone of the U-boat war came to mirror that of the entire Nazi war effort: Courage and fanaticism were invoked to match superior resources and technology, "inspired improvisation" substituted for analytical study of operations and weapons effectiveness, and massive sacrifices of life justified for vague gains in an unspecified future.

Yet loyalty to the regime never implied unconditional acceptance of Nazi ideology. Throughout the war the navy remained true to its own codes of conduct. U-boat crewmen proved steadfastly susceptible to American jazz and French women, firmly indifferent to political issues, and resolutely hostile to disciplinary strictures of their own military police and paper-pushers in headquarters. Even in the ruthless arena of unrestricted submarine warfare, U-boat commanders and crews followed their own consciences in the treatment of survivors of sunken enemy ships; Dönitz's open rejection of Hitler's suggestions to kill survivors defined his own limits to adulation of the Führer. Submariner virtues demanded improvisation and independence just as much as devotion and bravery. Such qualities would have been little valued in a peacetime environment shaped by Nazi visions. The men of the U-boat service fought and died for an ideology that had little impact in their daily lives or in their wartime conduct.

Still, the U-boat crews may represent the closest realization attainable of National Socialism in practice with mainstream segments of German society. Officered by a traditional elite that finally opened its ranks to those below, manned by working-class sons who aspired to social advancement, the U-boat service illustrated a German society in transition under the strains of war—the all-out perpetual warfare implicit in NS goals that precluded a proclaimed but illusory future of race-based social harmony. Instead of Hitlerian fantasies of Germanic colonists homesteading new frontiers in the Ukraine, Dönitz's submariners from 1939 to 1945 constituted the concrete reality of a warrior elite skilled in technology, egalitarian in spirit, dedicated in combat, and faithful unto death. And it is in death that most shared the final union with, and ultimate fate of, National Socialism.

12   Endings

War's end found the surviving men of the U-boat service scattered around the globe in various capacities. As was typical on
any given day, only a relative handful were at sea, and most of
these surrendered to Allied forces to begin their final journeys
to British or American ports. The crews of two submarines, *U-
530* (*Kaptlt.* Otto Wermuth) and *U-977* (*Oblt.z.S.* Heinz Schaeffer), refused to obey Dönitz's surrender order and snorkeled
across the Atlantic—the latter for sixty-six days underwater followed by another month on the surface—to Argentina, only to
be promptly turned over with their boats and belongings to the
U.S. Navy.[1]

Many crews scuttled their U-boats in their Norwegian and
German bases before the victorious Allies assumed control,
leading to several war crimes trials of individual officers by the
British for illegal destruction of submarines (one chief engineer
was convicted and sentenced to seven years' imprisonment,
later reduced to five).[2] Over 250 Kriegsmarine personnel at the
Far East bases of Penang and Singapore, including the complete
complements of two U-boats and survivors of others, served an
awkward internment among their erstwhile allies before British
forces arrived in September 1945, then waited another nine
months before transport was arranged to Britain.[3]

Many other former submariners ended the war as emergency infantrymen as the Third Reich stoked its funeral pyre
with the last reserves of manpower. In April 1945 *Oblt.z.S.*

Heinrich Gode and the seamen's division of his not-yet-completed Type XXI boat, *U-3536,* suddenly received marching orders to proceed to the defense of Berlin, where they were swallowed up in the maelstrom of the advancing Red Army.[4] *Korv.Kapt.* Reinhard Hardegen, who had opened the war flying a seaplane and then earned honors as captain of *U-123,* completed the circle in command of naval infantry fighting British forces advancing on Bremen. *Korv.Kapt.* Ali Cremer led a *Marine-Panzervernichtungs-Bataillon* (Naval Tank Destroyer Battalion)—a mix of U-boat and other naval personnel armed with the simplified German variants of bazookas known as *Panzerfausts,* machine guns, and one day's infantry training—into action against British armor south of Hamburg in late April 1945.[5]

Hundreds of miles behind the front, the German defenders of the former submarine base at Lorient held out to the bitter end; their numbers included nearly eight hundred U-boat support staff and personnel reserves that had once supplied replacements to outbound submarines. Their commander, *Kapt.z.S.* Ernst Kals, formerly in command of the 2d U-boat Flotilla and a Knight's Cross winner as captain of *U-130,* was severely wounded by a land mine during the siege.[6] Other U-boat trainees awaiting assignment found themselves ordered into ground action against Soviet forces in eastern Germany as early as January 1945.[7]

Wherever the location, whatever the circumstances, the last combatants of the *U-Boot-Waffe* laid down their arms after more than sixty-eight months' continuous fighting. Sadly, the dying could not be stopped by mere signatures on a surrender document but continued like the destructive spasms of a great dying beast. *Kapt.z.S.* Wolfgang Lüth, second in sinkings only to Otto Kretschmer and commandant of the naval academy at the age of thirty, was accidentally killed by one of his own sentries on 13 May 1945.[8] Admiral von Friedeburg committed suicide a few days later when the Allies came to arrest the short-lived Dönitz government in Flensburg.[9] On 20 May *Kaptlt.* Friedrich Steinhoff, CO of *U-873,* slashed his wrists in a Boston jail after being "slapped around" by his American interrogators.[10] Three months later American authorities at Ft. Leavenworth, Kansas, hanged the seven crewmen from *U-352, U-199,* and *U-615* who had been convicted of the murder in prison of their former comrade Werner Drechsler.[11] And on 30 November, *Kaptlt.* Heinz Eck and two officers from *U-852* died before a British firing squad for their killing of survivors of the Greek steamer *Peleus,* the only such confirmed case among all U-boat attacks during World War II.[12]

Unexploded U-boat torpedoes would continue to claim lives through the years. The last recorded victims were eight of twelve crewmen aboard the American trawler *Snoopy,* lost on 19 July 1965 when the captain tried to disarm a torpedo snared in his net off the North Carolina coast.[13]

The U-boats themselves disappeared quickly, almost as if their continued presence embarrassed everyone concerned. German crews scuttled or destroyed 218 submarines in early May. Of the 154 that surrendered or fell into Allied hands, 31 (mostly representing the newer models) were kept by Britain and the United States for tests or allocated to the Soviet Union, France, and Norway as additions to their own navies. For the rest, only the manner of their destruction remained to be determined. The disposal action, code-named Operation "Deadlight," took place from 25 November 1945 through 12 February 1946, when 110 U-boats were towed into the deep waters northwest of Ireland and sunk, partly by scuttling charges, partly in British air and naval attack exercises, and half through foundering en route.[14]

Those U-boats retained by Britain and America for tests soon followed their comrades to the bottom; the handful allocated to other Allied countries lasted a while longer before being scrapped, with one exception. *U-995,* recommissioned as RNS *Kaura* in 1952, served as a training submarine in the Norwegian navy until 1962. Negotiations with Germany eventually led to the submarine's return and permanent display near the German Navy Memorial at Laboe outside Kiel, where it remains today. It joins *U-505,* captured at sea by U.S. Navy forces and preserved since 1954 at the Chicago Museum of Science and Industry, as the only two U-boats intact and never sunk during World War II that may be visited today.

Two additional submarines have been restored after salvaging: *U-2540* (raised and recommissioned in 1957 in the Bundesmarine as *U-Wilhelm Bauer,* now permanently anchored at Bremerhaven as a technical museum) and *U-534* (raised off the Danish coast in 1993 and brought to Birkenhead, England, in 1996, currently being restored).[15] They are all that is left of the German U-boat fleet, inert and rendered harmless as testament to the fear they once aroused.

BUT WHAT OF the men who manned them?

For a very fortunate few, the end of hostilities brought a quick transition to peace and home. *Obermaschinist* Carl Möller's incredible streak of good luck continued: A veteran of the prewar *U-Boot-Waffe,* Möller survived more than four years and four months' combat duty aboard three different U-boats, missing or transferring off of each submarine just before she was destroyed. In February 1944 he had become an engineering instructor at Neustadt for members of the new *Kleinkampfverbände,* the formations of midget submarines, manned torpedoes, and frogmen who operated in coastal and riverine waters. In the war's final days he returned to his home outside Hamburg, destroyed all personal papers and decorations that identified him as a U-boat sailor, and passed himself off to British occupation authorities as a Kriegsmarine administrative official. Because of his command of English, the British employed Möller as a translator, allowing the former *Elektro Maschinenmaat* and his family and closest friends to manage rather comfortably during postwar Germany's beginnings.[16]

Möller's precautions in concealing his U-boat service proved well-founded, for submarine duty generally meant extended detention in Allied custody and prolonged hardship for wives and children forced to get by on little. U-boat officers and crews on active duty who capitulated in May 1945 joined their five thousand comrades taken prisoner during the war. Some of those stationed in Norway (including *Oblt.z.S.* Herbert Werner, former *Kommandant* of *U-415* and *U-953*) traveled by ship and rail to Frankfurt, there to be entrained to camps in France. Other enlisted personnel returning from United States captivity in the spring of 1946 to what they assumed was home also found themselves instead beginning a new captivity in France. The labor and living conditions in these camps were extremely harsh. Werner managed to escape aboard a Frankfurt-bound train in October 1945, but some would remain until 1948 before strong pressure from the American government induced the French to release them.[17]

For most U-boat POWs, the final return to Germany lay through Great Britain. Captives in the United States worked on farms, picked cotton, and attended educational classes for the remainder of 1945 until the need to find jobs for returning servicemen influenced Washington to accelerate repatriation. In early 1946 former submariners began moving from POW camps to transport centers, then taking ships to Antwerp. Once there, some proved fortunate enough to be allowed to return home, especially if one could find a way to be certified as unfit for heavy labor. However, many others were put back on vessels bound for Britain, where labor shortages made U-boat NCOs and enlisted men attractive as skilled yet inexpensive workers on farms, in clearing war debris, and in building new housing. This additional term averaged six months to a year before British authorities granted final passage home. For example, the men of *U-515*, captured by the Americans in April 1944, did not return to Germany until September–October 1947.[18]

Longer delays, however, awaited U-boat commanders and crewmen captured by or surrendered to British forces. *Funkmaat* Heinz Guske, a radioman aboard *U-764* when it surrendered at Loch Alsh, Scotland, on 16

May 1945, typified the experience of his crew as he spent the next two years, ten months, and two weeks in six different British POW camps before his release on 2 March 1948.[19] The U-boat crews from the Far East, who had already waited there for more than a year after Germany's capitulation, finally arrived in Liverpool in July 1946 with promises of imminent transport home. Instead they too were shifted around POW camps and allocated to farms; repatriations did not begin until April 1947 and were not completed until April 1948.[20]

Transfers of POWs from Canada to Britain generally began in late 1946, but here British authorities took pains to detain those considered hard-core Nazis or Prussian militarists. Forty U-boat commanders—that is, virtually all of those recovered as survivors from engagements with British forces—were deemed "unrelenting militarists" in early 1947 and sent with Waffen-SS and Luftwaffe officers to Watten Camp in Caithness, Scotland. After a month of further questioning the British approved the release of fifteen of these former captains. One of them, *Korv. Kapt.* Gerhard Glattes, had put out to sea with his *U-39* on 19 August 1939 and had been captured after her loss on 14 September 1939; he returned to Germany 8 April 1947 without ever having seen Germany at war and long after the nation's reconstruction had begun. The remaining twenty-five commanders first moved to Featherstone Camp near Haltwhistle, England, then to an internment camp in the Rhineland and eventually to Neuengamme, site of a former Nazi concentration camp near Hamburg, for final processing before a British Naval Review Board. *Freg.Kapt.* Otto Kretschmer, captured on 17 March 1941, was not released until 31 December 1947; *Korv.Kapt.* Heinrich Timm did not depart for home until 9 April 1948.[21]

Last among the national contingents of U-boat POWs to be returned, as for the Wehrmacht in general, were the handful of men in Soviet custody. They included the six survivors of *U-250* and an unknown number of former U-boat men captured in ground operations. If the experience of *Maschinengefreiter* Rudolf Tscharnke is typical, they divided their period in captivity between chopping wood and working in a coal mine before returning to Germany in July 1949.[22]

The very last U-boat man to return home from prison, fittingly, was former *Grossadmiral* Karl Dönitz. Brought to trial before the International Military Tribunal at Nuremberg—over the objections, ironically, of the British Admiralty—his conviction on charges of war crimes and crimes against humanity ultimately represented a difficult compromise among the judges between condemning unrestricted submarine warfare and recognizing its universal use.[23] Dönitz served his full ten-year prison sentence at Spandau, his belief in himself and the U-boat arm unshaken. A few minutes after midnight on 1 October 1956, the former BdU and navy commander-in-chief walked out of his cell, stepped into his wife's automobile, and drove off into a new Germany.[24]

Much had changed during those ten years. Two German states now occupied the reduced realm of what had been the Reich, and the former members of the *U-Boot-Waffe* had disappeared into the fabric of German society. With the support of the Marshall Plan, West Germany had rebuilt from the ruins into a strong and prosperous member of both the European Community and the North Atlantic Treaty Organization.

The wartime U-boat effort served as a both an indicator and contributor to this process. The accelerated production of Types XXI and XXIII submarines in 1944–45 came too late to affect the campaign, but as one historian noted:

So, in 1944–45, U-boat construction was actually only a symbol of the efficiency of German industry, which was producing the most modern submarines in the world using advanced building methods under extremely difficult conditions. In this way it was more a testbed for Germany's postwar "economic miracle."[25]

Links to the U-boat past also extended into the new Bundesmarine established in 1955, despite the dampened enthusiasm felt by many submariners at Dönitz's treatment by the Allies. The first three submarines commissioned into Bundesmarine service from 1957 to 1960 consisted of two former Type XXIIIs and one XXI boat, under the overall command of *Kapt.z.S.* Otto Kretschmer and *Kapt.z.S.* Erich Topp, successively. *Kapt.z.S.* Werner Hartmann, who as a member of Crew 21 had commanded *U-26* in 1936, joined the new navy in 1956 as head of a naval training unit before retiring in 1972. Former U-boat CO Fritz Guggenberger eventually rose to rear admiral before retiring in 1964. Of the former U-boat officers in our sample, seventeen (10 percent) also entered the Bundesmarine (as officers), accompanied by fifteen of the former enlisted personnel (less than 2 percent).[26]

These reenlistment percentages testify to both the continuity in naval leadership and the veterans' successful integration into the new society. A recent study of Crew 34's contribution to the Bundesmarine indicates an inclination among highly successful former Kriegsmarine officers toward renewed military service, while those highly successful in postwar civilian life preferred to remain in the private sector.[27] While the data in our sample do not permit a direct contrast, they do confirm that many former officers proved quite content to enjoy successful private careers. Not less than thirty of their number became professional engineers; others held positions as lawyers and jurists, doctors, chemists, and architects. In business they served as managers and especially as sales representatives, particularly for industrial and export firms. Others chose occupations in the public field, including administrative posts in state government or the German rail system and at least twelve in the area of teaching. Two joined the theater.[28]

Most interesting are the postwar careers of former NCOs and enlisted men. Not only did their metalworking and craftsmanship skills serve them well in the rebuilding tasks confronting postwar Germany but their experiences in the U-boat arm provided them an invaluable perspective in dealing with difficulties after 1945. Men inured to hard work in the confines of a submarine and exposed to the omnipresent threat of annihilation would not be daunted by reconstructing their society. "When we were on patrol and being depth-charged, I swore to myself that if I survived I was never going to let another problem really bother me," recalls *U-518* veteran Peter Petersen, "and I've stuck to that."[29]

Within both Germanies, former submariners devoted themselves to their families and their new careers. Among the much smaller number of our sample who lived in the German Democratic Republic, the reconstitution of heavy industry to match developments in the Bundesrepublik offered new opportunities for employment. After his return from captivity, Dresden native and former *Maschinenmaat* Fritz Weinrich discovered that East German authorities prohibited his employment except as a manual laborer because of his naval background; with the return of heavy industries after 1950, however, Weinrich suddenly regained his qualifications as a machinist, eventually rising to the status of civil engineer.[30] Others of the sample sought their fortunes outside of either Germany, beginning new lives in the United States, Great Britain, or Canada.

Wherever they settled, former U-boat NCOs and enlisted men became civilians again and contributed their skills to the new economic prosperity. Some increase in social mobility is evident: Where their fathers were roughly equally divided between working-class and *Mittelstand* backgrounds, now seven out of ten could claim membership in the middle class. Although the doors to the upper class generally remained closed, they were not locked, as demonstrated by the more than 10 percent of all sample members of the *Funker, Mechaniker,* and *Obersteuermann* career-tracks who joined the ranks of managers, higher civil servants, independent entrepreneurs, and academic professionals. The greatest concentrations of professions—accounting for more than 35 percent of our sample— consisted of lower- and middle-grade white-collar employees in business (including many office managers and shop foremen) and lower- and middle-grade civil servants, especially teachers, technicians, employees of the German rail system, postal workers, and policemen. More than a quarter of the sample became master craftsmen or nonacademic professionals (including draftsmen, pharmacists, and engineers); and over 20 percent returned to the skilled labor professions—machinists, electricians, mechanics, bakers, carpenters—they had started a lifetime ago.[31]

As with World War II veterans everywhere, U-boat crewmen locked away their memories of the war and got on with the daily business of their lives. Although friends and former comrades who lived in the same city or town might see each other regularly and former officers maintained contact with fellow members of their Crew, reunions for those who served on individual U-boats remained a rare occurrence. Only with retirement came the time and reflection needed for perspective, for the opportunity to see former comrades, and for the willingness to openly share memories of the past, often with Englishmen and Americans who formerly opposed them. Not until the early 1980s did annual reunions of former U-boat crews become a common event for veterans, and many boats' reunions did not begin before the 1990s.[32]

By that time, many aspects and conditions of postwar Germany had passed, to be replaced by new concerns and issues. German reunification facilitated easier contact with comrades across the former border, but pensioners now had greater difficulty making ends meet. Attitudes particularly changed as a new generation of Germans came to power, more critical of the past and less inclined to accept the answers they received to ultimately unanswerable questions. When Karl Dönitz died on 24 December 1980, the Bundesrepublik denied him a state funeral and forbade the wearing of military uniforms at the private graveside service: The grand admiral's identification with Hitler and the National Socialist regime could not be evaded, as the West German defense minister explained.[33] In March 1994 and November 1995, local U-boat veterans' groups in Kiel had to improvise resources to pay nearly DM 7,000 in repairing damage and graffiti at the Möltenort Memorial.[34]

Each U-boat veteran reacted to these events in his own way, as he had to the controversies over the U-boat service that followed the publication of Lothar-Günther Buchheim's novel *Das Boot*.[35] Despite the assumptions and generalizations sometimes made by contemporary historians, the reactions and attitudes of former submariners to the events of a half-century ago remain intensely private, just as each had long ago come to his own terms with the mystery: Why so many others and not me?

What is shared at the reunions is the cameraderie of the past, anecdotes of deceased comrades, jokes at one another's expense, and wistful regrets over expanded waists and receding hairlines. After two or three days, the community still bound by fate departs and returns home to nurse their modest pensions, babysit their grandchildren, and enjoy that which remains to them. Those who live near Kiel lay annual wreaths for their comrades at the U-boat Memorial at Möltenort, even as the shadows overtake them.

And for their far more numerous comrades to whom the wreaths are dedicated, there remains only the silence of the sea that entombs them. No trace remains of the unimaginable violence in which they killed and were killed, no roses bloom upon their graves. What History says of them will always depend on whose History it is, and which generation momentarily holds History in its grasp. But we may at least be sure that History will not forget them.

Appendix One

Survey of U-boat Veterans

At the heart of this book is a survey of background information obtained from more than one thousand U-boat veterans from May 1991 through December 1994. Most of the data were collected at the *U-Boot-Archiv* in Cuxhaven, Germany, during visits to that institution by individuals or groups. The *Archiv*'s director, Mr. Horst Bredow—himself a former U-boat officer—kindly forwarded the questionnaires to the author while retaining copies for his own files. Data for additional individuals were collected by the author in Germany and North America. Questionnaires submitted by a handful of such specialized personnel as propaganda officers, surgeons, and naval architects were not used in the compilation of data as they were not representative of operational U-boat crews.

Each veteran filled out a simple questionnaire on his personal and service background. Information requested in the questionnaire included date and place of birth, father's occupation, preservice and postwar occupations, religion, educational level, date of service entry, service speciality and highest rank attained, dates of U-boat service, and identification of individual submarines on which served. Most veterans chose to sign their names and many added comments or supplemental biographical data.

Upon receipt, completed questionnaires were first divided

between officers and enlisted personnel and thereunder arranged by ca-reer-track (*Laufbahn*) and rank. Each questionnaire received a unique num-ber that reflected this arrangement pattern. The information provided was then coded into numerical values to facilitate easy manipulation of the data: German provinces and states were assigned particular numbers, for example, while ages, years of service entry, and number of submarines on which served acted as their own numerical values.

The manner of the survey's conduct was intended to obviate any inher-ent biases. Veterans who chose not to participate in reunions or to visit the U-Boot-Archiv, I hoped, should be evenly distributed among U-boat sur-vivors and not overly representative of any group. This proved not to be the case regarding engine room personnel. Based on the ratios within a typical U-boat crew, engineering officers are underrepresented within the sample (32 among 167 officers, or 1:5 instead of the usual 1:3), and ma-chinist NCOs and enlisted men are overrepresented (395 against 229 ordi-nary seamen, a 1:1.7 ratio against what should be approximately 1:1). I offer possible accountings for this phenomenon in chapter 6; in any case, these numbers do not affect the characteristics identified for the various classification groups within the sample.

The extent and completeness with which veterans answered the queries naturally varied. Where categories had been left blank, a numerical code for "no data" was entered. Some men furnished exact dates of their service aboard every submarine; others simply indicated the year or combined their basic and specialized training periods ashore with duty at sea in a summary date span. All, however, identified the specific U-boats on which they served, and by consulting such basic reference works as Erich Gröner's *German Warships, 1815–1945*, the earliest and latest dates for submarine service could be fixed. And, like military veterans of every nation, nearly every submariner remembered the exact date he entered service.

Another potential difficulty concerned the identification of small towns and villages as birthplaces. Modern gazetteers of reunified Germany usually came through for locales within the current borders, and the 1932 edition of *Herders Welt- und Wirtschaftsatlas* proved invaluable for both the eastern provinces lost as a consequence of World War II and the internal boundaries of German states at that time. In the end, locations were identified for all but sixteen (less than 2 percent) of the birthplaces for enlisted personnel.

Attempts to categorize German civilian occupations and social status for the Weimar–Third Reich period differ greatly among historians who have studied the sociological structure of the Nazi party, the SS, and the SA. I have relied on the classification model developed by Detlef Mühlberger in his *Hitler's Followers: Studies in the Sociology of the Nazi Movement* because it appears the most comprehensive and at least provides one common framework of sociological analysis.

The final tallies of individuals covered in this survey, including their specialization categories and final ranks achieved, are as follows (ranks are given in German, approximate equivalents for which are provided in the "Table of Comparative Ranks").

Officers: 167

Line officers (*Seeoffiziere*): 128
- *Korvettenkapitän:* 5
- *Kapitänleutnant:* 27
- *Oberleutnant z.S.:* 71
- *Leutnant z.S.:* 20
- *Leutnant (T):* 1
- *Oberfähnrich z.S.:* 3
- *Fähnrich z.S.:* 1

Of this total, 55 served as U-boat commanders, the remainder as watch officers. The ranks of *Oberfähnrich* and *Fähnrich* are here counted as officers-in-training, although their formal naval status remained that of NCOs.

Engineer officers (*Marine-Ingenieuroffiziere*): 32
- *Fregattenkapitän (I):* 1
- *Korvettenkapitän (I):* 1
- *Kapitänleutnant (I):* 3
- *Oberleutnant (I):* 18
- *Leutnant (I):* 8
- *Fähnrich (I):* 1

Communications officers (*Marinenachrichtenoffiziere*): 7
- *Oberleutnant:* 1
- *Leutnant:* 4
- *Oberfähnrich:* 1
- *Fähnrich:* 1

NCOs and Enlisted Men: 937

Mechaniker (Mechanics): 117 (T=Torpedo, A=Artillerie)
- *Stabsobermechaniker (T):* 1
- *Obermechaniker (T):* 9
- *Obermechanikersmaat (T):* 17
- *Mechanikersmaat (T):* 21
- *Mechanikersmaat (A):* 2
- *Mechanikershauptgefreiter (T):* 1
- *Mechanikersobergefreiter (T):* 36

- *Mechanikersobergefreiter (A):* 9
- *Mechanikersgefreiter (T):* 14
- *Mechanikersgefreiter (A):* 7

Funker (Radiomen): 139
- *Oberfunkmeister:* 10
- *Oberfunkmaat:* 37
- *Funkmaat:* 30
- *Funkhauptgefreiter:* 3
- *Funkobergefreiter:* 50
- *Funkgefreiter:* 9

Sanitätsdienst u.a. (Medical and other): 11
- *Sani. Obermaat:* 2
- *Sani. Maat:* 7
- *Verwaltungsmaat:* 1
- *Küstenverpflegungsmaat:* 1

Bootsmann (Boatswain, ordinary seamen): 229
- *Oberbootsmann:* 1
- *Bootsmann:* 2
- *Oberbootsmannsmaat:* 29
- *Bootsmannsmaat:* 42
- *Matrosenhauptgefreiter:* 20
- *Matrosenobergefreiter:* 115
- *Matrosengefreiter:* 19
- *Matrose II:* 5

Obersteuermann (Navigator): 46
- *Stabsobersteuermann:* 7
- *Obersteuermann:* 34
- *Obersteuermannsmaat:* 4
- *Steuermannsmaat:* 1

Maschinisten (Machinists): 395
- *Stabsobermaschinist:* 11
- *Obermaschinist:* 40
- *Obermaschinenmaat:* 44
- *Maschinenmaat:* 114
- *Maschinenhauptgefreiter:* 16
- *Maschinenobergefreiter:* 144
- *Maschinengefreiter:* 24
- *Maschinenmatrose:* 2

Appendix Two

Numbers and Losses of the U-boat Service

In modern military history, no service or command of any nation has suffered the casualty rate of Nazi Germany's *U-Boot-Waffe*. Depending on the figures used, Dönitz lost between 70 and 80 percent of the men who served on his submarines. This singular quantitative dimension of the U-boat service, however, reveals a paradox: While the name of every U-boat officer and enlisted man known to have perished is carefully recorded on the bronze tablets of the U-boat Memorial at Möltenort near Kiel, there are no precise figures on the number of their comrades who survived.

The 28,748 names currently displayed at the memorial for the 1939–45 conflict represent more than five decades' careful work by U-boat veterans organizations and German government agencies in compiling and reconstructing data from various sources.[1] Both the exhaustive research to yield these data and the paucity of precise information on non-casualties reflect the problematic nature of available German documentation, much of which is lost or otherwise unavailable for research. Strength returns, crew lists, and other administrative records were regularly maintained by individual U-boat flotillas, but these records were generally destroyed by the Germans themselves in the French and Norwegian ports prior to surrender in the last year of the war. The personnel files maintained by the U-boat organizational branch were mostly destroyed by Polish workers in Neustadt (Holstein) after war's end. Kriegsmarine personnel files are held, not with equivalent German army and Luftwaffe records in the Bundesarchiv-Abt. Zentralnachweisstelle at Aachen-Kornelimünster but by the Deutsche Dienststelle (WASt) in Berlin. There records of U-boat crewmen are intermixed with those of all other naval personnel but, as of 1993, these could not be used for sampling or systematic research.[2]

There is no final figure of U-boat deaths, however, because the lists are constantly updated and revised as new information comes to light. The losses of individual crewmen washed overboard or killed in air attacks or gun misfires, for example, were largely unavailable until a systematic finding aid to microfilmed U-boat war diaries, prepared by the National Archives, permitted a ready identification of those incidents.[3]

Thus the painstaking compilation of the names of nearly 29,000 dead and forever missing *U-Boot-Fahrer* constitutes a major achievement as both a testament to their memory and the starting point of any personnel study. As additional but less-permanent casualties must be added the approximately five thousand U-boat prisoners of war recovered by British and American forces from sunken submarines during the war,[4] and approximately 150 to 200 officers and men who were interned in Spain, Turkey, and Ireland, representing most or all of the crews of six U-boats lost or scuttled off those neutral powers' coasts in 1943–45.[5]

Completely untabulated, however, are casualties suffered by U-boat personnel outside the context of submarine operations. How many, for example, were killed or crippled in Allied bombings of French ports or German cities while home on leave? No figures are available, although such victims included at least one U-boat CO, *Oblt.z.S.* Jürgen Vockel *(U-2336).*[6] Some 227 submariners are known to have been wounded in air attacks on their vessels, principally during the 1943–44 period.[7] How many of these did not return to submarine duty? And how many men in the French bases were lost in the ground fighting around those cities in 1944–45? We know, for example, that allegations of poor combat performance and some desertions by U-boat reserve personnel in the besieged fortress of Brest precipitated a flurry of Kriegsmarine telegrams in September 1944, leading only to the commonsense conclusion that naval personnel "entirely untrained for ground combat ought not to be compared with paratroopers." Two flotilla commanders and former submarine aces, *Korv.Kapt.* Werner Winter and *Kapt.z.S.* Ernst Kals, and an unknown number of U-boat veterans were captured or surrendered with the Brest and Lorient garrisons, respectively.[8] In addition, a number of U-boat officers belonging to the 29th U-boat Flotilla at Toulon were taken prisoner in the attempted evacuation of the Mediterranean port.[9]

Finally, no data have been compiled on how many veterans in the training establishment were killed or captured after their conversion to infantry in the war's final days. Given the conditions that prevailed then and the lack of documentation, the numbers will never be known.

Perhaps more significant numerically are those submariners released from duty for medical reasons unrelated to wounds, and especially on psychological/psychiatric grounds. Some information is available from a postwar interview with a Luftwaffe medical specialist, *Oberstarzt* Dr. Hans Luxenburger, the chief psychiatric consultant to the Luftwaffe surgeon general. After estimating that 15 percent of Luftwaffe flying personnel became disabled by anxiety neuroses, Luxenburger stated that "flying personnel and submarine personnel had the highest incidence of neurosis in the German armed forces," an observation which he later reiterated: "For the U-boat personnel in the navy, the problem of psychoneuroses was of similar relative magnitude as for flying personnel in the Luftwaffe." He added that in treating air force cases, about 30 percent could be returned to flying duties but the remainder were thereafter given ground assignments.[10]

Luxenburger's data can be compared with the most recent assessment of emotional and psychiatric casualties among Allied bomber crews during World War II, which concludes that approximately 5 percent of all Eighth Air Force and Bomber Command flying personnel had to be hospitalized or permanently grounded for this reason.[11] If the same rate is applied to the conventional figure of approximately forty thousand German submariners, then at least two thousand U-boat crewmen developed psychological stress of sufficient degree to require their release from submarine duty. The condition was sufficiently widespread that U-boat crews referred to it as *Blechkrankheit* or *Blechkoller,* literally "tin disease."[12] If similar posttreatment reassignment rates prevailed as in the Luftwaffe, most of these men did not return to the U-boats but probably received employment in the training establishment. The total number of psychiatric casualties, however, might well be more, simply because the total strength of Germany's U-boat force has never been fully tabulated.

Here the numbers are far more problematic than those memorialized at Möltenort. At Nuremberg Dönitz gave the figure of those who served in the U-boat service as 40,000, a number barely revised in recent studies to 40,900 or 41,300.[13] The first postwar German history of the U-boat campaign referred to a total strength of 39,000.[14] Calculations of the U-Boot-

Archiv in Cuxhaven point to a total of 41,500, with a plus or minus error range of 250.[15] None of these cases, however, offers an explanation of how this number was determined, much less a breakdown of personnel strengths at different periods of the war.

The problem with a total of only 41,000 becomes apparent through simple arithmetic. When the war ended, 154 operational U-boats surrendered to Allied forces and 218 others were scuttled by their crews, a total of 372 submarines. If nearly 34,000 permanent casualties had been suffered by the U-boat service through 8 May, and assuming crews of the 154 operational boats alone averaged no more than forty-five officers and men, then a total of approximately 41,000 has already been reached. It may well be that the 7,000 active submariners who manned these 154 U-boats provided the final foundation for the 41,000, by simply adding them to the known losses in killed and captured. This, however, leaves no margin for the partial or complete crews of the remaining 218 U-boats, nor for the psychiatric cases, nor for the considerable number of former submariners serving in other capacities by war's end.

As noted in chapter 8, at least 369 former U-boat *Kommandanten*—more than a quarter of all those who held submarine command—had transferred to other duties at the time of Germany's capitulation. If a similar percentage of NCOs and enlisted men were affected, then more than 10,000 personnel would have to be added to the 34,000 casualties and 7,000 front-line sailors at war's end. It is probable that former commanders represent a larger relative group than other ranks. On the other hand, no data exist to indicate how many former U-boat crewmen were serving in other naval capacities or had been mobilized for ground combat in 1944–45. In addition, Dönitz himself described the increasing assignment of former U-boat captains and junior officers to the *Kleinkampfverbände* (special service units of midget submarines, manned torpedoes, and frogmen) from the end of 1944.[16]

Thus the figure for World War II U-boat crewmen that has been accepted for the last fifty years is simply too low. This was acknowledged in a 1979 study of submarine training by a Bundesmarine officer, who concluded that "during the five war years between 40,000 and 50,000 men of all ranks, including some full captains in special cases, passed through U-boat training."[17] As the existing front-line strength of the U-boat force in September 1939 numbered 3,000, a conservative estimate would place the total of *U-Boot-Fahrer* at a minimum of 45,000 officers and men and more likely in the range of 48,000–50,000.

This figure, it should be clear, represents the cumulative number of men who served aboard U-boats throughout the war. The number at any given time, of course, varied greatly. Casualty rates fluctuated as well, although in no month did losses ever approach the ultimate proportions evident at war's end; rather their effect became cumulative as the U-boat fleet contracted in 1944–45. Dönitz's peak combat strength, achieved with 240 *Frontboote* in May 1943, numbered approximately 12,000, of whom perhaps 9,250 were actively engaged on Atlantic operations. That month's loss of 38 U-boats, with nearly all of their 1,900 crewmen killed or captured, represented a loss rate strong enough to compel Dönitz to temporarily suspend convoy operations. In August 1944 the Kriegsmarine maintained an average front-line strength of 158 boats with approximately 7,900 crewmen; 32 were sunk that month, a 20 percent rate, but because many boats were bombed or scuttled in port the loss in personnel amounted to less than 1,000 (under 13 percent).

The overall strength and personnel structure of the U-boat service must also be considered. Some available evidence allows quantitative insights into the numbers and ratios of personnel necessary to maintain as well as to man the U-boat fleet, but at the same time demonstrates the difficulty of differentiating active submariners within the *U-Boot-Waffe*. On 1 July 1942, for example, detailed statistics for the entire organization under the authority of *Befehlshaber der Unterseeboote* reveal a grand total of 45,362 personnel, of whom 32,247 (71 percent) served in what were identified as "home units" *(Heimatverbände)*. (A complete reproduction of the organization of U-boat Command at this time is provided as appendix 3.) These included the crews of 155 future front-line U-boats undergoing training, the crews of 44 "school boats" *(Schulboote)* permanently assigned to the training establishment, a personnel pool of 234 officers and enlisted men at Wilhelmshaven available for U-boat assignment, and an unspecified number of U-boat veterans retired to training duties.

By contrast, the "front-line units" *(Frontverbände)* numbered 13,115 men, or only 29 percent of the U-boat service. The majority comprised the crews of 150 operational boats, but the remainder included such varied elements as dockyard personnel in the U-boat bases, administrative staffs and personnel pools for nine submarine flotillas, the U-boat command staff for the Mediterranean, and the headquarters staff of BdU. This means that, in addition to an average crew of fifty, each front-line U-boat required approximately twenty-seven shore-based personnel to maintain it.[18]

Less-detailed summary data for May 1943, the apogee of German submarine strength, indicate that the U-boat service had grown to approximately 58,000 officers and enlisted men and 5,000 administrative officials.[19] Given the same ratios as applied the previous year, about 18,000 manned the front-line units, which in turn translated into 12,000 actual U-boat crew-men, of whom 9,500 were deployed in the Atlantic.

To gain some perspective into the place of the U-boat service in the overall German war effort, it need only be recalled that the *Feldheer* (Field Army) never fell below a strength of four million (exclusive of replacement units and Waffen-SS formations) throughout the period 1942–44. And as horrific as U-boat personnel casualties were, the grand totals of 34,000 dead and captured at sea never approached the Wehrmacht's monthly average of over 44,800 killed and missing on the Eastern Front throughout 1942 alone.[20]

If the true number of submariners amounted to 48,000–50,000, does that alter their status or the measure of their sacrifice? First, the total number of personnel who served in the German navy during World War II amounts to approximately 72,000 officers and 1,123,000 NCOs and enlisted men;[21] thus, even a total of 50,000 *U-Boot-Fahrer* represents a total just over 4 percent, truly a select if not entirely voluntary service. And even for a 50,000 total, the casualty rate of killed and captured remains 68 percent, with deaths and drownings totaling more than 57 percent. These figures moreover exclude the additional categories of casualties discussed earlier in this section. Such figures remain unequaled by any modern military service arm or branch over the course of a war.

Appendix Three

Organization of the U-boat Arm, 1 July 1942

Befehlshaber der Unterseeboote (BdU): Adm. Karl Dönitz
BdU/Op: *Freg.Kapt.* Eberhard Godt
Headquarters: Boulevard Suchet, Paris

FdU West (administrative position only): *Kapt.z.S.* Rösing
Headquarters: Paris
1. *Ubootsflottille* (*Korv.Kapt.* Winter), Brest (16 Type VIIB and VIIC boats, 2 XB boats)
2. *Ubootsflottille* (*Korv.Kapt.* Schütze), Lorient (27 Type IX boats)
3. *Ubootsflottille* (*Korv.Kapt.* Zapp), La Rochelle (15 Type VII boats)
6. *Ubootsflottille* (*Kaptlt.* W. Schulz), La Baule (11 Type VII boats)
7. *Ubootsflottille* (*Korv.Kapt.* Sohler), St.-Nazaire (18 Type VIIC boats)
9. *Ubootsflottille* (*Kaptlt.* Lehmann-Willenbrock), Brest (2 Type VIIC boats, 3 VIID boats)

Source: "Organisation, Stellenbesetzung und Personalbestand im B.d.U.-Bereich am 1.7.1942," T1022/4038/PG 31794; supplemented by organizational information in Herzog, *Deutsche U-Boote*, 226–31; Showell, *U-boats under the Swastika* (2d ed.), 104–8; and Rössler, "Die deutsche U-Bootausbildung," 453–66.

10. Ubootsflottille (Kaptlt. Kuhnke), Lorient (11 Type IXC boats, 3 XIV U-tankers)
11. Ubootsflottille (Korv.Kapt. Cohausz), Bergen, Trondheim, and Narvik (24 Type VIIC boats)

FdU Italien (operational command for Mediterranean U-boats): *Kapt.z.S.* Kreisch
Headquarters: Rome
29. Ubootsflottille (Kaptlt. Frauenheim; from May 1942 incorporated the former 23. Ubootsflottille in the eastern Mediterranean), Pola, La Spezia, Toulon, and Salamis (19 Type VIIC boats)
Total Strength, Front-line Units: 151 U-boats
Total Strength, Front-line Personnel: 730 officers, 203 ensigns, 799 senior NCOs, 2,480 NCOs, 7,912 enlisted men (active duty); 179 officers, 130 senior NCOs, 313 NCOs, 419 enlisted men (reservists); 109 civilians (total = 13,115)
Flotillas later added: *12. Ubootsflottille*, established October 1942 in Bordeaux for Type IXD, XB, and XIV boats; *13. and 14. Ubootsflottillen* established in Trondheim, June 1943, and Narvik, December 1944, respectively, for additional Type VIIC boats to combat Allied convoys to Russia; *30. Ubootsflottille*, established at Constanza, Romania, October 1942 to operate against Soviet forces in the Black Sea; and *33. Ubootsflottille*, established September 1944 for U-boats operating in the Far East

2. Admiral der Unterseeboote: *Kapt.z.S.* Hans-Georg von Friedeburg (training and administration)
Headquarters: Kiel
1. Ubootslehrdivision (1. ULD, Kapt.z.S. A. Schmidt), Hamburg
21. Ubootsflottille (Korv.Kapt. Büchel), Hamburg (21 Type II boats, 1 VIIC; all as Schulboote)
2. Ubootslehrdivision (2. ULD, Freg.Kapt. Hashagen), Gotenhafen
22. Ubootsflottille (Korv.Kapt. Ambrosius), Gotenhafen (22 Type II boats, all as Schulboote)
1. Ubootsausbildungsabteilung (1. UAA, Kapt.z.S. Zechlin), Plön
2. Ubootsausbildungsabteilung (2. UAA, Freg.Kapt. Schünemann), Neustadt/Zeven
4. Ubootsflottille (Freg.Kapt. Fischer), Stettin (34 boats, nearly all Types IXC and IXD, undergoing training and in final fitting-out before departing for the front)
5. Ubootsflottille (Korv.Kapt. Moehle), Kiel (59 Type VIIC boats undergoing training and in final fitting-out before departing for the front)

8. *Ubootsflottille* (*Korv.Kapt.* Eckermann), Königsberg and Danzig (49 Type VIIC boats undergoing training and in final fitting-out before departing for the front)

24. *Ubootsflottille* (*Korv.Kapt.* Weingärtner), Memel (13 Type VII *Schulboote* for training commanders in shooting torpedoes)

25. *Ubootsflottille* (*Korv.Kapt.* Jasper), Danzig (no U-boats assigned; provided instruction in torpedo shooting to new boats)

26. *Ubootsflottille* (*Korv.Kapt.* von Stockhausen), Pillau (no U-boats assigned; provided instruction in torpedo shooting to new boats)

27. *Ubootsflottille* (*Freg.Kapt.* Hartmann), Gotenhafen (no U-boats assigned; provided tactical training to new boats)

Technische Ausbildungsgruppe für Front-Uboote (*Agru-Front*) (*Korv.Kapt.* [I] H. Müller), Hela (no U-boats assigned; provided technical training under simulated emergency conditions)

Ubootsabnahmekommando (*UAK, Kapt.z.S.* Bräutigam), Kiel (no U-boats assigned; tested new boats for seaworthiness)

Kriegsschiffbaulehrabteilung U-Boote Ostsee (*KLAU O*), six *Baulehrkompanien* in shipyards at Kiel, Flensburg, Lübeck, Danzig (18 new Type VIIC boats under construction, with skeleton crews)

Kriegsschiffbaulehrabteilung U-Boote Nordsee (*KLAU N*), five *Baulehrkompanien* at shipyards in Bremen, Emden, and Wilhelmshaven (23 new Types VIIC, IXC, and IXD2 boats under construction, with skeleton crews)

8. *Kriegsschiffbaulehrabteilung,* seven *Baulehrkompanien* at shipyards in Hamburg (41 Types VIIC and IXC boats at various stages of construction, with skeleton crews or assigned personnel)

Marineärztliches Forschungsinstitut für Ubootmedizin (*Flottenarzt* Dr. Lepel), Carnac, France

Total Strength, Home Units: 142 Front U-boats in training, 57 U-boats for training only, 82 U-boats under construction

Total Strength, Home Units Personnel: 1,366 officers, 399 ensigns, 1,684 senior NCOs, 5,082 NCOs, 18,388 enlisted men (active duty); 212 officers, 531 senior NCOs, 704 NCOs, 1,031 enlisted men (reservists); 2,850 civilians (total = 32,247)

Training flotillas later added: 18. *Ubootsflottille,* established January 1945 for underwater detection for advanced submarine models; 19. *Ubootsflottille,* established October 1943 for boat handling and visual observation; 20. *Ubootsflottille,* established June 1943 for initial tactical training; 23. *Ubootsflottille,* established August 1943 for submerged torpedo training; and 31. and 32. *Ubootsflottillen,* established September 1943 and April 1944, respectively, for initial U-boat training

Notes

Preface

1. Raeder's comment of 3 September 1939 is published in *Fuehrer Conferences*, 37–38.
2. An annotated bibliography of this topic through the early 1980s is provided by Bird, *German Naval History*, 571ff., esp. 675–93, but a massive amount of new literature has appeared over the past fifteen years as is evident from a glance at the bibliography. A comprehensive guide to English-language primary and secondary sources is provided by Blair, *Hitler's U-boat War*, vol. 1, *The Hunters*, currently available in the publisher's website (www.randomhouse.com/uboat/biblio.html) and scheduled for publication in 1998 in vol. 2, *The Hunted*. Hadley's *Count Not the Dead* offers a unique, critical review of U-boat memoirs and other accounts by German participants.
3. The most recent include Kemp, *U-boats Destroyed*, and Wynn, *U-boat Operations*. The latter, released in the United States in April 1998, arrived too late for inclusion in this work.
4. For example, Buchheim, *Das Boot* (*The Boat*), and Ott, *Haie und Kleine Fische* (*Sharks and Little Fish*), both available in translation.
5. See Mulligan, *Lone Wolf*, esp. 75ff., 164–65, and Mulligan, "Sociology of an Elite," 261–81.
6. See Heinsius, "Verbleib des Aktenmaterials," 82–85; Granier, et al., *Bundesarchiv und seine Bestände*, 267–68.
7. A start has been made with the *Stiftung Traditionsarchiv Unterseeboote*, more commonly known as the U-Boot-Archiv, located in the small town of Altenbruch near Cuxhaven. The archive represents the decades-long efforts of its director, U-boat veteran Horst

Bredow, to collect copies of official and personal records, photographs, and artifacts from fellow veterans.

Chapter 1. A Community Bound by Fate

1. Monsarrat, *Cruel Sea,* 225.
2. Dönitz, *U-Bootswaffe,* 26–27.
3. Except where otherwise noted, the descriptions that follow are taken from the collected "Befehle für den Dienstbetrieb auf U-Booten," in folder "UWO-Lehrgänge," U-Boot-Archiv, Cuxhaven; *Bestimmungen für den Dienst an Bord, Heft III: Wach- und Sicherheitsdienst,* 10ff.; Showell, *U-boats,* 115; and Stern, *Type VII U-boats,* 63–68. The best descriptions of a Type IXC's characteristics and onboard systems is provided in the handbook translated by the U.S. Navy as "Preliminary Knowledge of U-boats, Typ IXc," located in Bureau of Ships central correspondence files, 1940–45, in classification C-EF30/55, vol. 5, Record Group 19, Records of the Bureau of Ships, NA.
4. This issue is discussed in chapters 4 and 7; the specialized navy career-tracks are detailed in chapter 6.
5. Interview with Reinhard Hardegen, Bremen, 6 November 1995; quotation of *Kaptlt.* Kurt Neide in Middlebrook, *Convoy,* 59.
6. Quotation from Wolfgang Lüth's "Menschenführung auf einem U-Boot," in Tarrant, *U-boat Offensive,* 177, 185; interview with former U-boat officer Hans Schultz, Neukirchen, 25 June 1996.
7. Bräckow, *Marine-Ingenieuroffizierkorps,* 248.
8. Buchheim, *U-boat War,* 53.
9. Metzler, *Sehrohr,* 89.
10. The extensive data presented in the British Ministry of Defence's study, "The U-boat Logs, 1939–45," regrettably omit comparisons between surface and submerged attacks. The relationship, however, is revealed in the torpedo data for such U-boats as *U-48* (96 surface vs. 30 submerged shots over 22 months) and *U-515* (61 surface vs. 9 submerged shots over 20 months). See Herzog, "Torpedoverbrauch von U-48," 135, and Mulligan, *Lone Wolf,* 228.
11. Lüth, "Menschenführung," in Tarrant, *U-boat Offensive,* 182.
12. See the description in Merten, *Nach Kompass,* 208.
13. Naval surgeons aboard U-boats are described in more detail in chapter 5.
14 Reports and correspondence of these men and their units are reproduced on National Archives Microfilm Publication T77, Records of the German Armed Forces High Command, rolls 1020–22, frames 2489427ff. For a discussion of the themes and significance of such postwar writers as Harald Busch, Wolfgang Frank, and Lothar-Günther Buchheim, see Hadley, *Count Not the Dead,* 110–17, 140ff.
15. Kaiser, *QXP,* 157.
16. See *Guides to the Microfilmed Records of the German Navy, 1850–1945,* no. 2,

Records Relating to U-boat Warfare, 1939–1945, compiled by Timothy P. Mulligan (Washington, D.C.: National Archives and Records Administration, 1985), hereafter cited as *Guide No. 2,* passim. U-boat rescues of German refugees (not found in extant war diaries) are discussed in chapter 4; the number of patrols is provided in the unpublished British study, "U-boat Logs," 29. *U-380*'s extraordinary exploit is detailed in her war diary for 5–16 May 1943 (T1022/2889/PG 30442/6). Some additional rescues (e.g., that by *U-481* of 25 to 30 shipwrecked Estonians in the Gulf of Finland, August 1944) are not recorded in war diaries (Nöldeke and Hartmann, *Sanitätsdienst,* 82).

17. Lüth, "Menschenführung," in Tarrant, *U-boat Offensive,* 182.

18. Hirschfeld, *Feindfahrten,* 192.

19. The term *Unteroffiziere mit Portepee* has been translated as warrant officers—the wartime choice of the U.S. Navy—or even (incorrectly) as chief petty officers. I have accepted the translation used in Angolia and Schlicht, *Uniforms and Traditions,* vol. 1, 38ff.

20. A detailed picture of the *Obersteuermann*'s navigational duties is provided in Buchheim, *U-boat War,* 162–63.

21. Interview with Hermann Kaspers, Neukirchen, 26 June 1996; Plottke, *Fächer,* 56, 90.

22. Gasaway, *Grey Wolf, Grey Sea,* 118–19; Brennecke, *Jäger-Gejagte,* 371–72; and interview with Hermann Brandt, Neukirchen, 26 June 1996.

23. See the extensive data and findings in Dr. Karl E. Schaefer, "Man and Environment in the Submarine (Bioclimatology of the Submarine)," Study B-I, 6ff., and Dr. Jürgen Tonndorf, "Influence of Service on Submarines on the Auditory Organ," Study D-II, 17–20, both in Schaefer, ed. "Monograph on Submarine Medicine" (temperatures have been converted from Celsius to Fahrenheit readings).

24. Kahn, *Seizing the Enigma,* 197–98; Kaiser, *QXP,* esp. 61ff.; Guske, *War Diaries,* esp. 147–49, 169–74.

25. Descriptions based on Stern, *Type VII U-boats,* 33, 91; Busch, *So war,* 14–16; Buchheim, *U-boat War,* 90–91, and *Jäger,* 20–36; Lüth and Korth, *Boot greift wieder an!,* 201–3; and interview with Werner Hirschmann, Toronto, 8 February 1996. An excellent cross-section schematic of the *Zentrale* is provided in Lakowski, *Deutsche U-Boote Geheim,* 67–70, a book based on German naval construction records long held in Soviet archives.

26. Stern, *Type VII (U-boats),* 76; Showell, *U-boats,* 95; Gasaway, *Grey Wolf,* 37–38. Partial instructions for toilet use aboard a 1943 Type VIIF boat are published in Lakowski, *Deutsche U-Boote Geheim,* 78–79.

27. Cf. the version in Brennecke, *Jäger-Gejagte,* 383–86, and the captain's account in Högel, *Embleme,* 266; three crewmen were lost with the boat.

28. Schaefer, "Ernährung des U-Bootsfahrers," 156c-d, 157; Plottke, *Fächer Loos!,* 8–10.

29. Mulligan, *Lone Wolf,* 75–83, 86.

30. KTB (War Diary) *U-47,* 8–17 October 1939, reproduced on National Archives

Microfilm Publication T1022, Records of the German Navy, 1850–1945, Received from the Naval Historical Division, roll 2970, item PG 30044 (hereafter cited in the format T1022/2970/PG 30044); Köhl and Niestlé, *Original zum Modell: Uboottyp IXC,* 13; Ministry of Defence study, "U-boat Logs," 29. Complete listings of Atlantic patrols for 1939–42 are provided in Blair, *U-boat War: The Hunters,* 709–32, but these omit war cruises of Type II boats in the early months.

31. Stern, *U-boats in Action,* 64–65.

32. Most of these are cited by Lüth in his lecture on "Menschenführung" in Tarrant, *U-boat Offensive,* 177–84 (see also Gallery, *U-505,* 142, and Gasaway, *Grey Wolf,* 192); examples of a U-boat's newspaper and titles of typical phonograph records and library books are available among the reels 78–82 of the microfilmed German Submarine Materials for *U-505* and *U-805,* Manuscripts Division, Library of Congress, Washington, D.C. (hereafter cited as Mss. Division, LC).

33. See the catalogues of recordings (*Schallplattenverzeichnisse*) for *U-505* (87 records) and *U-805* (118 records) reproduced on reels 81–82 of the German Submarine Materials, Mss. Division, LC.

34. Lüth, "Problems of Leadership," in Tarrant, *U-boat Offensive,* 183–84; *U-505 Schallplattenverzeichnis,* reel 81 of the German Submarine Materials, Mss. Division, LC; interview with Werner Hirschmann, Toronto, 30 September 1995.

35. See Mulligan, *Lone Wolf,* 68.

36. Hirschfeld, *Feindfahrten,* 251; Gannon, *Operation Drumbeat,* 281; letter, Werner Hirschmann to author, 22 May 1995.

37. Memorandum No. 658 for Op-16-W, "American Radio Programs for U-boat Men," 15 June 1943, file "Memorandums" in Op-16-Z subject files, Records of the Special Activities Branch (Op-16-Z), Office of Naval Intelligence (ONI), Records of the Chief of Naval Operations, Record Group 38, National Archives, College Park, Md. (hereafter cited RG 38, NA).

38. War Department Classified Incoming Message CM-IN-8460, Curaáao to WDGBI, 25 June 1942, in file 383.6 Germany 6-25-42, Army Intelligence project decimal file, 1941–45, Records of the G-2 (Intelligence) Division, RG 319, NA. Additional information on this captive and his hosts (*U-126, Kaptlt.* Ernst Bauer) can be found in chapter 10.

39. Examples of these humor forms are provided in: Buchheim, *Boat,* passim; Mulligan, *Lone Wolf,* 30–31, 36n, 89; Högel, *Embleme,* 219, 272–73, 313, 315–16; and Hadley, *U-boats against Canada,* 233–34, 307–11. Collected Crew newsletters, which contain many doggerel-verse examples for officers, are in the custody of the Wehrgeschichtliches Ausbildungszentrum at the Marineschule Mürwik, Flensburg; the best collection of certificates and verse pertaining to individual boats can be found at the U-Boot-Archiv, Cuxhaven.

40. Kaiser, *QXP,* 199; Gasaway, *Grey Wolf,* 67; Giese and Wise, *Shooting,* 120–21; letter from Werner Hirschmann to author, 7 August 1998.

41. Stern, *Type VII U-boats,* 55–58; British Director of Naval Intelligence, "Summary

of Information on German U-boats," 29 November 1943 (esp. 10), in subject file "British Final Reports," Op-16-Z subject files, RG 38, NA (hereafter cited as British Naval Intelligence, "Summary").

42. Data on losses in Högel, *Embleme,* 282–84; *U-106* described in Busch, *So war,* 139–41.

43. ONI interrogation report on *U-94,* Op-16-Z files, RG 38, NA.

44. Examples from the war diaries of *U-485,* December 1944 (T1022/3657/PG 30602/2); *U-1064,* 13 February 1945 (T1022/3764/PG 30849/2); and *U-1228,* 19 September 1944 (T1022/3463/PG 30867/2). *Schnorchel* conditions were described in interviews with Werner Hirschmann, Toronto, 30 September 1995, and Peter Petersen, Chicago, 6 June 1996 (both of whom also reviewed and corrected this chapter with regard to terminology and shipboard routine).

45. Dr. Günther Malorny, "Carbon Monoxide on Submarines," Report B-III, and Dr. Hellmut Uffenorde, "Otological Experience with 'Schnorchel'-equipped Submarines," Report D-III, both in Schaefer, ed., "Monograph on Submarine Medicine."

46. See Showell, *U-boats,* 83–84; Tarrant, *Last Year,* 84–85.

47. Malorny, "Carbon Monoxide on Submarines," and Uffenorde, "Otological Experience with 'Schnorchel'-equipped Submarines."

48. See the original and translated lyrics in Hadley, *U-boats against Canada,* 233–34, 308–11.

49. Angolia and Schlicht, *Kriegsmarine,* 1:287–307, 2:288–99; Stern, *U-boats in Action,* 65–68.

50. Buchheim, *U-boat War,* 90–96; Stern, *Type VII U-boats,* 76–77; Morison, *Atlantic Battle Won,* 163.

51. Churchill, *Their Finest Hour,* 529.

Chapter 2. First Generation

1. ONI preliminary interrogations and final interrogation report on survivors of *U-487,* Op-16-Z interrogation reports, RG 38, NA.

2. Data on the individuals discussed in this and the following two paragraphs (except where otherwise noted) are taken from Stoelzel, ed., *Ehrenrangliste,* 232, 349, 351–53, 403, 483, 500, 782, and 806; Lohmann and Hildebrand, *Kriegsmarine,* vol. 3, 291/30, 306, 312–13, 328, 362, 408; Herzog and Schomaekers, *Ritter der Tiefe,* 75–91, 270–71; and Busch and Röll's *U-Boot-Kommandanten,* 152, 202–3, and 255. U-boat "family dynasties" are discussed in Herzog, *U-Boote im Einsatz,* 30; Ludwig Becker's data are taken from my survey of U-boat veterans (sample 5529). Dönitz's *Wechselvolles Leben,* 109–22, provides the most details on his World War I U-boat career, but the cited claim comes from his *Memoirs,* 4.

3. See Bräckow, *Marine-Ingenieuroffizierkorps,* 247ff.

4. For more on Rose, see Herzog and Schomaekers, *Ritter der Tiefe,* 157–70, 283–85.

5. An example of the latter was *Oblt.z.S.d.R.* Gustav Lange, personnel officer for the 24th U-boat Flotilla in Memel (Merten, *Nach Kompass*, 351).

6. On these men's contribution, see Saville, "Development," 320–31, 420ff., 515–26, and Rössler, *U-boat*, 90–98; highlights of their careers are provided in Stoelzel, ed., *Ehrenrangliste*, 289, 364, 388, and Lohmann and Hildebrand, *Deutsche Kriegsmarine*, vol. 3, 291/88, /340, /364.

7. Vause, *Wolf*, 27–28 (the quote is that of Victor Oehrn, later U-boat ace, BdU staff officer, and FdU Mittelmeer). An exception was Lothar von Arnauld de la Perière, the greatest U-boat ace of all time (194 ships sunk, totaling 453,716 tons): Promoted to the rank of *Vizeadmiral z.V.* (vice admiral "at disposal," a German designation similar to but not identical with "acting"), he served successively as *Marinebefehlshaber Bretagne* (naval commander, Brittany) and *Marinebefehlshaber Westfrankreich* (naval commander, Western France) before being named *Admiral Südost* (admiral, Southeast), in command of all naval forces in southeastern Europe, in February 1941. On 24 February 1941, en route to his new post, he died in an airplane crash at Paris (see Herzog, *Deutsche U-Boote*, 151–52, and Herzog and Schomaekers, *Ritter der Tiefe*, 30–51). Why he had no connection with the U-boat arm is not known, but a difficult and uncomfortable situation would have arisen had either Dönitz or his more successful elder been subordinated to the other.

8. Dönitz, *Vierzig Fragen*, 29.

9. Herzog, *U-Boote im Einsatz*, 30; questionnaire no. 5529; author's conversation with a crewman aboard *U-17* during the submarine's visit to Alexandria, Va., 7 June 1997.

10. Rössler, *U-boat*, 10–13.

11. See Herwig, *"Luxury" Fleet*, 77–78; Lakowski, *U-Boote*, 59, 121; and Rössler, *U-boat*, 32–33.

12. This is the thesis of Eckart Kehr, *Schlachtflottenbau und Parteipolitik, 1894–1901* (Berlin, 1930), and more particularly of Volker Berghahn, *Der Tirpitz-Plan: Genesis und Verfall einer innenpolitischen Krisenstrategie unter Wilhelm II* (Düsseldorf: Droste, 1971).

13. See especially the important works by Gary E. Weir: *Building the Kaiser's Navy*, 83–89, 97, 105–9; "Origins of German Seapower: Military-Industrial Relationships in the Development of the High Seas Fleet," 205–6, 228; and "Tirpitz, Technology, and Building U-boats," 174–90. See also Herzog, *Deutsche U-Boote*, 11–14, 77; Lakowski, *U-Boote*, 62–63; and Rössler, *U-boat*, 25–35. Parliamentary debates on the role of the submarine are reviewed in Sutton, "Imperial German Navy," 299–303.

14. Herwig, *"Luxury" Fleet*, 90, 111.

15. Harrod, *Manning the New Navy*, 34ff., 54, 174.

16. Sutton, "Imperial German Navy," 336–38.

17. Güth, *Von Revolution zu Revolution*, 122–26; Kapt.z.S. von Kühlwetter, "Personnel of the German Navy," 132–50 (with slight variations in the percentages noted by Güth).

18. Cf. the sociological data from Herwig, *"Luxury" Fleet,* 118–28, and the same author's *Elitekorps des Kaisers,* 38–53, with that in Rust, *Crew 34,* 20–21; quotation from von Kühlwetter, "Personnel," 140–41.

19. Herzog, *U-Boote,* 13; Lakowski, *U-Boote,* 53–54; and Michelsen, *U-Bootskrieg,* 136–37.

20. See Spindler, *Handelskrieg mit U-Booten,* vol. 1, 153–55, and Rössler, *U-boat,* 36.

21. Dönitz, *Memoirs,* 32–33.

22. Weddigen's exploit is described in Groos, *Der Krieg in der Nordsee,* vol. 2, 49–64; on the popular reaction, see Hadley, *Count Not,* 21–22, 25–26.

23. Kramsta, *Aus dem Logbuch,* 64–69.

24. Hurd and Castle, *German Sea-Power,* 157–58.

25. Horn, *War, Mutiny and Revolution,* 75.

26. Spindler, "Value of the Submarine," 838–39.

27. Horn, *German Naval Mutinies,* 24–25; Güth, *Revolution,* 141.

28. Tarrant, *U-boat Offensive,* 10–12.

29. See Lundeberg, "German Naval Critique," 107–9, and Tarrant, *U-boat Offensive,* 17–22.

30. See Tarrant, *U-boat Offensive,* 44ff.; Marder, *Dreadnought,* vol. 4, 99ff.; and most recently Halpern, *World War I,* 340ff.

31. Bauer, *Als Führer,* 133–35; Thomas, *Raiders,* 270–71. Jünger was a controversial German writer who, as a World War I participant, extolled the virtues of the individual soldier.

32. Thomas, *Raiders,* 133.

33. On the UB III and its link to the VIIC, see Rössler, *U-boat,* 56–59, 76–80, 97–98; Herzog, *Deutsche U-Boote,* 56–61, 114–15 (contrasting the sinking achievements of each class of U-boats); Möller, *Kurs Atlantik,* 137–41; and Stern, *Type VII U-boats,* 10–13.

34. Rössler, *U-boat,* 80–87, 90–92, 97, 100–101, 105–8, 328–32; and Möller, *Kurs Atlantik,* 130–49.

35. On the general subject, see Saville, "Development," 2, 9–17, 25ff., but his emphasis on the fact of German covert evasion overlooks its relative insignificance in the face of the net loss in submarine development.

36. Bauer, *Als Führer,* 5; Spindler, *Handelskrieg,* vol. 4, 2–3, 41ff.; Michelsen, *U-Bootskrieg,* 140–41, 182–85. The average duration of World War II patrols is discussed in chapter 1.

37. The publication, Kurt Galster's *Welche Seekriegsrüstung braucht Deutschland?,* is quoted in Herzog, *Deutsche U-Boote,* 174n.

38. Spindler, *Handelskrieg,* vol. 4, 39–40; Lundeberg, "Critique," 115–16; KTB *U-53,* 1–30 Sep 1939, T1022/2930/PG 30050.

39. Cf. Jeschke, *U-Boottaktik,* 37ff., esp. 48–58, and Herzog, *Deutsche U-Boote,* 169–75, who disagree on the relative significance of these efforts. See also the discussion in chapter 3.

40. Tarrant, *Offensive,* 36, 43, 56–57, 148–49; Spindler, *Handelskrieg,* vol. 4, 2–3.

41. Padfield, *Dönitz,* 61–89; Dönitz, *wechselvolles Leben,* 109–22.

42. See the "Monatsberichte des BdU Pola" for June–August 1918, reproduced on T1022/928/PG 76421; summary data appear in Halpern, *Mediterranean,* 535, 539.

43. The compiled data are presented in the BdU Brieftelegrammen of 12 July and 13 August 1917, T1022/95/PG 62022.

44. See the discussion in Lundeberg, "German Naval Critique," 116–18. Dönitz's concept of "tonnage war" is described in chapter 3.

45. See Michelsen, *U-Bootskrieg,* 134–39.

46. The standard practice is cited in a World War II document, Flottenkommando an das OKM, "Kriegspersonalwirtschaft," 20 November 1939, 2, T1022/2066/PG 33541; "Interrogation of Acting Warrant Officer Haack (UC 32)," February 1917, in ONI subject files, 1911–27, Naval Records Collection of the Office of Naval Records and Library, RG 45, NA.

47. Führer der U-Boote, "Niederschrift über die Besprechung mit den Ubootskom-mandanten am 17.I.1917," 27 January 1917, in Nachlass Werner Rüting, U-Boot-Archiv, Cuxhaven. For contrasts in World War I U-boat commanders' treatment of survivors, cf. Thomas, *Raiders,* 118–23, 160–65, 178–79, and Gray, *Killing Time,* 139–43, 202–3. Similar World War II incidents are discussed in chapter 10.

48. Commander casualties compiled from the data in Stoelzel, ed., *Ehrenrangliste,* 164ff. (World War II commander casualty data are treated in chap. 8); Comp-ton-Hall, *Submarines and the War at Sea,* 303; Showell, *U-boats,* 18.

49. The detailed calculation appears in Schwarte, ed., *Weltkampf um Ehre und Recht: Der Seekrieg,* 284–86; the same data are used in Bauer, *Als Führer,* 464, and simi-lar arguments appear in Michelsen, *U-Bootskrieg,* 73–103. On Dönitz, see *Vierzig Fragen,* 117–19, and the discussion in chapters 3 and 9.

50. See Lundeberg, "Critique," 113–17; Spindler, "Meinungsstreit," 235–45; and Herwig, *"Luxury" Fleet,* 224–25.

51. "Notiz zur Einleitung," comment by an unidentified historian of the Kriegswis-senschaftliche Abteilung as a preface to a December 1944 chapter outline, "Die Seekriegsleitung und die Mittelmeerkriegführung 1941; Kurze Darstellung der Entstehung des Weltkriegeswerkes 1914/18," T1022/3468/PG 31052.

52. Dönitz letter of June 1963, cited in Lundeberg, "German Naval Critique," 117n.

53. Hirschfeld, *Feindfahrten,* 9.

Chapter 3. The Framework of the U-boat War

1. There is no satisfactory biography of Dönitz, possibly because his own (three) memoirs have intimidated the effort. Padfield's *Dönitz* provides much useful information but remains a prosecution brief. A more balanced but still critical assessment is offered by Hartwig, "Karl Dönitz," 133–52. Rewarding insights into different aspects of Dönitz's character and command style can also be found in Salewski, *Seekriegsleitung,* vol. 2, 225–29; Vause, *Wolf,* 26–28; and

Showell, *U-boats*, 15, 125–26. A collection of his papers has been donated to the Bundesarchiv-Abt. Militärarchiv (Freiburg i.Br.) as Nachlass N 236; other papers remain in family custody.

2. Dönitz, *Wechselvolles Leben*, 7–19.

3. Excerpted evaluations by his superiors appear in Padfield, *Dönitz*, 120–25, and Gannon, *Drumbeat*, 73–74; IQ and Nuremberg observations in Gilbert, *Nuremberg Diary*, 34, and Kelley, *Twenty-two Cells*, 96–97.

4. Dönitz's post–World War I assignments included command of torpedo boat *T.157* (April 1920–March 1923), staff positions with the Torpedo and Mine Inspectorate and the Naval High Command (1923–27), navigations officer aboard the cruiser *Nymphe* (October 1927–October 1928), commander of the 4th Torpedo Boat (Half) Flotilla (October 1928–October 1930), a senior staff posting with the command of Naval Station North Sea (October 1930–September 1934), and commander of the light cruiser *Emden* (September 1934–July 1935).

5. Showell, *U-boats*, 15. On those who refounded the U-boat arm, see Saville, "Development," esp. 522ff. The reorganization of U-boat offices is described in Rössler, *U-boat*, 102–3, and the same author's "U-boat Development and Building," 120–22.

6. Dönitz, *Memoirs*, 13.

7. See Cremer, *U-boat Commander*, 14; Topp, *Fackeln*, 91–92; and Suhren, *Nasses Eichenlaub*, 102. On general treatment of U-boat men, see chapter 9.

8. The incident is recalled in Kaiser, *QXP*, 37 (although erroneously identified as a greeting of Dönitz's U-boat); for more information on the sons, see Padfield, *Dönitz*, 7, 266, 282–94, 297–99, and 359–61.

9. See Hirschfeld, *Feindfahrten*, 83–84.

10. BdU signal of 21 May 1943, a translation of the decrypted intercept of which is provided in the U.S. Navy's signals intelligence history, "Battle of the Atlantic," vol. 2, "U-boat Operations (December 1942–June 1945)," 76–77, Study No. SRH– 008, Records of the National Security Agency/Central Security Service, Record Group 457, National Archives (hereafter cited RG 457, NA).

11. Hadley, *U-boats*, 196, 259, 269, 271.

12. For example, Churchill's signal to Gen. A. P. Wavell on 10 February 1942 regarding the Singapore situation:

> There must at this stage be no thought of saving troops or sparing the population. The battle must be fought to the bitter end at all costs. The 18th Division has a chance to make its name in history. Commanders and senior officers should die with their troops. The honour of the British Empire and the British Army is at stake. I rely on you to show no mercy to weakness [*sic*] in any form. . . . The whole reputation of our country and our race is involved. (Churchill, *Hinge of Fate*, 87)

13. Schaeffer, *U-boat 977*, 135.

14. Dönitz, *Memoirs*, 42–45, and *Vierzig Fragen*, 40. Blum's estimate is discussed in chapter 2.

15. Quoted in Showell, ed., *Fuehrer Conferences*, 37–38.
16. Dönitz, *Vierzig Fragen*, 50–51. Padfield, citing the same source and a letter from a staff officer, revises Dönitz's final comment to "If each does his duty we will win" (*Dönitz*, 188). Günter Hessler, a U-boat commander, BdU staff officer, and Dönitz's son-in-law, ascribed the "draw at best" sentiments of his chief shortly after the fall of France (Hessler letter of 13 July 1956, quoted in Dönitz, *Vierzig Fragen*, 63–64).
17. See Price, *Aircraft versus Submarine*, 155–57, and the KTB of *U-441* for 12 July 1943 (T1022/2978/PG 30495). The upgraded flak armament is described in Rössler, *U-boat*, 188, 192–94.
18. See Salewski, *Seekriegsleitung*, vol. 2, 239, 305–7.
19. Dönitz did relieve Adm. Eberhard Maertens, chief of naval communications (and ciphers), in May 1943, but not in association with a general review of the cipher situation (Kahn, *Seizing the Enigma*, 260–62).
20. Hans-Georg von Friedeburg, born 15 July 1895 in Strasbourg, Alsace (then a part of Germany), entered the navy in 1914 and spent most of World War I aboard the battleship *Kronprinz*, but served in the U-boat arm throughout the war's final year. Thereafter he held the typical variety of mixed assignments, both at sea and on shore, until joining the U-boat arm. There he rose to the rank of admiral in his organizational capacity and in May 1945 became commander-in-chief of the navy when Dönitz succeeded Hitler as head of the government. Von Friedeburg acted as the chief negotiator with the Western Allies in the final German surrender and committed suicide on 23 May 1945 (Busch and Röll, *U-Boot-Kommandanten*, 72). A collection of his papers is available in the Bundesarchiv-Abt. Militärarchiv (Freiburg) as Nachlass N 374.
21. See Showell, *German Navy*, 177.
22. Dönitz, *Memoirs*, 120–21; service data in Busch and Röll, *U-Boot-Kommandanten*, 72. On U-boat training, see chapter 7.
23. Unidentified quotation in Frank, *Wölfe und der Admiral*, 320.
24. See, e.g., Merten, *Nach Kompass*, 152, 191–92, and Schulz, *Nassen Abgrund*, 203.
25. Correspondence and interviews with Inge Molzahn (née Karpf), February–November 1983. Mrs. Molzahn's father was *Korv.Kapt.* Hans Karpf, lost with *U-632* in the North Atlantic shortly after his daughter's birth; her mother, a native of the Canary Islands who came to Germany with her husband shortly before the war, remembers with gratitude the assistance and kindness she received from von Friedeburg.
26. Interview with Armin Müller-Arnecke (Crew 33, staff officer in the U-boat Personnel Department), Bremen, 6 November 1993. Müller-Arnecke served under von Friedeburg from late 1940 through the end of 1944.
27. See the quoted comments of von Friedeburg and accompanying assessments in Thomas, *German Navy*, 87, 93–94, and Müller, *Heer und Hitler*, 75n, 82n, 108n.
28. Interview with Müller-Arnecke.
29. See von Friedeburg's letter to Himmler, 19 October 1943, reproduced on National Archives Microfilm Publication T175, Records of the Reichsführer-SS and

Chief of the German Police, roll 33, frames 2541663–666 (hereafter cited in the format T175/33/2541663–666). For a full description of the incident, see Mulligan, *Lone Wolf,* 157–59, 169–71.

30. The incident is recounted in Suhren and Brustat-Naval, *Nasses Eichenlaub,* 68; Suhren's relationship with von Friedeburg is also described on pp. 65–66, 142, 151, 153, 162–63. On Suhren's anti-Nazi anecdote, see chapter 11.

31. Showell, *U-boat Command,* 136–37, apparently quoting Otto Köhler's (*U-377*) account.

32. See Merten, *Nach Kompass,* 362, 365–66, 378, 384, 390.

33. Topp, *Fackeln,* 114.

34. BdU headquarters locations and dates are provided in Showell, *German Navy,* 101; a description of Kerneval appears in Merten, *Nach Kompass,* 233; frontline U-boat strength taken from Tarrant, *U-boat Offensive,* 96, 106, 116.

35. See Price, *Aircraft versus Submarine,* 120–21; Showell, *German Navy,* 100–101 (including names of the principal staff officers); Showell, *U-boat Command,* 110; and Frank, *Wölfe,* 181, for a description of each officer's duties. The radio bunker is described in Kahn, *Seizing the Enigma,* 195.

36. Dönitz, *Memoirs,* 129. On Hessler, see Alman, *Ritter,* 287; on the Western Approaches HQ, see Chalmers, *Max Horton,* 152–53, and Terraine, *U-boat Wars,* 304–7.

37. See especially the BdU KTB for 18 April and 16 September 1941, T1022/4063/PG 30286 and PG 30297, respectively.

38. See Showell, *U-boat Command,* 109–10 (the officer quoted is not identified). For general comments on the BdU staff, see Salewski, *Seekriegsleitung,* vol. 2, 305–7.

39. See Waddington, *OR in World War 2,* 18 and esp. 32ff., for detailed O.R. data on Coastal Command's operations against U-boats; data on ASWORG and the influence of O.R. on American anti-U-boat efforts, see the Office of Scientific Research and Development report, *A Survey of Subsurface Warfare in World War II,* 75ff.; Tidman, *Operations Evaluation Group,* 35ff.; and Meigs, *Slide Rules and Submarines,* 54–63, 93ff. An excellent overview of the subject is provided by McCue, *U-boats in the Bay of Biscay,* passim.

40. See Syrett, *Defeat,* 191–92, 198–99, for the general context, and Bercuson and Herwig, *Deadly Seas,* 250–75, for a detailed account of part of that engagement.

41. On the T–5 and its operational use, see Rössler, *Torpedos,* 142–50; on acoustic countermeasures, see Hackmann, *Seek and Strike,* 318–20.

42. Cf. KTB BdU of 24 May 1943, T1022/4064/PG 30324, and Hessler, *U-boat War,* vol. 2, 112 (including British Admiralty comments on 112n).

43. The source of this revelation is the BdU KTB for 13 August 1943 (Teil VI. Allgemeines), which was excised from the original war diary and neither microfilmed nor restituted to Germany, but maintained as Item ZEMA 06 Nr. 36419A in the Historic Cryptographic Collection, Pre–World War I through World War II, of the National Security Agency. In 1996 this series was declassified and accessioned by the National Archives, where it became part of RG 457. The context of the Abwehr report indicates that the intelligence source in-

volved a Swiss contact within the U.S. Navy Department in Washington. To the author's knowledge, no subsequent study has been made of this incident; one is urgently needed.

44. For a study of an earlier investigation into cipher security, see Mulligan, "German Navy Evaluates," 75–79. Dönitz's own concerns about possible cipher compromise actually predate ULTRA's success against naval codes: See KTB BdU for 18 April and 7 June 1941 (T1022/4063/PG 30287, 30290). And as late as July 1944, captured U-boat officers sent coded warnings home with strong suspicions of cipher compromise (Op 20 GI-a, "German Awareness of Cipher Compromise," in Study SRMN– 054, 202, RG 457, NA).

45. KTB BdU, 15 January 1944, T1022/3981/PG 30338. Many of the advisories and instructions are reproduced in the KTB BdU for the previous two weeks.

46. Vause, *Wolf*, 186, quoting *Freg.Kapt.* Victor Oehrn.

47. Background data in Busch and Röll, *U-Boot-Kommandanten*, 162, and Kurowski, *Knight's Cross*, 169. On a war patrol in October–November 1940, Moehle had a narrow escape when one of his six victims nearly entangled *U-123* beneath it as it sank (Herzog, *U-Boote im Einsatz*, 83).

48. See the testimony by Moehle and Godt in *Trial of the Major War Criminals before the International Military Tribunal Nuremberg* (hereafter cited as *TMWC*), vol. 5, 230–45, and vol. 13, 534, 548; the issue is more generally discussed in chapter 10.

49. The two instructions are discussed in Salewski, *Seekriegsleitung*, vol. 2, 415–16; Cremer, *U-boat Commander*, 179–80, also provides the text of the April directive and a discussion of its significance.

50. The original account, by Karl Heinz Marbach (*U-953*) as related to Harald Busch, named Winter (*So war*, 328); Herbert Werner (*U-415*) identifies Rösing in his memoirs (*Iron Coffins*, 288–91). If the statement was made, Rösing is the more likely candidate in view of tentative plans for FdU West to assume operational command of the anti-invasion force (KTB BdU, Anlage z. KTB 7 June 1944, T1022/4065/PG 30348). The veracity of Werner's memoirs, however, has been strongly questioned by Jürgen Rohwer in several reviews that identify numerous errors and distortions and are noted in Bird, *German Naval History*, 690, 1032; Salewski, *Seekriegsleitung*, vol. 2, 416n; and Hadley, *Count Not*, 133.

51. Vause makes this point in *Wolf*, 192.

52. KTB BdU of 6 June 1944, T1022/4065/PG 30348, and the much more informative account in Showell, *U-boat Command*, 201, apparently based on Godt's statements. A useful summary of anti-invasion operations appears as a supplement to the KTB of BdU for 1–15 August 1944 ("Ubootseinsatz im Invasions- und invasionsgefährdeten Raum"), T1022/4066/PG 30352.

53. This is discussed in chapter 11.

54. Examples of the former include Morison, *Atlantic Battle Won*, 58–59, and Farago, *Tenth Fleet*, 240–41; an example of the latter is Kuenne, *Attack Submarine: A Study in Strategy*, 126–48.

55. BdU KTB, 5 November 1940, T1022/4063/PG 30276.

56. See Hessler, *U-boat War*, vol. 1, 87–97; Showell, *U-boat Command*, 88–89; Salewski, *Seekriegsleitung*, vol. 1, 475ff.

57. KTB BdU of 15 April 1942, quoted in Dönitz, *Memoirs*, 228.

58. See Tarrant, *U-boat Offensive*, 105–7; Hessler, *U-boat War*, vol. 2, 8–10; Showell, *U-boat Command*, 93–95; and Dönitz, *Memoirs*, 206–12.

59. "Vortrag des B.d.U. beim Führer am 14.5.1942 in Gegenwart des Oberbefehlshabers der Kriegsmarine," in Wagner, ed., *Lagevorträge*, 393–96. BdU's intelligence estimates of Allied shipbuilding in 1942 (8.2 million tons) actually exceeded the final totals (6.99 million tons), but the estimates for 1943 (10.3 million tons) fell well below actual production (14.39 million tons); see Hessler, *U-boat War*, vol. 2, 17.

60. 1/Skl, "Denkschrift zum gegenwärtigen Stand der Seekriegführung gegen England Juli 1941," in Salewski, *Seekriegsleitung*, vol. 3, 207. The head of the operations department within the Skl, however, more optimistically considered Britain in the summer of 1942 to be in a "fatal" position if 800,000 tons per month could be sunk, but the context of his argument concerned potential Allied amphibious assaults on U-boat bases (Salewski, *Seekriegsleitung*, vol. 2, 142).

61. Memorandum of 3/Skl, "Einfluss der Schiffsversenkungen," 9 September 1942, in KTB 1/Skl, Teil C, Heft IV, 1942 (T1022/1727/PG 32174). Long after the war Dönitz considered these estimates of Allied shipbuilding exaggerated (*Memoirs*, 343).

62. During November 1942, U-boats sank 118 merchant ships totaling 743,321 tons (their claims at the time were 149 ships and 955,200 tons), much of which was accomplished against unprotected independently routed ships in the eastern Atlantic; only 31 vessels (less than 180,000 tons) were sunk in the North Atlantic (Herzog, *Deutsche U-Boote*, 247–50).

63. Dönitz, *Memoirs*, 343.

64. This strategy shift is discussed in chapter 4.

65. See Jeschke, *U-Boottaktik*, esp. 48–60.

66. Dönitz, *wechselvolles Leben*, 118–19, and *Memoirs*, 1–3.

67. Wassner's comments quoted in Rössler, *U-boat*, 121. Information on his background can be found in Stoelzel, ed., *Ehrenrangliste*, 273; Spindler, *Handelskrieg mit U-Booten*, vol. 4, 152, 328, 451, and vol. 5, 72–75, 100, 303; and Thomas, *Raiders*, 240.

68. Von Heimburg (Chef des Stabes, Kommando der Marinestation der Nordsee) an Chef der Marineleitung, "Gegenmassnahmen gegen U-Bootsabwehr," 10 September 1927, in T1022/2100/PG 33382. Von Heimburg's First World War service included command of *UB-14*, *UC-22*, *UB-68* (turning over command to *Oblt.z.S.* Karl Dönitz on 1 September 1918), and *U-35* (see Stoelzel, ed., *Ehrenrangliste*, 294).

69. Von Heimburg was interviewed at length by American journalist Lowell Thomas in *Raiders* (132–41); additional data on his sinkings are provided in Spindler, *Handelskrieg mit U-Booten*, vol. 4, 176, 354, 478, and vol. 5, 165, 197, 201, 266.

70. Von Heimburg (promoted to *Vizeadmiral* in April 1942) spent much of World War II in administrative backwaters, serving as inspector for the naval replacement office in Bremen from January 1940 through April 1943; thereafter he was detailed to the staff of *Marineoberkommando Nord*. His thoughts on the U-boat campaign that he had foreseen are not known; he died in October 1945 in Russian captivity (Lohmann and Hildebrand, *Kriegsmarine*, vol. 3, 291/122).

71. Cf. Jeschke, *U-Boottaktik*, 65, 68, and Rössler, *U-boat*, 120, with Saville, "Development of the U-boat Arm," 358–63, 433–35. Fürbringer also made it clear in a spring 1939 memorandum that he considered U-boat warfare against convoys pointless until "stealth" technology could be developed to protect submerged submarines from asdic (quoted in Rössler, *Sonaranlagen*, 82).

72. See Dönitz, *Vierzig Fragen*, 29–32, and *Memoirs*, 13–15, 32–34; excerpts of the conclusions drawn from the exercises are provided in Padfield, *Dönitz*, 163–64, 171–80.

73. On the general subject, Neitzel's *Einsatz der deutschen Luftwaffe* stands alone, esp. 74ff., 123–25, 142–47, and 158ff.; on the transfer of officers, see chapter 7.

74. *Korv.Kapt.* Ernst Sobe, commander of *U-Flottille* "Wegener" aboard *U-53*, described the problems of tactical leadership at sea in an appendix to the *U-53* war diary for 1–30 September 1939 (T1022/2930/PG 30050); other attempts were made with *Korv.Kapt.* Werner Hartmann aboard *U-37* in October 1939 and February 1940 (*U-37* KTB, T1022/3039/PG 30034). See also Jeschke, *U-Boottaktik*, 73, and esp. Dönitz, *Memoirs*, 60–63, for the abandonment of the idea.

75. On the organization of "packs," see Hessler (a former BdU staff officer), *U-boat War*, vol. 1, 64–67. Torpedo attack procedures are described in *U-boat Commander's Handbook*, a translation of the 1943 (!) edition of the German manual.

76. Ministry of Defence study, "U-boat Logs," 19–20, 47.

77. See Blair, *Hitler's U-boat War: The Hunters*, 698, and Roskill, "CAPROS Not Convoys," 1052.

78. Von Heimburg, "Gegenmassnahmen," T1022/2100/PG 33382.

79. Möller, *Kurs Atlantik*, 130–49 (limited improvement from First to Second World War models) and 154 (quote). These sentiments are echoed in Brennecke, "Seit dem Weltkrieg I," 28–31. For a detailed review of Walter's design, see Rössler, *U-boat*, 168ff.

80. There is no full study of the Z-Plan and its implications, although invaluable discussions are offered in Dülffer, *Weimar, Hitler, und die Marine*, 471ff., and Salewski, *Seekriegsleitung*, vol. 1, 38ff. The literature to 1980 is reviewed in Bird, *German Naval History*, 556–65.

81. See Rössler, *U-boat*, 97–117, and Dülffer, *Weimar, Hitler, und die Marine*, 468–72, 484–85, 493–98; on the divisions among navy strategists regarding U-boats, see Salewski, *Seekriegsleitung*, vol. 1, 21ff. Summary data on the major characteristics, construction dates, and fates of individual boats of each class are provided in Gröner, *German Warships*, vol. 2, 39ff.

82. See the British Government Code and Cypher Section (G.C. & C.S.) Naval His-

tory, "The German Navy: The U-boat Arm," Item CBBD 53 in the NSA Historic Cryptographic Collection, RG 457, NA (hereafter cited as G.C. & C.S. Naval History, followed by volume and page numbers), vol. 7, 184–87; Showell, *U-boats*, 71–72; Stern, *U-boats in Action*, 10–12; and Enders, *Auch kleine Igel*, passim, for data on Black Sea operations.

83. Data from Busch and Röll, *U-Bootbau*, 41 (omitted from the grand totals are captured submarines placed in German service). Other Type VII variants comprised VIIA (10 boats), VIIB (24), VIID (6), and VIIF (4); on the evolution of these categories see Stern, *Type VII U-boats*, 14–23.

84. Although the terms of this treaty accorded the German navy parity in submarine tonnage with the Royal Navy, the former announced its intention to build no more than 45 percent, or about 22,000 tons. With construction for several models already underway, the 500-ton class offered the most economical return of oceangoing submarines for the remaining available tonnage. On the treaty, see Norbert T. Wiggershaus, "Der Deutsch-Englische Flottenvertrag vom 18. Juni 1935. England und die geheime deutsche Aufrüstung 1933–1935" (Ph.D. dissertation, Rheinische Friedrich-Wilhelms-Universität Bonn, 1972); on its implications for the Type VII, see Rössler, *U-boat*, 102–4, and Stern, *Type VII U-boats*, 13.

85. Rössler, *U-boat*, 105–8.

86. More information on the three aces is available in chapters 4 and 8; on *U-48*, see Herzog, "Torpedoverbrauch von U-48," 121–46.

87. Calculated from the data in Showell, *U-boats*, 16 and 33, supplemented by data for U-73 in Rohwer, *Axis Submarine Successes*, 44, 48–49, 235–36, 238, 241, 246–48, 251–53.

88. On the "S"-*Gerät*, see Rössler, *Sonaranlagen*, 64–65 (only one VIIC, *U-134*, actually received the equipment for which the design was nominally created); on general modifications, see Stern, *Type VII U-boats*, 17–20, 129, and Rössler, *U-boat*, 115–16, 154–60.

89. Commissioning data from Busch and Röll, *U-Bootbau*, 7 and 40; on conning tower variations, see Rössler, *U-boat*, 188–94.

90. Data on construction, commissioning, and fates compiled from Rössler, *Uboote und ihre Werften*, 203–7, and Gröner, *German Warships*, vol. 2, 52; data on successes based on Showell, *U-boats*, 135, corrected by information in Rohwer, *Axis Submarine Successes*, 175, 177, 181, 185–89, 191–93, 195, 204–11.

91. KTB BdU, 11 December 1941, T1022/4063/PG 30301a, and quoted in Dönitz, *Memoirs*, 197–98. For a good contrast of Type VIIC and IXC qualities, see Middlebrook, *Convoy*, 68–69.

92. U-boat strength in April 1943 amounted to 166 Type VIIs and 50 Type Ixs. By BdU calculations, losses of the former in March–April 1943 amounted to eleven (six in convoy operations) versus thirteen Type IXs (seven against convoys); see KTB BdU, 1 and 5 May 1943, T1022/4064/PG 30323.

93. Stern, *U-boats in Action*, 38; Herzog and Schomaekers, *Ritter der Tiefe*, 308 (see also the discussion of *Korv.Kapt.* Viktor Schütze's success in command of Type

IXB *U-103,* fourth most successful U-boat of the war, pp. 214–23). The five most successful U-boats of the war were *U-48* (VIIB), *U-99* (VIIB), *U-124* (IXB), *U-103* (IXB), and *U-107* (IXB) (Herzog, "Torpedoverbrauch von U-48," 124).

94. Köhl and Niestlé, *Vom Original zum Modell: Uboottyp IXC,* 14.

95. See Showell, *U-boats,* 76, and Möller, *Kurs Atlantik,* 144–48.

96. Rössler, *U-boat,* 103–5, 117–21.

97. Skl/Amtsgruppe U-Bootswesen (*Kaptlt.* Langer), "Auswirkungen der Arbeiterlage und des Rohstoffsmangels auf die Führung des U-Bootskrieges," 22 January 1942, in KTB 1/Skl, Teil C, Heft IV, 1942 (T1022/1726/PG 32174); published with commentary in Rahn, "Einsatzbereitschaft und Kampfkraft," 86–98.

98. The final IXC/40 to enter service was *U-889* (*Kaptlt.* Friedrich Braeucker), commissioned 4 August 1944 at the Deschimag AG Weser yard in Bremen (Busch and Röll, *U-Bootbau,* 35).

99. On the IXD boats' evolution, see Rössler, *U-boat,* 110–17, 150–51, 337; on their general use in the Far East, see Brennecke, *Haie,* 175–76, 212–19.

100. See Vause, *U-boat Ace,* 148–85.

101. See Stevens, *U-boat Far from Home,* 114ff.

102. See Schley, "Mit 'U 861' nach Ostindien," 282–83, 60–61, 250–51, 285–86, 316–17.

103. On the design, specific operations, and fates of Type XIV boats, see Rössler, *U-boat,* 151–52, 161–62, 166–67, 338; the significance is discussed in Rahn, "Long-Range German U-boat Operations," passim. Their specific targeting for destruction is described in Study SRH-008, 131–59, RG 457, NA, and Beesly, *Very Special Intelligence,* 195–97, 208–9.

104. Rössler, *U-boat,* 110–12, 161–62, 167; Gröner, *German Warships,* vol. 2, 76–77.

105. The most succinct assessment of Type XVII boats appears in Stern, *U-boats in Action,* 45–46; their evolution and Dönitz's plans are discussed in Rössler, *U-boat,* 168–87. For detailed histories, see Köhl and Rössler, *Vom Original zum Modell: Uboottyp XVII,* passim, and the articles by Sieche and Wilson, "Walter Submarine," in the October 1981 issue of *Warship.*

106. Van der Vat, *Atlantic Campaign,* 346.

107. See Rössler, *U-boat,* 208–10, 214ff.

108. Sixty-five XXIII boats were completed in 1944–45, sixty-two of which were commissioned; of these, six conducted patrols off the British coast before war's end. See Köhl and Rössler, *Vom Original zum Modell: Uboottyp XXIII,* esp. 10–12, 33–37, 45–46.

109. Among postwar submarine developments, the Soviet Navy's "W" class, the American "Guppy" fleet submarine conversion, and the British "T" class all incorporated features of the Type XXI (Hackmann, *Seek and Strike,* 336). The historian of naval operations research wrote that in assessing the Soviet submarine threat of 1950, "the potential threat . . . loomed large, however. The Type XXI U-boat . . . was regarded as the model for the future threat" (Tidman, *Operations Evaluation Group,* 118).

110. For the best overview of the Type XXI boats and their operational history, see Wetzel, *U 2540*, passim. Technical aspects are described in Köhl and Rössler, *Anatomy of the Ship: The Type XXI U-boat*, esp. 8–11, 59ff., and the two works by Rössler, *U-Boottyp XXI*, passim, and *U-boat*, 214–34.

Chapter 4. Patterns of the U-boat War, 1939–1945

1. Examples of variations in the chronological phases in the U-boat war can be seen in Rohwer, "U-boat War," 260ff.; Tarrant, *U-boat Offensive*, 81ff.; and Showell, *U-boat Command*, 11–15.

2. While this work was in preparation, the first volume of Clay Blair's massive study *Hitler's U-boat War: The Hunters, 1939–1942* appeared, with volume 2 (*The Hunted, 1943–1945*) scheduled for publication later in 1998. Although they promise to be the most detailed operational narratives of the U-boat campaign, they were received too late for other than occasional citation here but are mandatory for any future review of U-boat operations.

3. Showell, *U-boats*, 16–18, and Showell, *U-boat Command*, 27.

4. Herzog, "Torpedoverbrauch von U-48," 141 (the author does not identify his source material).

5. See Korganoff, *Prien gegen Scapa Flow*, and Snyder, *Royal Oak Disaster*, for accounts of the operation; Prien gave his own version in *Mein Weg*, 166ff., while Dönitz offers his perspective in *Memoirs*, 67–71. On the work of others in planning the operation, see Vause, *Wolf*, 41–54.

6. On general developments see Hessler, *U-boat War*, vol. 1, 7–27; on the torpedo crisis, see Rössler, *Torpedos*, 90–96, and Dönitz, *Memoirs*, 84–99, 482–85. Dönitz's earliest wartime notations on the torpedo problem are included in the BdU KTB entry for 21 January 1940 (T1022/3979/PG 30256).

7. Van der Vat, *Atlantic Campaign*, 126–27.

8. BdU/Operationsabteilung an OKM/M, "Ein Jahr U-Bootskriegführung," 24 August 1940, in KTB 1/Skl, Teil C, Heft IV, T1022/1724/PG 32011; U-boat commissionings in Busch and Röll, *U-Bootbau*, 6–7. The selection and ages of U-boat commanders and crews are discussed in chapters 5, 6, and 8.

9. KTB FdU West, 2 October 1939, T1022/4185/PG 30902.

10. Based on a review of COs and command dates for *U-1* through *U-52* in *Guide No. 2*, 23–35, supplemented by Dönitz's note on the relief of the CO of *U-53* in the BdU KTB of 29 November 1939, T1022/3979/PG 30252.

11. On the resolution of the torpedo crisis but continued problems with torpedoes, see Blair, *Hitler's U-boat War: The Hunted*, 159–60; Rössler, *Torpedos*, 93–96; and Dönitz, *Memoirs*, 91–99. The implications of this crisis for the U-boat campaign might extend far beyond naval ordnance issues, for it revealed to all how a branch of the navy's technical support staff had let down its combat forces. When the same issue resurfaced with a different branch—the ciphers section of Naval Communications—the failure to vigorously investigate technical as-

pects of cipher compromise might reflect a reluctance to confront further failures by responsible authorities. The revelation of incompetence among technical experts in 1940 might thus have discouraged later investigations in other areas lest front-line morale be completely undermined.

12. See Showell, *U-boat Command,* 30–41, and Tarrant, *U-boat Offensive,* 89–90.

13. BdU/Organisationsabteilung to Kommando der Marinestation Ostsee, "Personalbedarf der U-Boote auf Grund des Schiffbauneubauplanes," 13 November 1939, and accompanying Anlage "Ausbildungsmöglichkeiten U-Schule Neustadt u. Gotenhafen vom 1. April 1940 bis 1. Juli 1943," T1022/2066/PG 33541. The date for *U-1053* is derived from the data in Busch and Röll, *U-Bootbau,* 4–32.

14. The recruitment and training of submariners is treated in chapter 7.

15. See Rössler, *U-boat,* 122–26, 168–72, and his "U-boat Development and Building," 126–28; and Dönitz, *Memoirs,* 123–26. Comparative production data are from Busch and Röll, *U-Bootbau,* 9, 30–31.

16. The instability at Fleet Command is described in Salewski, *Seekriegsleitung,* vol. 1, 137–39, 162–73, and 203–7, and the forthcoming work by Güth, *Erich Raeder und die Englische Frage.*

17. Data in Tarrant, *U-boat Offensive,* 89–96.

18. "Historians looking for the turning point of the U-boat war would do well to analyze the events of this period in detail. It marks a drastic change in the war at sea from which U-boats never recovered" (Showell, *U-boat Command,* 63). Supporting this argument is the fact that the three aces named sank many of their victims in convoys; by March 1941 convoy escorts had gained sufficiently in numbers and experience to eliminate such opportunities. Thereafter the U-boat "ace" who achieved impressive totals on the North Atlantic convoy lanes was rare indeed. See also Rohwer, "U-boat War," 263–64.

19. See Kahn, *Seizing the Enigma,* esp. 161ff., 191ff.; Hinsley, et al., *British Intelligence,* vol. 2, 163ff.; Beesly, *Very Special Intelligence,* 92ff.; and Rohwer, "Auswirkungen der deutschen und britischen Funkaufklärung," 167–73, 386–90.

20. On training and the significance of *U-570,* see chapter 7.

21. See Hessler, *U-boat War,* vol. 1, 87–92; Showell, *U-boat Command,* 89–91; and the BdU KTB for 1 January 1942, T1022/3979/PG 30302. On diversions of U-boats to secondary tasks, see the valuable essay by Neitzel, "Deployment of the U-boats," 276–301.

22. See BdU an den Oberbefehlshaber der Kriegsmarine, 26 November 1941, in Wagner, ed., *Lagevorträge,* 320–25; and the memorandum of *Konteradmiral* Lange of Amtsgruppe U-Bootswesen 2/Skl, "Auswirkungen der Arbeiterlage und des Rohstoffmangels auf die Führung des U-Bootskrieges," 22 January 1942, and "Vortrag Kapt.z.S. Ernst Kratzenberg (Chef der Abt. UII der Amtsgruppe U-Bootswesen) vor dem Oberbefehlshaber der Kriegsmarine am 14. Juli 1942 über 'Erhöhung der Einsatzmöglichkeiten der U-Boote,'" both published in Rahn, "Einsatzbereitschaft und Kampfkraft," 86–107.

23. Neitzel, *Deutschen Ubootbunker,* esp. 41–45, 51–62, 70–72, 77–82, 154–60; and Rohwer, "U-boat War," 287–88.

24. E.g., Hoyt, *U-boats Offshore;* Hickam, *Torpedo Junction;* Gentile, *Track of the Grey Wolf;* Gannon, *Operation Drumbeat;* Wiggins, *Torpedoes in the Gulf;* and Kelshall, *U-boat War in the Caribbean.*

25. Dönitz, *Memoirs,* 206–12, 223–24.

26. See Bonatz, *Seekrieg im Äther,* 235–37; Hinsley, et al., *British Intelligence,* 228–33; Rahn, "Long Range German U-boat Operations," 8–11; and Hessler, *U-boat War,* vol. 2, 20–34.

27. Cf. the memorandum of 1/Skl Referat IIIa, "U-Bootsbau," ca. 30 July 1941 in KTB 1/Skl, Teil C, Heft IV (T1022/1724/PG32173), and the Lange memorandum "Auswirkungen der Arbeiterlage und des Rohstoffmangels auf die Führung des U-Bootskrieges," 22 January 1942, in Rahn, "Einsatzbereitschaft," 92.

28. Zilbert, *Albert Speer,* 149.

29. Data in Tarrant, *U-boat Offensive,* 106–7.

30. Rössler, *U-boat,* 174.

31. Fernschreiben (teletype message) vom 4.7.42: "Besuch BdU bei Jeschonnek 2.7. betr. Luftlage Biskaya," KTB 1/Skl Teil C, Heft IV, 1942 (T1022/1726/PG 32174). As a result of these efforts, the Luftwaffe committed additional Ju-88 units to help protect U-boats in the Bay of Biscay and exacted a price from RAF operations there, but long-range air support in convoy operations remained lacking (Neitzel, *Einsatz der deutschen Luftwaffe,* 142–46).

32 See Hessler, *U-boat War,* vol. 2, 48, and Showell, *U-boat Command,* 95.

33. See, for example, Dönitz's letter sent to several Naval High Command offices, "Waffenentwicklung für Uboote," 5 September 1942, in KTB 1/Skl, Teil C, Heft IV, 1942 (T1022/1727/PG 32174). The apparent project Dönitz had in mind was a surface-to-surface rocket to be used against Allied escorts, discussed in the text below.

34. On recruitment changes and contrasts in age, see chapters 6 and 7.

35. See the information on training in chapter 7.

36. Compare the *U-47* crew lists for the two periods in Snyder, *Royal Oak,* 268–69, and in the custody of the U-Boot-Archiv, Cuxhaven. The most recent research into the loss of *U-47,* long attributed to HMS *Wolverine* during an attack on convoy OB 293, discards this cause and rates an accident as the most likely possibility (Kemp, *U-boats Destroyed,* 68).

37. Skl/Amtsgruppe U-Bootswesen, "Aufstellung U-Bootsverluste Stand 24.8.42," 3 September 1942, in KTB 1/Skl, Teil C, Heft IV, 1942 (T1022/1727/PG 32174).

38. BdU, "Personalbestand im B.d.U. Bereich am 1.7.1942," Anl. 52 to "Organisation, Stellenbesetzung und Personalstand im B.d.U.-Bereich am 1.7.42," T1022/4038/PG 31794. A complete breakdown of the U-boat Command at this time is provided in appendix 3.

39. Convoy operations are discussed in Hessler, *U-boat War,* vol. 2, 31–37, 50–51. For a listing of U-boat successes and context in November 1942, see Herzog and Schomaekers, *Ritter der Tiefe,* 304–7; on the March convoy battles, see Roh-

wer, *Critical Convoy Battles,* 195–200, and Middlebrook, *Convoy,* 276–82. The Admiralty comment appears in Roskill, *War at Sea,* vol. 2, 367.

40. See Rössler, *Torpedos,* 101, 114–21; Hessler, *U-boat War,* vol. 2, 84–85; and Stern, *Type VII U-boats,* 82–86.

41. The best operational narrative is Syrett, *Defeat of the German U-boats,* passim; the German perspective is provided in Hessler, *U-boat War,* vol. 2, 99ff., and Showell, *U-boat Command,* 123ff. The latest and best summary of the May 1943 battles can be found in Gannon, *Black May,* passim. The various German technological stopgaps are described in Niestlé, "German Technical and Electronic," 438–50; "hunter-killer" operations are described in Y'Blood, *Hunter-Killer,* and signals intelligence aspects are discussed in Hinsley, et al., *British Intelligence,* vol. 2, 547ff.; Beesly, *Very Special Intelligence,* 180ff., and Study SRH-008, "Battle of the Atlantic," RG 457, NA.

42. KTB BdU, 21 August 1942, T1022/3980/PG 30310b (the translation of this passage in Middlebrook, *Convoy,* 286, is more dramatic but too negative). Dönitz reiterated this view in his KTB of 3 September (T1022/3980/PG 30911).

43. KTB BdU, 26 August 1942 (T1022/3980/PG 30310b); Showell, *U-boat Command,* 146.

44. The most detailed account of this meeting is provided by participant Waas, "Zeitzeuge zum Walter-U-Boot-Bau," 19–27; the official minutes in Wagner, ed., *Lagevorträge,* 420–25, are more complete than the translation in *Führer Conferences,* 294–97.

45. By November, concrete plans had been prepared for production of twenty-four of the original Walter boats (designated Type XVII) and two of a larger model (Type XVIII); see Rössler, *U-boat,* 179–82.

46. See Salewski, "Raeder zu Dönitz," esp. 109–112 on BdU's exceeding his technical authority.

47. See Salewski, *Seekriegsleitung,* vol. 2, 225–26.

48. On the Speer negotiations, see Eichholtz, *Geschichte der Deutschen Kriegswirtschaft,* 131–36, and Dönitz, *Memoirs,* 350–52; Luftwaffe discussions are summarized in Neitzel, *Einsatz der deutschen Luftwaffe,* 160–65.

49. The principal developments are described in Hessler, *U-boat War,* vol. 2, 99ff., and Showell, *U-boat Command,* 137ff.; sources for casualty data are given in table 5.

50. Data from Lakowski, *U-Boote,* 344 (for a broader discussion, see appendix 2).

51. U-boat strength from Tarrant, *U-boat Offensive,* 128; on training, see chapter 7.

52. On the background to the 1943 fleet program (including some documentation), see Salewski, *Seekriegsleitung,* vol. 2, 268–81 and 623–30. See also Rössler, "U-boat Development and Building," 129–30; Dönitz, *Memoirs,* 342–52; and the record of Dönitz's conference with Hitler on 11 April 1943 in Wagner, ed. *Lagevorträge,* 475–90.

53. "Niederschrift über die Sitzung am 8.4.43 bei Chef MPA," 14 April 1943, in KTB 1/Skl, Teil B, Heft V, 1943, T1022/1707/PG 32119. See also the information documented in note 56, below.

54. For the most complete record of the conference, see "Niederschrift über die Besprechung des Ob.d.M. beim Führer am 31.5.1943 auf dem Berghof," 5 June 1943, in Wagner, ed., *Lagevorträge*, 507–11; an abbreviated translation is available in *Führer Conferences*, 331–36. Revised production schedules developed in July 1943 are detailed in Rössler, "U-boat Development and Building," 132–33.

55. "Niederschrift," in Wagner, ed., *Lagevorträge*, 510.

56. Naval personnel planning for 1943/44 is provided in the memorandum of the Allgemeines Marinehauptamt (Admiral Warzecha), "Vortragsnotiz über eine notwendige vermehrte Rekrutenzuteilung für die Kriegsmarine" (with six accompanying Anlagen), 28 May 1943, in KTB 1/Skl Teil B, Heft V, 1943, T1022/1707/PG 32119. Dönitz's revised data are reproduced as an appendix to "Niederschrift über den Vortrag des Ob.d.M. beim Führer am 15.6.43 auf dem Berghof," 29 June 1943, in Wagner, ed., *Lagevorträge*, 513–16.

57. Five boats were lost in Asian waters, five returned to Europe (one sunk en route from Norway to Germany), one was sunk in passage home, and one surrendered after Germany's capitulation (as did two U-boats that had recently departed for Japan); seven submarines (including two ex-Italian boats) were given to or taken over by the Japanese. Excluded are two U-boats intended for *Monsun* but diverted to other activities and lost and one boat (*U-1224*) taken over by a Japanese crew in Germany and sunk en route to Japan (see Stevens, *U-boat Far From Home*, 83, 230–39). For general information on Far East operations, see Brennecke, *Haie im Paradies*, passim, and Giese and Wise, *Shooting the War*, 179ff.

58. See Hessler, *U-boat War*, vol. 3, 35–54; Kelshall, *U-boat War in the Caribbean*, 423–30; and Mulligan, *Lone Wolf*, 175–89. The morale crisis of 1943–44 is discussed in chapter 8.

59. On the snorkel, see Rössler, *The U-boat*, 198–204, and Bräckow, *Marine-Ingenieuroffizierkorps*, 260; a document on its earliest installation is reproduced in Lakowski, *Deutsche U-Boote Geheim*, 153. Dates of 1944 installation work aboard Type IXC boats are provided in Köhl and Niestlé, *Original zum Modell: Uboottyp IXC*, 30.

60. Price, *Aircraft versus Submarine*, 235; KTB BdU, Anlage z. KTB 1 January 1945, T1022/4066/PG 30362.

61. See Study SRH-008, 229–30, RG 457, NA, and Syrett, "Weather-Reporting U-boats," 16–18.

62. See Roskill, *War at Sea*, vol. 3 (pt. 2), 179–85, 285–92; Sarty, "Limits of Ultra," 44–68; Tarrant, *Last Year*, 71–93, 155ff.; Hadley, *U-boats against Canada*, 224ff.

63. The minutes of the Anti-U-boat Warfare Cabinet meeting quoted below note that U-boats sank fifteen merchant vessels and five warships from 20 December 1944 to 20 January 1945 against only three confirmed kills of U-boats. One of the vessels sunk in the English Channel, the Belgian steamer *Leopoldville*, took with her over eight hundred American soldiers of the 66th Infantry Division (see Sanders, *A Night before Christmas*).

64. War Cabinet, Anti-U-boat Warfare, "Minutes of the Meeting Held in the Cabi-

net War Room on Friday, 26th January 1945, at 11.30 a.m." (including attached memorandum of the First Lord of the Admiralty, 20 January 1945), formerly top secret 1945 correspondence of the Chief of Naval Operations, RG 38, NA.

65. Roskill, *War at Sea*, vol. 3 (pt. 2), 285–90, 298–301; Tarrant, *Last Year*, 194–201.

66. The two were *U-2511* (*Korv.Kapt.* Adalbert Schnee) and *U-3008* (*Kaptlt.* Helmut Manseck); see Rössler, *U-Boottyp XXI*, 50–51, and G.C. & C.S. Naval History, vol. 7, 243–44. The latter study, however, omits reference to *U-3008*.

67. Price, *Aircraft versus Submarine*, 224–25; Roskill, *War at Sea*, vol. 3 (pt. 2), 300–301, 467–69.

68. See Merten, *Nach Kompass*, 370–77; Brustat-Naval, *Unternehmen Rettung*, 30–31.

69. For general information, see Rössler, "U-Boot-Typ XXI" in *Technikmuseum U-Boot Wilhelm Bauer*, 95, and Brustat-Naval, *Unternehmen Rettung*, 81–82; for accounts by the commanders of *U-791* and *U-56*, see Högel, *Embleme*, 235–38, 255.

70. See Zilbert, *Albert Speer*, 166–79, and Speer, *Inside*, 355–58. No explanation accounts for the large discrepancy between this number of submarines completed and the 229 U-boats that were officially commissioned during the year (see Busch and Röll, *U-Bootbau*, 32–38), unless some categories of midget submarines are also included.

71. See Dönitz, *Memoirs*, 370, Matthes, *Seehunde* (the best general history of these units), 50, and Schulz, *Im Kleinst-U-Boot*, 21–26, the last by a U-boat recruit detailed to the small units.

72. See Rössler, "U-boat Development and Building," 135–36, and Rössler, *U-boat*, 246–65.

73. On the numbers of U-boats, see Hessler, *U-boat War*, vol. 1, 2, and vol. 3, 101. On the comparative ages of U-boat crewmen, see chapter 8. The most recent research, however, reveals that fifty-eight U-boats were at sea on 8 May 1945; see Axel Niestlé, *German U-Boat Losses during World War II: Details of Destruction* (Annapolis, Md.: Naval Institute Press, 1998), 203–5.

74. NSA Study SRH-008, "Battle of the Atlantic," 237, RG 457, NA.

Chapter 5. Spirit and Soul

1. Dönitz, *U-Bootswaffe*, 27; Lüth, "Menschenführung," in Busch, *So war*, 350 (in this case translated directly from the German, rather than the translation used in Tarrant, *U-boat Offensive*, 181).

2. Stöckel, "Entwicklung der Reichsmarine," Anlage 7.

3. Merten, *Nach Kompass*, 27; Rust, *Crew 34*, 18.

4. Quotation from Ott, *Sharks*, 34; the tests are discussed in Wiedersheim, "Officer Personnel Selection," 445–49, and their effectiveness is noted in Rust, *Crew 34*, 53.

5. Examples of Crew yearbooks, newsletters, and other publications, arranged

chronologically by Crew, are held at the Wehrgeschichtliches Ausbildungszentrum at the Marineschule Mürwik, Flensburg. On Crew cohesion through the postwar era, see Rust, *Crew 34*, 19–20, 74–76, 124–29, 143–49.

6. See C. R. W. Thomas, "Making Naval Officers," 39–48; Rahn, "Ausbildung zum Marineoffizier," 123–31; and Rust, *Crew 34*, 54–56, 68. Confirmation of the Prussian tradition appears in Schulz, *Nassen Abgrund*, 80.

7. See Güth, "Funktion und Charakter," 240–45; Thomas, *German Navy*, 208–10; and Hoch, "Zur Problematik der Menschenführung," 202–6.

8. *Personalakte* (personnel file) *Korv.Kapt.* Werner Henke (copy courtesy of Albrecht Henke).

9. *Rangliste der Deutschen Kriegsmarine nach dem Stande vom 1. November 1937*, 132–42, and *Rangliste . . . vom 1. November 1938*, 34–40; on the detail of cadets to the air force, see Rust, *Crew 34*, 64–65. To date no major study has been attempted of the aborted German naval air arm; one is badly needed.

10. Güth, "Funktion und Charakter" (Teil III), 243.

11. Data compiled from Rahn, "Ausbildung zum Marineoffizier," 128; the sources cited in Mulligan, *Lone Wolf*, 26–32; Rust, *Crew 34*, 37ff.; Güth, "Bild einer Crew," 131–32; and Thomas, "Making Naval Officers," 40ff.

12. Peter, "Fähnrichausbildung," 150; Werner, *Iron Coffins*, 23–25; Schaeffer, *U-boat 977*, 15–34.

13. Interview with Werner Hirschmann, Toronto, 10 August 1997.

14. Ibid., and Peter, "Fähnrichausbildung," 150–52, as well as his memoirs *Acht Glas*, 97–98.

15. Compiled from data in Busch and Röll, *U-Boot-Kommandanten*, 15ff.

16. Cf. BdU, "Personalbestand im B.d.U. Bereich am 1.7.1942," Anlage 52 zu "Organisation, Stellenbesetzung und Personalstand im B.d.U.-Bereich am 1.7.42," T1022/4038/PG 31794, and Förster, "Dynamics," 208.

17. Interview with Wilhelm Müller-Arnecke, Bremen, 6 November 1993. After a brief stint as a U-boat commander, Müller-Arnecke served most of the war as a staff officer under von Friedeburg, generally responsible for U-boat personnel issues relating to NCOs and enlisted men.

18. Data on promoted *Obersteuermänner* taken from Busch and Röll, *U-Boot-Kommandanten*, 16ff., and Trompelt, "Vom Obermechaniker-Maat," 43–46.

19. See chapter 8, especially table 18.

20. The watch officer plan is described in BdU's "Erläuterung zu Stellenbesetzung für Neubau—U-Boote 1942/43," Anlage 50 zu "Organisation, Stellenbestzung und Personalstand im B.d.U.-Bereich am 1.7.42," T1022/4038/PG 31794; figures on U-boat strength in July 1942 in Tarrant, *U-boat Offensive*, 106. Dönitz's 1943 plans are further discussed in chapter 6.

21. Chart and data provided by Heinz Trompelt in letter and enclosures to author, 9 November 1994. Trompelt hopes to publish his findings in the near future.

22. Rust, *Crew 34*, 43.

23. Data compiled from various sources in Rust, *Crew 34*, 16.

24. Thomas, *German Navy*, 124.

25. Güth, "Bild einer Crew," 132; on accelerated promotion of machinist petty officers, see chapter 6.
26. Tabulated in Rust, *Crew 34*, 16.
27. All data that follow are taken from the officer questionnaires from our sample.
28. The population data are that for the German Reich as of May 1939, as furnished in *Statistisches Jahrbuch für das Deutsche Reich 1939/40;* complete population data for the areas cited with definitions of partial or consolidated regions can be found in table 11 in chapter 6. The sample here expands to 123 officers with the background data furnished by the four officers omitted in table 7.
29. Rust, *Crew 34*, 20; Güth, "Bild einer Crew," 133.
30. See Rust, *Crew 34*, 23–24, 28; data from officers' questionnaires of sample.
31. On early Crews, see Herwig, *Elitekorps*, 39–55; priorities are quoted in Wentzel, "Werden einer Crew," 18; quote from Rust, *Crew 34*, 22.
32. For overviews of research into class structure in modern Germany, see Dahrendorf, *Society and Democracy,* passim, and Hartmut Kaelble, "Social Stratification in Germany in the Nineteenth and Twentieth Centuries: A Survey of Research since 1945," *Journal of Social History* 10, no. 2 (Winter 1976): 144–65.
33. For a review of the *Mittelstand* arguments and literature, see Paul Madden, "The Social Class Origins of Nazi Party Members as Determined by Occupations, 1919–1933," *Social Science Quarterly* 68, no. 2 (June 1987): 263–80. Detlef Mühlberger, who places skilled workers in crafts and industry in the working class (*Hitler's Followers*, 11–17), believes the NSDAP represented a *Volkspartei* with significant support from all classes.
34. See Mühlberger, *Hitler's Followers*, 5–25, for a discussion of his methodology in correlating German occupations and social status. None match his comprehensive organization of specific occupations into socio-economic groups, which have been used for both officers and enlisted personnel (in the next chapter) and allow comparisons with Mühlberger's research into Nazi party membership.
35. Kroener, "Heeresoffizierkorps," 669–70.
36. See Kaelble, "Social Mobility," 451–53.
37. See Dahrendorf, *Society and Democracy,* 73.
38. On the *Niobe* crew losses, see Thomas, *German Navy*, 134n.
39. Two engineering officers provided no or insufficient data on their fathers' backgrounds.
40. Data from the personal papers of the historian of German naval engineering officers, Werner Bräckow, cited in Thomas, *German Navy*, 139n.
41. Marinewaffenamt, "Sofortmassnahmen zur Behebung des Mangels an technischen Personal: Niederschrift über den Vortrag beim Ob.d.M. am 8. März 1939," 14 March 1939, T1022/2066/PG 33540.
42. Based on the presence of seven *Volksoffiziere* as chief engineers among thirty U-boats sunk by U.S. forces among ONI interrogation reports (in RG 38, NA) that furnish background information on engineer officers.

43. Letter of Carl Möller to author, 21 November 1987, and subsequent interview in Hamburg, 30 August 1989; author's interviews with Hermann Brandt, Clausthal-Zellerfeld, 12 May 1994, and Neukirchen, 26 June 1996 (the latter together with fellow machinist Kurt Hanisch). A brief account of the incident appears in Mulligan, *Lone Wolf*, 143, 149–50.

44. These issues are detailed in Bräckow, Marine-*Ingenieuroffizierkorps*, 229–35, and the speech reproduced on 347–55; the situation is admirably summarized in Thomas, *German Navy*, 127–33.

45. Examples of the former are cited in Rust, *Crew 34*, 69; an example of the latter is Werner Hirschmann, former L.I. on *U-190*, interviewed by author in Toronto, 10 August 1997.

46. Bräckow, *Marine-Ingenieuroffizierkorps*, 235–36.

47. On communications officers' status, see Angolia and Schlicht, *Kriegsmarine*, vol. 1, 44; German naval signals intelligence numbers are taken from Bonatz, *Marine-Funkaufklärung*, 86, 104–5.

48. KTB *U-664*, May–June 1943, T1022/3397/PG 30963; ONI interrogation report of *U-664*, RG 38, NA.

49. The best source for medical aspects of U-boat operations is Nöldeke and Hartmann, *Der Sanitätsdienst*, esp. 39, 63–64, for the information here; the memoir of a U-boat doctor is available in Schütze, *Operation*, passim. The emergency operation is described in Kaiser, *QXP*, 154–66.

50. See Nöldeke and Hartmann, *Der Sanitätsdienst*, 33–34, 79–82, 156–57. The authors' sources include several medical war diaries maintained by surgeons attached to the individual U-boat flotillas, most of them today in the custody of the Krankenbuchlager in Berlin; these sources deserve more detailed treatment.

51. See Schaefer, "Ernährung des U.-Bootfahrers," esp. 157–158b for recommended daily menus on extended patrols.

52. Translations of twenty-four studies were subsequently prepared by the U.S. Navy and collectively issued as "Monograph on Submarine Medicine," edited by Dr. K. E. Schaefer; other studies have appeared in military medical journals (e.g., Dr. H. Nothdurft's articles "Das CO_2-Problem in U-Booten" and "Über die Klima-Hygiene auf Ubooten" in 1992–93 issues of *Wehrmedizinische Monatsschrift*).

53. For a provocative if not always convincing assessment of the attitudes and values of the naval officer corps, see Salewski, "Offizierkorps der Reichs- und Kriegsmarine," 211–29.

Chapter 6. The Right Man in the Right Place

1. *Hamburger Illustrierte*, vol. 25, no. 7 (13 February 1943), copy in the U-Boot-Archiv, Cuxhaven.

2. Mierke, "Auswahl," 185.

3. Lüth, "Menschenführung," in Busch, *So war*, 340–42.

4. "The Age-Structures of the U-boat Arm and the G.A.F. (British source, 10 January 1944)," Report B-578, 3 February 1944, and "Social Structure of U-boat Arm and of the G.A.F. Air Crews (British source, 26–27 January 1944)," Report B-595, 17 February 1944, both in Records of the G-2 Division (MIS-Y), RG 165, NA.

5. Cf. Mulligan, "German U-boat Crews," 261–81, and Gannon, *Drumbeat*, 109–12.

6. On the economic differences between the Ruhr and Saxony-Thuringia, see Turner, *German Big Business*, xviii, 192–96, and the Office of Strategic Services' (OSS) Research and Analysis Branch Report No. 1757, "Central Industrial Region of Germany," 4 August 1944, RG 226, NA.

7. On the army's principle of regional organization, see van Creveld, *Fighting Power*, 45, 75; much more needs to be done contrasting this with the other services' practices.

8. "Social Structure," Report B-595, RG 165, NA.

9. See Frederick C. Howe, *Socialized Germany* (New York: Charles Scribner's Sons, 1917), 220ff., and Dahrendorf, *Society and Democracy*, 80. I am also indebted to Werner Hirschmann for his comments on this matter.

10. "Social Structure," Report B-595, RG 165, NA.

11. The classification is that used by Detlef Mühlberger in his *Hitler's Followers;* see especially pp. 11–25 for detailed explanations of his methodology. Unlike other historians, Mühlberger groups skilled craft workers as working-class rather than lower-middle-class. I concur with this view, particularly as the educational levels evident for U-boat crewmen do not support a middle-class context.

12. Data from questionnaires no. 5529, 5105, 1246, 1253, 2903, 2985, 3702, and 3718.

13. Stöckel, "Entwicklung der Reichsmarine," 94–95. The backgrounds of 21 percent were not specified.

14. See Mulligan, "German U-boat Crews," 275–77.

15. Bry, *Wages*, 109–112.

16. Gillingham, "Vocational Training," 426–27; Grunberger, *Twelve-Year Reich*, 206–7.

17. Kroener, "Personelle Ressourcen," *Deutsche Reich* V/1, 810–17; Mason, *Sozialpolitik*, 220–23.

18. On the German Army's draft classification system and recruitment of specific job categories, see the postwar manuscripts by Helmuth Reinhardt, et al., "Personnel and Administration, Project #2b (Parts II and III)," Foreign Military Studies manuscripts P-008 (esp. 23–30) and P-012 (esp. 95–100, 138–53) (U.S. Army Europe, Historical Division, 1949).

19. U.S. naval attaché's report, "Requirements for Entry into the German Navy," 1 October 1935, file EF30/74, general correspondence files 1925–40, Bureau of Navigation/Personnel, RG 24, NA.

20. Franke, *Handbuch*, 306 (also 265).

21. U.S. naval attaché's report, "Careers of Volunteers (Enlisted Men) in the Ger-

man Navy," 7 February 1939, file E-6-e No. 15849, naval attaché reports 1886–1939, RG 38, NA.

22. See Busch, *Buch von der Kriegsmarine,* 160.

23. U.S. naval attaché report, "Translation of German Newspaper Article 'Who Wants to Join the Navy?,'" 19 May 1941, file EF30/223, general correspondence files 1941–45, Bureau of Navigation/Personnel, RG 24, NA.

24. Mierke, "Auswahl," 186–87.

25. Details of the various *Laufbahnen* and promotion standards in 1939 are provided in the naval publication *Bestimmungen über die Beförderung der Unteroffiziere und Mannschaften,* 9ff., most of which is summarized in *Wie komme ich zur Kriegsmarine,* 9–19; wartime changes are described in the British intelligence G.C.& C.S. Naval History, vol. 4, "The German Navy: Organisation," appendixes G–O.

26. Information on the individual career-tracks is taken from Angolia and Schlicht, *Kriegsmarine,* vol. 1, 49–61, 88ff.

27. See Burkard Freiherr von Müllenheim-Rechberg, *Schlachtschiff Bismarck: Ein Überlebender in seiner Zeit* (Frankfurt/Main: Ullstein Verlag, 1987), 45.

28. Angolia and Schlicht, *Kriegsmarine,* vol. 1, 47–49, 57–58, 77–78, 101; OKM, *Wie komme ich,* 10; and ONI (Op-16-Z) report, "German Naval Training Establishments," 15 May 1943, subject file "Handbook of Interrogations," Op-16-Z subject files, RG 38, NA (hereafter cited as ONI report, "Naval Training Establishments").

29. Survey questionnaire no. 3907, Heinz Theen.

30. Angolia and Schlicht, *Kriegsmarine,* vol. 1, 47–50, 57–60, 70–77, 101.

31. Bräckow, *Marine-Ingenieuroffizierkorps,* 267.

32. See the memorandum prepared within the navy's Allgemeines Marineamt by *Korv.Kapt.* Wenninger, "Vortragsnotiz: Lage der Personalwirtschaft," 25 November 1940, file RM 7/1206, BA-MA.

33. ONI, Interrogation report on survivors of *U-841* and *U-848* (sunk 17 October and 5 November 1943), RG 38, NA.

34. Angolia and Schlicht, *Kriegsmarine,* vol. 1, 47–50, 57–58, 93ff.; ONI report, "Naval Training Establishments," RG 38, NA.

35. The remaining metalworker categories consisted of tinsmiths (3), plumbers (3), mechanical engineers (3), and electricians (2), with single representatives for watchmakers, industrial technicians, and professional engineers.

36. Angolia and Schlicht, *Kriegsmarine,* vol. 1, 47–50, 70ff.; G.C. & C.S. Naval History, vol. 4, app. G–2.

37. Data from sample; the three authors are Wolfgang Hirschfeld, Ernst Kaiser, and Hans Guske (full citations provided in the bibliography).

38. See Hirschfeld, *Story,* passim.

39. On the *Sani-Laufbahn,* see Angolia and Schlicht, *Kriegsmarine,* vol. 1, 47–49, 58–61, 72ff., and Nöldecke and Hartmann, *Sanitätsdienst,* 79–81.

40. Busch, *Buch von der Kriegsmarine,* 160.

41. See, for example, the familiar listings of preferred occupations and skills for the

successors to *Maschinisten* and *Mechaniker* career-tracks in Giese, *Alte und Neue Marine*, 75–77.

Chapter 7. Quality before Quantity

1. Quoted in Robertson, *Golden Horseshoe*, 14.
2. See Deighton, *Blood*, 130, and Terraine, *U-boat Wars*, 199. Deighton proceeds to confuse inadequate training vis-à-vis Allied antisubmarine measures (true) with inadequate training in basic seamanship (false), blaming the latter for such onboard accidents as fingers lost in machinery, crewmen lost overboard, and sailors falling down companionways.
3. Letter, Horst Bredow (U-Boot-Archiv, Cuxhaven) to author, 15 May 1990.
4. Interview with Carl Möller, Steinhude am Meer, 26 May 1991. Möller's Kriegsmarine career reflects a remarkable defiance of the odds: Entering the navy and the U-boat service in 1938, he served aboard *U-25*, *U-107*, and *U-515* from September 1939 to January 1944, departing each just before the submarine's final patrol. Promoted to Obermaschinist and a recipient of the *Deutsches Kreuz in Gold* (German Cross in Gold), Möller ended the war as an instructor for the *Kleinkampfverbände* that used midget submarines and manned torpedoes. He enjoyed a successful postwar business career and died in Hamburg in December 1995.
5. BdU/Organisationsabteilung to Kommando der Marinestation Ostsee, "Personalbedarf der U-Boote auf Grund des Schiffsbauneubauplanes" (with Anlagen), 13 November 1939, T1022/2066/PG 33541.
6. See the report by the British Naval Staff, Intelligence Division, "*U. 48:* Interrogation of Survivors," December 1917, in ONI subject files (JU-U48), 1911–27, RG 45, NA. This information is confirmed by statements of POWs recovered from *UB-26*, *UB-52*, and *UC-65* in the same series.
7. Hoch, "Problematik der Menschenführung," 197.
8. Whitley, *Destroyer!*, 139–40.
9. See KTB 1/Skl, Teil A, 22–23 October 1940, T1022/1664/PG 32034.
10. Führer der Zerstörer an das Flottenkommando, "Personelle Kriegsbereitschaft," 13 October 1941, RM 7/1206, BA-MA.
11. Statements of Koitschka, Töpfer, and *Oblt.(I)* Walter Lorch, quoted in Middlebrook, *Convoy*, 60; Mulligan, *Lone Wolf*, 42–43.
12. Hoch, "Problematik der Menschenführung," 195.
13. See Just, *Seeflieger zum U-Bootfahrer*, 44–45.
14. Statement of *Fähnrich z.S.* Wolfgang Jacobsen (*U-305*), quoted in Middlebrook, *Convoy*, 60–61.
15. Legro, *Cooperation*, 52–62; Salewski, "Offizierkorps," 226–27.
16. Hirschfeld and Brooks, *Hirschfeld*, 6–7 (this English translation of Hirschfeld's *Feindfahrten* contains more background information than the German original).

17. Statement of *Obermaschinist* Artur Kolbe (*U-406*), quoted in Middlebrook, *Convoy,* 61.

18. Letter, Heinz Trompelt to author, 9 November 1994.

19. Interrogation report of *U-233* in Op-16-Z files, RG 38, NA.

20. ULTRA intercept ZTPGM/12032, cited in the G.C. & C.S. Naval History, vol. 7, 91.

21. Monitored room conversation (S.R.N. 1105), 30 September 1942, CPMB report #B-54, Extracts of British Reports, in Enemy POW Interrogation files (MIS-Y), G-2 Division, RG 165, NA.

22. Quotation from author's interview with Peter Petersen, Chicago, 11 June 1997; see also the comment by former radioman Heinz Guske in his *War Diaries,* 21–22.

23. Allgemeines Marinehauptamt (*Korv.Kapt.* Wenninger), "Vortragsnotiz: Lage der Personalwirtschaft (Anfang Juni 1941)," 19 June 1941, RM 7/1206, BA-MA.

24. See the *Marinekommandoamt* memorandums "Seemännische Bevölkerung," 14 April 1936, and "Ergebnis der Besprechung über den Wehrdienst der seemännischen Bevölkerung am 24.4.1936," both in T1022/2066/PG 33540.

25. Anecdote quoted in Ansel, *Hitler Confronts,* 214–15.

26. The figures for 1939–41 are taken from Kroener, "Personellen Ressourcen," 854, 906–7; data for 1942–43 appear in Allgemeines Marinehauptamt/Ia (Admiral Warzecha), "Vortragsnotiz über eine notwendige vermehrte Rekrutenzuteilung für die Kriegsmarine," 28 May 1943, in KTB 1/Skl, Teil B, vol. 5, on T1022/1707/PG 32119.

27. See Wagner, ed., *Vorträge,* 512–16.

28. Interview with Eduard Vogt, Silver Spring, Md., 27 January 1990; on the fluctuations in personnel policy, see also chapter 8.

29. For example, several Polish-German draftees were recovered by American forces as survivors of *U-118* (*Kaptlt.* Werner Czygan), sunk 12 June 1943, and *U-487* (*Oblt.z.S.d.R.* Helmut Metz), sunk 13 July 1943; survivors of *U-512* (*Kaptlt.* Wolfgang Schultze), sunk 2 October 1942, referred to three Polish-German conscripts among the crew. See the interrogation reports for these boats and the raw interrogations of *U-505* crewmen in Op-16-Z files, RG 38, NA.

30. Statement of Hermann Lawatsch, quoted in Middlebrook, *Convoy,* 61.

31. Letter, Horst Bredow to the author, 15 May 1990.

32. Interview with Werner Hirschmann, Toronto, 10 August 1997.

33. U-boat personnel strength is discussed in appendix 2. An example of a U-boat captain who had no formal training beyond the commanders' course was *Kaptlt.* Friedrich Kloevekorn, who survived the war after stints in command of *U-471* (May 1943–August 1944) and *U-3012* (December 1944–April 1945) (Busch and Röhl, *U-Boot-Kommandanten,* 125); examples of untrained crewmen are located in the ONI interrogation reports for *U-67, U-210,* and *U-960,* Op-16-Z files, RG 38, NA. Koch data from questionnaire no. 7001.

34. For a detailed assessment of the UAS and early U-boat plans, see Saville, "Development," 513ff., 523–528, 588ff. The first actual training of U-boat personnel, however, took place in January–April 1933 (Saville, 515–18).

35. Saville, "Development," 619–20; Prien, *Mein Weg,* 112–20.

36. Rössler, "U-Bootausbildung," 457–58; Dönitz, *Memoirs,* 15–16.

37. Dönitz, *Vierzig Fragen,* 29.

38. Quoted in Dönitz, *Memoirs,* 16–17.

39. Wilke, "Unterseebootsabwehrschule," 11–12. The UAS acquired independent status (this time as a true antisubmarine warfare center) in September 1939.

40. KTB BdU, 30 April 1940, T1022/3979/PG 30263.

41. The *Königsberg* incident is recounted in detail in Showell, *U-boats,* 60–62; Showell describes Köhler's later experience in *U-boat Command,* 134–36.

42. Rössler, "U-Bootausbildung," 458.

43. Bräckow, *Marine-Ingenieuroffizierkorps,* 252.

44. BdU an das Kommando der Marinestation der Ostsee, "Personalbedarf," 13 November 1939, T1022/2066/PG 33541.

45. Rössler, "U-Bootausbildung," 458–59; Dönitz's prevention of the proposed commitment of training boats to combat in 1940 is claimed in his *Vierzig Fragen,* 63. The observation on von Friedeburg is from Frank, *Wölfe und der Admiral,* 320.

46. Dr. Jürgen Tonndorf, "The Influence of Service on Submarines on the Auditory Organ," Study D II, 36ff., in Schaefer, ed., "Monograph on Submarine Medicine." On the *Dräger* apparatus, see Shelford, *Subsunk,* 143–46, 237; an illustration of the exercises appears in Elting and Mulligan, eds., *Wolf Packs,* 66–67.

47. Information on the training establishment taken from Rössler, "U-Bootausbildung," 459–61; G.C. & C.S. Naval History, vol. 7, 90–95; and ONI interrogation report of *U-128,* Op-16-Z files, RG 38, NA.

48. Questionnaires no. 2204, 2237, 22144, 2421–22, 2429, and 2498 from the sample.

49. Figures on Gotenhafen from Tonndorf, "Influence of Service," 38. On the UAA establishments, see the G.C. & C.S. Naval History, vol. 7, 97–102. The *F-Gerät* is described in the British report "U 593—Interrogation of Survivors, February 1944," file Germany: 915–510, in ONI monograph files, RG 38, NA; illustrations of some training devices are provided in Elting and Mulligan, eds., *Wolf Packs,* 62–66.

50. Comments of *Kaptlt.* Klaus Bargsten in ONI interrogation report of *U-521,* Op-16-Z files, RG 38, NA.

51. See Rössler, "Ausbildung," 460–62; Merten, *Nach Kompass,* 351ff.; and Rössler, "U-Bootausbildung," 466. The daily schedule is described by Hirschmann, "Recollections," who served as the L.I. on *U-612,* one of the boats in the 24th U-Flotilla.

52. Information on the *Agru-Front* from Rössler, "U-Bootausbildung," 465; Bräckow, *Marine-Ingenieuroffizierkorps,* 253–54; and ONI interrogation reports for *U-210* and *U-512,* RG 38, NA. Information and an illustration of the emblem is provided in Högel, *Embleme,* 30, 149.

53. Daily schedule from Hirschmann, "Recollections"; experience of *Kaptlt.* Claus Korth in charge of the pretactical exercises of the final training phase, quoted in Showell, *U-boats,* 112.

54. On the final training stages see Rössler, "U-Bootausbildung," 465–66; ONI interrogation report of *U-1059*, Op-16-Z files, RG 38, NA; and British Naval Intelligence, "Summary," 19–21. For a description of difficulties in the group exercises, see Hirschfeld, *Feindfahrten*, 17–23, abbreviated in *Hirschfeld*, 12–16.

55. British naval intelligence, "Summary," 21; ONI interrogation report for *U-512*, Op-16-Z files, RG 38, NA.

56. Data compiled from the listing of U-boats lost by cause, prepared by the Marine-Ehrenmal Laboe and included as an enclosure to Wetzel, *U 995*, together with ships' data in Gröner, *German Warships*, vol. 2, 40–41, 47ff. On British minelaying, see Roskill, *War at Sea*, vol. 3 (pt. 2), 140–42, 294, 472.

57. Summary data compiled from Busch and Röll, *U-Bootbau*, 6, and Kemp, *U-boats Destroyed*, 63–65; specific data for the dates indicated from KTB *U-55*, T1022/2882/PG 30052, and KTB *U-63*, T1022/3114/PG 30060.

58. The fate of *U-70* is taken from her reconstructed war diary, reproduced on T1022/3032/PG 30067; data on the seven other boats (*U-556*, Kaptlt. Herbert Wohlfarth; *U-651*, Kaptlt. Peter Lohmeyer; *U-401*, Kaptlt. Gero Zimmermann; *U-452*; *U-501*, Kaptlt. Hugo Forster; and *U-207*, Kaptlt. Fritz Meyer) are compiled from the commissioning and loss dates in Kemp, *U-boats Destroyed*, 71–73.

59. The reconstructed KTB of *U-570* is reproduced on T1022/4185/PG 30606; for a dramatic but undocumented account of *U-570*'s capture, see Noli, *Admiral's Wolfpack*, 99–114. Postwar statements by Rahmlow and crew members appeared in the German periodical *Kristall*, nos. 12–15 and 19–20 ("Denn wir fuhren . . . Weisse Flagge auf U 570?"), 1956.

60. Noli (*Admiral's Wolfpack*, 98–99, 125–26) attributes the abbreviated training directly to Hitler, rescinded after *U-570* at Dönitz's insistence of five months as the minimum training period necessary. The explanation offered by von Friedeburg at the time appears more convincing.

61. KTB BdU, 24 October 1941, T1022/4063/PG 30299.

62. Data compiled from Busch and Röll, *U-Bootbau*, 8–15.

63. Peak strength in Tarrant, *U-boat Offensive*, 116; loss rates quoted in Hessler, *U-boat War*, vol. 2, 100.

64. Rössler, "U-Bootausbildung," 460–62; Herzog, *Deutsche U-Boote*, 228–29.

65. ONI interrogation reports for *U-1059* and *U-1229*, Op-16-Z files, RG 38, NA; Wetzel, *U 995*, 92; and the KTBs for cited dates for *U-327* (T1022/3042/PG 30401), *U-1002* (T1022/3764/PG 30825), *U-1051* (T1022/3380/PG 30841), *U-1169* (T1022/3463/PG 30853), *U-1172* (T1022/3463/PG 30854), *U-1209* (T1022/3463/PG 30862), and *U-1273* (T1022/3463/PG 30873). The names of commanding officers are here omitted (several changed from the date of commissioning through the training period).

66. Rössler, *U-Boottyp XXI*, 41.

67. Only *U-995* and *U-1002* escaped destruction; the fates of the remainder are provided in Kemp, *U-boats Destroyed*, 179ff.

68. Merten, *Nach Kompass*, 364.

69. Several examples are cited in Showell, *U-boat Command,* 149–52, and probably account for the numerous problems described in Guske, *War Diaries,* 12ff.
70. Suhren and Brustat-Naval, *Nasses Eichenlaub,* 146–47.
71. Showell, *U-boats,* 112 (emphasis in original).
72. Data cited in Hoch, "Problematik zur Menschenführung," 200.
73. Loss rates in Hessler, *U-boat War,* vol. 2, 100, and vol. 3, 21; KTB BdU, 25 July 1942, T1022/3980/PG 30309b.
74. Comments by Werner Hirschmann, "RE: Topp's speech 'Manning and Training the U-boat Fleet,' 1994," copy furnished to the author by Werner Hirschmann.
75. See, e.g., Glover, "Manning and Training," 188–213, and Calmers, *Horton,* 170–73.
76. See Cremer, *U-boat Commander,* 165–66, describing a meeting between himself and Werner Henke in January 1944.
77. On changes in U-boat onboard technology see, e.g., Mulligan, *Lone Wolf,* 163–64, 175–77, 191; the stream of messages is noted in KTB BdU, 15 January 1944, T1022/3981/PG 30338.
78. ONI interrogation report of *U-128,* Op-16-Z interrogation reports, RG 38, NA.
79. Interview with Horst Bredow, Cuxhaven, 15 May 1994.

Chapter 8. A Children's Crusade?

1. Buchheim, *Zu Tode Gesiegt,* 56.
2. Salewski, *Von der Wirklichkeit des Krieges,* 29.
3. Topp, "Manning and Training," 216.
4. "Grossadmiral Dönitz, Schlussansprache auf der Tagung für Befehlshaber der Kriegsmarine in Weimar am Freitag, dem 17. Dezember 1943," Document 443–D, *TMWC,* 35:105–16.
5. Bryant, *Submarine Commander,* 32.
6. E.g., Lohmann and Hildebrand, *Deutsche Kriegsmarine;* and Busch and Röll, *U-Boot-Kommandanten.* The access question reflects the author's experiences in 1993.
7. Güth and Brennecke, "Hier irrte," pp. 45–46. It is worth noting here that the average age of a German Army *Oberleutnant* in 1942 was twenty-two years, three months (Kroener, "Personellen Ressourcen," 903).
8. Showell, *U-boats,* 18.
9. Data compiled from Dörr, *Ritterkreuzträger,* passim; and Busch and Röll, *U-Boot-bau,* 9–15. One IXC boat, *U-125,* was commissioned into service in March 1941 by Knight's Cross winner Günther Kuhnke, who transferred command in December to former watch officer Ulrich Folkers, who earned his own Knight's Cross with *U-125;* I have here substituted Folkers for Kuhnke in my calculations.
10. From Busch and Röll, *U-Boot-Kommandanten,* passim. Instead of the total of 1,410 commanders included in this study, I have omitted those whose com-

mands were limited to the prewar period, commander-designates for boats never commissioned, and watch officers who assumed commands only under unusual circumstances (e.g., death or incapacitation of commander). The data have sometimes been supplemented by that found in Lohmann and Hildebrand, *Kriegsmarine*, vol. 3, passim.

11. KTB BdU, 20 October 1940, T1022/4063/PG 30275.

12. Data from sample; Busch and Röll, *U-Boot-Kommandanten*, 267–72; on Dobratz, see Dörr, *Ritterkreuzträger*, 40–42, 261.

13. See KTB FdU West, 2 October 1939, T1022/4185/PG 30902.

14. The spring 1941 incidents are described in chapter 4; on the fate of *U-109*'s first commander, see Hirschfeld and Brooks, *Hirschfeld*, 15–16, 54–56.

15. On Bleichrodt, see Hirschfeld and Brooks, *Hirschfeld*, 185, 223–25; on Zschech, see Herlin, *Verdammter Atlantik*, 85ff.

16. General biographical information drawn from Busch and Röll, *U-Boot-Kommandanten*, 71, 103, 266.

17. Letter, Werner Hirschmann to the author, 13 December 1995.

18. See Blair, *Silent Victory*, 107n, 199–201, 361, 818.

19. Hessler, *U-boat War*, vol. 2, 26, 43, 86; Showell, *U-boat Command*, 105; Niestlé, "German Technical and Electronic Development," 438–43.

20. Based on a review of career data in Kurowski, *Knight's Cross*, 13ff.

21. General data compiled from Busch and Röll, *Kommandanten*, passim; data on 1940 Type IX commanders supplemented by Dörr, *Ritterkreuzträger*, passim.

22. Data on submarine commanders from Busch and Röll, *U-Boot-Kommandanten*, passim; submarine losses in Tarrant, *U-boat Offensive*, 88, and Mars, *British Submarines*, 109.

23. Numbers are from Saville, "Development of the German U-boat Arm," 619n, and Hoch, "Problematik der Menschenführung," 195.

24. Topp, "Manning and Training," 216.

25. Office of Naval Intelligence (Op-16-Z), "Age Study of the Crews of German U-boats from the Outbreak of War in 1939 to the End of 1942," 22 February 1943, Op-16-Z subject files, RG 38, NA.

26. These figures are described in some detail in chapter 4; for an example of one historian's account, see Terraine, *U-boat Wars*, 262.

27. Tarrant, *U-boat Offensive*, 88, 96, 103; Dönitz, *Memoirs*, 122–25.

28. See BdU/Organisationsabteilung, "Personalbedarf der U-Boote auf Grund des Schiffbauneubauplanes," 13 November 1939, and Flottenkommando, "Kriegspersonalwirtschaft," 20 November 1939, reproduced on T1022/2066/PG 33541. Dönitz's training efforts are discussed in chapter 3.

29. These problems are detailed in two memorandums prepared by a *Korv.Kapt.* Wenninger, both entitled "Lage der Personalwirtschaft" and dated 25 November 1940 and 19 June 1941, file RM 7/1206, BA-MA. For personnel statistical data, see Marinekommandoamt/AIIb to AMA, 4 April 1941, reproduced on T1022/2066/PG 33541.

30. KTB 1/Skl, Teil A, 22–23 October 1940, T1022/1664/PG 32034; see also the dis-

cussion in Salewski, *Seekriegsleitung,* vol. 1, 265. In the end *Tirpitz* was commissioned on 25 March 1941; *Leipzig* was formally recommissioned (after suffering damage during the Norwegian campaign) on 1 December 1940, but never became fully operational again.

31. Kroener, "Personellen Ressourcen," in *Dritte Reich und der Zweite Weltkrieg,* vol. 5/1, 853–54.

32. Op-16-Z, "Age Study," tables 3–4, RG 38, NA.

33. Based on crew casualty lists in the U-Boot-Archiv for *U-47, U-100, U-204, U-206, U-207, U-208, U-556,* and *U-557,* a combined total loss of 269 NCOs and enlisted men.

34. See Mulligan, "Tracking *Das Boot,*" 203–11.

35. Hessler, *U-boat War,* vol. 1, 72; Tarrant, *U-boat Offensive,* 106–7; Dönitz, *Memoirs,* 223, 243.

36. From Lüth's lecture "Menschenführung" in Busch, *So war,* 341.

37. See Mulligan, "German U-boat Crews," 270–71. The 1944 data derive from sixty-seven crewmen captured from four boats in July–August 1944.

38. Dönitz, *Memoirs,* 353–55.

39. Transcripts of the conferences and accompanying appendices are reproduced in Wagner, ed., *Lagevorträge,* 507–16; additional material in Salewski, *Seekriegsleitung,* vol. 2, 277–89, 506–7.

40. Cf. Allgemeines Marinehauptamt (Admiral Warzecha), "Vortragsnotiz für Vortrag Od.d.M. beim Führer über die personelle Entwicklung des U-Bootsprogramms Stand 1.11.1943," 13 November 1943, and Keitel's responding letter to Dönitz (with Anlage), 23 November 1943, both in file RM 7/1238, BA-MA. These issues had been previously discussed among Dönitz, Keitel, and Hitler in conferences on 15 June and 8 July 1943 (see Wagner, ed., *Lagevorträge,* 512–22).

41. See Rössler, "U-boat Development and Building," 134–35.

42. Plottke, *Fächer Loos!,* 89–96, 106.

43. Showell, *U-boat Command,* 179–80.

44. U-boat losses are those provided in Möller, *Kurs Atlantik,* 202. Even more striking are the alternative figures compiled from German base records in Tarrant, *U-boat Offensive,* 165–69, which list 251 U-boats destroyed from 1939–May 1943 against 570 lost thereafter. For U-boat personnel losses, see table 5 and appendix 2.

45. Casualty data compiled from Gröner, *Warships,* vol. 2, 48ff. (for sunken U-boats), and Högel, *Embleme,* 282–84 (for additional losses on boats not sunk); general information from Tarrant, *U-boat Offensive,* 127–32.

46. *Annual Report,* 16.

47. Hoch, "Problematik der Menschenführung," 196–97, 200–201; British Naval Intelligence Division, "Summary of Statements Made by German Prisoners of War," no. 120 (week ending 23 March 1945), 17, in Op-16-Z subject file "British Summaries," RG 38, NA.

48. See the discussions in Rohwer, "U-boat War," 308–12, and at the end of chapter 4.

Chapter 9. More One Cannot Be

1. Churchill, *Triumph,* 464.
2. See, e.g., Hoch, "Problematik zur Menschenführung," 202ff. An exception is the perceptive assessment by Bundesmarine *Kaptlt.* Matthias Faermann (Ubootflottille "U 20"), "Die Einsatzmotivation von Uboot-Besatzungen im Zweiten Weltkrieg, trotz starker Überlegenheit der Gegner" (unpublished ms., 1994, copy in the custody of the U-Boot-Archiv, Cuxhaven).
3. Roskill, *War at Sea,* vol. 2, 355; Edwards, *Dönitz and the Wolf Packs,* 213. Neither author cites supportive evidence; for both, the wish may be father to the thought.
4. Excerpt of a poem by Fritz Thomas (killed in action 13 October 1939) on display in the U-Boot-Archiv, Cuxhaven, quoted and discussed in Hadley, *Count Not,* 172–73.
5. See the brief but invaluable assessments in van Creveld, *Fighting Power,* 11–17, and Dupuy, *Genius for War,* 7–11.
6. Merten, *Nach Kompass,* 155.
7. The general subject is superbly described in Hadley, *Count Not,* 48ff.; the quote appears in Fürbringer, *Alarm!,* 257–58.
8. Mueller-Hillebrand, *Heer,* vol. 3, 254.
9. Compare the data in chapter 6 and van Creveld, *Fighting Power,* 66–67.
10. For a description of training and the ceremony, see Harlinghausen, *Ein Junge,* 24–30; the oath and its significance are superbly described by Peter, *Acht Glas,* 32–37.
11. Quotation of Hans Göbeler (*U-505*) in Turkel, *Good War,* 403 ("three fingers" refers to the German form of swearing in, with the thumb and two forefingers).
12. See Grossman, *On Killing,* 58–59, and chapter 10, below.
13. The indispensable source of U-boat crews' dietary information is Dr. Jobst Schäfer's wartime study, "Die Ernährung der U-Boot-Fahrer," based on his extensive U-boat experience and research. The data given here appear on pp. 165c–d and 168–70 of that study. See also the ONI study "Morale and its Maintenance in the German Navy" (part 1, sec. 3), January 1943 (esp. pp. 29–31), OSS R&A Report No. 28761, RG 226, NA.
14. Data from *Besoldungstabellen für Soldaten,* especially the detailed tables on 124ff.; ONI study, "Morale and Its Maintenance," 34–35, OSS Research and Analysis Branch Report no. 28761, Records of the Office of Strategic Services, RG 226, NA; and Absalon, *Wehrgesetz,* 299–304.
15. OKM booklet (December 1939), *Wie komme ich,* 19. See also the discussion of more rapid promotions within specific career-tracks in chapter 6.
16. Absalon, *Wehrgesetz,* 228; G.C. & C.S. Naval History, vol. 4, 10–11, 70. See also table 10.
17. Additional data on naval pay in "Memorandum No. 103 for Op-16-W: Pay in the German Navy," 30 January 1943, in Op-16-Z subject file "Memoranda for Op-16-W," RG 38, NA; quotation of Peter Petersen in Wiggins, *Torpedoes,* 216.

18. For examples, see Mulligan, *Lone Wolf,* 155, and Werner, *Iron Coffins,* 182–89.

19. Quotation from the personal correspondence of *Ritterkreuzträger Korv.Kapt.* Siegfried Freiherr von Forstner (*U-402*) in Waters, *Bloody Winter,* 267–68. Von Forstner was killed in the North Atlantic shortly thereafter.

20. Faermann, "Einsatzmotivation," 56; Werner, *Iron Coffins,* 189; and see the discussion of the crisis in morale later in this chapter.

21. *Merkblatt über die neue Urlaubsregelung (21.2.1944),* in file "Handakte für den Kommandanten ('U 977')," T1022/4186/fr. 468. On German army leave, see van Crefeld, *Fighting Power,* 107–8 and John A. English and Bruce I. Gudmundsson, *On Infantry* (Westport, Conn.: Praeger, 1994), 120n.

22. Edwards, *Dönitz and the Wolf Packs,* 213; interview with Carl Möller, Hamburg, 16 May 1994 (the scrounger was *Matrosenobergefreiter* Herbert Bölke).

23. For descriptions of conditions in port, see the report "U-boat Bases," 15 July 1943, in Op-16-Z subject files, RG 38, NA, and Mulligan, *Lone Wolf* (based on interviews with *U-515*'s crew), 153–56. The author's study of the operations of *U-515* reveal that, during her operational history through the first five patrols, the U-boat spent a total of 330 days at sea and 190 days in port.

24. See Shils and Janowitz, "Cohesion and Disintegration," 285. Other works in the field include S. L. A. Marshall, *Men against Fire* (New York: William Morrow and Co., 1947); and S. A. Stouffer, et al., *The American Soldier: Combat and Aftermath* (Princeton, N.J.: Princeton University Press, 1949).

25. The authoritative source on U-boat insignia is Högel, *Embleme,* passim, especially the introductory information regarding their history (pp. 7–11) and the index of subjects, city coats of arms, Crew symbols, and types of figures used as insignia (pp. 285–88).

26. Ibid., 26–29, 285–86. A few U-boats also maintained pets as mascots aboard their boats, the most distinctive being the piglet "Sonja" on *U-992* (*Oblt.z.S.* Hans Falke) in 1943–44 (ibid., 261–63).

27. KTB U-123, 30 May–1 June 1942, T1022/2973/PG 30113; Hoyt, *U-boats,* 82.

28. Peillard, *Laconia Affair,* 5; interview in Washington, D.C., 22 February 1998, with Nigel Turner, who visited the Plauen city archives in researching a forthcoming documentary on the *Laconia* incident.

29. Dönitz, *Memoirs,* 118–19.

30. Observation by Victor Oehrn, quoted in Vause, *Wolf,* 227–28n.

31. Showell, *German Navy,* 158–60; Absolon, *Wehrgesetz,* 270–72.

32. Absolon, *Wehrgesetz,* 261–62; Mueller-Hillebrand, *Heer,* vol. 3, 253–61 for computation of army strength.

33. Herlin, *Verdammter Atlantik,* 35; Metzler, *Sehrohr,* 294.

34. Marbach's comments quoted in Busch, *So war,* 332; Lüth, "Problems of Leadership," in Tarrant, *U-boat Offensive,* 178; crew list of *U-515* in the U-Boot-Archiv, Cuxhaven (on her fifth patrol, see Mulligan, *Lone Wolf,* 175–86); ONI interrogation report of *U-1059* in Op-16-Z interrogation reports, RG 38, NA.

35. For general information, see Showell, *German Navy,* 171, and *U-boats,* 115; and

Herzog, "Ritterkreuz," 246–50, and "Torpedoverbrauch," 125. Detailed biographical data on Knight's Cross winners is provided in the standard reference
by Dörr, *Ritterkreuzträger.*

36. The award is described in Showell, *German Navy,* 172; data compiled from Ger-
    icke, *Deutschen Kreuzes,* 7–8, 41ff. (percentages based on data from 532 ran-
    domly selected recipients).

37. E.g., Vause, *Ace,* 188–89 ("German military honors weren't worth much more
    than the metal from which they were minted"); Herzog, "Ritterkreuz," 252 ("It
    is scandalous for the submarine service"). Neither critic notes any comparison
    with inflated claims by other nations' services: see Blair, *Silent Victory,* 877–78,
    for examples of similar exaggerations by American submariners but who kept
    their medals despite postwar adjustments to their credited kills.

38. See Middlebrook, *Convoy,* 73n, and the decrypted intercept of the proxy mar-
    riage of a *U-515* radioman, 31 December 1942, SRGN No. 8444, RG 457, NA.

39. These incidents are detailed in Hadley, *U-boats against Canada,* 168–84; less re-
    liable is the account in Farago, *Tenth Fleet,* 235–40.

40. See Hoch, "Problematik der Menschenführung," 205.

41. See Mulligan, *Lone Wolf,* 156–59, 169–71; Wiggins, *Torpedoes,* 216–18; and
    "Auszug aus dem Wachebuch des Wachoffiziers der 2. U.-Flottille vom 3.6.42,"
    on T1022/4186/frame 325.

42. Vause, *Ace,* 148; Lüth, "Problems of Leadership," in Tarrant, *U-boat Offensive,*
    177–85.

43. Giese and Wise, *Shooting,* 170–72.

44. Interview with Peter Petersen, Chicago, 11 June 1997; Loewe account cited in
    Gallery, *U-505,* 89–92.

45. For a full account of the incident, see Hadley, *U-boats against Canada,* 235.

46. See the data in Högel, *Embleme,* 282–84, and the specific examples recorded in
    the war diaries of *U-134* (*Kaptlt.* Rudolf Schendel) for 15 January 1943
    (T1022/2835/PG 30124/7), *U-205* (*Kaptlt.* Franz-Georg Reschke) for 30 Septem-
    ber 1941 (T1022/3039/PG 30193/2), and *U-1302* (*Kaptlt.* Wolfgang Herwartz)
    for 18 September 1944 (T1022/3463/PG 30877). Omitted are the reported and
    unknown instances of suicide that occurred when a U-boat was lost.

47. ONI interrogation report of *U-606,* Op-16-Z interrogation reports, RG 38, NA.

48. ONI interrogation report of survivors of *U-664* (sunk 8 July 1943 in the North
    Atlantic), quoted in Y'Blood, *Hunter-Killer,* 88.

49. ONI interrogation report of *U-591,* Op-16-Z interrogation reports, RG 38, NA.

50. BdU KTB of 6 August 1943, quoted in Y'Blood, *Hunter-Killer,* 82. For the contin-
    ued effects into March 1944, see Hessler, *U-boat War,* vol. 2, 54.

51. Dönitz, *Memoirs,* esp. 89–90.

52. KTB BdU of 13 November 1943, T1022/3980/PG 30334. On the failed opera-
    tions of September–November 1943, see Syrett, *Defeat,* 181ff.

53. See Schaeffer, *U-boat 977,* 112, who adds that crews had been recently ordered
    to prepare their wills before departing on mission.

54. Hannemann, *Justiz,* 260–61, 308–16, 356–57; the author discusses his methodology on pp. 230ff. The "submariners" here include all those serving in the U-
boat arm, not just combat crews.

55. A captured U-boat officer describes the lectures in Op-16-Z Spot Item No. 286,
"Morale of Officers in the U-boat Arm as of December 1943," 14 June 1944,
Op-16-Z subject file "Spot Items," RG 38, NA; the quotation is that of
Korv.Kapt. Siegfried Freiherr von Forstner in Waters, *Bloody Winter,* 267.

56. ONI interrogation report of survivors of *U-231,* Op-16-Z interrogation reports,
RG 38, NA.

57. Averages computed from data in Tarrant, *U-boat Offensive,* 116, 128. In May
1944 the average daily number of U-boats at sea dipped to forty-three.

58. According to eyewitnesses, *Kaptlt.* Horst Höltring took his own life as his command, *U-185,* began her final plunge to the bottom after a fatal air attack in
the Central Atlantic on 24 August 1943: See ONI interrogation report on survivors of *U-604* and *U-185,* Op-16-Z interrogation reports, RG 38, NA.

59. There is still no authoritative account of Zschech's death. The KTB of *U-505* offers nothing more than "Kommandant tot"; the accounts by Gallery, *U-505,*
178–93, and Herlin, *Verdammter Atlantik,* 85–114, are undocumented and mix
literary imagination with fact.

60. The key source is Walle, *Tragödie,* passim; see also chapter 11.

61. See McLachlan, *Room 39,* 173–74.

62. Documentation on the collaboration of Coreth and other U-boat POWs (although not of the full significance of their assistance) can be found in the Op-
16-Z day files, 1/1/44–12/31/44 and 1/1/45–; and Op-16-Z subject files
"Berthing Lists 1944" and "P/W Special 1945," RG 38, NA.

63. The collected reports, "German U-boat Communications, Codes, and Ciphers," not declassified until their accessioning by the NA in 1996, are located
as Item CBIK56 Nr. 5315 among the NSA Historic Cryptographic Collection,
Pre–World War I through World War II, RG 457, NA.

64. ONI interrogation report of survivors of *U-1059,* in Op-16-Z interrogation reports, and letter, Lt. Cmdr. V. R. Taylor to Cmdr. John Riheldaffer, 8 December
1944, in file "Taylor, V. R. (NY) Incoming Letters 1/1/43–4/30/45," Op-16-Z administrative files, both in RG 38, NA.

65. Documentation of Drechsler is located in his interrogations among the German POW alphabetical 201 files, G-2 Division (MIS-Y Branch), RG 165, NA;
and the Op-16-Z Day Files from 6/30–12/28/43 and file "Transfer of P/Ws" in
Op-16-Z subject files, both in RG 38, NA. For a general account of Drechsler
and his killing, see Whittingham, *Martial Justice,* 37ff., 62ff. Dönitz's role is discussed in Messerschmidt, *Wehrmacht,* 420–21n, and his directive to promote
Drechsler's killers ("Geheim-Erlass des Grossadmirals Dönitz von 11.4.45")
constitutes Document GB-212, RG 238, NA.

66. Schaeffer, *U-boat 977,* 128–30.

67. See Vause, *Ace,* 97–98, 195; Lüth's complete address is provided in translation

in Tarrant, *U-boat Offensive*, 177–85; the German original (but edited to remove some National Socialist remarks) appears in Busch, *So war*, 340–58.

68. Hannemann, *Justiz*, 348–55.

69. McLachlan, *Room 39*, 175–76.

70. KTB BdU, 30 November 1943, T1022/30335/3980; award of decorations listed in *Marineverordnungsblatt*, 15 August 1943–15 April 1944, RG 242, NA.

71. See the data and sources summarized in Mulligan, *Lone Wolf*, 130–35.

72. McLachlan, *Room 39*, 175–76.

73. Intercepted message of 7 November 1944, quoted in U.S. Navy signals intelligence study SRH–008, "The Battle of the Atlantic," vol. 2, "U-boat Operations (Dec 1942–May 1945)," 216, RG 457, NA. See also Hessler, *U-boat War*, vol. 2, 57–59, 72ff.

74. Hoch, "Problematik der Menschenführung," 200.

75. See Moore, *Faustball*, esp. 119ff.

76. Faermann, "Einsatzmotivation," 51, 62–63.

77. Chalmers, *Horton*, 225–26.

Chapter 10. Humanity vs. Necessity

1. See Rogers, *Enemy*, 154.

2. Examples include the motion pictures *Civilization* (1916), *Lest We Forget* (1918), *Lifeboat* (1943), *Action in the North Atlantic* (1943), and *Murphy's War* (1971), and specific episodes in the television series "Victory at Sea" (1952–53) and "The Twilight Zone" (1959). When the German film studio Bavaria-Atelier approached Hollywood in 1977 for coproduction of *Das Boot*, cooperation foundered on American scriptwriters' redrawing of the character of the first officer to a Nazi fanatic who machine-gunned shipwrecked survivors in the water (*Der Spiegel* 36, no. 53 (29 December 1980), 81–82).

3. Roskill, *War at Sea*, vol. 3 (pt. 2), 306.

4. Padfield, *Dönitz*, 253–60, 353, although he cites no more evidence than that considered insufficient by the International Military Tribunal at Nuremberg; Terraine, *U-boat Wars*, 467–68 (with additional invective on 672–73). Neither offers an objective treatment of the U-boat campaign.

5. Bird, *German Naval History*, 590–91.

6. Nimitz's affidavit is published in *TMWC*, 40:108–11; the incident off New Guinea is described in Blair, *Silent Victory*, 383–85.

7. Kennedy, "War Crimes," 57–58, and de Zayas, *War Crimes*, 251–57. Kennedy concludes, "There can be no doubt that Miers' action was in every way as cold-blooded as what Eck was to do in the *U-852*" (discussed later in chapter).

8. See, e.g., Bartov, *Hitler's Army*, 199n, for the quotation; Padfield, *Dönitz*, 353.

9. Robertson, *Golden Horseshoe*, 78–79.

10. Cremer, *Commander*, 43.

11. E.g., Legro, *Cooperation,* 52–62. While Legro is correct in Dönitz's anticommerce emphasis in prewar doctrine, his thesis cannot be reconciled with such actions as the patrol of *U-35* discussed later in this chapter, and his statement that Germany commenced unrestricted submarine warfare in autumn 1939 is in error: Not until 17 August 1940 did Germany fully extend unrestricted operations to the seas west of Ireland.

12. Prien, *Mein Weg,* 133–40.

13. See Schmoeckel, *Menschlichkeit,* 29–33, and Edwards, *Dönitz and the Wolf Packs,* 18–19.

14. KTB *U-35,* T1022/3039/PG 30032. The U-boat was sunk on her next patrol, but (perhaps fittingly) her entire crew survived as prisoners of war.

15. Sobe's report and the drift toward a general submarine campaign is described in Manson, *Diplomatic Ramifications,* 98ff. Dönitz's proposals are contained in a memorandum of 22 September 1939 subsequently published as Document 191-C in *TMWC,* 34:776–78; see also the KTB of BdU for 23 October 1939, T1022/3979/PG30250, where Dönitz supposed that two of his boats had been sunk by armed merchantmen. The danger of Q-ships (*U-Bootsfallen*) is discussed in navy publication M.Dv. Nr. 28, *Kriegserfahrungen der deutschen U-Boote im Weltkriege, 1914–1918,* 1939, 5–18.

16. See the KTB of 1/Skl, Teil A, 23 September 1939, on T1022/1660/PG 32021.

17. Cf. the text of the order in *TMWC,* 35:267–70, with Dönitz's testimony as to its context in *TMWC,* 13:272–75.

18. Schmoeckel, *Menschlichkeit,* 63–67; Herzog, *U-Boote im Einsatz,* 70; Robertson, *Golden Horseshoe,* 51–52, 68, 74–77; and KTB *U-30,* 3 May 1940, T1022/2831/PG 30027.

19. British Foreign Office, "Enemy Attacks on Merchant Shipping, September 1, 1940–February 28, 1941," 10 March 1941, Exhibit GB-191, RG 238, NA.

20. See, e.g., Morison, *Battle of the Atlantic,* 292–302 and esp. 392–97.

21. See Barker, *Children,* esp. 147–49; Lawrence, *Bloody War,* 58–59, 85, 105–6; Middlebrook, *Convoy,* 170, 232; Miller and Hutchings, *Transatlantic Liners,* 28, 31; and Hughes and Costello, *Battle,* 304.

22. Bell and Lockerbie, *In Peril,* 49–56, 279.

23. Gretton, *Crisis Convoy,* 125–26.

24. See Oehrn's account in Vause, *Wolf,* 59–60, and the subsequent discussion during the Nuremberg Trial in *TMWC,* 13:370–75.

25. Statements of survivors of the *Noreen Mary* and *Antonico* constitute Nuremberg Documents 645-D and 647-D, reproduced in *TMWC,* 35:282–91; Dönitz testimony, *TMWC,* 13:389–90. It is possible in the case of *Noreen Mary* that Matschulat was carrying out the "suggested" killing of survivors as per the guidance of 5th U-boat Flotilla commander Moehle.

26. Schulz, *Nassen Abgrund,* 154–56, 221–26.

27. See Metzler, *Sehrohr,* 136–48; Moore, *A Careless Word,* 242–43.

28. KTB *U-108,* 10 June 1941, T1022/3035/PG 30104/3.

29. Brennecke, *Jäger-Gejagte,* 211–13.

30. Cremer and Brustat-Naval, *Cremer: U 333,* 70–72.

31. Data taken from the descriptions of U-boat war diaries in *Guide No. 2,* passim.

32. See Document Dönitz-23 and Dönitz testimony in *TMWC,* 13:276–77.

33. Data from *Guide No. 2,* passim; Dönitz estimate from his testimony at Nuremberg, *TMWC,* 13:277.

34. Gannon, *Operation Drumbeat,* 286–92, 362–66.

35. See Kelshall, *U-boat War in the Caribbean,* 53, 95, 121–22; Moore, *A Careless Word,* 269; British report, "Devices on Submarines Seen in the Western Atlantic," November 1942, in Op-16-Z administrative files ("Canadian Correspondence 1942"), RG 38, NA; Parker, *Running the Gauntlet,* 122–23, 126–27; Gallery, *U-505,* 125–27; Mulligan, *Lone Wolf,* 95–96; Schmoeckel, *Menschlichkeit,* 112; the KTB of *U-161* for 16–17 June 1942, T1022/2834/PG 30148; and Hirschfeld, *Feindfahrten,* 328.

36. Sources for these incidents are Naval Liaison Officer, Curaçao, NWI, "Interview with subject (Gibbs)," 21 June 1942, file F-6-e 22845-B, Formerly Confidential Reports of Naval Attachés, 1940–46; and cable ALUSNOS SANTOS to OPNAV, 2 July 1942, Naval Armed Guard Reports: *M. F. Elliott,* both in RG 38, NA.

37. See Alman, *Graue Wölfe in blauer See,* 209, and the KTB of *U-565* for 29 July 1942, T1022/3074/PG 30601/7.

38. Descriptions of all incidents are provided in Irving, *Destruction of Convoy PQ. 17,* 144–45, 196, 213, 233–34, 237, 294–95, based on the U-boats' war diaries and Allied survivors' accounts.

39. "Memorandum on the Conversation between the Führer and Ambassador Oshima, in Presence of the Reich Foreign Minister in the Wolfsschanze on 3 January 1942," Document D-423, *Nazi Conspiracy and Aggression* (Washington, D.C.: Government Printing Office, 1946), vol. 7, 53–54.

40. "Conference of the C.-in-C., Navy, with the Führer at the Führer's Headquarters, Wolfsschanze, on May 13 and 14, 1942," in *Führer Conferences,* 279–83; Document Dönitz-17, Raeder affidavit of 18 April 1946 regarding 14 May 1942 Führer conference, in *TMWC,* 40:23–24.

41. Grossmith, *Sinking of the Laconia,* 64, 77.

42. On the *Laconia* Incident, see Peillard, *Laconia Affair,* passim; Dönitz testimony, *TMWC,* 13:278–91 (esp. 288); Dönitz, *Memoirs,* 255–64; Terraine, *U-boat Wars,* 472–73; and Rohwer and Hümmelchen, *Chronology,* 163.

43. *Guide No. 2,* 140–41.

44. The eyewitness to this discussion was Dr. Heinrich Waas, whose account is provided in "Zeitzeuge zum Walter-U-Boot-Bau," 19–27; a slightly different version is published with an introduction by Karl-Dietrich Erdmann, "Eine Besprechung über den U-Boot-Krieg," 684–95.

45. See, e.g., the comments of then-*Oblt.z.S.* Joachim Schramm, I.W.O. of *U-109,* quoted in Hirschfeld, *Feindfahrten,* 332–33, and *Hirschfeld,* 175. Schramm succeeded to command of *U-109* in March 1943 and was killed with his crew two months later.

46. See the comments by Merten in *Nach Kompass,* 321–24.

47. E.g., Terraine, *U-boat Wars,* 466 ("Allied navies did not leave German submariners to drown except in very rare circumstances").

48. Robertson, *Escort Commander,* 202.

49. Syrett, *Defeat of the German U-boats,* 50, 90, 140; Kemp, *U-boats Destroyed,* 150.

50. Hughes and Costello, *Battle,* 304; data from *Guide No. 2,* passim; and KTB BdU for 4 and 8 February 1943, on T1022/4064/PG 30317.

51. KTB *U-238,* T1022/2938/PG30221/2; KTB BdU, 28 November 1943, T1022/3980/PG 30335.

52. KTB *U-753,* 27 February 1943, T1022/3389/PG 30732; KTB *U-336,* 5 April 1943, T1022/3043/PG 30406.

53. Letter of Able Seaman Harry Weeks, quoted in Georg Högel, *Embleme,* 66.

54. Vause, *Ace,* 157–60, 172–78.

55. Ges. Leitner, Auswärtiges Amt (AA) cable of 14 December 1942, and OKW/Amt Ausland/Abwehr an AA, 18 December 1942, both in T1022/2097/PG 33350; the figure for Allied merchant seamen is taken from Middlebrook, *Convoy,* 298.

56. KTB 1/Skl, Teil C, 4 April 1943. T1022/1734/PG 32195 (a partial translation was used at the Nuremberg Trial as Document Dönitz-42, RG 238, NA).

57. Operation Order "Atlantic" No. 56 for U-boats in the Atlantic, 7 October 1943, Document D-663, *Nazi Conspiracy and Aggression,* vol. 7, 170.

58. Moehle testimony, *TMWC,* 5:230–45; Moehle's "advisories" were already known to the Allies through statements by captured U-boat commanders (see interrogation report for *U-1059,* Op-16-Z interrogation reports, and interrogation statement of Commanding Officer, *U-681,* "Summary of Statements Made by German Prisoners of War," no. 120 (week ending 23 March 1945), Op-16-Z subject files, both in RG 38, NA). There is no evidence that Moehle's counterparts, the commanders of the 4th and 8th U-boat Flotillas, provided any such instructions to the submarine commanders whom they fitted out for front-line duty.

59. Affidavits of U-boat commanders are reproduced as Documents Dönitz-13, -29, and -53 in *TMWC,* 40:11–19, 43–47, 80–83; the incident regarding British fliers is reproduced as Document Dönitz-27, *TMWC,* 40:41–43.

60. *Guide No. 2,* 28, 174–75, 182.

61. See Cameron, *"Peleus" Trial,* passim, esp. 54, 58, 63; Herlin, *Verdammter Atlantik,* 219ff.; Messimer, "Heinz-Wilhelm Eck: Siegerjustiz and the *Peleus* Affair," in Savas, ed., *Silent Hunters,* 137–83; and NID.1/PW/REP/9/44, "U 852. Interrogation of Survivors," November 1944, subject file "British—NID/1/PW—Final Reports," Op-16-Z subject files, RG 38, NA. The L.I. and another crew member who participated in the shooting received prison sentences.

62. Hughes and Costello, *Atlantic,* 304.

63. Memorandum for Mr. Justice Jackson (Lt. Cmdr. John P. Bracken), "Grand Admiral Karl Dönitz as a War Criminal," 24 August 1945, in "Interrogation Summaries: Dönitz," Chief Justice Jackson Main Office Files, RG 238, NA.

64. Smith, *Reaching Judgment,* 259–65 (Biddle quote on 261).

Chapter 11. Disinterested Service

1. Cf. Bartov, *Hitler's Army,* and the review by R. J. Overy, *Journal of Military History* 66, no. 4 (December 1994), 878–79; see also Bartov's earlier work *The Eastern Front.*
2. Ansel, *Hitler Confronts,* 331.
3. Raeder, *Life,* 239–45; Dönitz, *Memoirs,* 310–14. The literature is critically reviewed in Bird, *Guide,* 550ff.
4. The literature to 1980 is summarized by Bird, *Guide,* 537–52, 589–95; recent additions include Thomas, *German Navy,* and Padfield, *Dönitz.* The official statement of the Bundesministerium der Verteidigung regarding Dönitz's funeral, with accompanying commentaries, is found in the "Forum" section of *Marineforum* (April 1981), 116–18.
5. Vause, *Ace,* esp. 7, 123–26.
6. Hoyt, *U-boats,* 51–55. Hoyt's observation is based on a review of the U.S. Navy interrogation reports in ONI's Op-16-Z files, RG 38, NA. Instructive of national prejudice is a World War I British interrogation report that characterizes one captured U-boat officer as "a typical middle-class Hun . . . brutal to the crew . . . and offensive when he was being interrogated" (British Naval Staff, Intelligence Division, "'U.C. 65': Interrogation of Survivors," November 1917, ONI subject files, 1911–27, RG 45, NA).
7. Polygram Video International production, "Battlefield: The Battle of the Atlantic" (PBS telecast July 1996).
8. NSDAP Master file *Ortsgruppenkartei* (geographic registry), Berlin Document Center (BDC) Accessioned Microfilm A3340, series MFOK, roll X027, NA; Topp, *Fackeln,* 21, 181ff. For an assessment of Topp's autobiography, see Hadley, *Count Not,* 181–84.
9. Neither name appears in the most comprehensive registry of Nazi party membership, the *Ortsgruppenkartei,* BDC Accessioned Microfilm A3340, series MFOK, rolls M008 and T031. See Schepke's memoir, *Ubootfahrer von heute* (esp. p. 22), and the discussion in Hadley, *Count Not,* 84–85.
10. Documentation of Prien's party membership is located among the NSDAP applications (*Anträge*) on BDC Accessioned Microfilm A3340-NSDAP-A roll 082; see his *Mein Weg,* 96.
11. The literature here is extensive and growing: In addition to the already-cited works by Mühlberger and Brustein, the most significant secondary works include Jürgen Falter, *Hitlers Wähler* (Munich: Verlag C. H. Beck, 1991); Richard F. Hamilton, *Who Voted for Hitler?* (Princeton, N.J.: Princeton University Press, 1982); Thomas Childers, *The Nazi Voter: The Social Foundations of Fascism in Germany, 1919–1933* (Chapel Hill: University of North Carolina Press, 1983); and Michael Kater, *The Nazi Party: A Social Profile of Members and Leaders, 1919–1945* (Cambridge, Mass.: Harvard University Press, 1983).
12. Cf. Mühlberger, *Hitler's Followers,* 14–17, 44–49, 94–96, 203–9, and Brustein, *Logic,* 149–59, 179–80.

13. Examples include *Funkgefreiter* Werner Hess of *U-530* (*Kaptlt.* Otto Wermuth), cited in Middlebrook, *Convoy,* 61, and the ill-fated *Mechanikersobergefreiter* Werner Drechsler of *U-118,* discussed in chapter 9.

14. Hitler, *Mein Kampf,* 273–74.

15. Raeder, *Life,* 142.

16. See Höhne, *Canaris,* esp. 54ff.

17. The most extensive treatment of the naval *Freikorps* is Bird, *Weimar,* 44–83; see also Dülffer, *Weimar,* 59–60; Rahn, *Reichsmarine,* 29–33; and Robert G. L. Waite, *Vanguard of Nazism: The Free Corps Movement in Postwar Germany, 1918–1923* (New York: W. W. Norton & Co., 1969), 38, 149–51. The information on Kukat appears in Dönitz, *Wechselvolles Leben,* 127; that on Zapp, in Merten, *Nach Kompass,* 55. For a different perspective on the Ehrhardt Brigade, see Ruschenbuch, "Reaktionäre Offiziere," 252–54.

18. Dülffer, *Weimar,* 47–52.

19. Hadley, *Count,* 72; Valentiner's party card is located among the NSDAP Master file *Ortsgruppenkartei,* BDC Accessioned Microfilm A3340, series MFOK, roll X059.

20. Background information on Steinbrinck's career is included in the published record of the war crimes trial, U.S.A. vs. Friedrich Flick, et al., in *Trials of War Criminals Before the Nuernberg Military Tribunals Under Control Council Law No. 10,* vol. 6 (Washington, D.C.: Government Printing Office, 1950), 202–4, 226–29, 342–60; Niemöller's affidavit on Steinbrinck's behalf is reproduced on pp. 340–41. On Niemöller, see Victoria Barnett, *For the Soul of the People: Protestant Protest against Hitler* (New York: Oxford University Press, 1992), passim.

21. Bird, *Weimar,* 286–89.

22. Rust, *Crew 34,* 32–33.

23. Merten, *Nach Kompass,* 110–13.

24. Bird, *Weimar,* 261–69, 278–83.

25. On *Gleichschaltung* and the army, see Messerschmidt, *Wehrmacht,* 48ff.; Müller, *Heer und Hitler,* 82ff.; and O'Neill, *Army,* 19ff.

26. Messerschmidt, *Wehrmacht,* 45–46; Müller, *Heer und Hitler,* 82n; and Raeder, *Life,* 263–64, 416–17; for the Army's reaction, see O'Neill, *Army,* 63–64, 114–15.

27. Thomas, *German Navy,* 154, and Rust, *Crew 34,* 58–59; for an example of noncompliance with dancing strictures, see Mulligan, *Lone Wolf,* 18, 29.

28. Crew 35's album of its world cruise aboard *Emden,* entry during a visit to Baltimore in April 1936, quoted in Bercuson and Herwig, *Deadly Seas,* 45.

29. See Raeder, *Life,* 264; Dönitz, *Vierzig Fragen,* 35; Merten, *Nach Kompass,* 161; and Rust, *Crew 34,* 72.

30. Thomas, *German Navy,* 157–59; Raeder, *Life,* 256–63.

31. The most detailed account appears in Irving, *War Path,* 212–14.

32. Baum, "Marine," 22–25; Dülffer, *Marine,* 471ff.; Salewski, *Seekriegsleitung,* vol. 1, 51ff., and vol. 3, 27–63.

33. This research is summarized in Messerschmidt, "German Military Effectiveness," 233–35. For a contrasting view that details the improvised and often

contradictory manner of warship design and construction, see Treue, Möller, and Rahn, *Marinerüstung*, 41ff.

34. Stöckel, "Entwicklung," 94ff. (esp. 106–9) and Anlage 7.

35. Sorge, *Marineoffizier*, esp. 7–9, 16–18, 37, 56, 61, 64, 72, 76, 97, 142–43; for an exaggerated view of the acceptance of NS ideology in Sorge's work, see Thomas, *German Navy*, 150–52.

36. Vause, *Ace*, 123–25; Merten, *Kompass*, 155.

37. Rust, *Crew 34*, 58.

38. Ibid., 54.

39. Op-16-Z Spot Item No. 286, "Morale of Officers in the U-boat Arm, December 1943," 14 June 1944, Op-16-Z subject files, RG 38, NA.

40. On the change in command (including Raeder's farewell address), see Salewski, "Raeder zu Dönitz," esp. 129–30, 139–45, and the same author's *Seekriegsleitung*, vol. 2, 218–24.

41. Kelley, *Twenty-two Cells*, 99.

42. Dönitz address of 5 February 1943, quoted in Salewski, "Raeder zu Dönitz," 146.

43. E.g., Thomas, *German Navy*, 230–31.

44. Dönitz's note following conversations with Hitler on 9 and 11 August 1943, quoted in *Fuehrer Conferences*, 360.

45. Dönitz, "Schlussansprache auf der Tagung für Befehlshaber der Kriegsmarine in Weimar am Freitag, dem 17. Dezember 1943," Document 443-D, published in *TMWC*, 25:105–16 (quotation on 106).

46. Dönitz's membership card is located in the geographic registry of the NSDAP *Ortsgruppenkartei*, BDC Accessioned Microfilm A3340, series MFOK, roll D032, fr. 2932.

47. Speer, *Spandau*, 369.

48. "Erlass gegen die Kritiksucht und Meckerei," 9 September 1943, reproduced in Salewski, *Seekriegsleitung*, vol. 2, 638–39.

49. Messerschmidt, *Wehrmacht*, 475–77; Messerschmidt correctly notes that the navy's assured loyalty rendered much of the staff's task unnecessary.

50. Quoted in Rust, *Crew 34*, 57.

51. Commentary by Werner Hirschmann on Topp's speech "Manning and Training the U-boat Fleet," accompanying letter of 13 December 1995 to author.

52. E.g., Hoyt, *U-boats*, 54, and van der Vat, *Atlantic*, 175 (the two books published in 1987 and 1988, respectively).

53. Quoted in Padfield, *Dönitz*, 349–51.

54. See Rohwer, *Versenkung*, esp. 45–56. Rohwer's examination of evidence regarding the sinking of two transports, in February 1942 and August 1944, leads to the conclusion that the actions were committed by Soviet submarines operating in these waters.

55. Schmoeckel's own account appears in Steinhoff, et al., *Voices*, 55–56, 181–82; see also Busch and Röll, *U-Boot-Kommandanten*, 211.

56. Rust, *Crew 34*, 28.

57. Ibid., 125.

58. Interrogation of Josef Fellinger (*U-515*), 9 May 1944, in alphabetical POW 201 files, War Department G-2 Division (MIS-Y Branch), RG 165, NA.

59. Monitored room conversation of three survivors of *U-569*, 19 June 1943, Extract of Information No. 390, Interrogation Reports: German, among the general interrogations and intelligence materials of the G-2 Division (MIS-Y Branch), RG 165, NA.

60. The Himmler speech of 4 October 1943 at Posen is reproduced as Document 1919-PS, *TMWC*, 29:110–73; for the case that Dönitz attended the speech, see Padfield, *Dönitz*, 322–26.

61. "Wortlaut der Rede des Reichsführer-SS Heinrich Himmler auf der Tagung der Befehlshaber der Kriegsmarine in Weimar am 16.12.1943," T175/91/2613339ff.

62. Mulligan, *Lone Wolf*, 158–59, 169–70; Suhren and Brustat-Naval, *Nasses Eichenlaub*, 123–24. One of those present was *Leutnant* Max von Arnim, an army officer later involved in the July 1944 conspiracy (von Nayhauss, *Zwischen Gehorsam und Gewissen*, 253–54).

63. Suhren and Brustat-Naval, *Nasses Eichenlaub*, 123–24, 153ff.; Rohwer, *Axis Submarine*, 69, 89, 91, 105, 109–10, 132, 162; and Gericke, *Inhaber*, 195. Uphoff died in August 1943 when *U-84* was sunk (Busch and Röll, *U-Boot-Kommandanten*, 246).

64. ONI final interrogation on survivors of *U-801*, Op-16-Z interrogations, RG 38, NA; Busch and Röhl, *U-Boot-Kommandanten*, 36.

65. ONI interrogation report on *U-1059*, Op-16-Z interrogation reports, and letter of Lt. V. R. Taylor to Cmdr. John L. Riheldaffer, 6 December 1944, Op-16-Z subject file "Taylor VLR (Ltr)," RG 38, NA.

66. Abel's party membership card (no. 996,997) is located among the NSDAP geographic registry, BDC Accessioned Microfilm A3340-, series FOK, roll A001; additional biographical data is provided in Walle, *Tragödie*, 44–45.

67. See chapter 9.

68. The best work on the subject, including extensive documentation through the present, is Walle, *Trägodie*, esp. 89ff. Walle published an English-language summary of his findings as "Individual Loyalty and Resistance in the German Military: The Case of Sub-Lieutenant Oskar Kusch," in Nicosia and Stokes, eds., *Germans*, 323–50. For an earlier and opposing interpretation, see Karl Peter, "Der Fall des Oberleutnants zur See Kusch" (unpublished ms. in the U-Boot-Archiv, Cuxhaven).

69. Speer, *Spandau*, 369.

70. Baum, "Marine," 24ff.; Hoffmann, *Resistance*, 344–45, 392.

71. Höhne, *Canaris*, 582.

72. On changes in the officer corps, see Förster, "Dynamics," 207–8; Müller-Hillebrand, *Heer*, vol. 3, 255, 264; and Kroener, "Auf dem Weg," 679–81. On the conspirators' regiments, see von Nayhauss, *Zwischen Gehorsam and Gewissen*, passim.

73. See esp. Salewski, "Selbstverständnis," 65ff.

74. See Hoffmann, *Resistance*, 264–69, 324–25.

75. On the general staff comparison, cf. the essays by Salewski, "Das Offizier-korps," esp. 219–21, and Absolon, "Offizierkorps," esp. 254–56, both in Hoff-mann, ed., *Offizierkorps*.

Chapter 12. Endings

1. See Schaeffer, *U 977*, 144ff., for an account of this voyage. For the story of a surrendered U-boat and the subsequent experiences of its crew, see Hirschfeld, *Das letzte Boot*, 7ff.
2. See "The Scuttled U-boats Case," in *Law Reports of Trials of War Criminals*, 55–70, and Madsen, *Royal Navy and German Naval Disarmament*, 180–81.
3. See Giese and Wise, *Shooting the War*, 232ff., and Stevens, *U-boat Far from Home*, 202–16.
4. Busch and Röll, *U-Boot-Kommandanten*, 79–80, 285n.
5. Gannon, *Operation Drumbeat*, 22–23, 408–9; Cremer, *U-boat Commander*, 199–200. This infantry duty may have benefited Cremer when a sympathetic British naval officer arranged for his release from captivity shortly after Ger-many's surrender (*U-boat Commander*, 212–13).
6. A garrison strength return of 31 October 1944 listed 780 men of the former *U-Stützpunkt* Lorient as defenders: See Farmbacher and Matthiae, *Lorient: Entste-hung und Verteidigung*, 36–39, 101.
7. This was the experience of *Maschinenobergefreiter* Heinrich Goral, questionnaire no. 1228.
8. Vause, *U-boat Ace*, 197, 201–8.
9. According to Showell, *U-boats*, 15, von Friedeburg had told his wife that he would take his own life rather than submit to humiliation as an Allied pris-oner.
10. An account of Steinhoff's death appears in Högel, *Embleme*, 258–59; the cir-cumstances leading to his death remain unclear, but some information is sum-marized in the U.S. Navy's investigation, "Irregularities Connected with the Handling of Surrendered German Submarines and Prisoners of War at the Navy Yard, Portsmouth, NH," 19 June 1945, in file A16–2(3)/EF30, 1945 formerly se-cret SecNav/CNO correspondence files, General Records of the Department of the Navy, RG 80, NA.
11. The Drechsler story is related in chapter 9; the execution is described in Whit-tingham, *Martial Justice*, 7ff., 257–81.
12. The best summary of the Eck case is Messimer, "Heinz-Wilhelm Eck," 138ff.; the trial record is synthesized in Cameron, ed., *"Peleus" Trial*, passim. See also Herlin, *Verdammter Atlantik*, 217ff.
13. Herzog, *U-Boote im Einsatz*, 254.
14. A painstaking accounting for the location and disposition of individual U-boats in May–June 1945 is provided in Rohwer and Hümmelchen, *Chronology*, 353–55, 357; "Deadlight" is detailed in "Where Are They Now? Operation

Deadlight," 43–49. On general Royal Navy policy vis-à-vis the dismantlement of Germany's navy 1945–47, see the recent study by Madsen, *Royal Navy and German Naval Disarmament,* passim.

15. On the histories and preservation of these submarines see Wetzel, *U 995;* Gallery, *U-505;* and Wetzel, *U 2540.* Doubtless a similar account of *U-534* will be forthcoming.

16. Data on Carl Möller from questionnaire no. 2701; author's correspondence with Möller, 11 November 1987, and interviews in Hamburg, 30 August 1989, and Steinhude am Meer, 26 May 1991. Additional information on Möller's combat service is provided in note 4 in chapter 7.

17. Werner, *Iron Coffins,* 340–56; Just, *Seeflieger zum Uboot-Fahrer,* 218–20; and Engelhardt, "Vom U-Boot in die französische Gefangenschaft," 24–26. On general conditions and mortality of German prisoners in France, 1945–48, see Günter Bischof and Stephen E. Ambrose, eds., *Eisenhower and the German POWs: Facts against Falsehood* (Baton Rouge: Louisiana State University Press, 1992), 149–52.

18. Examples of divisions after arrival in Belgium are given in Moore, *Faustball Tunnel,* 236–38. A radioman's assistance from a U-boat surgeon in being declared "unfit" and thus arriving home by June 1946 is described in Hirschfeld, *Das letzte Boot,* 233ff. The *U-515* experiences are from interviews with Rolf Taubert and Frau Ursula Eckert, Clausthal-Zellerfeld, 11 May 1994.

19. Guske, *War Diaries,* 158ff. and end papers; Guske questionnaire no. 5418.

20. Giese and Wise, *Shooting,* 252–54; Stevens, *U-boat Far from Home,* 215–16.

21. Robertson, *Golden Horseshoe,* 185–91; Busch and Röll, *U-Boot-Kommandanten,* 133, 242, 342–43; Stevens, *U-boat Far from Home,* 216.

22. Karschawin, *U 250,* 65.

23. See the incisive discussion in Smith, *Reaching Judgment,* 247–65.

24. On Dönitz's time in Spandau, see Speer, *Spandau,* esp. 88–89, 130–32, 203, 237–39, 243–45, 331–32.

25. Rössler, "U-boat Development and Building," 135.

26. Specific information from Herzog, *Deutsche U-Boote,* 297–300, and Alman, *Ritter,* 44–45; general data from the sample (an eighteenth became an officer with the border security police). Topp discusses his reenlistment in *Fackeln,* 201ff.; general recruitment of former officers is described in Rust, *Crew 34,* 151–61. Some invaluable personal insights into the reestablishment of the Bundesmarine are offered in Peter, *Acht Glas,* 144–52.

27. Rust, *Crew 34,* 154–55.

28. Data collected from questionnaires in officers' sample.

29. Interview with Peter Petersen, Chicago, 10 June 1997.

30. Weinrich data in questionnaire no. 2737 of the sample.

31. Data accumulated from the sample; cf. table 14 for a comparison with their fathers' occupations. Using the same categories defined in that table, 220 sample members (23.5 percent) entered postwar working-class careers; 653 (70 percent) held lower-middle and middle-middle class professions; and 52 (5.5 per-

cent) moved into upper-class occupations (12 sample members provided no or insufficient information). Social stratification in the Bundesrepublik, however, proved less rigid than that of the 1930s, especially with greater income possibilities for specific skilled labor careers. Precise delineations of working versus middle class are therefore inappropriate in the postwar context.

32. Reunion information taken from the regular announcements of the September/October 1995 issue of *Schaltung Küste* (the bulletin of the U-boat Veterans' Association), pp. 22–32. Forty-two reunions listed the number of previous annual meetings, with the earliest in 1971. Eight had started by 1979, and sixteen began in the period 1980–85; eight, however, commenced only in 1991 or later.

33. Dönitz's death and funeral are described in Padfield, *Dönitz*, 489–90; for an exchange of letters on the official reaction, including the note of the *Bundesministers der Verteidigung*, see *Marineforum*, 4/1981, 116–18.

34. Described in the "Jahresbericht 1995" of the Vorstand, Stiftung U-Boot-Ehrenmal Möltenort, in *Schaltung-Küste*, no. 162 (March/April 1996), 14–16.

35. The controversies are reviewed in Salewski, *Von der Wirklichkeit*, passim, and Hadley, *Count Not*, 140ff.

Appendix 2. Numbers and Losses of the U-boat Service

1. The figure is provided by the U-Boot-Archiv (letter of Horst Bredow to the author, 28 February 1990).

2. Heinsius, "Verbleib," 84; author's correspondence from the Bundesarchiv-Abt. Zentralnachweisstelle, 5 August 1993, and Deutsche Dienststelle (WASt), 15 December 1993. Crew lists for some U-boats, kept by individual veterans, have been donated to the U-Boot-Archiv, Cuxhaven.

3. See *Guide No. 2*, passim. The data was then tabulated in Högel, *Embleme*, 282–84.

4. Naval Intelligence Division (Admiralty), "German U-boats from Which Prisoners Were Taken during Hostilities by British and American Forces," n.d., in ONI Op-16-Z subject files, RG 38, NA. This source gives the figure of 5,009 POWs, but a number of these died or were killed in captivity and are included among the list of dead; a few others (usually severely wounded) were repatriated. Omitted from this report are six U-boat prisoners recovered from *U-250* by Soviet forces (Karschawin, *Unterseeboot U 250*, 24).

5. The six boats were *U-19*, *U-20*, *U-23* (all scuttled off the Turkish coast, September 1944), *U-760*, *U-966* (crews permanently interned in Spain, September and November 1943, respectively), and *U-260* (crew interned in Ireland, March 1945). Descriptions of their losses are provided in Kemp, *U-boats Destroyed*, 145, 157, 217, 237; further documentation is cited in *Guide No. 2*, 27–28, 161, 176.

6. Vockel, who entered the U-boat service in March 1942, served as a watch offi-

cer aboard *U-198* and *U-969* before taking command of the Type XXIII boat *U-2336* on 30 September 1944. He died exactly six months later in an air raid on Hamburg; his U-boat was sunk on 3 January 1946 as part of Operation "Deadlight" (Busch and Röll, *U-Boot-Kommandanten*, 247; Köhl and Rössler, *Original zum Modell: Uboottyp XXIII*, 45).

7. Compiled from the descriptions in U-boat war diaries in *Guide No. 2,* passim.

8. The exchange of telegrams, 6–8 September 1944, is found in decrypted intercepts, SRGN nos. 39171–172, 39273–274, RG 457, NA; data on Kals and Winter from Busch and Röll, *U-Boot-Kommandanten*, 118, 256.

9. These prisoners included the flotilla commander and former CO of *U-596,* *Korv.Kapt.* Gunter Jahn, and his staff officer and former captain of *U-380,* *Kaptlt.* Josef Röther (Busch and Röll, *U-Boot-Kommandanten*, 112–13, 195).

10. Combined Intelligence Objectives Subcommittee (CIOS) report, no. 28-49, "German Military Neuropsychiatry and Neurosurgery," 87–88, ca. May 1945, Formerly security-classified G-2 intelligence library "P" publications files, 1946–51, RG 319, NA.

11. See Wells, *Courage and Air Warfare,* esp. 70–73.

12. Noted in Busch, *So war,* 335.

13. Dönitz testimony, *TMWC,* 13:295. The former figure is cited in Mason, *Secret Menace,* 154; Hughes and Costello, *Battle,* 303; and van der Vat, *Atlantic,* 382, and the higher figure in Rahn, "Grundzüge," 66, although none identify a source or explanation as to how their figure was derived.

14. Busch, *So war,* 316.

15. Letter of Horst Bredow to author, 28 February 1990.

16. Dönitz, *Memoirs,* 370.

17. *Freg.Kapt.* Wolfgang Steinort, "Die Ausbildung in der U-Bootwaffe im 2. Weltkrieg," paper presented 5 September 1979 before the Arbeitskreis Reserveoffiziere Marine Hamburg (copy courtesy of the U-Boot-Archiv, Cuxhaven).

18. BdU, "Personalbestand im B.d.U. Berich am 1.7.1942" (Anlage 52 zu "Organisation, Stellenbesetzung und Personalstand im B.d.U.-Bereich am 1.7.42"), T1022/4038/PG 31794.

19. See Lakowski, *U-Boote,* 344, using (uncited) sources available in former DDR archives.

20. See Mueller-Hillebrand, *Heer,* vol. 3, 251, 266.

21. Figure from the Deutsche Dienststelle (WASt), "Vorgezogener Arbeitsbericht 1989/1990," 44.

Selected Bibliography

Bibliographies, Source Guides, and Finding Aids

Bird, Keith W. *German Naval History: A Guide to the Literature*. New York: Garland Publishing, 1985.

Burdick, Charles. "The Tambach Archive: A Research Note." *Military Affairs* 36, no. 4 (December 1972): 124–26.

Deutsche Dienststelle (WASt) für die Benachrichtigung der nächsten Angehörigen von Gefallenen der ehemaligen deutschen Wehrmacht. *Vorgezogener Arbeitsbericht 1989/1990*.

Granier, Gerhard, Josef Henke, and Klaus Oldenhage. *Das Bundesarchiv und seine Bestände*. 3d ed. Boppard/Rhein: Harald Boldt, 1977.

Heinsius, Paul. "Der Verbleib des Aktenmaterials der deutschen Kriegsmarine: Das ehemalige Marinearchiv, Marinegerichtsakten und Personalakten, Krankenakten sowie Druckschriften und Bibliotheken." *Der Archivar* 8, no. 2 (April 1958): 75–86.

National Archives and Records Administration. *Guides to the Microfilmed Records of the German Navy, 1850–1945. No. 1, U-boats and T-boats 1914–1918*. Washington, D.C.: National Archives and Records Service, 1984.

———. *Guides to the Microfilmed Records of the German Navy, 1850–1945. No. 2, Records Relating to U-boat Warfare, 1939–1945*. Washington, D.C.: National Archives and Records Administration, 1985.

———. *Guides to the Microfilmed Records of the German Navy, 1850–1945. No. 3, Records of the German Naval High Command, 1935–1945*. Washington, D.C.: National Archives and Records Administration, 1998.

Salewski, Michael. "Das Kriegstagebuch der deutschen Seekriegsleitung

im Zweiten Weltkrieg." *Marine-Rundschau* 64, no. 3 (June 1967): 137–45.
Wolfe, Robert, ed. *Captured German and Related Records: A National Archives Conference*. Athens, Ohio: Ohio University Press, 1974.

Primary Sources: Unpublished

National Archives, College Park, Md.

Record Group 242, National Archives Collection of Seized Enemy Records, 1942–. Microfilm Publication T1022, *Records of the German Navy, 1850–1945:* War diaries of 1/Seekriegsleitung (Teile A, B, C), Befehlshaber der Unterseeboote, and various U-boats, all for the 1939–45 period; selected records of the Admiralstab files on U-boat warfare, 1917–18; Marineleitung (AU files), 1927, 2/Skl BdU Op, 1942–43; and Kriegswissenschaftliche Abteilung, 1944. Microfilm Publication T175, *Records of the Reichsführer-SS and Chief of the German Police:* Persönlicher Stab, Reichsführer-SS, 1943–44. *Berlin Document Center Accessioned Microfilm A3340, NSDAP-MFOK (Ortsgruppenkartei,* geographic registry) and *NSDAP-Anträge* (applications): Nazi party membership records for various individuals.
Record Group 38, Records of the Office of the Chief of Naval Operations, Office of Naval Intelligence, Special Activities Branch (Op-16-Z). Administrative correspondence, interrogation reports and raw interrogations, and subject files, 1941–45; ONI Monograph Files: Germany; Naval Attaché Reports, 1939–46; Naval Armed Guard Reports, 1942; Chief of Naval Operations, formerly top secret 1945 correspondence.
Record Group 457, Records of the National Security Agency. Cryptologic studies and decrypted intercepts (SRH-, SRGN-, and SRMN- series); Historic Cryptographic Collection, Pre–World War I through World War II
Record Group 24, Records of the Bureau of Naval Personnel. General correspondence files, 1925–40 and 1941–45.
Record Group 80, General Records of the Department of the Navy. Formerly security-classified SecNav/CNO correspondence files, 1945 formerly secret correspondence.
Record Group 165, Records of War Department General and Special Staffs, G-2 (Intelligence) Division. Formerly security-classified interrogation reports and correspondence on POWs (MIS-Y Branch), 1942–45.
Record Group 238, National Archives Collection of World War II War Crimes Records, International Military Tribunal Nuremberg. Chief Justice Jackson main office files, British (GB-) exhibits, Dönitz defense exhibits.
Record Group 45, Naval Records Collection of the Office of Naval Records and Library. Office of Naval Intelligence subject files, 1911–27 (File JU, Interrogations of U-boat POWs).
Record Group 319, Records of the Army Staff G-2 (Intelligence) Division. Army Intelligence formerly security-classified project decimal file, 1941–45; formerly security-classified G-2 intelligence library "P" publications files, 1946–51.

Record Group 226, Records of the Office of Strategic Services (OSS). Research and Analysis (R&A) Branch Reports (nos. 1757, 28761).

Bundesarchiv-Abt. Militärarchiv, Freiburg i.Br.

Bestand RM 7, Seekriegsleitung.
RM 7/1206, Personalwirtschaft 1940–41.
RM 7/1238, Personalbedarf 1943–44.

Stiftung Traditionsarchiv Unterseeboote, Cuxhaven

Collected historical materials, including crew lists for U-boats, Personalakten for commanding officers, unpublished memoirs and studies (listed later in the bibliography), and photographs.

Library of Congress, Washington, D.C.

Manuscripts Division: German Submarine Materials, reels 78–82.

Wehrgeschichtliches Ausbildungszentrum, Marineschule Mürwik

Crew yearbooks, newsletters, and other publications relating to specific Crews.

Questionnaires, Interviews, and Correspondence

Questionnaires were completed by 167 former naval officers and 937 former NCOs and enlisted men, for the most part during their visits to the U-Boot-Archiv in Cuxhaven between May 1991 and December 1994. Copies of individual questionnaires are on file, arranged by the number of the U-boat on which the sample member served, at the U-Boot-Archiv.
A number of veterans and survivors also provided information through interviews (I) and/or correspondence (C) on their experiences in the U-boat arm: Günther Altenburger (I/C); Hermann Brandt (I); Horst Bredow (I/C); Günter Eckert (I); Ursula Eckert (I); Rolf Güth (C); Reinhard Hardegen (I); Werner Hirschmann (I/C); Hermann Kaspers (I); Carl Möller (I/C); Inge Molzahn (I/C); Wilhelm Müller-Arnecke (I/C); Peter Petersen (I); Hans Schultz (I/C); Rolf Taubert (I); Heinz Trompelt (C); and Eduard Vogt (I).

Primary Sources: Published

Cameron, John, ed. *The "Peleus" Trial.* Vol. 1 of the War Crimes Trials series, edited by Sir David Maxwell Fyfe. London: William Hodge and Co., 1948.
Fuehrer Conferences on Naval Affairs, 1939–1945. Foreword by Jak P. Mallmann Showell. Annapolis, Md.: Naval Institute Press, 1990.

Nazi Conspiracy and Aggression. 8 vols. and 2 supps. Washington, D.C.: Office of the U.S. Chief of Counsel for Prosecution of Axis Criminality, 1946.

Trial of the Major War Criminals before the International Military Tribunal, Nuremberg, 14 November 1945–1 October 1946. 42 vols. Nuremberg: International Military Tribunal, 1947–1949.

Wagner, Gerhard, ed. *Lagevorträge des Oberbefehlshabers der Kriegsmarine vor Hitler, 1939–1945.* Munich: J. F. Lehmanns Verlag, 1972.

German Navy and Government Publications

Besoldungstabellen für Soldaten: Stand, January 1941. Berlin: Verlag Bernard & Graefe, 1941.

Bestimmungen für den Dienst an Bord. Heft 3, *Wach- und Sicherheitsdienst (M.Dv. Nr. 49).* Berlin: E. S. Mittler & Sohn, 1938.

Bestimmungen über die Beförderung der Unteroffiziere und Mannschaften der Kriegsmarine im Frieden (M.Dv. Nr. 15). Berlin: E. S. Mittler & Sohn, 1938.

Kriegserfahrungen der deutschen U-Boote im Weltkriege, 1914–1918 (M.Dv. Nr. 28). Berlin: E. S. Mittler & Sohn, 1939.

Marineverordnungsblatt, 15 August 1943–15 April 1944.

Rangliste der Deutschen Kriegsmarine nach dem Stande vom 1. November 1937–1. November 1938 (M.Dv. Nr. 293). Berlin: E. S. Mittler & Sohn, 1937–38.

Statistisches Jahrbuch für das Deutsche Reich, 1939/40. Berlin: Statistisches Reichsamt, 1940.

The U-boat Commander's Handbook (U.S. Navy translation of *M.Dv. Nr. 906,* 1943 ed.). Introduction by E. J. Coates. Gettysburg, Pa.: Thomas Publications, 1989.

Wie komme ich zur Kriegsmarine? Ein Merkheft für Freiwillige. Berlin: Oberkommando der Kriegsmarine, 1939.

Memoirs and Autobiographies of German Participants

Bauer, Hermann. *Als Führer der U-Boote im Weltkriege: Der Eintritt der U-Boot-Waffe in die Seekriegführung.* Leipzig: Koehler & Amelang, 1941.

Cremer, Peter, and Fritz Brustat-Naval. *Ali Cremer: U 333.* Berlin: Ullstein Verlag, 1982. Translated by Lawrence Wilson as *U-boat Commander Peter Cremer. A German Sub Commander's View of the Battle of the Atlantic* (Annapolis, Md.: Naval Institute Press, 1984). Page citations in text are to the Jove paperback edition (New York: Berkeley Publishing Group, 1986).

Dönitz, Karl. *Zehn Jahre und Zwanzig Tage.* Frankfurt/M.: Athenäum Verlag, 1958. Translated by R. H. Stevens and David Woodward as *Memoirs. Ten Years and Twenty Days,* introduction and afterword by Prof. Dr. Jürgen Rohwer (Annapolis, Md.: Naval Institute Press, 1990).

———. *Mein wechselvolles Leben.* Göttingen: Musterschmidt Verlag, 1968.

———. *Vierzig Fragen an Karl Dönitz*. 4th ed. Munich: Bernard & Graefe Verlag, 1980.

Ernst, Georg. *Bis zur letzten Stunde: Illusion und Wirklichkeit*. Hamburg: E. S. Mittler & Sohn, 1995.

Fürbringer, Werner. *Alarm! Tauchen!!: U-Boot in Kampf und Sturm*. Berlin: Im Deutschen Verlag, 1933.

Giese, Otto, and James E. Wise, Jr. *Shooting the War: The Memoir and Photographs of a World War II U-boat Officer*. Annapolis, Md.: Naval Institute Press, 1994.

Hartmann, Werner, and Gerhart Weise. *Feind im Fadenkreuz. U-Boot auf Jagd im Atlantik*. Foreword by *Vizeadmiral* Karl Dönitz. Berlin: Verlag die Heimbücherei, 1942.

Hirschfeld, Wolfgang. *Feindfahrten: Das Logbuch eines U-Boot-Funkers*. Munich: Wilhelm Heyne, 1985.

———. *Das letzte Boot: Atlantik Farewell*. Munich: Universitas Verlag, 1989.

Hirschfeld, Wolfgang, and Geoffrey Brooks. *Hirschfeld: The Story of a U-boat NCO, 1940–1946*. Foreword by Jak P. Mallmann Showell. Annapolis, Md.: Naval Institute Press, 1996.

Kaiser, Ernst. *QXP: Im U-Boot auf Feindfahrt*. Herford: Koehler, 1981.

Lüth, Wolfgang, and Claus Korth. *Boot greift wieder an!: Ritterkreuzträger erzählen*. Berlin: Verlag Erich Klinghammer, 1944.

Merten, Karl-Friedrich. *Nach Kompass: Lebenserinnerungen eines Seeoffiziers*. Berlin: E. S. Mittler & Sohn, 1994.

Metzler, Jost. *Sehrohr Südwärts: Ritterkreuzträger Kapitänleutnant Jost Metzler erzählt*. Berlin: Wilhelm-Limpert Verlag, 1943.

Michelsen, Andreas. *Der U-Bootskrieg, 1914–1918*. Leipzig: Von Hase & K. F. Koehler, 1925.

Peter, Karl. *Acht Glas (Ende der Wache): Erinnerungen eines Offiziers der Crew 38*. Reutlingen: Preussischer Militär-Verlag, 1989.

Prien, Günther. *Mein Weg nach Scapa Flow*. Berlin: Im Deutscher Verlag, 1940.

Raeder, Erich. *My Life*. Translated by Henry W. Drexel. Annapolis, Md.: United States Naval Institute, 1960.

Schaeffer, Heinz. *U-boat 977*. New York: W. W. Norton & Co., 1952. New York: Bantam Books, 1981 (paperback).

Schepke, Joachim. *U-Bootfahrer von heute: Erzählt und gezeichnet von einem U-Boot-Kommandanten*. Berlin: Im Deutscher Verlag, 1940.

Schulz, Werner. *Im Kleinst-U-Boot: Aus dem Nachlass eines "Seehund"-Fahrers*. Berlin: Brandenburgisches Verlagshaus, 1995.

Schulz, Wilhelm. *Über dem nassen Abgrund: Als Kommandant und Flotillenchef im U-Boot-Krieg*. Berlin: E. S. Mittler & Sohn, 1994.

Schütze, H. G. *Operation unter Wasser*. Herford: Koehler, 1985.

Speer, Albert. *Spandau: The Secret Diaries*. Translated by Richard and Clara Winston. New York: Pocket Books, 1977. Originally published as *Spandauer Tagebücher* (Frankfurt/M.: Ullstein Verlag, 1975).

Suhren, Teddy, and Fritz Brustat-Naval. *Nasses Eichenlaub: Als Kommandant und F.d.U. im U-Boot-Krieg*. 2d ed. Herford: Koehler, 1985.

Topp, Erich. *Fackeln Über dem Atlantik: Lebensbericht eines U-Boot-Kommandanten.* Herford: E. S. Mittler & Sohn, 1990.

Werner, Herbert. *Iron Coffins. A Personal Account of the German U-boat Battles of World War II.* New York: Holt, Rinehart and Winston, 1969.

Secondary Sources: Books

Absalon, Rudolf. *Wehrgesetz und Wehrdienst, 1935–1945: Das Personalwesen in der Wehrmacht.* Boppard/Rh.: Harald Boldt, 1960.

Alman, Karl [Franz Kurowski]. *Ritter der sieben Meere.* Rastatt: Erich Pabel, 1963.

————. *Graue Wölfe in blauer See: Der Einsatz der deutschen U-Boote im Mittelmeer.* Munich: Wilhelm Heyne, 1977.

Angolia, John R., and Adolf Schlicht. *Die Kriegsmarine: Uniforms and Traditions.* 3 vols. San Jose, Calif.: R. James Bender, 1991–93.

Ansel, Walter. *Hitler Confronts England.* Durham, N.C.: Duke University Press, 1960.

Barker, Ralph. *Children of the Benares: A War Crime and Its Victims.* London: Methuen, 1987.

Bartov, Omer. *Hitler's Army: Soldiers, Nazis, and War in the Third Reich.* New York: Oxford University Press, 1992.

Beesly, Patrick. *Very Special Intelligence: The Story of the Admiralty's Operational Intelligence Centre, 1939–1945.* Garden City, N.Y.: Doubleday & Co., 1978.

Bell, Robert W., and D. Bruce Lockerbie. *In Peril on the Sea: A Personal Remembrance.* Garden City, N.Y.: Doubleday & Co., 1984.

Bercuson, David J., and Holger H. Herwig. *Deadly Seas: The Duel between the St. Croix and the U305 in the Battle of the Atlantic.* Toronto: Random House of Canada, 1997.

Bird, Keith W. *Weimar, the German Naval Officer Corps, and the Rise of National Socialism.* Amsterdam: B. R. Grüner Publishing Company, 1977.

Blair, Clay, Jr. *Silent Victory: The U.S. Submarine War against Japan.* New York: Bantam Books, 1975.

————. *Hitler's U-boat War.* Vol. 1, *The Hunters.* New York: Random House, 1997.

Bonatz, Heinz. *Die Deutsche Marine-Funkaufklärung, 1914–1945.* Darmstadt: Wehr und Wissen Verlagsgesellschaft, 1970.

————. *Seekrieg im Äther: Die Leistungen der Marine-Funkaufklärung, 1939–1945.* Herford: Verlag E. S. Mittler & Sohn, 1981.

Bräckow, Werner. *Die Geschichte des deutschen Marine-Ingenieuroffizierkorps.* Oldenburg: Stalling, 1974.

Brennecke, Jochen. *Jäger-Gejagte: Deutsche U-Boote, 1939–1945.* Herford: Koehler, 1956; Munich: Wilhelm Heyne, 1986 (paperback).

————. *Haie im Paradies: Der deutsche U-Boot-Krieg 1943/45 in Asiens Gewässern: Tatsachenbericht.* Munich: Wilhelm Heyne, 1983.

————. *Die Wende im U-Boot-Krieg: Ursachen und Folgen, 1939–1943.* Herford: Koehler, 1984.

Brustat-Naval, Fritz. *Unternehmen Rettung.* Herford: Koehler, 1970.

Brustein, William. *The Logic of Evil: The Social Origins of the Nazi Party, 1925–1933.* New Haven: Yale University Press, 1996.

Bry, Gerhard. *Wages in Germany, 1871–1945.* Princeton, N.J.: Princeton University Press, 1960.

Bryant, Ben. *Submarine Commander.* New York: Ballantine Books, 1960.

Buchheim, Lothar-Günther. *Jäger im Weltmeer.* Berlin: Suhrkamp Verlag, 1943. Reprint. Hamburg: Hoffmann und Campe, 1996.

———. *Das Boot: Roman.* Munich: R. Piper Verlag, 1973. Translated by Denver and Helen Lindley as *The Boat* (New York: Alfred A. Knopf, 1975).

———. *U-boat War.* Translated by Gudie Lawaetz. New York: Bantam Books, 1979.

———. *Die U-Boot-Fahrer: Die Boote, die Besatzungen, und ihr Admiral.* Munich: C. Bertelsmann, 1985.

———. *Zu Tode Gesiegt: Der Untergang der U-Boote.* Stuttgart: C. Bertelsmann, 1988.

Busch, Fritz Otto, ed. *Das Buch von der Kriegsmarine.* Berlin: Verlagshaus Bong & Co., 1939.

Busch, Harald. *So war der U-Boot-Krieg.* Bielefeld: Deutscher Heimat-Verlag, 1952. Translated by L. P. R. Wilson as *U-boats at War* (New York: Ballantine Books, 1955).

Busch, Rainer, and Hans-Joachim Röll. *U-Bootbau auf deutschen Werften 1935–1945 (Indienststellungen, Bauwerften und Kommandanten).* Cuxhaven: Stiftung Traditionsarchiv U-Boote, 1994.

———. *Der U-Boot-Krieg, 1939–1945: Die Deutschen U-Boot-Kommandanten.* Hamburg: Verlag E. S. Mittler & Sohn, 1996.

Chalmers, W. S. *Max Horton and the Western Approaches. A Biography of Admiral Sir Max Kennedy Horton.* London: Hodder and Stoughton, 1954.

Churchill, Sir Winston. *Their Finest Hour.* Vol. 2 of *The Second World War.* Boston: Houghton Mifflin, 1950.

———. *The Hinge of Fate.* Vol. 4 of *The Second World War.* Boston: Houghton Mifflin, 1950.

Compton-Hall, Richard. *Submarines and the War at Sea, 1914–1918.* London: Macmillan, 1991.

Creveld, Martin van. *Fighting Power. German and U.S. Army Performance, 1939–1945.* Westport, Conn.: Greenwood Press, 1982.

Dahrendorf, Ralf. *Society and Democracy in Germany.* Translation by Doubleday & Co. New York: Anchor Books, 1967. Originally published as *Gesellschaft und Demokratie in Deutschland* (Munich: R. Piper Verlag, 1965).

Deighton, Len. *Blood, Tears, and Folly.* Vol. 1, *An Objective Look at World War II.* New York: HarperPaperbacks, 1996.

Dönitz, Karl. *Die U-Bootswaffe.* 3d ed. Berlin: E. S. Mittler & Sohn, 1940.

Dörr, Manfred. *Die Ritterkreuzträger der Deutschen Wehrmacht, 1939–1945.* Teil 4, *Die U-Boot-Waffe.* 2 vols. Osnabrück: Biblio Verlag, 1988.

Dülffer, Jobst. *Weimar, Hitler, und die Marine: Reichspolitik und Flottenbau, 1920–1939.* Dusseldorf: Droste Verlag, 1973.

Edwards, Bernard. *Dönitz and the Wolf Packs*. London: Arms and Armour, 1996.

Eichholtz, Dietrich. *Geschichte der deutschen Kriegswirtschaft, 1939–1945*. Band 2, *1941–1943*. Berlin: Akademie-Verlag, 1985.

Elting, John R., and Timothy P. Mulligan, eds. *Wolf Packs*. Alexandria, Va.: Time-Life Books, 1989.

Enders, Gerd. *Auch kleine Igel haben Stacheln: Deutsche U-Boote im Schwarzen Meer*. Herford: Koehler, 1984.

Fahrmbacher, Wilhelm, and Walter Matthiae. *Lorient: Entstehung und Verteidigung des Marine-Stützpunktes, 1940/1945*. Weissenburg: Prinz-Eugen-Verlag, 1956.

Farago, Ladislas. *The Tenth Fleet*. New York: Paperback Library, 1964.

Frank, Wolfgang. *Die Wölfe und der Admiral: Triumph und Tragik der U-Boote*. Oldenburg: Stalling, 1953. Translated by R. O. B. Long as *The Sea Wolves* (New York: Rinehart & Co., 1955).

Franke, Hermann, ed. *Handbuch der neuzeitlichen Wehrwissenschaften*. Band 3, Teil 1, *Die Kriegsmarine*. Berlin: Verlag von Walter de Gruyter & Co., 1938.

Gallery, Daniel V. *U-505* (original title: *Twenty Million Tons under the Sea*). New York: Paperback Library, 1967.

Gannon, Michael. *Operation Drumbeat: The Dramatic True Story of Germany's First U-boat Attacks along the American Coast during World War II*. New York: Harper & Row, 1990.

———. *Black May: The Epic Story of the Allies' Defeat of the German U-boats in May 1943*. New York: HarperCollins, 1998.

Gasaway, E. B. *Grey Wolf, Grey Sea*. New York: Ballantine Books, 1970.

Gentile, Gary. *Track of the Gray Wolf: U-boat Warfare on the U.S. Eastern Seaboard, 1942–1945*. New York: Avon Books, 1989.

Gericke, Bernd. *Die Inhaber des Deutschen Kreuzes in Gold, des Deutschen Kreuzes in Silber der Kriegsmarine und die Inhaber der Ehrentafelspange der Kriegsmarine*. Osnabrück: Biblio Verlag, 1993.

Giese, Fritz E. *Die Alte und die Neue Marine*. Bonn: Athenäum-Verlag, 1957.

Gilbert, G. M. *Nuremberg Diary*. New York: Farrar, Straus and Cudahy, 1947. Reprint. New York: Signet Books, 1961.

Gretton, Sir Peter. *Crisis Convoy*. New York: Zebra Books, 1974.

Gröner, Erich. *German Warships, 1815–1945*. Vol. 2, *U-boats and Mine Warfare Vessels*. Revised and expanded by Dieter Jung and Martin Maass. Annapolis, Md.: Naval Institute Press, 1991.

Groos, Otto. *Der Krieg in der Nordsee*. Band 2, *Von Anfang September bis November 1914*. (Volume 2 of the German official history *Der Krieg zur See, 1914–1918*, issued by the Marine-Archiv under the general editorship of *Vizeadmiral a.D. E. Mantey*.) Berlin: E. S. Mittler & Sohn, 1922.

Grossman, Dave. *On Killing: The Psychological Cost of Learning to Kill in War and Society*. Boston: Backpay Books, 1996.

Grossmith, Frederick. *The Sinking of the* Laconia: *A Tragedy in the Battle of the Atlantic*. Stamford, England: Paul Watkins, 1944.

Guske, Heinz F. K. *The War Diaries of U-764: Fact or Fiction?* Gettysburg, Pa.: Thomas Publications, 1992.

Güth, Rolf. *Von Revolution zu Revolution: Entwicklungen und Führungsprobleme der Deutschen Marine (1848–1918)*. Herford: E. S. Mittler & Sohn, 1978.

Hackmann, Willem. *Seek and Strike: Sonar, Anti-submarine Warfare and the Royal Navy, 1914–1954*. London: Her Majesty's Stationery Office, 1984.

Hadley, Michael L. *U-boats against Canada: German Submarines in Canadian Waters*. Kingston, Ont.: McGill-Queen's University Press, 1985.

———. *Count Not the Dead: The Popular Image of the German Submarine*. Montreal: McGill-Queen's University Press, 1995.

Halpern, Paul G. *The Naval War in the Mediterranean, 1914–1918*. Annapolis, Md.: Naval Institute Press, 1987.

———. *A Naval History of World War I*. Annapolis, Md.: Naval Institute Press, 1994.

Hannemann, Ludwig C. R. *Die Justiz der Kriegsmarine 1939–1945 im Spiegel ihrer Rechtsprechung*. Regensburg: S. Roderer Verlag, 1993.

Harlinghausen, C. Harald. *Ein Junge geht zur Kriegsmarine: Ein Bild vom Leben und vom Dienst in unserer heutigen Kriegsmarine*. Minden/W.: Wilhelm Köhler, n.d. (ca. 1938).

Harrod, Frederick S. *Manning the New Navy: The Development of a Modern Naval Enlisted Force, 1899–1940*. Westport, Conn.: Greenwood Press, 1978.

Herlin, Hans. *Verdammter Atlantik: Schicksale deutscher U-Boot-Fahrer: Tatsachenbericht*. Hamburg: Christian Wegner Verlag, 1982.

Herwig, Holger H. *Das Elitekorps des Kaisers: Die Marineoffiziere im Wilhelminischen Deutschland*. Hamburg: Hans Christians Verlag, 1977.

———. *"Luxury" Fleet: The Imperial German Navy, 1888–1918*. London: Ashfield Press, 1987.

Herzog, Bodo. *U-Boote im Einsatz, 1939–1945: Eine Bilddokumentation*. Dorheim/H.: Podzun-Verlag, 1970.

———. *Deutsche U-Boote, 1906–1966*. Erlangen: Karl Müller Verlag, 1993.

Herzog, Bodo, and Günter Schomaekers. *Ritter der Tiefe—Graue Wölfe: Die erfolgreichsten U-Boot-Kommandanten der Welt*. Munich: Verlag Welsermühl, 1976.

Hess, Hans Georg. *Die Männer von U 955: Gespräche mit ehemaligen Besatzungsangehörigen des Bootes von Laboe*. 2d ed. Wunstorf-Idensen: Hess-Press, 1987.

Hessler, Günter. *The U-boat War in the Atlantic, 1939–1945*. Published under the auspices of the British Ministry of Defence. London: Her Majesty's Stationery Office, 1989.

Hickam, Homer H., Jr. *Torpedo Junction: U-boat War off America's East Coast, 1942*. Annapolis, Md.: Naval Institute Press, 1989.

Hinsley, F. H., et al. *British Intelligence in the Second World War*. 5 vols. in 6 parts. New York: Cambridge University Press, 1979–81, and London: Her Majesty's Stationery Office, 1979–90.

Hoffmann, Peter. *The History of the German Resistance, 1933–1945*. Translated by Richard Barry. Cambridge, Mass.: MIT Press, 1977.

Högel, Georg. *Embleme, Wappen, Malings deutscher U-Boote, 1939–1945*. Herford: Koehler, 1987.

Höhne, Heinz. *Canaris: Hitler's Master Spy*. Translated by J. Maxwell Brownjohn. Garden City, N.Y.: Doubleday & Co., 1979.

Horn, Daniel. *The German Naval Mutinies of World War I.* New Brunswick, N.J.: Rutgers University Press, 1969.

———, ed. and trans. *War, Mutiny and Revolution in the German Navy: The World War I Diary of Seaman Richard Stumpf.* New Brunswick, N.J.: Rutgers University Press, 1967.

Howarth, Stephen, and Derek Law, eds. *The Battle of the Atlantic, 1939–1945: The Fiftieth Anniversary International Naval Conference.* London: Greenhill Books, and Annapolis, Md.: Naval Institute Press, 1994.

Hoyt, Edwin P. *U-boats Offshore.* New York: Playboy Paperbacks, 1980.

———. *U-boats: A Pictorial History.* New York: McGraw-Hill, 1987.

Hughes, Terry, and John Costello. *The Battle of the Atlantic.* New York: Dial Press/James Wade, 1977.

Hurd, Archibald, and Henry Castle. *German Sea-Power: Its Rise, Progress, and Economic Basis.* London: John Murray, 1913. Reprint. Westport, Conn.: Greenwood Press, 1971.

Irving, David. *The Destruction of Convoy PQ. 17.* New York: Simon and Schuster, 1968.

———. *The War Path: Hitler's Germany, 1933–1939.* New York: Viking Press, 1978.

Jeschke, Hubert. *U-Boottaktik: Zur deutschen U-Boottaktik, 1900–1945.* Freiburg/Br.: Verlag Rombach, 1972.

Jones, Geoffrey. *Autumn of the U-boats.* London: William Kimber, 1984.

———. *Defeat of the Wolf Packs.* London: William Kimber, 1986.

Kahn, David. *Seizing the Enigma: The Race to Break the German U-boat Codes, 1939–1943.* Boston: Houghton Mifflin, 1991.

Karschawin, Boris A. *Das deutsche Unterseeboot U 250: Neue Dokumente und Fakten.* Translated by Gunter Fuhrmann. Jena: André Fuhrmann, 1994.

Kelley, Douglas M. *Twenty-two Cells in Nuremberg.* New York: MacFadden Books, 1961.

Kelshall, Gaylord T. M. *The U-boat War in the Caribbean.* Annapolis, Md.: Naval Institute Press, 1994.

Kemp, Paul. *U-boats Destroyed: German Submarine Losses in the World Wars.* Annapolis, Md.: Naval Institute Press, 1997.

Köhl, Fritz, and Axel Niestlé. *Vom Original zum Modell: Uboottyp VII C.* Koblenz: Bernard & Graefe Verlag, 1989.

———. *Vom Original zum Modell: Uboottyp IX C.* Koblenz: Bernard & Graefe Verlag, 1990.

Köhl, Fritz, and Eberhard Rössler. *Anatomy of the Ship: The Type XXI U-boat.* Annapolis, Md.: Naval Institute Press, 1991.

———. *Vom Original zum Modell: Uboottyp XXIII.* Bonn: Bernard & Graefe Verlag, 1993.

———. *Vom Original zum Modell: Uboottyp XVII (Walter-Uboote).* Koblenz: Bernard & Graefe Verlag, 1995.

Korganoff, Alexandre. *Prien Gegen Scapa Flow: Tatsachen, Geheimnisse, Legenden.* Translated from the French by Hans and Hanne Meckel. Stuttgart: Motorbuch Verlag, 1992.

Kramsta, E., ed. *Aus dem Logbuch des I. Wachoffiziers U 66: Auszüge aus Briefen und Tagebuchblättern.* Hannover: Verlag Industrie- und Handelsdienst, 1931.

Kuenne, Robert E. *The Attack Submarine: A Study in Strategy.* New Haven: Yale University Press, 1965.

Kurowski, Franz. *Knights of the Wehrmacht: Knight's Cross Holders of the U-boat Service.* Translated by David Johnston. Altglen, Pa.: Schiffer Publishing, 1995.

Lakowski, Richard. *U-Boote: Zur Geschichte einer Waffengattung der Seestreitkräfte.* Berlin: Militärverlag der Deutschen Demokratischen Republik, 1989.

————. *Deutsche U-Boote Geheim 1935–1945.* Berlin: Brandenburgisches Verlagshaus, 1991.

Lawrence, Hal. *A Bloody War: One Man's Memories of the Canadian Navy, 1939–1945.* New York: Bantam Books (originally published by Nautical & Aviation), 1982.

Legro, Jeffrey W. *Cooperation under Fire: Anglo-German Restraint during World War II.* Ithaca: Cornell University Press, 1995.

Lohmann, Walter, and Hans H. Hildebrand. *Die Deutsche Kriegsmarine, 1939–1945: Gliederung, Einsatz, Stellenbesetzung.* 3 vols. Bad Nauheim: Podzun-Verlag, 1956–64.

Madsen, Chris. *The Royal Navy and German Naval Disarmament, 1942–1947.* London: Frank Cass, 1998.

Manson, Janet M. *Diplomatic Ramifications of Unrestricted Submarine Warfare, 1939–1941.* New York: Greenwood Press, 1990.

Mason, David. *U-boat, the Secret Menace.* New York: Ballantine Books, 1968.

Mason, Timothy W. *Sozialpolitik im Dritten Reich: Arbeiterklasse und Volksgemeinschaft.* 2d ed. Opladen: Westdeutscher Verlag, 1978.

Mattes, Klaus. *Die Seehunde, Klein-U-Boote: Letzte deutsche Initiative im Seekrieg, 1939–1945.* Hamburg: E. S. Mittler & Sohn, 1995.

McCue, Brian. *U-boats in the Bay of Biscay: An Essay in Operations Analysis.* Washington, D.C.: National Defense University Press, 1990.

McLachlan, Donald. *Room 39: Naval Intelligence in Action, 1939–1945.* London: Weidenfeld & Nicolson, 1968.

Meigs, Montgomery C. *Slide Rules and Submarines: American Scientists and Subsurface Warfare in World War II.* Washington, D.C.: National Defense University Press, 1990.

Messerschmidt, Manfred. *Die Wehrmacht im NS-Staat: Zeit der Indoktrination.* Hamburg: R. v. Decker's Verlag, 1969.

Middlebrook, Martin. *Convoy.* New York: William Morrow & Co., 1976.

Militärgeschichtliches Forschungsamt, comp. *Das Deutsche Reich und der Zweiten Weltkrieg.* 6 vols. to date. Stuttgart: Deutsche Verlags-Anstalt, 1979–90.

Miller, William H., and David F. Hutchings. *Transatlantic Liners at War: The Story of the Queens.* London: David & Charles, 1985.

Möller, Eberhard. *Kurs Atlantik: Die Deutsche U-Boot-Entwicklung bis 1945.* Stuttgart: Motorbuch Verlag, 1995.

Monsarrat, Nicholas. *The Cruel Sea.* New York: Alfred A. Knopf, 1951. Reprint. New York: Bantam Books, 1970.

Moore, Arthur R. *A Careless Word . . . A Needless Sinking.* Kings Point, N.Y.: American Merchant Marine Museum, 1983.

Moore, John Hammond. *The Faustball Tunnel: German POWs in the United States and Their Great Escape.* New York: Random House, 1978.

Morison, Samuel Eliot. *The Battle of the Atlantic, 1939–1943.* Vol. 1 of *History of United States Naval Operations in World War II.* Boston: Little, Brown and Co., 1975.

———. *The Atlantic Battle Won, May 1943–May 1945.* Vol. 10 of *History of United States Naval Operations in World War II.* Boston: Little, Brown and Co., 1975.

Mueller-Hillebrand, Burckhart. *Das Heer.* Band 3, *Der Zweifrontenkrieg.* Frankfurt/M.: E. S. Mittler & Sohn, 1969.

Mühlberger, Detlef. *Hitler's Followers: Studies in the Sociology of the Nazi Movement.* London: Routledge, 1991.

Müller, Klaus-Jürgen. *Das Heer und Hitler: Armee und nationalsozialistisches Regime, 1933–1940.* Stuttgart: Deutsche Verlags-Anstalt, 1969.

Mulligan, Timothy P. *Lone Wolf: The Life and Death of U-boat Ace Werner Henke.* Westport, Conn.: Praeger, 1993.

Nayhauss, Mainhardt Graf von. *Zwischen Gehorsam und Gewissen.* Bergisch Gladbach: Bastei/Lübbe Taschenbuch (Gustav Lübbe Verlag), 1994.

Neitzel, Sönke. *Die deutschen Ubootbunker und Bunkerwerften.* Koblenz: Bernard & Graefe Verlag, 1991.

———. *Der Einsatz der deutschen Luftwaffe über dem Atlantik und der Nordsee, 1939–1945.* Koblenz: Bernard & Graefe Verlag, 1995.

Nöldeke, Hartmut, and Volker Hartmann. *Der Sanitätsdienst in der deutschen U-Boot-Waffe und bei den Kleinkampfverbänden.* Hamburg: E. S. Mittler & Sohn, 1996.

Noli, Jean. *The Admiral's Wolf Pack.* Translated by Doubleday & Co. New York: Zebra Books, 1974.

Office of Scientific Research and Development (OSRD). *A Summary of Antisubmarine Warfare Operations in World War II.* Summary Technical Report of Division 6, National Defense Research Committee. Washington, D.C.: OSRD, 1946.

O'Neill, Robert J. *The German Army and the Nazi Party, 1933–1939.* Foreword by Sir Basil Liddell Hart. London: Corgi Books, 1968.

Ott, Wolfgang. *Sharks and Little Fish.* Translated by Ralph Manheim. New York: Ballantine Books, 1966. Originally published as *Haie und kleine Fische* (Munich: Albert Langer-Georg Müller, 1956).

Padfield, Peter. *Dönitz: The Last Führer.* New York: Harper & Row, 1984.

Parker, Mike. *Running the Gauntlet: An Oral History of Canadian Merchant Seamen in World War II.* Halifax: Nimbus, 1994.

Peillard, Léonce. *The Laconia Affair.* Translated by Jonathan Cape, Ltd., and G. P. Putnam's Sons. New York: Bantam Books, 1983. Originally published as *L'Afaire du Laconia* (Paris: Robert Laffont, 1961).

Plottke, Herbert. *Fächer Loos!: U 172 im Einsatz in den Weltmeeren von Rio bis Kapstadt: Ein Tatsachenbericht aus den Jahren 1942/43.* Wölfersheim-Berstadt: Podzun-Pallas-Verlag, 1994.

Price, Alfred. *Aircraft versus Submarine: The Evolution of the Anti-submarine Aircraft, 1912 to 1972.* Annapolis, Md.: Naval Institute Press, 1973.

Rahn, Werner. *Reichsmarine und Landesverteidigung, 1919–1928.* Munich: Bernard & Graefe Verlag für Wehrwesen, 1976.

Robertson, Terence. *Escort Commander.* New York: Bantam Books, 1979. Reprint of *Walker, R.N.* (London: Evans Brothers, 1956).

———. *The Golden Horseshoe.* London: Pan Books, 1957.

Rogers, Stanley. *Enemy in Sight!* New York: Thomas Y. Crowell Co., 1943.

Rohwer, Jürgen. *Die Versenkung der jüdischen Flüchtlingstransporter Struma und Mefkure im Schwarzen Meer (February 1942, August 1944).* Schriften der Bibliothek für Zeitgeschichte Weltkriegsbücherei, Heft 4. Frankfurt/M.: Bernard & Graefe Verlag für Wehrwesen, 1965.

———. *Axis Submarine Successes, 1939–1945.* Annapolis, Md.: Naval Institute Press, 1983. Updated translation of *Die U-Boot-Erfolge der Achsenmächte, 1939–1945* (Munich: J. F. Lehmanns Verlag, 1968).

———. *The Critical Convoy Battles of March 1943.* Translated by Derek Masters. Annapolis, Md.: Naval Institute Press, 1977.

Rohwer, Jürgen, and Gerd Hümmelchen. *Chronology of the War at Sea, 1939–1945: The Naval History of World War II.* 2d ed. Annapolis, Md.: Naval Institute Press, 1992.

Roskill, Stephen W. *The War at Sea, 1939–1945.* 3 vols. in 4 parts. London: Her Majesty's Stationery Office, 1954–61.

Rössler, Eberhard. *The U-boat: The Evolution and Technical History of German Submarines.* Translated by Harold Erenberg. Annapolis, Md.: Naval Institute Press, 1981.

———. *Die Torpedos der deutschen U-Boote.* Herford: Koehler, 1984.

———. *U-Boottyp XXI.* 4th ed. Koblenz: Bernard & Graefe Verlag, 1986.

———. *Die deutschen Uboote und ihre Werften: Eine Bilddokumentation über den deutschen Ubootbau von 1935 bis heute.* Koblenz: Bernard & Graefe Verlag, 1990.

———. *Die Sonaranlagen der deutschen U-Boote.* Herford: Koehler, 1991.

Runyan, Timothy J., and Jan M. Copes, eds. *To Die Gallantly: The Battle of the Atlantic.* Boulder, Colo.: Westview Press, 1994.

Rust, Eric C. *Naval Officers under Hitler: The Story of Crew 34.* Westport, Conn.: Praeger, 1991.

Salewski, Michael. *Die deutsche Seekriegsleitung, 1935–1945.* 3 vols. Frankfurt/M.: Bernard & Graefe Verlag, 1970–75.

———. *Von der Wirklichkeit des Krieges: Analysen und Kontroversen zu Buchheims "Boot."* Munich: Deutscher Taschenbuch Verlag, 1976.

Sanders, Jacquin. *A Night before Christmas: The Sinking of the Troopship* Leopoldville. New York: G. P. Putnam's Sons, 1963.

Savas, Theodore P., ed. *Silent Hunters: German U-boat Commanders of World War II.* Campbell, Calif.: Savas Publishing Co., 1997.

Schmoeckel, Helmut. *Menschlichkeit im Seekrieg?* Herford: E. S. Mittler & Sohn, 1987.

Shelford, W. O. *Subsunk: The Story of Submarine Escape.* New York: Popular Library, 1962.

Showell, Jak P. Mallmann. *The German Navy in World War II: A Reference Guide to the Kriegsmarine, 1935–1945*. Annapolis, Md.: Naval Institute Press, 1979.

———. *U-boats under the Swastika*. 2d ed. Annapolis, Md.: Naval Institute Press, 1987.

———. *U-boat Command and the Battle of the Atlantic*. Lewiston, N.Y.: Vanwell, 1989.

Smith, Bradley F. *Reaching Judgment at Nuremberg*. New York: Basic Books, 1977.

Snyder, Gerald S. *The* Royal Oak *Disaster: The Tragic Story of U-47's Bloody Raid on Scapa Flow*. London: Granada Publishing, 1978.

Sorge, Siegfried. *Der Marineoffizier als Führer und Erzieher*. 4th ed. Berlin: E. S. Mittler & Sohn, 1940.

Spindler, Arno. *Der Handelskrieg mit U-Booten*. 5 vols. (Part of the German official history *Der Krieg zur See, 1914–1918*, issued by the Marine-Archiv under the general editorship of *Vizeadmiral a.D.* E. v. Mantey.) Berlin: E. S. Mittler & Sohn, 1932–41 (Bände 1–4); Frankfurt/M.: E. S. Mittler & Sohn, 1966 (Band 5).

Steinhoff, Johann, Peter Pechel, and Dennis Showalter, eds. *Voices from the Third Reich: An Oral History*. New York: Da Capo Press, 1994.

Stern, Robert C. *U-boats in Action*. Carrollton, Texas: Squadron/Signal Publications, 1977.

———. *Type VII U-boats*. Annapolis, Md.: Naval Institute Press, 1991.

Stevens, David. *U-boat Far from Home: The Epic Voyage of U 862 to Australia and New Zealand*. St. Leonards, Australia: Allen & Unwin, 1997.

Stoelzel, *Konteradmiral a.D.* Albert, ed. *Ehrenrangliste der Kaiserlich Deutschen Marine, 1914–1918*. Berlin: Marine-Offizier-Verein e.V., 1930.

Syrett, David. *The Defeat of the German U-boats: The Battle of the Atlantic*. Columbia: University of South Carolina Press, 1994.

Tarrant, V. E. *The U-boat Offensive, 1914–1945*. Annapolis, Md.: Naval Institute Press, 1989.

———. *The Last Year of the Kriegsmarine, May 1944–May 1945*. Annapolis, Md.: Naval Institute Press, 1994.

Terraine, John. *The U-boat Wars, 1916–1945*. New York: Henry Holt and Co., 1989.

Thomas, Charles S. *The German Navy in the Nazi Era*. Annapolis, Md.: Naval Institute Press, 1990.

Thomas, Lowell. *Raiders of the Deep*. Garden City, N.Y.: Garden City Publishing Co., 1928.

Tidman, Keith R. *The Operations Evaluation Group: A History of Naval Operations Analysis*. Annapolis, Md.: Naval Institute Press, 1984.

Treue, Wilhelm, Eberhard Möller, and Werner Rahn. *Deutsche Marinerüstung, 1919–1942: Die Gefahren der Tirpitz-Tradition*. Herford: E. S. Mittler & Sohn, 1992.

Turkel, Studs. *"The Good War": An Oral History of World War II*. New York: Ballantine Books, 1985.

Van der Vat, Dan. *The Atlantic Campaign: World War II's Great Struggle at Sea*. New York: Harper & Row, 1988.

Vause, Jordan. *U-boat Ace: The Story of Wolfgang Lüth*. Annapolis, Md.: Naval Institute Press, 1990.

————. *Wolf: U-boat Commanders in World War II.* Annapolis, Md.: Naval Institute Press, 1997.

Waddington, C. H. *OR in World War II: Operational Research against the U-boat.* London: Elek Science, 1973.

Walle, Heinrich. *Die Tragödie des Oberleutnants zur See Oskar Kusch.* Beiheft 13 der Historische Mitteilungen im Auftrage der Ranke-Gesellschaft. Stuttgart: Franz Steiner Verlag, 1995.

Waters, John M., Jr. *Bloody Winter.* Princeton, N.J.: D. Van Nostrand Co., 1967.

Wegner, Bernd. *Hitlers Politische Soldaten: Die Waffen SS, 1933–1945.* Paderborn: Ferdinand Schöningh, 1982.

Weir, Gary E. *Building the Kaiser's Navy: The Imperial Naval Office and German Industry in the von Tirpitz Era, 1890–1919.* Annapolis, Md.: Naval Institute Press, 1992.

Wells, Mark K. *Courage and Air Warfare: The Allied Aircrew Experience in the Second World War.* London: Frank Cass, 1997.

Wetzel, Eckard. *U 995: Das U-Boot vor dem Marine-Ehrenmal in Laboe.* Kiel: Paschke Verlag, 1985.

————. *U 2540: Das U-Boot beim Deutschen Schiffahrtsmuseum in Bremerhaven.* Schwedeneck: Wetzel, 1989.

Whitley, M. J. *Destroyer!: German Destroyers in World War II.* Annapolis, Md.: Naval Institute Press, 1983.

Whittingham, Richard. *Martial Justice: The Last Mass Execution in the United States.* Chicago: Henry Regnery, 1971. Reprint. Annapolis, Md.: Naval Institute Press, 1996.

Wiggins, Melanie. *Torpedoes in the Gulf: Galveston and the U-boats, 1942–1943.* College Station: Texas A&M University Press, 1995.

Wynn, Kenneth. *U-boat Operations of the Second World War.* Vol. 1, *Career Histories, U1–U510.* Annapolis, Md.: Naval Institute Press, 1997.

Y'Blood, William T. *Hunter-Killer: U.S. Escort Carriers in the Battle of the Atlantic.* Annapolis, Md.: Naval Institute Press, 1983.

Zayas, Alfred M. de. *The Wehrmacht War Crimes Bureau, 1939–1945.* Lincoln: University of Nebraska Press, 1989. Originally published as *Die Wehrmacht-Untersuchungsstelle* (Munich: Universitas/Langen-Müller, 1980).

Zilbert, Edward R. *Albert Speer and the Nazi Ministry of Arms: Economic Institutions and Industrial Production in the German War Economy.* London: Associated Universities Presses, 1981.

Secondary Sources: Articles

Absolon, Rudolf. "Das Offizierkorps des Deutschen Heeres, 1935–1945." In *Das deutsche Offizierkorps 1860–1960,* edited by Hanns H. Hoffmann. Boppard/Rh.: Harald Boldt Verlag, 1980, 247–68.

Baum, Walter. "Marine, Nationalsozialismus und Widerstand." *Vierteljahreshefte für Zeitgeschichte* 11, no. 1 (January 1963): 16–48.

Brennecke, Jochen. "Seit dem Weltkrieg I: Unveränderte U-Boot-Konzeption trotz zunehmender Zahl und Bedeutung der Flugzeuge." *Schiff und Zeit,* no. 26 (1987): 28–31.

"Denn wir fuhren . . . Weisse Flagge auf U 570?" *Kristall,* nos. 12–15 and 19–20, 1956.

Engelhardt, Walter. "Vom U-Boot in die französische Gefangenschaft." *Schaltung-Küste, Nachrichtenblatt Verband Deutscher U-Bootfahrer e.V.,* no. 161 (January/February 1996): 24–26.

Erdmann, Karl Dietrich. "Eine Besprechung über den U-Boot-Krieg bei Hitler in der Reichskanzlei im Herbst 1942 und ihre Bedeutung für den Kriegsverlauf." *Geschichte im Wissenschaft und Unterricht,* 1987/11, 684–95.

Förster, Jürgen. "The Dynamics of *Volksgemeinschaft:* The Effectiveness of the German Military Establishment in the Second World War." In *Military Effectiveness,* vol. 3, *The Second World War,* edited by Allan R. Millett and Williamson Murray, 180–220. Boston: Allen & Unwin, 1988.

"Forum: Stimmen zum Thema 'Beisetzung des Grossadmirals.'" *Marine-Forum* 4 (1981): 116–18.

Gillingham, John. "The 'Deproletarianization' of German Society: Vocational Training in the Third Reich." *Journal of Social History* 19 (1986): 423–32.

Güth, Rolf. "Bild einer Crew: Ein Beitrag zur Frage der Struktur, Soziologie und Haltung des Marineoffizierkorps." *Marine-Rundschau* 61, no. 3 (June 1964): 131–41.

———. "Funktion und Charakter: Technische Entwicklungen und soldatische Führung in der deutschen Marine 1848 bis 1945." *Truppenpraxis,* Hefte 1–3 (1980), 73–78, 157–62, 240–45.

Güth, Rolf, and Jochen Brennecke. "Hier irrte Michael Salewski: Das Trauma vom 'Kinderkreuzzug' der U-Boote." *Schiff und Zeit,* no. 28 (1989): 43–47.

Hartwig, Dieter. "Karl Dönitz: Versuch einer kritischen Würdigung." *Deutsches Schiffahrtsarchiv* 12 (1989): 133–52.

Herzog, Bodo. "Der Torpedoverbrauch von U-48, dem erfolgreichsten Unterseeboot des zweiten Weltkrieges, in der Zeit von September 1939 bis Juni 1941." *Deutsches Schiffahrtsarchiv* 4 (1981): 121–46.

———. "Ritterkreuz und U-Boot-Waffe: Bemerkungen zur Verleihungspraxis." *Deutsches Schiffahrtsarchiv* 10 (1987): 245–60.

Hoch, Gottfried. "Zur Problematik der Menschenführung im Kriege." In *Die Deutsche Marine: Historisches Selbstverständnis und Standortbestimmung,* compiled by Deutsches Marine Institut/Deutsche Marine Akademie, 191–216. Herford: E. S. Mittler & Sohn, 1983.

Kaelble, Hartmut. "Social Mobility in Germany, 1900–1960." *Journal of Modern History* 50, no. 3 (September 1978): 439–61.

Kennedy, Ludovic. "War Crimes of the Ocean." *Telegraph Magazine,* 1 June 1991, 18–20, 55–58.

Kroener, Bernhard R. "Die personellen Ressourcen des dritten Reiches im Spannungsfeld zwischen Wehrmacht, Bürokrätie und Kriegswirtschaft 1939–1942." In Militärgeschichtliches Forschungsamt, *Das Deutsche Reich und der Zweite*

Weltkrieg, Bd. 5/1, *Organisation und Mobilisierung des deutschen Machtbereichs. Kriegsverwaltung, Wirtschaft und personelle Ressourcen, 1939–1941*, 693–1001. Stuttgart: Deutsche Verlags-Anstalt, 1988.

———. "Auf dem Weg zu einer 'nationalsozialistischen Volksarmee.'" In *Von Stalingrad zur Währungsreform: Zur Sozialgeschichte des Umbruchs in Deutschland*, 3d ed., edited by Martin Broszat, Klaus-Dietmar Henke, and Hans Woller, 651–82. Munich: R. Oldenbourg Verlag, 1990, 651–82.

Kühlwetter, Friedrich von. "The Personnel of the German Navy." *The Naval Annual*, 1913, 132–50.

Lundeberg, Philip K. "The German Naval Critique of the U-boat Campaign, 1915–1918." *Military Affairs* 27, no. 3 (Fall 1963): 105–18.

Messerschmidt, Manfred. "German Military Effectiveness between 1919 and 1939." In *Military Effectiveness*, vol. 2, *The Interwar Period*, edited by Allan R. Millett and Williamson Murray, 218–55. Boston: Unwin Hyman, 1988.

Messimer, Dwight R. "Heinz-Wilhelm Eck: Siegerjustiz and the *Peleus* Affair." In *Silent Hunters: German U-boat Commanders of World War II*, edited by Theodore P. Savas, 136–83. Campbell, Calif.: Savas Publishing Co., 1997.

Mierke, Karl. "Der Auswahl der Fachsoldaten der Kriegsmarine." *Nauticus*, 1942, 185–96.

Mulligan, Timothy P. "Tracking *Das Boot:* Records of U-96 in the National Archives." *Prologue: Journal of the National Archives* 14, no. 4 (Winter 1982): 203–11.

———. "The German Navy Evaluates Its Cryptographic Security, October 1941." *Military Affairs* 49, no. 2 (April 1985): 75–79.

———. "German U-boat Crews in World War II: Sociology of an Elite." *Journal of Military History* 56, no. 2 (April 1992): 261–81.

Niestlé, Axel. "German Technical and Electronic Development." In *The Battle of the Atlantic, 1939–1945: The Fiftieth Anniversary International Naval Conference*, edited by Stephen Howarth and Derek Law, 430–51. London: Greenhill Books, and Annapolis, Md.: Naval Institute Press, 1994.

Nothdurft, Hans. "Das CO_2 Problem in U-Booten." *Wehrmedizinische Monatsschrift* 36 (June 1992): 266–68.

Peter, Karl. "Fähnrichsausbildung während des zweiten Weltkrieges." In *Marineschule Mürwik*, 2d ed., edited by Deutsches Marine Institut, 141–53. Herford: E. S. Mittler & Sohn, 1989.

Rahn, Werner. "Die Ausbildung zum Marineoffizier zwischen den Weltkriegen, 1920–1939." In *Marineschule Mürwik*, 2d ed., edited by Deutsches Marine Institut, 123–31. Herford: E. S. Mittler & Sohn, 1989.

———. "Einsatzbereitschaft und Kampfkraft deutscher U-Boote 1942." *Militärgeschichtliche Mitteilungen* 47, no. 1 (1990): 73–132.

———. "Grundzüge des deutschen U-Boot-Krieges, 1939–1945." In *Technikmuseum U-Boot Wilhelm Bauer: Kleine Geschichte und Technik der deutschen U-Boote*, 57–69. Bremerhaven: Nordwestdeutsche Verlagsgesellschaft, 1990.

Rohwer, Jürgen. "The U-boat War against the Allied Supply Lines." In *Decisive Bat-*

tles of World War II: The German View, edited by H. A. Jacobsen and J. Rohwer, 259–312. Translated by Edward Fitzgerald. New York: G. P. Putnam's Sons, 1965.

———. "Die Auswirkungen der deutschen und britischen Funkaufklärung auf die Geleitzugoperationen im Nordatlantik." In *Die Funkaufklärung und ihre Rolle im 2. Weltkrieg,* edited by Jürgen Rohwer and Eberhard Jäckel, 167–200. Stuttgart: Motorbuch Verlag, 1979.

Roskill, Stephen W. "CAPROS not Convoy: Counterattack and Destroy!" *United States Naval Institute Proceedings* 82, no. 10 (October 1956): 1047–53.

Rössler, Eberhard. "Die deutsche U-Bootausbildung und ihre Vorbereitung, 1925–1945." *Marine-Rundschau* 68, no. 8 (1971): 453–66.

———. "Der U-Boot-Typ XXI: Entstehung, Konstruktion, Fertigung und Einsatz, 1943–1945." In *Technikmuseum U-Boot Wilhelm Bauer: Kleine Geschichte und Technik der deutschen U-Boote,* 73–100. Bremerhaven: Nordwestdeutsche Verlagsgesellschaft, 1990.

———. "U-boat Development and Building." In *The Battle of the Atlantic, 1939–1945: The Fiftieth Anniversary International Naval Conference,* edited by Stephen Howarth and Derek Law, 118–37. London: Greenhill Books, and Annapolis, Md.: Naval Institute Press, 1994.

Ruschenbuch, E. "Reaktionäre Offiziere contra sozialistische Regierung?" *Marine-Forum,* nos. 7/8 (July/August 1991), 252–54.

Salewski, Michael. "Selbstverständnis und historisches Bewusstsein der deutschen Kriegsmarine." *Marine-Rundschau* 67, no. 2 (1970): 65–88.

———. "Von Raeder zu Dönitz: Das Wechsel im Oberbefehl der Kriegsmarine, 1943." *Militärgeschichtliche Mitteilungen* 14, no. 2 (1973): 101–46.

———. "Das Offizierkorps der Reichs- und Kriegsmarine." In *Das deutsche Offizierkorps, 1860–1960,* edited by Hanns H. Hoffmann, 211–30. Boppard/Rh.: Harald Boldt Verlag, 1980.

Sarty, Roger. "The Limits of Ultra: The Schnorckel U-boat Offensive against North America, November 1944–January 1945." *Intelligence and National Security* 12, no. 2 (April 1997): 44–68.

Schley, Max. "Mit 'U 861' Nach Ostindien." *Marinezeitung "Leinen Los!"* 1958, no. 9:282–83; 1959, no. 2:60–61; 1959, no. 8:250–51; 1959, no. 10:316–17; and 1960, no. 9:285–87.

"The Scuttled U-boats Case: Trial of Oberleutnant Gerhard Grumpelt." *Law Reports of Trials of War Criminals* 1 (1947): 55–70.

Shils, Edward A., and Morris Janowitz. "Cohesion and Disintegration in the Wehrmacht in World War II," *Public Opinion Quarterly* 12, no. 2 (Summer 1948): 280–315.

Sieche, Erwin. "The Walter Submarine-1." *Warship,* no. 20 (October 1981): 235–46.

Spindler, Arno. "Der Meinungsstreit in der Marine über den U-Bootskrieg, 1914–1918." *Marine-Rundschau* 55, no. 5 (1958): 235–45.

Syrett, David. "Weather-Reporting U-boats in the Atlantic, 1944–1945: The Hunt for U-248." *The American Neptune* 52, no. 1 (Winter 1992): 16–24.

Thomas, C. R. W. "Making Naval Officers in Germany." *United States Naval Institute Proceedings* 64, no. 1 (January 1938): 39–56.

Topp, Erich. "Manning and Training the U-boat Fleet." In *The Battle of the Atlantic, 1939–1945: The Fiftieth Anniversary International Naval Conference,* edited by Stephen Howarth and Derek Law, 214–19. London: Greenhill Books, and Annapolis, Md.: Naval Institute Press, 1994.

Waas, Heinrich. "Zeitzeuge zum Walter-U-Boot-Bau und zu den Laconia-Fall-Folgen." *Schiff und Zeit,* no. 26 (1987): 19–27.

Walle, Heinrich. "Individual Loyalty and Resistance in the German Military: The Case of Sub-Lieutenant Oskar Kusch." In *Germans against Nazism: Nonconformity, Opposition, and Resistance in the Third Reich: Essays in Honour of Peter Hoffmann,* edited by Francis R. Nicosia and Lawrence D. Stokes, 323–50. New York: Berg, 1991.

Wentzel, Friedrich-Wilhelm. "Vom Werden einer Crew: Ein Beitrag zur Soziologie des Offizierkorps der Reichsmarine." *Marine-Forum,* nos. 1–2 (1981), 17–20.

"Where Are They Now? Operation Deadlight." *After the Battle Magazine,* no. 36 (1982): 43–49.

Wiedersheim, William A., III. "Officer Personnel Selection in the German Navy, 1925–1945." *United States Naval Institute Proceedings* 73, no. 4 (April 1947): 445–49.

Wilson, Michael. "The Walter Submarine-2." *Warship,* no. 20 (October 1981): 247–53.

Unpublished Materials

Directorate of Operational Analysis (Royal Navy), Ministry of Defence. "The U-boat Logs, 1939–1945." Part 2, "Operational Performance and Degradation." August 1966. Ms. in the possession of the U-Boot-Archiv.

Faermann, Matthias. "Die Einsatzmotivation von Uboot-Besatzungen im Zweiten Weltkrieg, trotz starker Überlegenheit der Gegner." 1994. Ms. in the possession of the U-Boot-Archiv.

Güth, Rolf. "Erich Raeder und die Englische Frage: Betrachtungen zur deutschen Marineführung 1928–1945." 1995. Draft ms. for future publication. (Copy furnished to author.)

Hirschmann, Werner. "Chief Engineer on *U-190:* Two War Memories," 1945. Translated 1985. Personal papers. (Copy furnished to author.)

———. "Re: Topp's Speech 'Manning and Training the U-boat Fleet.'" 1994. Personal papers. (Copy furnished to author.)

———. "Recollections of a Submariner," 1994. Personal papers. (Copy furnished to author.)

Peter, Karl. "Der Fall des Oberleutnants zur See Kusch. 'Wider besseres Wissen zum Tode verurteilt'—Stimmt das?" 1985. Ms. in the possession of the U-Boot-Archiv.

Rahn, Werner. "Long-Range German U-boat Operations in 1942 and their Logistical Support by U-Tankers." Paper presented at the Eighth Naval History Symposium, U.S. Naval Academy, Annapolis, Md., 25 September 1987. (Copy furnished to author.)

Reinhardt, Hellmuth, et al. "Personnel and Administration Project #2b." Parts 2 and 3. Mss. no. P-012 and P-008. Foreign Military Studies, Historical Division, U.S. Army Europe, 1949.

Saville, Allison Winthrop. "The Development of the U-boat Arm, 1919–1935." Ph.D. dissertation, University of Washington, 1963.

Schaefer, Jobst. "Die Ernährung des U-Bootsfahrers im Kriege." Inaugural dissertation for the Medical Department, Christian-Albrechts-Universität Kiel, 1943. (Copy in the U-Boot-Archiv.)

Schaefer, Karl E., ed. "Monograph on Submarine Medicine." 8 folios containing 21 articles and 2 annexes prepared by German medical researchers during the war. Translated by U.S. Fleet, U.S. Naval Forces, Germany, Technical Section (Medical), 1948. (Copy in the National Library of Medicine, Bethesda, Md.)

Steinort, Wolfgang. "Die Ausbildung in der U-Bootwaffe im 2. Weltkrieg." Paper presented before the Arbeitskreis Reserveoffiziere Marine Hamburg, 5 September 1979. (Copy in the U-Boot-Archiv.)

Stöckel, Kurt. "Die Entwicklung der Reichsmarine nach dem Ersten Weltkriege (1919–1935): Äusserer Aufbau und innere Struktur." Doctoral dissertation, Georg-August-Universität zu Göttingen, 1954.

Sutton, James E. "The Imperial German Navy, 1910–1914." Ph.D. dissertation, Indiana University, 1953.

Trompelt, Heinz. "Meine Marinedurchlauf" and "Der U-Boot-Krieg," personal reminiscences combined with research into U-boat operational data. (Copy furnished to author.)

Wilke, Kaptlt. Herbert. "Die Unterseebootsabwehrschule (UAS), 1933–1945." Ms. prepared at the Marine-Unterwasserwaffenschule, 1964. (Copy in the U-Boot-Archiv.)

Websites

http://uboat.net (U-Web, with extensive historical data on all aspects of U-boat warfare, 1939–45).

http://www.msichicago.org.u505 (*U-505* home page, offers a tour of the compartments of *U-505*, the captured German submarine on display at Chicago's Museum of Science and Industry).

http://www.randomhouse.com/uboat/biblio.html (bibliography of original sources and secondary works for Clay Blair's *Hitler's U-boat War*).

Index

About the Author

Timothy P. Mulligan is an archivist who specializes in captured German and World War II–era U.S. naval and military records. A native of Baltimore, he received his doctorate in history at the University of Maryland. In addition to numerous articles, he has written *Lone Wolf: The Life and Death of U-boat Ace Werner Henke* and edited the volume *Wolf Packs* in the Time-Life series *The Third Reich*.